lonely planet

SOUTHWEST USA'S

BEST TRIPS

32 AMAZING ROAD TRIPS

This edition written and researched by

**Amy C Balfour,
Michael Benanav, Greg Benchwick,
Ryan Ver Berkmoes, Lisa Dunford,
Mariella Krause, Carolyn McCarthy**

MAY 2014

SYMBOLS IN THIS BOOK

 Top Tips

 Link Your Trips

 Tips from Locals

Trip Detour

 History & Culture

 Family

 Food & Drink

Outdoors

 Essential Photo

 Walking Tour

 Eating

 Sleeping

🕿 Telephone Number
🕙 Opening Hours
🅿 Parking
🚭 Nonsmoking
❄ Air-Conditioning

@ Internet Access
📶 Wi-Fi Access
🥗 Vegetarian Selection
🏊 Swimming Pool

🍴 English-Language Menu
👪 Family-Friendly
🐾 Pet-Friendly

MAP LEGEND

Routes
Trip Route
Trip Detour
Linked Trip
Walk Route
Tollway
Freeway
Primary
Secondary
Tertiary
Lane
Unsealed Road
Plaza/Mall
Steps
Tunnel
Pedestrian Overpass
Walk Track/Path

Boundaries
International
State/Province
Cliff

Population
⊗ Capital (National)
◉ Capital (State/Province)
● City/Large Town
○ Town/Village

Transport
✈ Airport
Cable Car/ Funicular
🅿 Parking
Train/Railway
🚋 Tram
Ⓜ Underground Train Station

Trips
1 Trip Numbers
9 Trip Stop
Walking tour
Trip Detour

Highway Route Markers
97 US National Hwy
5 US Interstate Hwy
44 State Hwy

Hydrography
River/Creek
Intermittent River
Swamp/Mangrove
Canal
Water
Dry/Salt/ Intermittent Lake
Glacier

Areas
Beach
Cemetery (Christian)
Cemetery (Other)
Park
Forest
Reservation
Urban Area
Sportsground

PLAN YOUR TRIP

ON THE ROAD

CONTENTS

Utah,
Colorado & Nevada
p265

Arizona
p31

New
Mexico
p133

Texas
p223

Contents cont.

Classic Trips

Look out for the Classic Trips stamp on our favorite routes in this book.

Red rocks around Sedona Courthouse Butte and Bell Rock (Trip 8)

WELCOME TO
SOUTHWEST USA

Mother Nature had some fun in the Southwest. Red rock canyons crack across ancient plateaus. Hoodoos cluster like conspirators on remote slopes. Whisper-light sand dunes shimmer on distant horizons. Wildflowers, saguaros and ponderosa pines add the artistic flourish, luring you in for a closer look.

The 32 road trips in this book swoop from scrubby deserts to the majestic Grand Canyon, linking to the sandstone charms of Utah and the artistic sparkle of New Mexico. Texas two-steps across the page with big skies, sugary beaches and Hill Country wildflowers while Colorado says howdy with million-dollar views. Vast open spaces are the jackpot in Nevada.

But it's not just about the scenery. Dinosaur tracks, spectacular caverns, Old West towns, kitschy attractions, BBQ joints and wine-tasting rooms add history, geology and, well, oomph. If you've only got time for one trip, make it one of our seven Classic Trips, which take you to the very best of the Southwest.

→

SOUTHWEST USA

Classic Trips

5

What is a Classic Trip

All the trips in this book show you the best of Southwest USA, but we've chosen seven as our all-time favorites. These are our Classic Trips – the ones that lead you to the best of the iconic sights, the top activities and the unique Southwest experiences. Turn the page to see the map, and look out for the Classic Trip stamp throughout the book.

2 **Route 66: The Southwest** 'Get your kitsch' on this iconic drive.

5 **Fantastic Canyon Voyage** The Colorado River winds through the awesome canyon it carved over millennia.

31 **San Juan Skyway & Million Dollar Highway** Golden aspens colour the San Juan Mountains in fall.

31

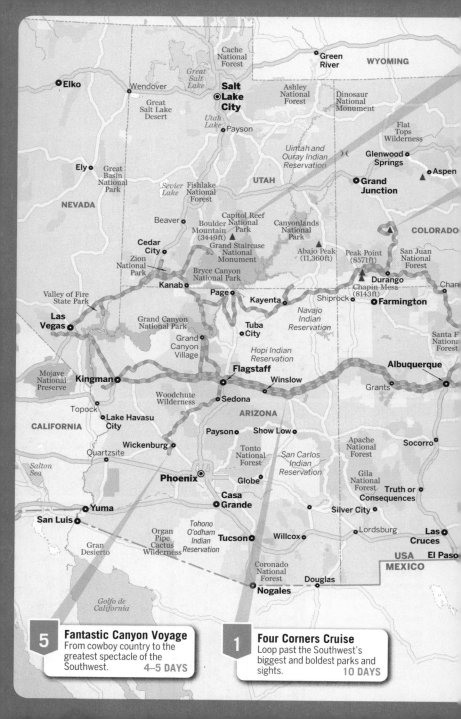

5 **Fantastic Canyon Voyage**
From cowboy country to the greatest spectacle of the Southwest. **4–5 DAYS**

1 **Four Corners Cruise**
Loop past the Southwest's biggest and boldest parks and sights. **10 DAYS**

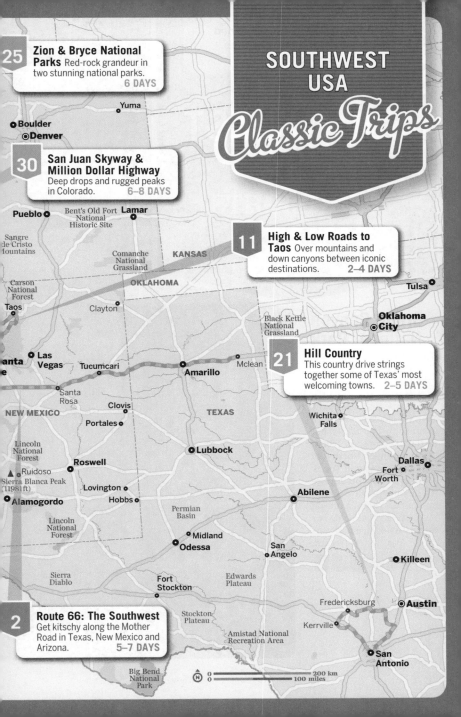

25 Zion & Bryce National Parks Red-rock grandeur in two stunning national parks. **6 DAYS**

Yuma

Boulder
Denver

30 San Juan Skyway & Million Dollar Highway Deep drops and rugged peaks in Colorado. **6–8 DAYS**

SOUTHWEST USA

Classic Trips

Pueblo
Bent's Old Fort National Historic Site **Lamar**

Sangre de Cristo Mountains

Comanche National Grassland **KANSAS**

11 High & Low Roads to Taos Over mountains and down canyons between iconic destinations. **2–4 DAYS**

Carson National Forest

OKLAHOMA

Tulsa

Taos

Clayton

Black Kettle National Grassland

Oklahoma City

Santa e
Las Vegas Tucumcari Amarillo Mclean

21 Hill Country This country drive strings together some of Texas' most welcoming towns. **2–5 DAYS**

Santa Rosa

Clovis

NEW MEXICO Portales

TEXAS

Wichita Falls

Lincoln National Forest

Roswell

Ruidoso
Sierra Blanca Peak (11981ft)

Lovington
Alamogordo Hobbs

Lubbock

Dallas
Fort Worth

Abilene

Lincoln National Forest

Permian Basin

Midland
Odessa

San Angelo

Killeen

Sierra Diablo

Fort Stockton

Edwards Plateau

Fredericksburg

Austin

2 Route 66: The Southwest Get kitschy along the Mother Road in Texas, New Mexico and Arizona. **5–7 DAYS**

Stockton Plateau

Amistad National Recreation Area

Kerrville

Big Bend National Park

San Antonio

0   200 km
0   100 miles

Southwest USA's best sights and experiences, and the road trips that will take you there.

SOUTHWEST USA
HIGHLIGHTS

Grand Canyon National Park

The sheer immensity of the canyon is what grabs you at first: it's a two-billion-year-old rip across the landscape that reveals the Earth's geologic secrets with commanding authority. But as you'll discover on **Trip 4: Grand Canyon North Rim & Lake Powell** and **Trip 5: Fantastic Canyon Voyage** it's the small-scale details – sun-dappled ridges, crimson buttes – that hold your attention and demand your return.

Trips

Grand Canyon National Park North Rim view

Sedona Bridge over Oak Creek Canyon

Sedona

The beauty of the red rocks hits you on an elemental level. Yes, the jeep tours, crystal shops and chichi galleries add to the fun, but it's the crimson buttes – strange yet familiar – that make Sedona unique. On **Trip 8: Highway 89A: Around Sedona**, soak up the beauty of the region by hiking to Airport Mesa, bicycling beneath Bell Rock or sliding through Oak Creek.

Trips

Zion National Park

The soaring red-and-white cliffs of Zion Canyon are one of Utah's most dramatic natural wonders. But **Trip 25: Zion & Bryce National Parks** also reveals more delicate beauties: weeping rocks, tiny grottoes, hanging gardens and meadows of mesa-top wildflowers. This vegetation, and the low elevation, distinguish Zion from more barren parks to the east.

Trips

Moab

Bike-thrashing slickrock. Class IV rapids. Hikes to sheer cliffs. It's just another day at the office for outdoor outfitters in this rugged playground. And as **Trip 27: Moab & Southeastern National Parks** proves, with activities this tough, you gotta have the appropriate support system: a sunrise java joint, a cool indie bookstore and a post-ride brewery that smells of beer and adventure.

Trips

Mesa Verde National Park Ladder to a cliff dwelling

BEST SMALL TOWNS

Bisbee This old mining town cleaned up nice. **Trip** 3

Jerome Gallery hopping and wine tasting come with red-rock views. **Trip** 5

Marfa An art scene with heart lures crowds to west Texas. **Trip** 22

Springdale Savor a locally sourced meal before canyoneering. **Trip** 25

Silver City Billy the Kid and summer monsoons keep things wild. **Trips** 17 18

Mesa Verde National Park

At Mesa Verde, the site of 600 ancient cliff dwellings, you explore the past by scrambling up 10ft ladders, scaling a 60ft rock face and crawling 12ft through a tunnel. As you'll discover on **Trip 30: San Juan Skyway & the Million Dollar Highway**, the park is also a place for contemplation. Ancestral Puebloans vacated it in AD 1300 for reasons still not fully understood.

Trips 1 30

15

Taos Pueblo Dancer at the summer pow-wow

Taos

Ruggedly beautiful Taos has drawn a range of admirers over the years. Nineteenth-century mountain man Kit Carson had a home downtown and creative types like Georgia O'Keeffe and DH Lawrence also stayed awhile. And Carl Jung and Dennis Hopper? Maybe they came for the quirky individualism, which you can experience on **Trip 15: Enchanted Circle & Eastern Sangres** in the wonderfully eccentric Adobe Bar and off-the-grid Earthship community.

Trips 11 15

BEST SCENIC ROUTES

Highway 89/89A Old West meets the New West.
Trips 1 4 5 8 10 25

High Road to Taos Paint your own adventure on a picturesque mountain romp. **Trip** 11

Million Dollar Highway Thar's gold in them thar views. **Trip** 31

Highway 50 In the spring, snow-capped peaks are the backdrop. **Trip** 32

Scenic Byway 12 Cruise forested plateaus and red-rock canyons. **Trip** 26

HIGHLIGHTS
★

Carlsbad Caverns National Park Subterranean wonders

Native American art A Navajo couple bedecked in turquoise jewelry

Carlsbad Caverns National Park

The elevator drops the length of the Empire State Building then opens onto a subterranean village that holds a snack bar, water fountains, restrooms and the impressive 255ft-high Big Room, where geologic wonders line a 2-mile path. Explore the inky depths on **Trip 16: Las Cruces to Carlsbad Caverns**.

Trip 16

White Sands National Monument

Frisbee on the dunes, umbrellas in the sand, kids riding wind-blown swells – the only thing missing is the water. But you don't mind, not with 275 sq miles of gypsum draping the landscape with a hypnotic whiteness. For full immersion on **Trip 16: Las Cruces to Carlsbad Caverns**, buy a disc and sled down the slopes.

Trip 16

Native American Art

The most compelling traditional crafts of today put a fresh spin on ancient traditions. At Phoenix's Heard Museum on **Trip 10: Tribal Trails**, you'll even see Harry Potter–themed pottery. From Hopi kachina dolls to Navajo rugs to Zuni jewelry, art is a window into the heart of native Southwest peoples.

Trips

1 10 11 14 19

Hoover Dam

Before you begin the Hoover Dam Tour on **Trip 1: Four Corners Cruise**, the guide points out the window, gesturing toward a tiny opening on the face of the 726ft-tall dam. It looks very far away. As you're smushed into the elevator, you pause, 'Do I really want to do–' and whoosh, you're dropping 50 stories into this concrete beast. Pretty cool.

Trips 1 9

Canyon de Chelly

This remote, multipronged canyon feels far removed from time and space. Used as a stronghold by the Navajo, it has been the site of great violence. But families still farm the canyon, and it remains a beautiful sight, with walls soaring 1000ft from the canyon floor. The last stop on **Trip 10: Tribal Trails**, it's a compelling place to consider the Southwest's native people.

Trip 10

(left) **Hoover Dam** Lake Mead towers;

(below) **Southwest cuisine** Green chile cheeseburger

Green Chiles & Texas BBQ

In the Southwest, gift stores are filled with chile-themed gifts and homes are hung with dried-chile ristras. As you'll see on **Trip 12: El Camino Real & Turquoise Trail**, New Mexican restaurants rely on chiles as a key ingredient. In Texas, the emphasis is on barbecue, and on **Trip 21: Hill Country** the fun is in sampling the variations.

Trips

BEST ROADSIDE ODDITIES

Cadillac Ranch Ten Cadillacs are jammed in the dirt. **Trip** 2

Wigwam Motel Sleep in concrete tipis on Route 66. **Trip** 2

New Shoe Tree Sneakers drape a lonely cottonwood tree. **Trip** 32

Very Large Array Radio Telescope Is anybody out there? **Trip** 18

21

IF YOU LIKE...

Red rock hiking Distinctive to the Southwest

Southwest Cuisine

From green-chile cheeseburgers to vegan BLTs to Navajo tacos, eating in the Southwest is as diverse as its cultures and landscapes.

7 Southern Desert Wanderings Oh, Tucson, we love your menu: Sonoran dogs, breakfast burritos and nuevo-Mexican masterpieces.

10 Tribal Trails Savor indigenous Native American dishes at Kai, fry bread in Phoenix and enjoy lamb-and-hominy stew on the Hopi Reservation.

12 El Camino Real & Turquoise Trail A cheeseburger topped with Hatch green chiles? Why yes.

24 Heart of Texas Laredo serves great Mexican eats while big steaks are the bait in Amarillo.

History & Culture

Ancient civilizations left behind cliff dwellings, gunslingers left bullet holes and Alamo heroes left legends to fill hundreds of books.

3 A Taste of the Old West Boothill Graveyard and the OK Corral spotlight mining-town lore in Tombstone.

10 Tribal Trails Cliff dwellings and petroglyphs provide clues about prehistoric lifestyles while museums cover the Indian Wars and cultural issues.

21 Hill Country Remember the Alamo then learn about President Lyndon Johnson at his ranch and his boyhood home.

11 High & Low Roads to Taos Santa Fe recently celebrated its 400th birthday, but Taos Pueblo is older by 200+ years.

Open Road

When people hear the term 'Open Road,' an image from the Southwest is what likely comes to mind: sandstone canyons, big skies, saguaro-dotted deserts and twisty mountain ridges.

2 Route 66: The Southwest Long, uninterrupted stretches of the Mother Road unfurl across Arizona, with nary a stoplight in sight.

5 Fantastic Canyon Voyage Curve over mountains, roll past red rocks then zip through pine trees.

22 Big Bend Scenic Loop With Marfa lights and a renegade Prada store, things get weird on this lasso loop.

32 Highway 50: The Loneliest Road In spring, this highway across the white-hot belly of Nevada is flanked to the east by snow-capped peaks.

La Chiripada vineyard Try a local drop outside Dixon (Trip 11)

Bringing Kids

Adventurous families and quiet families – both will have a blast in the Southwest.

3 A Taste of the Old West Ride a stagecoach, watch a shootout and explore an old copper mine.

16 Las Cruces to Carlsbad Caverns Enjoy livestock-milking demos, sled rides down a sand dune, and a cavernous wonderland.

27 Moab & Southeastern National Parks Welcome active families! Kids keep busy with junior ranger programs at two national parks and there's low-key rafting and hiking.

29 Dinosaur Diamond Prehistoric Byway Dinosaur bones and footprints are bait for budding paleontologists in Utah and Colorado.

Wine & Beer

Whether it's a post-hike microbrew in Flagstaff or a glass of wine after shopping in Sedona, it just feels right to celebrate your adventures.

2 Route 66: The Southwest Savor history and beer at Kelly's Brewery and the Museum Club.

5 Fantastic Canyon Voyage Wine-tasting rooms hug Hwy 89 while the Flagstaff Ale Trail loops past microbreweries.

7 Southern Desert Wanderings A special microclimate encourages fine grapes in Sonoita and Elgin.

11 High & Low Roads to Taos The art and the wine are locally grown in Dixon.

Hiking

The Southwest is a hiker's paradise, with scenery to satisfy every type of explorer: mountain, riparian, desert and red rock.

5 Fantastic Canyon Voyage To fully appreciate the age and immensity of the Grand Canyon, hike into its depths.

22 Big Bend Scenic Loop There are more than 200 miles of trails at this enormous park, with many good sunrise and sunset vistas.

25 Zion & Bryce National Parks Slot canyons, hidden pools and lofty scrambles are Zion highlights, and a Tolkien-esque forest of hoodoos wows 'em at nearby Bryce.

31 Colorado's High Country Byways Ramble through the Rockies or slide over sand dunes.

NEED ^{TO} KNOW

CELL PHONES
The only foreign phones that work in the the USA are GSM multiband models. Cell-phone reception can be nonexistent in remote or mountainous areas.

INTERNET ACCESS
Wireless internet is available at most hotels and cafes, often for free. Internet cafes are not common, but hotels and libraries often provide computers for internet access.

FUEL
Gas stations are ubiquitous in urban areas and along interstates. They can be few and far between in isolated areas. Expect to pay $3.35 to $3.89 per gallon.

RENTAL CARS
Avis (www.avis.com)

Enterprise (www.enterprise.com)

Hertz (www.hertz.com)

IMPORTANT NUMBERS
AAA (📞 800-222-4357)

Emergency (📞 911)

Road Conditions (📞 511)

Climate

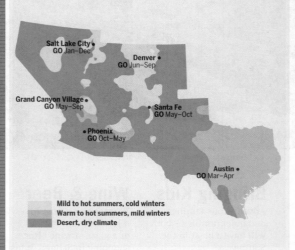

Mild to hot summers, cold winters
Warm to hot summers, mild winters
Desert, dry climate

When to Go

High Season (Jun–Aug)
» Enjoy warm temperatures and sunny skies in New Mexico, Utah and northern Arizona.

» In winter, hit the slopes in Utah, New Mexico and Colorado, or giddy-up at Arizona dude ranches (November to February).

Shoulder Season (Mar–May & Sep–Oct)
» In fall, check out colorful aspens and cottonwoods in southern Colorado and northern New Mexico.

» Cooler temperatures and lighter crowds on the Grand Canyon South Rim.

Low Season (Nov–Feb)
» National parks in northern Arizona and Utah clear out as the snow arrives.

» In summer, locals flee the heat in southern Arizona (June to August).

Your Daily Budget

Budget: Less than $100

» Campgrounds and hostels: $12–58

» Taquerias, sidewalk vendors, supermarkets for self-catering: $5–12

» Share a rental car; split cost of park vehicle entry fees: $13–20

Midrange: $100–250

» Mom-and-pop motels, low-priced chains: $60–100

» Diners, good local restaurants: $8–20

» Visit museums, theme parks, national and state parks: $5–25

Top End: Over $250

» Boutique hotels, B&Bs, resorts, national park lodges: $120–300

» Upscale restaurants: $18–63

» Hire an outdoor outfitter; take a guided tour; book ahead for top performances: from $25

Eating

Roadside diners Simple, cheap places with limited menus.

Taquerias and food stands Outdoor stalls selling tacos, frybread and Sonoran hotdogs.

Farm-to-table In mountain towns and big cities, the focus is increasingly about fresh and local.

Vegetarians Options can be limited in cattle country, but most cafes have vegetarian options.

Eating price indicators represent price of a main dish:

$	less than $10
$$	$10–20
$$$	more than $20

Sleeping

B&Bs Quaint accommodations, usually include breakfast.

Motels Affordable options, typically outside downtown.

Camping Facilities for tents, often at state and national parks. Some also offer simple cabins.

Resorts Popular in warm, sunny cities and beautiful backcountry areas; often have spas.

Price indicators represent the cost of a double room:

$	under $100
$$	$100-200
$$$	over $200

Arriving in Southwest USA

Denver International Airport

Rental Cars Courtesy shuttles to and from rental car offices stop on Level 5, Island 4 at Jeppesen Terminal.

Buses Outside door 506 in West Terminal and door 511 in East Terminal. Pay $9 to $13 to Stapleton, downtown and suburbs.

Taxis Around $60 to downtown.

Shuttles From $22 to Denver.

McCarran International Airport (Las Vegas)

Rental Cars Blue-and-white McCarran Rent-a-Car shuttles run from Terminals 1 and 2 to the rental car center 3 miles away.

Taxis Pay $12 to $21 to the Strip; 30 minutes in heavy traffic; per NV Taxi Authority, taking the tunnel will result in a higher fare.

Shuttles Cost $7 to the Strip; take exit door 9 to Bell Trans.

Money

ATMs widely available, but less prevalent on Native American land. Credit cards are accepted in most hotels and restaurants.

Tipping

Standard is 15% to 20% for waiters and bartenders, 10% to 15% for taxi drivers and $1 to $2 per bag for porters.

Time

Most of the Southwest is on Mountain Time. Arizona does not use daylight savings time (DST). The Navajo Reservation, which lies in Arizona, New Mexico and Utah *does* observe DST.

Useful Websites

Lonely Planet (www.lonelyplanet.com/usa/southwest) Summaries, travel news, links and traveler forum.

National Park Service (www.nps.gov) Current information about national parks.

Public Lands Information Center (www.publiclands.org) Provides descriptions, maps and book recommendations.

Recreation.gov (www.recreation.gov) Camping reservations on federally managed lands.

Arizona Scenic Roads (www.arizonascenicroads.com) Routes and summaries.

For more, see Driving in Southwest USA (p340).

CITY GUIDE

Las Vegas The Strip at dusk

LAS VEGAS

Las Vegas has been reinventing itself since the days of the Rat Pack. To grab your attention, and your cash, the old is constantly torn down for the new. What's hot right now? On the Strip, it's the swank charms of City Center casinos. Downtown, it's the Mob Museum and Fremont St.

Getting Around

Avoid driving on the Strip. If you're renting a car, self-park at your casino. From there, walk or ride the **monorail** (www.lvmonorail.com; 1 ride $5, 24/72hr pass $12/28, child under 6yr free; ⊙7am-midnight Mon, to 2am Tue-Thu, to 3am Fri-Sun), which runs from Sahara Station near Circus Circus south to MGM Grand, with stops along the way.

Parking

Casino parking lots are typically free. The catch? Remembering where you parked.

Where to Eat

The glitziest restaurants are on the Strip, with many bearing the names of celebrity chefs. The food is typically superb, if pricey, and cheap eats can be hard to find. The Strip is also famous for decadent buffets. Some of the best restaurants are off-Strip.

Where to Stay

The Strip stretches south on S Las Vegas Blvd from Circus Circus to Mandalay Bay. This is where the action is, and rooms are priced accordingly. Many hotels along the Strip charge a daily resort fee ($20 to $28). If you dig, you can find deals at older properties.

Bargains can be had in summer, midweek and after holidays. Rates are typically lower downtown or just off the Strip.

Useful Websites

Eater Vegas (www.vegas.eater.com) News about chefs and restaurants.

Vegas Chatter (www.vegaschatter.com) The latest happenings in Sin City.

Las Vegas.com (www.lasvegas.com) Run by the Las Vegas Convention and Visitors Authority.

Lonely Planet (lonelyplanet.com/usa/las-vegas) Where to eat, sleep, shop and hit the town.

Trips through Las Vegas 1 15

Phoenix City skyline

PHOENIX

Sprawling Phoenix has a bit of spring in its step. The new downtown dining-and-entertainment district, Cityscape, is welcoming guests, and officials are prepping for the 2015 Super Bowl. Swanky Scottsdale shines with upscale malls, art galleries and posh resorts. Camelback Mountain watches over it all.

Getting Around

A car is the best way to navigate the sprawl. At Sky Harbor International Airport, the free Phoenix Sky Train runs from economy parking to Terminal 4 and the METRO light-rail station at 44th St and E Washington St. **Valley Metro** (☎602-253-5000; www.valleymetro.org; tickets $2) operates buses all over the Valley. The free **Scottsdale Trolley** (www. scottsdaleaz.gov/trolley; ⏰11am-6pm Fri-Wed) loops through downtown Scottsdale.

Parking

Meters cost $1.50 per hour in downtown Phoenix (9am to 5pm weekdays). On-street parking in downtown Scottsdale is free, with time limits. At resorts, parking is usually included in the daily resort fee. Motels and smaller chain hotels do not typically charge guests for parking.

Where to Eat

Good restaurants are scattered across the metropolitan area, with clusters in downtown Phoenix, and in the Arts District and Southbridge in Scottsdale. Mexican restaurants, steakhouses and chic cafes are popular.

Where to Stay

Greater Phoenix is well-stocked with hotels and resorts, with a large concentration of resorts in Scottsdale. What you won't find is many B&Bs, cozy inns or charming mom-and-pop motels. Prices plummet in summer.

Useful Websites

Arizona Republic (www. azcentral.com) Arizona's largest newspaper.

Phoenix New Times (www. phoenixnewtimes.com) The major free weekly; lots of event and restaurant listings.

Visit Phoenix (www. visitphoenix.com) Greater Phoenix tourism website.

Trip through Phoenix

Santa Fe Distinctive adobe architecture

SANTA FE

The country's oldest state capital is a captivating place, energized by the easy melding of three cultures – Native American, Hispanic and Anglo. It's also beautiful, with the Sangre de Christo Mountains framing simple adobes. The historic Plaza links the 400-year-old city to the past, but artistic pursuits keep the vibe fresh.

Getting Around

The Plaza area is easily covered on foot, but you will want a car for exploring outside downtown.

Parking

Near the Plaza there are parking garages at 216 W San Francisco St and 100 E Water St. Both are $2 per hour with a $10 daily maximum.

Where to Eat

There are a number of good restaurants near the plaza, but some of the tastiest food is found at the city-licensed takeaway stalls on the Plaza lawn – try the beef fajitas with fresh guacamole. Many of Santa Fe's best eateries are in the Railyard District and along the adjacent Guadalupe St. Like to cook? Learn to make Southwestern dishes with a lesson at the **Santa Fe School of Cooking** (📞505-983-4511; www.santafeschoolofcooking.com; 125 N Guadalupe St; ⏱9:30am-5:30pm Mon-Fri, 9:30-5pm Sat, noon-4pm Sun).

Where to Stay

Low-budget and national chains line Cerrilos Rd. More expensive inns, posh B&Bs and boutique hotels tend to be closer to the Plaza. Generally, January and February offer the lowest rates.

Useful Websites

New Mexican (www.santafenewmexican.com) Daily paper with breaking news.

SantaFe.com (www.santafe.com) Listings for upcoming concerts, readings and openings in northern New Mexico.

Santa Fe Reporter (www.sfreporter.com) Free alternative weekly with thorough cultural listings.

Trips through Santa Fe

Austin Tangy trailer-stand tacos

AUSTIN

With its quirky, laid-back vibe and its standing as Live Music Capital of the World, Austin is one of the decade's definitive 'it' cities. Watch live music every night, stroll funky South Congress, dig into spicy Tex-Mex and tangy barbecue, and meet some of the friendliest people you'll find.

Getting Around

Downtown is easy to get around, and since Austin is pretty spread out, most everybody drives. However, you can always catch a Capital Metro bus (single ride $1) or take a taxi ($2.40 per mile) if you can find one – or call **Yellow Cab** (512-452-9999).

Parking

Aside from downtown and campus, parking is usually plentiful and free. Downtown meters (25c for 15 to 20 minutes) run late on weekends, including Sunday. The parking garage at 1201 San Jacinto is free for two hours and $2 per hour after that, maxing out at $8.

Where to Eat

Top restaurants are scattered all over town, but South Congress has the best concentration of interesting eateries. For cheap meals on the go, try the food trailer enclaves on South Congress, East 6th and Waller Sts, or S First and Elizabeth Sts. For Tex-Mex and a fun vibe, try the ever-popular **Güero's Taco Bar** (512-447-7688; 1412 S Congress Ave; mains $6-15; 11am-10pm).

Where to Stay

Downtown has everything from high-end chains to the historic Driskill Hotel to the Firehouse Hostel. Chains in every price range are found along I-35. South Congress (SoCo) has some quirky and cool digs. Look for bed and breakfasts in the Hyde Park area.

Useful Websites

Austin CVB (www.austintexas. org) Detailed travel planning.

Austin 360 (www.austin360. com) Listings, listings and more listings.

Austin Chronicle (www. austinchronicle.com) Events calendar from the local weekly.

Trip through Austin

Arizona Trips

ARIZONA IS WHERE SONGS ABOUT THE ROAD ARE BORN. And it's not just due to the scenery. Yes, the highways unfurl in front of stunning red rocks and deserts, but there's more to this place than beauty. There's a hint of the untamed. Something stubborn and disobedient. A little rock-and-roll, if you will.

Just look at the ornery characters and give-'em-hell stops along these drives. Wyatt Earp took no guff at the OK Corral. Geronimo gave the US Army fits in the Chiricahuas. The old mining town of Jerome clings to a crumbling hillside. A stubborn developer dropped London Bridge into the empty desert. And then there's the relentless Colorado River, carving the Grand Canyon for 6 million years. So get your motor runnin'...

Vermilion Cliffs Spectacular sandstone formations (Trip 4)

Arizona Trips

DON'T MISS

Audrey Headframe Park

Stand on a piece of glass over a 1920ft mining shaft. Look down, if you dare, on Trip 5

Pondering Petroglyphs

Solar calendars? The art of shamans? Or simply prehistoric graffiti? See for yourself on Trips 2 8

Horseshoe Bend

If you're a sucker for a gobsmacking view, stroll to this cliff-side perch over the Colorado River – 1100ft below – on Trips 1 4

Superstition Mountain Museum

Small and old-school, but a charmer; check out its its wacky wildlife dioramas and treasure maps on Trip 6

Airport Mesa

It's an easy scramble to a sweeping 360-degree view of Sedona's monolithic red rocks on Trips 5 8

Horseshoe Bend *A sheer drop – both beautiful and terrifying*

Classic Trip

Four Corners Cruise

1

This road trip is super-sized, covering the grandest views and biggest wows in the Southwest – from Vegas to Zion to the Grand Canyon and beyond. The timid should stay at a home.

TRIP HIGHLIGHTS

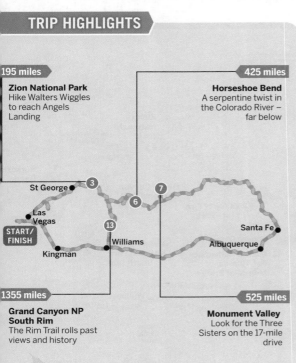

195 miles

Zion National Park
Hike Walters Wiggles to reach Angels Landing

425 miles

Horseshoe Bend
A serpentine twist in the Colorado River – far below

1355 miles

Grand Canyon NP South Rim
The Rim Trail rolls past views and history

525 miles

Monument Valley
Look for the Three Sisters on the 17-mile drive

10 DAYS
1850 MILES /
2980KM

GREAT FOR...

BEST TIME TO GO

Spring and fall for lighter crowds and pleasant temperatures.

  ESSENTIAL PHOTO

The glory of the Grand Canyon from Mather Point on the South Rim.

 BEST FOR OUTDOORS

Angels Rest Trail in Zion National Park.

Classic Trip

1 Four Corners Cruise

From a distance, the rugged buttes of Monument Valley look like the remains of a prehistoric fortress, red-gold ramparts protecting ancient secrets. But their sun-reflected beauty lures you in. Up close, the rocks are mesmerizing, an alluring mix of the familiar and elusive. Yes, they're recognizable from multitudes of Westerns, but the big screen doesn't capture the changing patterns of light, the imposing height or the strangeness of the angles. It's a captivating spell — one cast by breathtaking vistas across the Southwest.

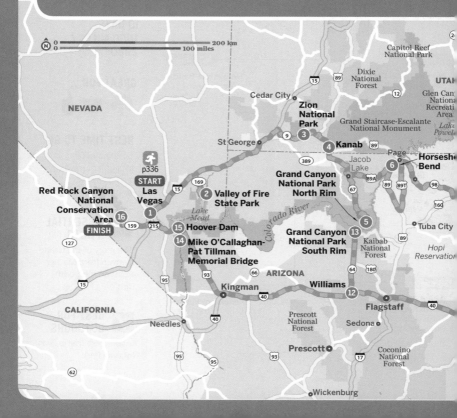

❶ Las Vegas

The giant pink stiletto in the lobby of Vegas' **Cosmopolitan** (www.cosmopolitanlasvegas.com; 3708 Las Vegas Blvd S; ⊘24hr) is an eye-catcher. Designed by Roark Gourley, the 9ft-tall shoe was supposed to be a piece of art on display. But its protective ropes were soon pushed aside by party girls who stepped inside the shoe to pose for photos. In response, the Cosmopolitan removed the ropes. After 16 months, the stiletto was sent out for repairs because of all the love, proving that what the crowd wants is what the crowd gets in Vegas.

Take in more of the city's excess with a morning walk past the icons of the Strip (see p336), then spend the afternoon downtown at the new **Mob Museum** (www.themobmuseum.org; 300 Stewart Ave; adult/child $20/14; ⊘10am-7pm Sun-Thu, to 8pm Fri & Sat),

LINK YOUR TRIP

11 High & Low Roads to Taos

Take the high road and the low road between Santa Fe and Taos, with fine craftwork, historic churches and mountain scenery.

27 Moab & Southeastern National Parks

From Monument Valley drive north on US 163 to US 191, continuing north to Moab and sandstone arches.

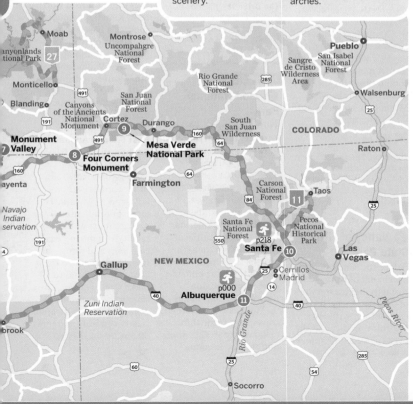

a three-story collection of exhibits examining the development of organized crime in America and the mob's connection to Las Vegas. One block south, you can zipline over **Fremont St** from Slotzilla's 11th-story launchpad (www.vegasexperience.com) then end the night with an illuminated stroll at the **Neon Museum** (☎702-387-6366; www.neonmuseum.org; 770 Las Vegas Blvd N; day tour adult/child $18/12, night tour $25/22; ☺9-10am & 7:30-9pm Jun-Aug, extended daytime hours beginning at 10am rest of the year). A money-saving combo ticket for the Mob Museum and the Neon Museum is now available for $30 per person.

✗ ⏟ p45

The Drive » Follow I-15 north for 37 miles then take exit 7. From here, Hwy 169/Valley of Fire Hwy travels 15 miles to the park.

❷ Valley of Fire State Park

Before the sandstone bacchanal of Utah, swing through this masterwork of desert scenery. It's an easy detour, with Hwy 169 running through the **park** (☎702-397-2088; www.parks.nv.gov/parks/valley-offire-state-park; per vehicle $10; ☺visitor center 8:30am-4:30pm) and passing close to the psychedelically shaped red rock outcroppings. From the visitor center, take the winding scenic side road out to **White Domes**, an 11-mile round-trip. En route you'll pass **Rainbow Vista**, followed by the turn-off to **Fire Canyon** and **Silica Dome** (where Captain Kirk perished in *Star Trek: Generations*).

Spring and fall are the best times to visit; summer temperatures typically exceed 100°F (more than 37°C).

The Drive » Return to I-15 north, cruising through Arizona and into Utah. Leave the highway at exit 16 and follow Hwy 9 east for 32 miles.

TRIP HIGHLIGHT

❸ Zion National Park

The climb up Angels Landing in **Zion National Park** (www.nps.gov/zion; Hwy 9; 7-day per vehicle $25; ☺24hr, Zion Canyon visitor center 8am-7:30pm Jun-Aug, closes earlier rest of year) may be the best day hike in North America. From Grotto Trailhead, the 5.4-mile round-trip crosses the Virgin River, hugs a towering cliffside, squeezes through a narrow canyon, snakes up Walters Wiggles, then traverses a razor-thin ridge where steel chains and the encouraging words of strangers are your only safety net. Your reward after the final scramble to the 5790ft summit? A bird's-eye view of Zion Canyon. The hike reflects what's best about the park: beauty, adventure and the shared community of people who love the outdoors.

The Drive » Take Hwy 9 east, driving almost 25 miles to Hwy 89. Follow Hwy 89 south to outdoorsy Kanab.

❹ Kanab

Sitting between Zion, **Grand Staircase-Escalante** (p281) and the Grand Canyon North Rim, Kanab is a good spot for a base camp. Hundreds of Western movies were filmed here, and John Wayne and other gun-slingin' celebs really put the town on the map. Today, animal lovers know that the town is home to the **Best Friends Animal Sanctuary** (☎435-644-2001; www.bestfriends.org; Angel Canyon, Hwy 89; admission free; ☺9:30am-5:30pm; ♿), the country's largest no-kill animal shelter. Tours of the facility – home to dogs, cats, pigs and birds – are free, but call ahead to confirm times and to make a reservation. The sanctuary's welcome center (open 8am to 5pm) is between mile markers 69 and 70 on Hwy 89.

✗ ⏟ p45

The Drive » Continue into Arizona – now on Hwy 89A – and climb the Kaibab Plateau. Turn right onto Hwy 67 at Jacob Lake and drive 44 miles to Grand Canyon Lodge.

----

5 Grand Canyon National Park North Rim

While driving through the ponderosa forest that opens onto rolling meadows in Kaibab National Forest, keep an eye out for mule deer as you approach the entrance to the **park** (per vehicle $25; ☺closed winter). Stop by the **North Rim Visitor Center** (☎928-638-7864; www.nps.gov/grca; ☺8am-6pm mid-May–mid-Oct, 9am-4pm Oct 16-31), beside Grand Canyon Lodge (p72), for information and to join ranger-led nature walks and night-time programs. Enjoy a cocktail from the **Roughrider Saloon** on the lodge terrace while soaking up the view.

For an easy but scenic half-day hike, follow the 4-mile **Cape Final Trail** (round-trip) through ponderosa pines to great canyon views. The difficult 14-mile **North Kaibab Trail** is the only maintained rim-to-river trail and connects with trails to the South Rim near Phantom Ranch. The trailhead is 2 miles north of Grand Canyon Lodge. For inner-canyon hiking, walk 0.75 miles down to Coconino

TOP TIP: NO BOTTLED WATER

As a conservation measure, Grand Canyon National Park no longer sells bottled water. Instead, fill your thermos at water filling stations along the rim or at Canyon View Marketplace. Water bottles had constituted 20% of the waste generated in the park.

Overlook or 2 miles to the Supai Tunnel.

For scenic drives and more hikes, see p67.

The Drive » At press time, the highway department had closed Hwy 89 between Bitter Springs and Page because a landslide had buckled the road. It should be closed until 2015. Hwy 89T is the temporary route. Turn right onto Hwy 89A heading east at Jacob Lake. Follow Hwy 89A down the Kaibab Plateau, past Lees Ferry and the closed section of Hwy 89, to Hwy 89T. Turn left onto Hwy 89T and take it north to Page.

TRIP HIGHLIGHT

6 Horseshoe Bend

The clifftop view at Horseshoe Bend will sear itself onto your memory. One thousand feet below, the Colorado River carves a perfect U through towering sandstone. It's simultaneously beautiful and terrifying. There are no railings – it's just you, a sheer drop and dozens of people you don't know. Free-range toddlers are not a good idea. From the parking lot it's a 0.75-mile one-way hike to the rim. There's a steep hill along the way, and the

trail is unshaded, but it's worth it. The trailhead is on Hwy 89 south of Page, south of mile marker 541.

The Drive » From the parking lot, turn left onto Hwy 89 and drive north a short distance to Hwy 98. Turn right onto Hwy 98 and follow it southeast to Hwy 160. Turn left and drive 32 miles, passing the entrance to Navajo National Monument. In Kayenta, turn left onto Hwy 163 north for almost 24 miles to Monument Valley, which sits beside the Arizona and Utah border.

TRIP HIGHLIGHT

7 Monument Valley

'May I walk in beauty' is the final line of a famous Navajo prayer. Beauty comes in many forms on the Navajo's sprawling reservation, but makes its most famous appearance at Monument Valley, a majestic cluster of buttes and spires. For up-close views of the formations, drive into the Monument Valley **Navajo Tribal Park** (☎435-727-5874; www.navajonationparks.org/htm/monumentvalley.htm; adult/child $5/free; ☺drive 6am-8:30pm May-Sep, 8am-4:30pm Oct-Apr; visitor center 6am-8pm May-Sep, 8am-5pm

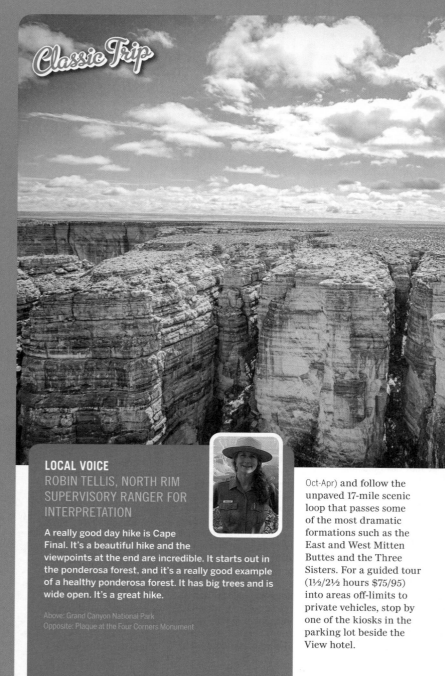

LOCAL VOICE
ROBIN TELLIS, NORTH RIM
SUPERVISORY RANGER FOR
INTERPRETATION

A really good day hike is Cape
Final. It's a beautiful hike and the
viewpoints at the end are incredible. It starts out in
the ponderosa forest, and it's a really good example
of a healthy ponderosa forest. It has big trees and is
wide open. It's a great hike.

Above: Grand Canyon National Park
Opposite: Plaque at the Four Corners Monument

Oct-Apr) and follow the
unpaved 17-mile scenic
loop that passes some
of the most dramatic
formations such as the
East and West Mitten
Buttes and the Three
Sisters. For a guided tour
(1½/2½ hours $75/95)
into areas off-limits to
private vehicles, stop by
one of the kiosks in the
parking lot beside the
View hotel.

FRANCKREPORTER/GETTY IMAGES ©

🛏 p45

The Drive >> Follow Hwy 163 back to Kayenta. Turn left and follow Hwy 160 east about 72 miles to tiny Tee Noc Pos. Take a sharp left to stay on Hwy 160 and drive 6 miles to the monument.

----

❽ Four Corners Monument

It's seriously remote, but you can't skip the **Four**

MICHAEL SAYLES/ALAMY ©

Corners Monument (☎928-871-6647; www. navajonationparks.org; admission $3; ⊗8am-7pm May-Sep, 8am-5pm Oct-Apr) in a road trips guide about the Southwest! Once you arrive, don't be shy: put a foot into Arizona and plant the other in New Mexico. Slap a hand in Utah and place the other in Colorado. Smile for the camera. It makes a

good photo, even if it's not 100% accurate – an April 2009 news story had government surveyors admitting that the marker is almost 2000ft east of where it should be, but it remains a legally recognized border point. Half the fun is watching the acrobatics performed on the marker.

The Drive >> Return to Hwy 160 and turn left. It's a 50-mile

Classic Trip

drive across New Mexico and into Colorado.

---

9 Mesa Verde National Park

Ancestral Puebloan sites are found throughout the canyons and mesas of **Mesa Verde** (☎970-529-4465; www.nps.gov/meve; 7-day pass car/motorcycle $15/8 Jun-Aug, low season $10/5; **P**🚻), perched on a high plateau south of Cortez and Mancos. According to the park, the Ancestral Pueobloans didn't 'disappear' 700 years ago, they simply migrated south, becoming the ancestors of today's Native Americans. If you only have time for a short visit, check out the **Chapin Mesa Museum** (p313) and walk through the **Spruce Tree House**, where you can climb down a wooden ladder into a kiva.

Mesa Verde rewards travelers who set aside a day or more to take the ranger-led tours of **Cliff Palace** and **Balcony House**, explore **Wetherill Mesa** (the quieter side of canyon), visit the museum or participate in one of the campfire programs at **Morefield Campground** (☎970-529-4465; www.visitmesaverde.

com; North Rim Rd; ⏱May-early Oct; 🚲). The park also offers plenty of hiking, skiing, snowshoeing and mountain-biking options. Camp out or stay in luxury at the lodge.

The Drive » Hop onto US 160, following it 35 miles east to Durango and then another 60 miles to join US 84 S. In New Mexico, US 84S passes through Abiquiú, home of artist Georgia O'Keeffe from 1949 until 1986. Continue toward Santa Fe, exiting onto N Guadalupe St to head toward the Plaza.

---

10 Santa Fe

This 400-year-old city is pretty darn inviting. You've got the juxtaposition of art and landscape, with cow skulls hanging from sky-blue walls and slender crosses topping century-old missions. And then there's the comfortable mingling of Native American, Hispanic and Anglo cultures, with ancient pueblos, 300-year-old haciendas and stylish modern buildings standing in easy proximity.

The beauty of the region was captured by New Mexico's most famous artist, Georgia O'Keeffe. Possessing the world's largest collection of her work, the **Georgia O'Keeffe Museum** (☎505-946-1000; www.okeeffemuseum.org; 217 Johnson St; adult/child $12/free; ⏱10am-5pm, to 7pm Fri) showcases the thick

brushwork and luminous colors that don't always come through on the ubiquitous posters; take your time to relish them firsthand. The museum is housed in a former Spanish Baptist church with adobe walls that has been renovated to form 10 skylit galleries.

The city is anchored by the Plaza, which was the end of the Santa Fe Trail between 1822 and 1880. For more sights, see Stretch Your Legs, p218.

✕ 🛏 p45

The Drive » The historic route to Albuquerque is the Turquoise Trail, which follows Hwy 14 south for 50 miles through Cerrillos and Madrid (see p147). If you're in a hurry, take I-25 south.

---

11 Albuquerque

Most of Albuquerque's top sites are concentrated in Old Town, which is a straight shot west on Central Ave from Nob Hill and the University of New Mexico (UNM).

The most extravagant route to the top of 10,378ft Sandia Crest is via the **Sandia Peak Tramway** (www.sandiapeak.com; Tramway Blvd; vehicles $1, adult/youth 13-20yr/child $20/17/12; ⏱9am-8pm Wed-Mon, from 5pm Tue Sep-May, 9am-9pm Jun-Aug). The 2.7-mile tram ride starts in the desert realm of cholla cactus and soars to the pine-topped summit. For exercise, take the beautiful 8-mile (one-way) **La Luz Trail** back down, connecting with the 2-mile Tramway Trail to return to your car. The La Luz Trail passes a small waterfall, pine forests and spectacular views. It gets hot, so start early. Take Tramway Blvd east from I-25 to get to the tramway. See p220 for an Old Town tour

 p45

The Drive » From Albuquerque to Williams, AZ, I-40 overlaps or parallels Route 66. It's 355 miles to Williams.

⑫ Williams

Train buffs, Route 66 enthusiasts and Grand Canyon–bound vacationers all cross paths in Williams, a small town with all the charm and authenticity of 'Main Street America.' If you only have time for a day visit to the park, the **Grand Canyon Railway** (📞800-843-8724, 928-635-4253; www.thetrain. com; Railway Depot, 233 N Grand Canyon Blvd; round-trip adult/child from $75/45; 🚻) is a fun and hassle-free way to get there and back. After a **Wild West show** beside the tracks, the train departs for its two-hour ride to the South Rim, where you can explore by foot or shuttle. Late May through early November passengers can ride in an open-air **Pullman** (adult/child $59/29).

On Route 66 the divey **Sultana Bar** (📞928-635-2021; 301 W Rte 66; ⏰10am-2am, from noon in winter), which once housed a speakeasy, recently had its 100th birthday.

TRIP HIGHLIGHT

⑬ Grand Canyon National Park South Rim

A walk along the **Rim Trail** in **Grand Canyon Village** brings stunning views of the **Grand Canyon** (www.nps.gov/grca; per vehicle $25, per person arriving on foot, bicycle or motorcycle $12, admission good for 7 days; ⏰visitor centre 8am-5pm) as well as historic buildings, Native American crafts and geologic displays.

Starting from the plaza at **Bright Angel Trailhead**, walk east on the Rim Trail to **Kolb Studio**, which holds a small bookstore and an art gallery. Next door is **Lookout Studio**, designed by noted architect Mary Colter to look like the stone dwellings of the Southwest's Puebloans. There's a small shop, and the popular **Condor Talks** are given here.

Step into the **El Tovar** hotel to see its replica Remington bronzes, stained glass, stuffed mounts and exposed beams, or to admire the canyon views from its porches. Despite renovations, this rambling 1905 wooden lodge hasn't lost any of its genteel historic patina.

Next door, the **Hopi House** has offered high-quality Native American jewelry and crafts since 1904. Just east, the **Trail of Time** interpretive display traces the history of the canyon's formation. End at the

PHOTO FINISH: KOLB STUDIO

Before digital photography, brothers Ellsworth and Emery Kolb were shooting souvenir photos of mule-riding Grand Canyon visitors as they began their descent down the Bright Angel Trail. The brothers would sell finished prints to the tourists returning to the rim at the end of the day. But in the early 1900s there was no running water on the South Rim – so how did they process their prints?

After snapping photos from their studio window that overlooked a bend in the trail, one of the brothers would run 4.6 miles down to the waters of Indian Garden with the negatives, print the photos in their lab there and then run, or perhaps hike briskly, back up the Bright Angel to meet visitors with their prints.

Classic Trip

big-windowed **Yavapai Museum** and its superb geology exhibit. 'For more about South Rim hiking trails, see p75.

🛏 p45

The Drive ›› Return to I-40 west. Drive 116 miles then take exit 48 for US 93 north. Take US 93 north for 72 miles, crossing into Nevada. In Nevada take exit 2 for Hwy 172 to the dam.

⑭ Mike O-Callaghan-Pat Tillman Memorial Bridge

This graceful span, dedicated in 2010, was named for Mike O'Callaghan, governor of Nevada from 1971 to 1979, and for NFL star Pat Tillman, a safety for the Arizona Cardinals who enlisted as a US Army Ranger after September 11. Tillman was killed by friendly fire during a battle in Afghanistan in 2004.

Open to pedestrians along a walkway separated from traffic on Hwy 93, the bridge sits 890ft above the Colorado River. It's the second-highest bridge in the US, and provides a bird's-eye view of Hoover Dam and Lake Mead behind it.

The Drive ›› Turn right onto the access road and drive a short distance down to the dam.

⑮ Hoover Dam

A statue of bronze winged figures stands atop **Hoover Dam** (📞866-730-9097, 702-494-2517; www.usbr.gov/lc/hooverdam; Hwy 93; visitor center $8, incl powerplant tour adult/child $11/9, all-inclusive tour $30; ⊙9am-6pm, last ticket sold 5:15pm), memorializing those who built the massive 726ft concrete structure, one of the world's tallest dams. This New Deal public works project, completed ahead of schedule and under budget in 1936, was the Colorado River's first major dam. Thousands of men and their families, eager for work during the Depression, came to Black Canyon and worked in excruciating conditions – dangling hundreds of feet above the canyon in 120°F (about 50°C) desert heat. Hundreds lost their lives.

Today, guided tours begin at the visitor center, where a video screening features original footage of the construction. After the movie take an elevator ride 50 stories below to view the dam's massive power generators, each of which alone could power a city of 100,000 people. Parking costs $7.

The Drive ›› Return to US 93, following it north as it joins I-515. Take exit 61 for I-215 north. After 11 miles I-215 becomes Clark County 215. Follow it just over 13 miles to Charleston Blvd/Hwy 159 at exit 26 and follow it west.

⑯ Red Rock Canyon National Conservation Area

The awesome natural forces in this **national conservation area** (📞702-515-5350; www.redrockcanyonlv.org; day-use per car/bicycle $7/3; ⊙scenic loop 6am-8pm Apr-Sep, earlier Oct-Mar, visitor center 8am-4:30pm) can't be exaggerated. Created about 65 million years ago, the canyon is more like a valley, with a steep, rugged red rock escarpment rising 3000ft on its western edge, evidence of tectonic-plate collisions.

The 13-mile, one-way scenic drive passes some of the canyon's most striking features, where you can access hiking trails and rock-climbing routes. The 2.5-mile round-trip hike to **Calico Tanks** climbs through the sandstone and ends atop rocks offering a grand view of the desert and mountains, with Vegas thrown in for sizzle.

National park passes are accepted for admission.

Eating & Sleeping

Las Vegas ❶

✕ Gordon Ramsay Steak
Steakhouse $$$

(📞877-346-4642; www.parislasvegas.com; 3655 Las Vegas Blvd S, Paris; mains $32-63; 🕐4:30-10:30pm, bar to midnight Fri & Sat) Ribboned in red and domed by a jaunty Union Jack, Gordon Ramsay's new steakhouse is one of the top seats in town.

✕ Lotus of Siam
Thai $$

(📞702-735-3033; www.saipinchutima.com; 953 E Sahara Ave; mains $9-30; 🕐11:30am-2:30pm Mon-Fri, buffet to 2pm, 5:30-10pm daily) According to *Gourmet Magazine*, this is the top Thai restaurant in the US. One bite of the simple pad Thai – or any of the exotic northern Thai dishes – will have you nodding in agreement.

🛏 Vdara
Hotel $$

(📞702-590-2767; www.vdara.com; 2600 W Harmon Ave; r $159-196; 🅿🛜🏊) Cool sophistication and warm hospitality merge seamlessly at new-on-the-scene Vdara, a no-gaming, all-suites hotel in City Center.

Kanab ❹

✕ Rocking V Cafe
American $$

(www.rockingvcafe.com; 97 W Center St; lunch $9-14, dinner $15-29; 🕐11:30am-10pm; 🍴) Fresh ingredients star in dishes like hand-cut buffalo tenderloin and char-grilled zucchini with curried quinoa. Local artwork decorating the 1892 brick storefront is as creative as the food. Off-season hours vary.

🛏 Quail Park Lodge
Motel $$

(📞435-215-1447; www.quailparklodge.com; 125 N 300 W; r $115-159; ❄@🛜🏊🍴) A colorful retro style pervades all 13 rooms at this refurbished 1963 motel. Mod cons include microwaves and minifridges.

Monument Valley ❼

🛏 View Hotel
Hotel $$$

(📞435-727-5555; www.monumentvalleyview.com; Hwy 163; r $209-265, ste $299-329; ❄@🛜) Southwestern-themed rooms that are nice but nothing compared to their balconies, which have straight-on views of the famous red rock formation. Wi-fi available in the lobby only.

Santa Fe ❿

✕ Horseman's Haven
New Mexican $

(4354 Cerrillos Rd; mains $8-12; 🕐8am-8pm Mon-Sat, 8:30am-2pm Sun; 🍴) The hottest green chile in town! (The timid should order it on the side.) Service is friendly and fast, and the enormous 3D burrito might fill you for the day.

🛏 El Rey Inn
Hotel $$

(📞505-982-1931; www.elreyinnsantafe.com; 1862 Cerrillos Rd; r incl breakfast $105-165, ste from $150; 🅿❄@🛜🍴) A classic courtyard hotel with super rooms, a great pool and hot tub, and a kids' playground scattered around 5 acres of greenery. Most rooms have air-con.

Albuquerque ⓫

✕ Flying Star Café
American $

(www.flyingstarcafe.com; 3416 Central Ave SE; mains $6-12; 🕐6am-11pm Sun-Thu, to midnight Fri-Sat; 🛜🍴🍴) With seven constantly packed locations, this is the place to go for creative diner food made with regional ingredients, including homemade soups, main dishes from sandwiches to stir-fry, and yummy desserts.

Grand Canyon ⓭

🛏 El Tovar
Lodge $$$

(www.grandcanyonlodges.com; d $178-273, ste $335-426; 🕐year-round; ❄🛜) Standard rooms are on the small side, so those in need of elbow room should go for the deluxe rooms. Both offer casual luxury and high standards of comfort.

High lights Neon relics from the heyday of the Mother Road

Classic Trip

Route 66: The Southwest

2

Concrete wigwams. A neon cowboy. Lumbering dinosaurs. 'Get Your Kitsch on Route 66' might be the best slogan for the scrubby patch of Mother Road connecting Texas, New Mexico and Arizona.

TRIP HIGHLIGHTS

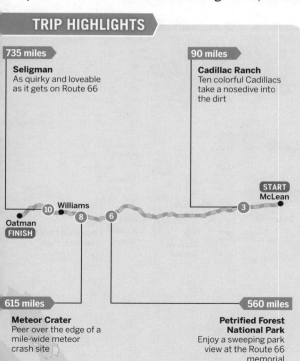

735 miles

Seligman
As quirky and loveable as it gets on Route 66

90 miles

Cadillac Ranch
Ten colorful Cadillacs take a nosedive into the dirt

START
McLean

Williams

Oatman
FINISH

615 miles

Meteor Crater
Peer over the edge of a mile-wide meteor crash site

560 miles

Petrified Forest National Park
Enjoy a sweeping park view at the Route 66 memorial

5–7 DAYS
910 MILES / 1464KM

GREAT FOR...

BEST TIME TO GO
April through September for the best conditions on the Colorado Plateau.

ESSENTIAL PHOTO
The concrete teepees at the Wigwam Motel in Holbrook.

BEST 2 DAYS
The natural wonders at Petrified Forest National Park and Meteor Crater.

Classic Trip

2 Route 66: The Southwest

The Snow Cap Drive-In encapsulates everything that's cool about Route 66. There's personal interaction — did the guy behind the counter just squirt me with fake mustard? It's old-fashioned — why yes, I will get a malt. And it draws a diverse sampling of humanity — from a busload of bleary-eyed tourists to a horde of tough-looking biker dudes, all linked at the Snow Cap by the simple joy of an ice-cream cone.

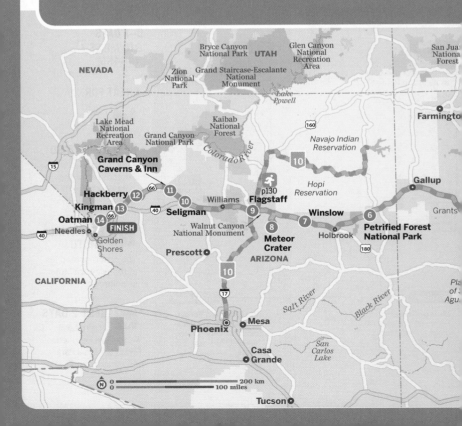

① McLean

Beyond the towns, the great wide open of the Texas Panhandle is punctuated only by the occasional windmill, and the distinct odor of cattle feedlots in the distance. The Mother Road cuts across this emptiness for 178 miles, and the entire route has been replaced by I-40 – but there are a few noteworthy attractions.

The sprawling grasslands of Texas and other western cattle states were once open range, where steers and cowboys could wander where they darn well pleased. That all changed in the 1880s when the devil's rope – more commonly known as barbed wire – began dividing up the land into private parcels. The

Devil's Rope Museum
(www.barbwiremuseum.com; 100 Kingsley St; admission free; ⊙9am-5pm Mon-Fri, 10am-4pm Sat Mar-Nov) in the battered town of McLean off exit 141 has vast barbed wire displays and a small but homey and idiosyncratic room

LINK YOUR TRIP

24 Heart of Texas
Swing south to the colorful Palo Duro Canyon from Amarillo.

10 Tribal Trails
Swap neon and kitsch for cliff dwellings and natural wonders at Walnut Canyon west of Meteor Crater.

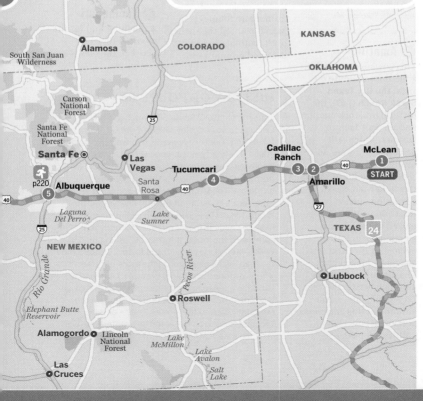

Classic Trip

devoted to Route 66. The detailed map of the road in Texas is a must. Also worth a look are the moving portraits of Dust Bowl damage and refugees from human-made environmental disaster.

The Drive » I-40 west of McLean glides over low-rolling hills. The landscape flattens at Groom, home of the tilting water tower and a 19-story cross at exit 112. Take exit 96 for Conway to snap a photo of the forlorn VW Beetle Ranch, aka the Bug Ranch, on the south side of the interstate. Take exit 74.

② Amarillo

This cowboy town holds a plethora of Route 66 sites: the **Big Texan Steak Ranch** (p57), the historic livestock auction and the San Jacinto District, which still has original Route 66 businesses.

As for the Big Texan, this hokey but classic attraction opened on Route 66 in 1960. It moved to its current location when I-40 opened in 1971 and has never looked back. The attention-grabbing gimmick here is the 'free 72oz steak' offer – you have to eat this enormous portion of cow plus a multitude of sides in

under one hour, or you pay for the entire meal ($72). Contestants sit at a raised table to 'entertain' the other diners. Less than 20% pass the challenge. Insane eating aside, the ranch is a fine place to eat, and the steaks are excellent.

🍴 p57

The Drive » Continue west on I-40. Take exit 60, about 5 miles west of the edge of downtown Amarillo, then backtrack a mile on the southern frontage road from the Love's gas station.

TRIP HIGHLIGHT

③ Cadillac Ranch

Controversial local millionaire Stanley Marsh planted the shells of 10 Cadillacs in the deserted ground west

of Amarillo in 1974 – an installation that's come to be known as Cadillac Ranch. He said he created it as a tribute to the golden age of car travel. The cars date from 1948 to 1959 – a period in which tail fins just kept getting bigger and bigger. Come prepared: the accepted practice is to leave your own mark by spray painting on the cars. It can also get quite windy.

The Drive » Follow I-40 west 60 miles to the New Mexico border. Tucumcari – and its 1200+ motel rooms – is 40 miles west.

④ Tucumcari

A ranching and farming town sandwiched between the mesas and

HISTORY OF ROUTE 66

Launched in 1926, Route 66 stretched from Chicago to Los Angeles, linking a ribbon of small towns and country byways as it rolled across eight states. The road gained notoriety during the Great Depression when migrant farmers followed it west from the Dust Bowl across the Great Plains. The nickname 'The Mother Road' first appeared in John Steinbeck's novel about the era, *The Grapes of Wrath*. Meanwhile unemployed young men were hired to pave the final stretches of muddy road. They completed the job, as it turns out, just in time for WWII. Hitchhiking soldiers and factory workers rode the road next. Things got a little more fun after WWII when newfound prosperity prompted Americans to hit the open road. Sadly, just as things got going, the Feds rolled out the interstate system, which eventually caused the Mother Road's demise. The very last town to be bypassed by an interstate was Arizona's very own Williams, in 1984.

the plains, Tucumcari is home to one of the best-preserved sections of Route 66 in the country. It's a great place to drive through at night, when dozens of neon signs – relics of the town's Route 66 heyday – cast a crazy rainbow-colored glow. Tucumcari's Route 66 motoring legacy and other regional highlights are recorded on 35 murals in downtown and the surrounding area. Pick up a map for the murals at the **Chamber of Commerce** (☑575-461-1694; www.tucumcarinm.com; 404 W Route 66; ⊙8:30am-5pm Mon-Fri).

The engaging **Mesalands Dinosaur Museum** (www.mesalands.edu/community/dinosaur-museum; 222 E Laughlin St; adult/child $6.50/4; ⊙10am-6pm Tue-Sat Mar-Aug, noon-5pm Tue-Sat Sep-Feb; 🚻) showcases real dinosaur bones and has hands-on exhibits for kids. Casts of dinosaur bones are done in bronze (not the usual plaster of paris), which shows fine detail.

✖ 🛏 p57

The Drive ≫ West on I-40, dry and windy plains spread into the distance, the horizon interrupted by flat-topped mesas. To stretch your legs, take exit 273 from Route 66/I-40 to downtown Santa Rosa and the Route 66 Auto Museum, which has upwards of 35 cars from the 1920s through the 1960s, all in beautiful condition.

5 Albuquerque

After 1936, Route 66 was re-aligned from its original path, which linked north through Santa Fe, to a direct line west into Albuquerque. Today, the city's Central Ave follows the post-1937 route. It passes through Nob Hill, the university, downtown and Old Town. For a walking tour, see p220.

The patioed **Kelly's Brewery** (www.kellysbrewpub.com; 3222 Central Ave SE; ⊙8am-10:30pm Sun-Thu, 8am-midnight Fri & Sat), in trendy Nob Hill, was an Art Moderne gas station on the route, commissioned in 1939. West of I-25, look for the spectacular tile-and-wood artistry of the **KiMo Theatre** (www.cabq.gov/kimo; 423 Central Ave NW, Downtown), across from the old Indian trading post. This 1927 icon of pueblo deco architecture blends Native American culture with art-deco design.

It also screens classic movies like *Singin' in the Rain* and *2001 A Space Odyssey*. For prehistoric designs, take exit 154, just west of downtown, and drive north 3 miles to Petroglyph National Monument (p168), which has more than 20,000 rock etchings.

✖ p57

The Drive ≫ Route 66 dips from I-40 into Gallup, becoming the main drag past beautifully renovated buildings, including the 1926 Spanish Colonial El Morro Theater. From Gallup, it's 21 miles to Arizona. In Arizona, take exit 311 to enter Petrified Forest National Park.

TRIP HIGHLIGHT

6 Petrified Forest National Park

The 'trees' of the **Petrified Forest** (☑928-524-6228; www.nps.gov/pefo; vehicle/walk-in, bicycle & motorcycle $10/5; ⊙7am-8pm Jun & Jul, shorter hours Aug-May) are fragmented, fossilized 225-million-year-old logs scattered over a vast area of

Classic Trip

Tourists
treated same as
Home Folks

WE'RE OPEN

CORVETTE DRIVE

ROUTE U.S. 66

ROUTE U.S. 66

fresh up · Ça ravigote

¡COWBOYS!

WHY THIS IS A CLASSIC TRIP
AMY C BALFOUR,
AUTHOR

My favorite section of Route 66 is the 115-mile stretch from Kingman east to Seligman. Things get quirky fast. You suddenly want to race a train. Tiny Hackberry draws an international crowd. Up pops a town called Valentine followed by a fake dinosaur. All linked by nutty Burma Shave signs. Then, for the finale, you get trapped inside Snow Cap Drive-In because you can't open the trick door.

Top: Route 66 memorabilia at Hackberry General Store
Left: Prehistoric kitsch
Right: The iconic highway shield

semidesert grassland. Many are huge – up to 6ft in diameter – and at least one spans a ravine to form a natural bridge. The trees arrived via major floods, only to be buried beneath silica-rich volcanic ash before they could decompose. Groundwater dissolved the silica, carried it through the logs and crystallized into solid, sparkly quartz mashed up with iron, carbon, manganese and other minerals. Uplift and erosion eventually exposed the logs.

The park, which straddles the I-40, has an entrance at exit 311 in the north and another off Hwy 180 in the south. A 28-mile paved scenic road, Park Rd, links the two. To avoid backtracking, westbound travelers should start in the north, eastbound travelers in the south.

The Drive » Drive west 25 miles to Holbrook, a former Wild West town now home to rock shops and the photo-ready Wigwam Motel (p57), which was added to the National Register of Historic Places in 2002. If someone is on the grounds before the 4pm check-in, they'll probably let you peek inside one of the wigwams. Continue west on I-40.

----

❼ Winslow

'Standing on a corner in Winslow, Arizona...' Sound familiar? Thanks

Classic Trip

to The Eagles' 1972 tune 'Take It Easy' (written by Jackson Browne and Glenn Frey), lonesome little Winslow is now a popular stop on the tourist track. Pose with the life-sized bronze statue of a hitchhiker backed by a charmingly hokey trompe l'oeil mural of that famous 'girl – my Lord! – in a flatbed Ford' at the corner of 2nd St and Kinsley Ave.

🛏 p57

The Drive » Twenty miles west of Winslow, take exit 233 off I-40 and drive 6 miles south.

TRIP HIGHLIGHT
❽ Meteor Crater

A fiery meteor crashed here 50,000 years ago, blasting a hole some 550ft deep and nearly 1 mile across. Today the privately owned **crater** (☎928-289-5898; www.meteorcrater.com; adult/senior/child $16/15/8; ⊙7am-7pm Jun–mid-Sep, 8am-5pm mid-Sep–May) is a major tourist attraction with exhibits about meteorites, crater geology and the Apollo astronauts who used its lunar-like surface to train for their moon missions. You're not allowed to go down into the crater, but there are a few look-out points as well as guided one-hour rim walking tours (free with admission). Look for the glinting piece of a plane that crashed inside the crater.

The Drive » Follow I-40 to exit 204 and pick up Route 66 into Flagstaff. This is also the exit for Walnut Canyon National Monument (p122). From the east, Route 66 passes a lengthy swath of cheap indie motels as well as the boot-kickin' Museum Club (3404 E Rte 66), a log-cabin-style roadhouse that's been entertaining roadtrippers since 1936. Chug into downtown Flagstaff alongside the railroad tracks.

---

❾ Flagstaff

This cultured college town still has an Old West heart. At the visitor center, which is inside the old train depot, pick up the free Route 66 walking tour guide. One of the buildings on the tour is the **Downtowner Motel**, formerly a brothel and now the Grand Canyon International Youth Hostel. Just north of Route 66 are two century-old hotels: the **Hotel Monte Vista** and the **Weatherford**. Both have plenty of character, not to mention convivial watering holes and lively ghosts. For more on these and other Flagstaff buildings, see p130.

If you're interested in architecture, stop by **Riordan Mansion State Historic Park** (☎928-779-4395; www.azstateparks.com/Parks/RIMA; 409 W Riordan Rd; adult/child $10/5;

SCENIC DRIVE: PETRIFIED FOREST NATIONAL PARK

The leisurely Park Rd, which travels through the park, has about 15 pullouts with interpretive signs and some short trails. North of I-40, enjoy sweeping views of the Painted Desert, where nature presents a hauntingly beautiful palette, especially at sunset. After Park Rd turns south, keep a lookout for the roadside display about Route 66, just north of the interstate.

The 3-mile loop drive out to Blue Mesa has 360-degree views of spectacular badlands, log falls and logs balancing atop hills with the leathery texture of elephant skin.

Two trails near the southern entrance provide the best access for close-ups of the petrified logs: the 0.6-mile Long Logs Trail, which has the largest concentration, and the 0.4-mile Giant Logs Trail, which is entered through the Rainbow Forest Museum and sports the park's largest log.

⏱9:30am-5pm Jun-Aug daily, 10:30am-5pm Thu-Mon Sep-May) just south. Having made a fortune from their Arizona Lumber Company, brothers Micahel and Timothy Riordan had this house built in 1904. The mansion's Craftsman-style design was the brainchild of architect Charles Whittlesey, who designed El Tovar on the South Rim.

The Drive » Route 66 rejoins I-40 just west of Flagstaff. Continue 30 miles to Williams, home of the Grand Canyon Railway and the Red Garter Bed & Bakery (p57). Williams was the last community along Route 66 to be bypassed by I-40. Route 66 runs one way in Williams, from west to east. Railroad Ave parallels Route 66 and heads one-way west. Rejoin I-40, only to leave it again at exit 139.

TRIP HIGHLIGHT

⓾ Seligman

This town takes its Route 66 heritage seriously – or with a squirt of fake mustard – thanks to the Delgadillo brothers, who for decades were the Mother Road's biggest boosters. Juan sadly passed away in 2004, but octogenarian Angel and his wife Vilma still run **Angel & Vilma Delgadillo's Route 66 Gift Shop** (📞928-422-3352; www.route66giftshop.com; 217 E Rte 66; ⏱9am-5pm), where you can poke

around for souvenirs and admire license plates sent in by fans from all over the world. Angel's madcap brother Juan used to rule supreme over the **Snow Cap Drive-In** (📞928-422-3291; 301 E Rte 66; dishes $3-6; ⏱10am-6pm mid-Mar–Nov), a Route 66 institution serving burgers, ice cream and pranks, now run by his sons Bob and John.

🍴 🛏 p57

The Drive » The Mother Road rolls northwest through scrub-covered desert, passing Burma Shave signs and lonely trains. Kitsch roars its dinosaury head at mile marker 115.

⓫ Grand Canyon Caverns & Inn

An elevator drops 210ft underground to artificially lit limestone caverns and the skeletal remains of a prehistoric ground sloth at **Grand Canyon Caverns** (📞928-422-3223; www.gccaverns.com; Rte 66, mile marker 115; 45 min tour adult/child $19/14; ⏱9am-5pm Jun-Sep, 10am-5pm Oct-May; 🚸). If you've seen other caverns, these might not be as impressive, but kids get a kick out of a visit. A shorter, wheelchair-accessible tour is also available (adult/child $16/12). Since 2010, the property has offered its Cavern Suite ($800) as an overnight lodging option.

This underground 'room' has two double beds, a sitting area and multicolored lamps. If you ever wanted to live in one of those postapocalyptic sci-fi movies, here's your chance! One of the DVDs on offer is an underground horror flick – watch it here only if you're especially twisted.

The Drive » Continue west through Peach Springs, Truxton and Valentine, for 35 miles.

⓬ Hackberry

Teensy Hackberry is one of the few still-kicking settlements on this segment of the Mother Road's original alignment. Inside an eccentrically remodeled gas station is the **Hackberry General Store** (📞928-769-2605; www.hackberrygeneralstore.com; 11255 E Rte 66; admission free; ⏱typically 8am-6pm). The life's work of highway memorialist Robert Waldmire, the building started as a general store in 1934, and is a great place to stop for an ice-cold Coke and Mother Road memorabilia. Check out the vintage petrol pumps, cars faded by decades of hot desert light, old toilet seats and rusted-out ironwork.

The Drive » From here, Route 66 arcs southwest, back toward I-40, then barrels into Kingman, which is 27 miles away.

ROUTE 66 READS

John Steinbeck's *Grapes of Wrath* is the classic novel of travel on the Mother Road during the Dust Bowl era. Woody Guthrie's *Bound for Glory* is the road-trip autobiography of a folk singer during the Depression. Several museums and bookshops along Route 66 stock Native American, Old West and pioneer writing with ties to the old highway.

13 Kingman

Founded in the heady 1880s railway days, Kingman is a quiet place today. The visitor center is at the western end of Kingman, in a 1907 powerhouse. The building also holds the small but engaging **Route 66 Museum** (☎928-753-9889; www.kingmantourism.org; 120 W Andy Devine Ave; adult/senior/child $4/3/ free; ◷9am-5pm), which has a great historical overview of the Mother Road. Check out the **former Methodist church** at 5th and Spring St where Clark Gable and Carole Lombard tied the knot.

In Kingman Route 66 is also called Andy Devine Ave, named after the hometown hero who acted in Hollywood classics like *Stagecoach*, in which he played the perpetually befuddled stagecoach driver.

The Drive » Route 66 corkscrews up a claustrophobic canyon and the rugged Black Mountains then passes falling rocks, cacti and tumbleweeds on its way over Sitgreaves Pass (3523ft) and into the old mining town of Oatman.

14 Oatman

Since the veins of ore ran dry in 1942, crusty Oatman has reinvented itself as a movie set and Wild West tourist trap, complete with staged gun fights (daily at 1:30pm and 3:30pm) and gift stores named Fast Fanny's Place and the Classy Ass.

Speaking of asses, there are plenty of them (the four-legged kind, that is) roaming the streets. Stupid and endearing, they're the descendants of pack animals left by the early miners. These burros may beg for food, but do not feed them carrots. Instead, buy healthier hay cubes for $1 per bag at nearby stores. Squeezed among the shops is the 1902 **Oatman Hotel**, a surprisingly modest shack (no longer renting rooms) where Clark Gable and Carole Lombard spent their wedding night in 1939. On July 4 the town holds a sidewalk egg-frying contest. Now that's hot!

From here, Route 66 twists down to Golden Shores and I-40.

Eating & Sleeping

Amarillo 2

✕ Big Texan Steak
Ranch   Steakhouse $$
(www.bigtexan.com; 7701 I-40 E, exit 74; mains $10-40; ⏱7am-10:30pm; 🚻) Consume the 72oz steak, plus all the fixin's, in an hour and it's free; otherwise you pay $72.

Tucumcari 4

✕ Kix on 66   Diner $
(www.kixon66.com; 1102 E Tucumcari Blvd; mains $5-10; ⏱6am-2pm; 🛜) A classic diner with a hint of style, Kix serves American and southwest specialties right beside the Mother Road.

🛏 Blue Swallow
Motel   Historic Motel $
(☎575-461-9849; www.blueswallowmotel.com; 815 E Tucumcari Blvd; r from $65; ❄🛜📺) Spend the night in this beautifully restored motel and feel time slide in reverse. The place has a great lobby, friendly owners and vintage, uniquely decorated rooms.

Albuquerque 5

✕ Frontier   New Mexican $
(www.frontierrestaurant.com; 2400 Central Ave SE; mains $3-11; ⏱5am-1am; 🚭🚻) Get in line for enormous cinnamon rolls and some of the best *huevos rancheros* in town. The food, people-watching and Western art are all outstanding.

Holbrook

🛏 Wigwam Motel   Motel $
(☎928-524-3048; www.galerie-kokopelli.com/wigwam; 811 W Hopi Dr; r $56-62; ❄) Each room is its own concrete tipi, with restored 1950s hickory log-pole furniture and retro TVs. Book ahead.

Winslow 7

🛏 La Posada   Historic Hotel $$
(☎928-289-4366; www.laposada.org; 303 E 2nd St; r $119-169; ❄🛜📺) The Mary Colter–designed 1930s hacienda features elaborate tile work, glass-and-tin chandeliers, Navajo rugs and other details that accent its rustic Western-style elegance. The period-styled rooms are named for illustrious former guests. Even if you're not staying here, enjoy modern Southwestern fare at its restaurant, the **Turquoise Room** (breakfast $8-12, lunch $9-13, dinner $19-40).

Williams

🛏 Red Garter Bed & Bakery   B&B $$
(☎928-635-1484; www.redgarter.com; 137 W Railroad Ave; d $135-160; ❄🛜) Up until the 1940s, gambling and girls were the draw at this 1897 bordello-turned-B&B across from the tracks. Nowadays, the place trades on its historic charm and reputation for hauntings. Rates include a 'continental-plus' breakfast with freshly-baked pastries.

- - - - - - - - - - - - - - - - - - - -

Seligman 10

✕ Westside Lilo's Cafe   Cafe $
(415 W Rte 66; breakfast $9-15, lunch $7-14, dinner $13-22; ⏱6am-9pm) Come here for friendly service and good American and German dishes. And resistance will be hard the minute you look in the dessert case.

🛏 Supai Motel   Motel $
(☎928-422-4153; www.supaimotel.com; 134 W Chino Ave; s/d $54/59; ❄🛜) A classic courtyard motel offering simple but perfectly fine rooms with refrigerators and microwaves. The neon sign is the best in town.

HERE LIES
GEORGE JOHNSON
HANGED BY
MISTAKE
1882
HE WAS RIGHT
WE
WAS WRONG
BUT WE STRUNG
HIM UP
AND NOW HE'S
GONE

Boothill Graveyard
Famed boneyard of gunslingers

UNKNOWN

BEN ALLENY

A Taste of the Old West

3

There are three certainties in southern Arizona: big skies, rowdy saloons and the 2pm shoot-out at the OK Corral – the marquee attraction in a land born of myths and mining claims.

TRIP HIGHLIGHTS

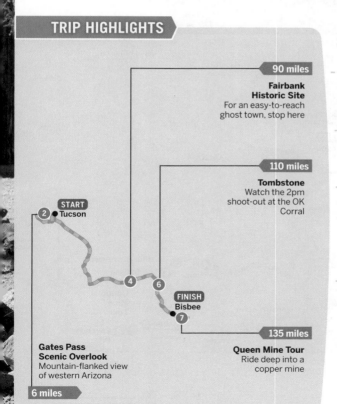

90 miles

Fairbank Historic Site
For an easy-to-reach ghost town, stop here

110 miles

Tombstone
Watch the 2pm shoot-out at the OK Corral

START
Tucson

FINISH
Bisbee

135 miles

Queen Mine Tour
Ride deep into a copper mine

Gates Pass Scenic Overlook
Mountain-flanked view of western Arizona

6 miles

**3 DAYS
135 MILES / 217KM**

GREAT FOR...

BEST TIME TO GO

Higher elevations keep things cool year-round.

ESSENTIAL PHOTO

A mountain-framed view of the Sonoran Desert at Gateway Pass Overlook.

BEST FOR HISTORY

Exhibits at the OK Corral and the Tombstone Courthouse State Historic Park.

3 | A Taste of the Old West

Murdered. Shot. Stabbed. Drowned. Killed by Indians. Cowboy Killed in Stampede. The epitaphs at Boothill Graveyard outside Tombstone are startlingly specific. One quick stroll around tells you everything you need to know about living – and dying – in mining towns in the late 1800s. Though legend may exceed reality, the discovery of gold, silver and copper deposits lured prospectors, gunslingers and outlaws – all part of a cast of characters that made Arizona a true frontier.

❶ Tucson

For an engaging primer about Arizona's Old West history, visit the **Arizona History Museum** (www.arizonahistoricalsociety.org; 949 E 2nd St; adult/child $5/4; ⏱10am-4pm Mon-Sat) beside the University of Arizona. The Arizona Mining Hall exhibit is a walk-through replica of an old copper mine. The Geronimo exhibit displays Geronimo's rifle and an 1880s photograph of his negotiations with Indian fighter Gen George Crook.

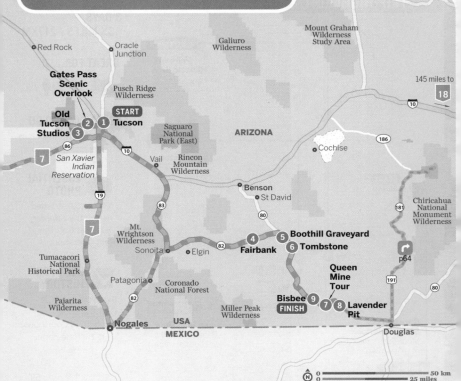

University Blvd, lined with bars and restaurants, is one block south. For more art and history, try the Tucson walking tour (p128).

 p65

The Drive » Drive north two blocks to E Speedway Blvd and turn left. Speedway becomes W Gates Pass Rd and swoops into Tucson Mountain Park. Watch for cops and cyclists. As you climb toward the pass, look for a one-way sign. Turn right here. If you miss it, turn around at the next parking lot.

TRIP HIGHLIGHT

2 Gates Pass Scenic Overlook

Named for Thomas Gates, who was looking for a short cut through the Tucson Mountains to his carbonate mine, this **overlook** (www.pima.

LINK YOUR TRIP

7 Southern Desert Wanderings

From Fairbank travel west on Hwy 82 to Sonoita for wine tasting and southern Arizona wanderings.

18 Into the Gila

Drive north from Tombstone to I-10 east for some green chile in southwestern New Mexico.

gov/nrpr/parks/tmp) **offers** a mountain-flanked view of western Arizona. On a clear day you can see Kitt Peak 36 miles away. There are trails, interpretive signs and lots of saguaros. It's a nice place to watch the sunset.

The Drive » Continue west until Gates Pass Rd ends. Turn left onto S Kinney Rd.

3 Old Tucson Studios

Nicknamed 'Hollywood in the Desert,' this **old movie set** (☎520-883-0100; www.oldtucson.com; 201 S Kinney Rd; adult/child $17/11; ⊙Fri-Sun Oct-Dec & May, daily Jan-Apr, closed Jun-Sep; ⊞) of 1860s Tucson was built in 1939 for the filming of *Arizona*. Hundreds of flicks followed, bringing in a galaxy of stars. Now a Wild West theme park, it caters to families hankering for shootouts, stagecoach rides, saloons, sheriffs and stunts (but no roller coasters or rides). The museum displays movie and TV memorabilia, including clothing worn by Clint Eastwood in *Joe Kidd* and and Michael Landon in *Little House on the Prairie*.

The Drive » Follow S Kinney St south to Hwy 86 E. Drive east to I-19, following it north to I-10 east. Continue 21 miles to exit 281 for Hwy 83 south. Pick up Hwy 82 east. Cross the

San Pedro River. The Fairbank turnoff is just ahead on the left. The total drive is almost 90 miles.

TRIP HIGHLIGHT

4 Fairbank Historic Site

It's the silence that grabs you on a stroll through the ghost town of Fairbank, where a handful of old buildings cluster near the road and the river. Established in 1881 to serve the New Mexico & Arizona Railroad, Fairbank was a transportation hub for nearby mining towns. The last residents left in the 1970s. Today, there's a **visitor center** (www.sanpedroriver.org/fairbank.htm; Fairbank; ⊙9:30am-4:30pm Fri-Sun, hours vary) in the restored 1920s school house. If it's closed, pick up the walking tour brochure from the kiosk. The tour loops past abandoned houses, a stable and an 1882 mercantile building.

The Drive » Drive east on Hwy 82 to Hwy 80. Turn right and drive south about 3 miles on Hwy 80.

5 Boothill Graveyard

Boot Hill was a name commonly given to graveyards for gunslingers and those who died violent deaths, ie they died with their boots on. For a list of the

3 A TASTE OF THE OLD WEST

graves – and causes of death – of those buried here, buy the $3 brochure at the entrance. The graves of Billy Clanton and Tom and Frank McClaury, all killed at the shoot-out at the OK Corral, are on Row 2. The marker for Lester Moore, a Wells Fargo agent, may be the most famous: 'Here lies Lester Moore, Four slugs from a .44, No Les, no More.'

The Drive » Turn left onto Hwy 80, which becomes E Fremont St in Tombstone, about 0.25 miles ahead.

TRIP HIGHLIGHT

➏ Tombstone

On October 26, 1881, Wyatt Earp, brothers Virgil and Morgan and their friend Doc Holliday gunned down outlaws Billy Clanton and Tom and Frank McLaury at the **OK Corral** (☎520-457-3456; www.ok-corral. com; Allen St btwn 3rd & 4th Sts; admission $10, without

gunfight $6; ◷9am-5pm). Today, the corral is the heart of Tombstone. It has models of the gunfighters and other exhibits, including CS Fly's early photography studio and a recreated 'crib,' the term for rooms used by hard-working, low-paid prostitutes. The town earned its name from first-on-the-scene prospector Ed Schieffelin, who was told all he would find in the dangerous region was his own tombstone.

The **Bird Cage Theater** (☎520-457-3421; 517 E Allen St; adult/child/senior $10/8/9; ◷9am-6pm) was a saloon, dance hall, gambling parlor and home for 'negotiable affections' in the 1880s. Today it's filled with bullet holes and dusty artifacts like Doc Holliday's old Faro gaming table. There's also a creepy 'merman.' Employees report ghost sightings. Doc Holliday's girlfriend's bar **Big Nose**

Kate's (www.bignosekates. info; 417 E Allen St; ◷10am-midnight) is full of Wild West character. It's a fun place for drinking, with great painted glass, historical photographs and live music in the afternoons.

For a less sensational look at the town's past, visit the informative **Tombstone Courthouse State Historic Park** (☎520-457-3311; http:// azstateparks.com/Parks/ TOCO/; 223 Toughnut St; adult/ child $5/2; ◷9am-5pm). Artifacts include Wyatt Earp's straight razor, the town's first piano and an invitation to a hanging.

🛏 p65

The Drive » Follow Hwy 80 southeast for 25 miles through desert scrub and the Mule Mountains.

TRIP HIGHLIGHT

➐ Queen Mine Tour

Could you have worked in the dark confines of an Arizona copper mine? Test your mental toughness on a tour of the **Queen Mine** (☎520-432-2071; www.queenminetour. com; 478 Dart Rd, off Hwy 80; adult/child $13/5.50; ◷tours 9am-3:30pm; 👪) near downtown Bisbee. Visitors wear miners' garb, carry lanterns and ride a mine train 1500ft into one of the area's most famous copper mines. In the early 20th century this was the most productive mine

LOCAL KNOWLEDGE: TINY'S SALOON & STEAKHOUSE

Pick-up trucks are lined-up like horses in front of **Tiny's Saloon & Steakhouse** (☎520-578-7700; 4900 W Ajo Hwy; mains $7-19; ◷11am-10pm, bar to midnight Fri; 👪), a weathered watering hole that's known for its burgers. Inside, once your eyes adjust, slide into a booth, nod at the regulars at the bar then order a steerburger. For a saloon, Tiny's is family friendly – at least during the day – and makes a nice stop after the Old Tucson Studios. Cash only but ATM on-site.

Bird Cage Theatre Tombstone's saloon, dance hall and gambling parlor

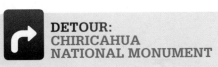

DETOUR: CHIRICAHUA NATIONAL MONUMENT

Start: ❾ Bisbee

Pronounced 'cheery-cow-wha', this remote **national monument** (📞520-824-3560; www.nps.gov/chir; Hwy 181; adult/child $5/free) is a wonderfully rugged yet whimsical wonderland. Rain, thunder and wind have chiseled volcanic rocks into fluted pinnacles, natural bridges, gravity-defying balancing boulders and soaring spires. The remoteness made Chiricahua a favorite hiding place of Apache warrior Cochise and his men. Today it's attractive to birds and wildlife. The paved **Bonita Canyon Scenic Drive** climbs 8 miles to Massai Point at 6870ft, where you'll see thousands of spires positioned on the slopes like some petrified army. To explore in greater depth, hit the trails. A hikers' shuttle bus leaves daily from the visitor center at 8:30am, going up to Massai Point for $2. Hikers return by hiking downhill.

If you're short on time, hike the **Echo Canyon Trail** at least half a mile to the Grottoes, an amazing 'cathedral' of giant boulders.

in Arizona, famous for producing particularly deep-shaded turquoise rocks known as Bisbee Blue. The tour, which lasts about an hour, is fun for kids.

The **Bisbee Visitor Center** (📞866-224-7233, 520-432-3554; www.discoverbisbee.com; 478 Dart Rd; ⏱9am-5pm Mon-Fri, 10am-4pm Sat & Sun) is also here.

The Drive ≫ Drive 0.5 miles south on Hwy 80.

- - - - - - - - - - - -

❽ Lavender Pit

The 'Scenic View' sign that points toward this immense stair-stepped gash in the earth is stretching the truth.

An open-pit mine, it produced about 600,000 tons of copper between 1950 and 1974. It's ugly but impressive.

The Drive ≫ Follow Hwy 80 north to Tombstone Canyon Rd, which leads into downtown Bisbee.

- - - - - - - - - - - -

❾ Bisbee

Bisbee built its fortune on ore found in the surrounding Mule Mountains. Between 1880 and 1975, underground and open-pit mines coughed up copper in sumptuous proportions, generating more than $6 billion worth of metals. Business really took off in 1892 when the Phelps Dodge Corporation brought in the railroad. By 1910 the population had climbed to 25,000, and nearly 50 saloons and bordellos crammed along Brewery Gulch.

As the local copper mines began to fizzle in the 1970s, hippies and artists arrived. The interweaving of the new creative types and the old miners has produced a welcoming bunch of eccentrics clinging to the mountainside.

The **Bisbee Mining & Historical Museum** (📞520-432-7071; www.bisbeemuseum.org; 5 Copper Queen Plaza; adult/child/senior $7.50/3/6.50; ⏱10am-4pm), a Smithsonian affiliate, does an excellent job documenting the town's past and the changing face of mining. From there, wander the galleries and indie shops on Main St, with a side trip into Brewery Gulch, where Arizona's oldest bar, the 100-year-old **St Elmo's** (36 Brewery Ave), attracts a boisterous crowd. Or try the **Old Bisbee Brewing Company** (www.oldbisbeebrewingcompany.com; 200 Review Alley), an easy-going watering hole in Brewery Gulch that crafts seven lip-smacking brews, including root beer.

✕ ⌫ p65

Eating & Sleeping

Tucson ❶

✕ Mi Nidito   Mexican $

(☎520-622-5081; www.minidito.net; 1813 S 4th Ave; mains $6-13; ⏱lunch & dinner Wed-Sun) The wait is worth it at this bustling spot, where Bill Clinton's order has become the signature president's plate: a heaping mound of tacos, tostados, burritos, enchiladas etc – groaning under melted cheese. Also give the prickly pear cactus chile a whirl.

✕ Pasco Kitchen & Lounge   American $$

(☎520-882-8013; www.pascokitchen.com; 820 E University Blvd; mains $10-15; ⏱11am-10pm Mon-Wed, 11am-11pm Thu, 10am-1am Fri & Sat, 10am-9pm Sun) The menu at this breezy eatery near the university offers fresh, locally sourced comfort food that's prepared with panache and tasty twists – think grass-fed all natural burgers topped by braised pork belly and a fried egg.

🛏 Catalina Park Inn   B&B $$

(☎520-792-4541; www.catalinaparkinn.com; 309 E 1st St; r $140-170; ⏱closed Jul & Aug; ✳@📶) Style, hospitality and comfort merge seamlessly at this inviting B&B, a Mediterranean-style villa just west of the University of Arizona and 4th Ave.

🛏 Hotel Congress   Historic Hotel $$

(☎520-622-8848; www.hotelcongress.com; 311 E Congress St; r $89-129; P✳@📶🐾) The historic but hip Hotel Congress is a hive of activity, mostly because of its popular cafe, bar and club. Infamous bank robber John Dillinger and his gang were captured here during a 1934 stay – check out the wall of photos and articles. Many rooms have period furnishings, rotary phones and wooden radios – but no TVs. Ask for a room at the far end of the hotel if you're noise-sensitive. Pets are $10 per night.

Tombstone ❻

🛏 Larian Motel   Motel $

(☎520-457-2272; www.tombstonemotels.com; 410 E Fremont St; r $69-79; ✳📶) Enjoy personalized attention, cute retro rooms named for historical characters (Doc Holliday, Curly Bill, Wyatt Earp) and a high standard of cleanliness. It's also close to the downtown action. Children 12 and under stay free.

Bisbee ❾

✕ Cafe Roka   New American $$$

(☎520-432-5153; www.caferoka.com; 35 Main St; dinner $17-24; ⏱5-9pm Thu-Sat) This sensuously lit grown-up spot serves innovative American cuisine that is at once smart and satisfying. The four-course dinners include salad, soup, sorbet and a rotating choice of mains. The central bar is great for solo diners. Reservations recommended.

✕ Screaming Banshee Pizza   Pizza $$

(☎520-432-1300; 200 Tombstone Canyon Rd; pizzas $7-14; ⏱4-9pm Tue & Wed, 11am-10pm Thu-Sat, 11am-9pm Sun) This is some good pizza. The ingredients are fresh, the crust is charred over a wood fire and the end result is unrelentingly delicious. There's a wide array of toppings too, from gorgonzola cheese to house-made fennel sausage. The decor is punk rock meets Mardi Gras float.

🛏 Bisbee Grand Hotel   Hotel $$

(☎520-432-5900; www.bisbeegrandhotel.com; 61 Main St; r incl breakfast $89-175; ✳📶)

You can sleep in a covered wagon at this quirky but fun hotel where the Old West comes to life (or maybe it never died) with Victorian-era decor and a kick-up-your-spurs saloon.

🛏 Shady Dell   Quirky $

(☎520-432-3567; www.theshadydell.com; 1 Douglas Rd; rates $87-145, closed early Jul-mid-Sep; ✳) Each unit at this fun-loving trailer park is an original 1950s travel trailer, meticulously restored and outfitted with period accoutrements such as vintage radios (playing '50s songs upon arrival). All have tiny kitchens, some have toilets, but showers are in the bathhouse.

Glen Canyon Dam *An ode to American ingenuity*

Grand Canyon North Rim & Lake Powell

4

Discover the secrets of the Colorado River on this ditch-the-crowds drive from Lake Powell to Lees Ferry to the North Rim of the Grand Canyon.

TRIP HIGHLIGHTS

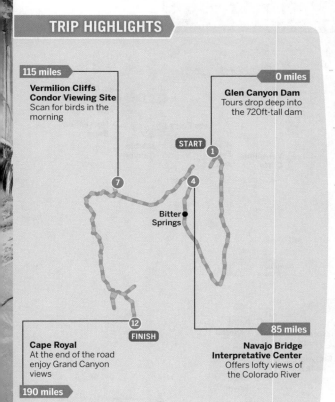

115 miles

Vermilion Cliffs Condor Viewing Site
Scan for birds in the morning

0 miles

Glen Canyon Dam
Tours drop deep into the 720ft-tall dam

START ①

④

Bitter Springs

⑦

⑫ FINISH

Cape Royal
At the end of the road enjoy Grand Canyon views

190 miles

85 miles

Navajo Bridge Interpretative Center
Offers lofty views of the Colorado River

**3 DAYS
190 MILES / 305KM**

GREAT FOR...

BEST TIME TO GO
May to October when the North Rim is open.

 ESSENTIAL PHOTO
Photograph the U-curve of the Colorado River at Horseshoe Bend.

✓ **BEST FOR OUTDOORS**
Hiking the wooded Widforss Trail along the edge of a North Rim side canyon.

4

Grand Canyon North Rim & Lake Powell

The Arizona Strip is the Land that Time Forgot. Just look around as you glide over Navajo Bridge. Below, the Colorado River cracks apart the earth. To the north, the Vermilion Cliffs stand like an impenetrable fortress, guarded by red-rock goblins on the verge of reanimation. To the south, ageless desert scrub sweeps mercilessly toward the horizon. And overhead? California condors swoop, blocking the sun with 9ft wingspans. Enjoy – and hold tight to the family chihuahua.

TRIP HIGHLIGHT

1 Glen Canyon Dam & Lake Powell

The 720ft-tall **Glen Canyon Dam** (☎928-608-6072; www.glencanyonnha.org) is a concrete ode to America's ingenuity and can-do spirit. Completed in 1963, it is the nation's second-highest concrete arch dam, only 16ft shorter than the Hoover Dam to the west. You can take guided 45-minute tours, departing from the **Carl Hayden Visitor Center** (☎928-608-6404;

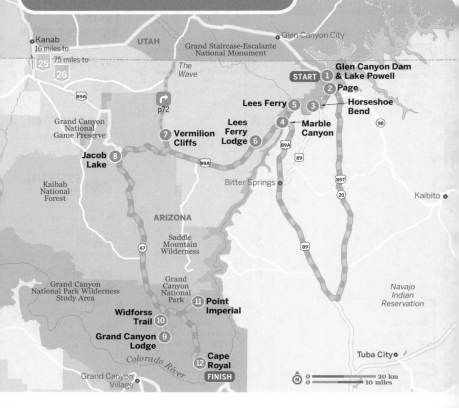

www.nps.gov/glca; Hwy 89; tour adult/child $5/2.50; ⏱tours 8:30am-4pm mid-May–mid-Sep, varies rest of year). Tours drop you deep inside the dam via elevators. Displays and videos in the visitor center tell the story of the dam's construction and provide technical facts about its operation.

The adjacent sparkling swath of blue is **Lake Powell**, part of the **Glen Canyon National Recreation Area** (📞928-608-6200; www.nps.gov/glca; 7-day pass per vehicle $15). The 186-mile-long lake was named for John Wesley Powell, the one-armed Union veteran who led the first Colorado River expedition though the Grand Canyon in 1869. The lake straddles the Utah–Arizona border, with its shoreline set against striking red

LINK YOUR TRIP

25 Zion & Bryce National Parks

Leave the Kaibab Plateau on Hwy 89A and continue to Hwy 9, which makes a stunning red-rock descent into Zion.

26 Scenic Byway 12

Swing north from Monument Valley for Ancestral Puebloan Ruins.

rocks. Rent kayaks ($45 per day) at Wahweap Marina at the **Lake Powell Resort** (📞928-645-2433; www.lakepowell.com; 100 Lakeshore Dr).

The Drive » Take Hwy 89 south past Navajo Dr. For an expansive view of the dam, turn right onto Scenic View Rd, following it behind the Denny's to get to the viewpoint parking area.

❷ Page

Established to house the workers who built Glen Canyon Dam, Page today is a great base camp for exploration of the area. It's also the place to join a tour of the stunning **Antelope Canyon** (www.navajonationparks.org/htm/antelopecanyon.htm), a slot canyon on the Navajo Reservation, which is open by Navajo-led tour only. In the more popular upper canyon, about a quarter-mile long, water and wind have carved the sandstone into an astonishingly sensuous temple of nature. Tours can feel a little like a cattle call, but the uniqueness of the experience makes it worthwhile. Try **Roger Ekis's Antelope Canyon Tours** (📞928-645-9102; www.antelopecanyon.com; 22 S Lake Powell Blvd; adult/child 5-12yr from $35/25).

  p73

The Drive » Follow Hwy 89 south out of Page. Continue 2

miles south after the junction of Hwy 89 and Hwy 98.

❸ Horseshoe Bend

For a short hike with a dramatic payoff, it's hard to beat Horseshoe Bend. Here, a 0.75-mile, one-way path leads to a lofty view of the Colorado River wrapping around a monolithic stone outcropping to form a U. Though it's short, the sandy, shadeless trail and moderate incline can be a slog. Watch your step. There are no guardrails at the viewpoint and the river is more than 1000ft below. If you're afraid of heights, stop at the covered hilltop shelter – the view is still impressive.

The Drive » At press time, Hwy 89 between Page and Bitter Springs was closed for major repairs after a landslide buckled the road. The temporary detour is the newly paved Indian Route 20, renamed Hwy 89T. To get to it from Horseshoe Bend, head north toward Page. Turn right onto Hwy 98. Follow it a short distance east to Hwy 89T south. Take Hwy 89T south to Hwy 89 then follow Hwy 89 north. Hwy 89 turns into Hwy 89A as you approach Marble Canyon. For closure updates visit www.azdot.gov/us89/.

TRIP HIGHLIGHT

❹ Marble Canyon

Hwy 89A crosses the Navajo Bridge over the Colorado River at Marble Canyon. Actually, there are two bridges: a modern one for motorists

that opened in 1995, and a historical one from 1929. Walking across the latter you'll enjoy fabulous views down Marble Canyon to the northeast lip of the Grand Canyon. The **Navajo Bridge Interpretive Center** (📞928-355-2319; www.nps. gov/glca; Hwy 89A; 🕙9am-5pm mid-Apr–mid-Oct), located on the west bank, has good background information about the bridges and the area. Keep an eye out for California condors.

The Drive ⟫ Return to Hwy 89A and turn right. Turn right again, almost immediately, onto Lees Ferry Rd. Follow it 5 miles.

- - - - - - - - - - - -

⑤ Lees Ferry

Lees Ferry is the premier put-in for Grand Canyon rafting trips on the Colorado River. The river here is also popular for fly-fishing. The area, which is a fee site within Glen Canyon National Recreation Area (p69), was named for John D Lee, the Mormon leader of the 1857 Mountain Meadows Massacre, in which 120 emigrants from Arkansas were murdered by Mormon and Paiute forces. To escape prosecution, Lee moved his wives and children to this remote outpost where they lived at the **Lonely Dell Ranch** and operated the area's only ferry service. Lee was tracked down and executed in 1877, but the ferry operated until the Navajo Bridge opened in 1929. You can walk around the ranch.

🛏 p73

The Drive ⟫ Take a right onto Hwy 89A and continue about 3 miles. This region, along the Colorado River north of the national park, is called Marble Canyon.

Grand Canyon View of the North Rim

6 Lees Ferry Lodge

This scrappy **roadside bar** (www.vermilioncliffs. com) is one of those joints where you're never quite sure who's going to roar off the highway and push through the door – rebel motorcyclist, park ranger, lonely travel writer – but they'll surely have a good story. There's a pool table and an impressive selection of beer.

📖 p73

The Drive ≫ Enjoy the quirky sites, from goblin-like red rocks to an 'Adopt the Highway' sign sponsored by Scary Larry.

TRIP HIGHLIGHT
7 Vermilion Cliffs

To increase your chances of spotting a California condor, stop at the **Condor Viewing Site** (www.blm.gov/az), near their release point. The birds, whose ancestors patrolled the skies in prehistoric times, were almost driven to extinction in the 1980s. The remaining condors were placed in captive breeding programs. Six were released here in 1997, and their numbers have grown. To get here turn right onto the graded House Rock Valley Rd (BLM Rd 1065) at the base of the Kaibab Plateau. Drive 3 miles. There are interpretive panels and a vault toilet.

The Drive ≫ Hwy 89A climbs 5000ft through the Kaibab National Forest to the lakeless outpost of Jacob Lake.

8 Jacob Lake

For the region, Jacob Lake is the closest thing to a metropolis – and all it offers is a gas station, a handful of campgrounds, an inn with a bakery and restaurant, and the USFS **Kaibab Plateau Visitor Center** (☏928-643-7298;

DETOUR:
THE WAVE

Start: ❼ Vermilion Cliffs

The Wave is a trail-free expanse of slick rock that ends at a smooth, orange-and-white striped rock, shaped into a perfect wave. This sinuous sandstone swirl, which is located in the Paria Canyon-Vermilion Cliffs Wilderness, is a favorite of photographers. A hike to the Wave requires a North Coyote Buttes permit ($7), which can be tough to obtain in spring and fall. To order a permit online, visit www.blm.gov and search for 'Coyote Buttes'. They're available four months in advance. The website also provides details about walk-up permits, awarded by lottery at the Grand Staircase Escalante-National Monument Visitor Center in Kanab, UT. If you win a spot, your permit is good for the *following* day. Plan for a six-hour hike.

cnr Hwys 89A & 67; ⊘8am-5pm mid-May–mid-Oct). The bakery at the Jacob Lake Inn (p73) is known for its homemade cookies.

 p73

The Drive » The 44 miles between Jacob Lake and the Grand Canyon Lodge via Hwy 67 south is one of the Southwest's finest drives. It rolls through hills of ponderosa forest that open onto lush meadows in Kaibab National Forest.

- - - - - - - - - - - - - -

❾ Grand Canyon Lodge

For immediate inspiration, walk through the stunning sunroom at the Grand Canyon Lodge to the narrow, quarter-mile path that leads to **Bright Angel Point**. Here you'll enjoy huge, unobstructed views into the canyon

and across to the South Rim. On clear days, look for the San Francisco Peaks more than 80 miles south.

At 8200ft, the **North Rim** (www.nps.gov/grca) is about 10°F (6°C) cooler than the south – even on summer evenings you'll need a sweater. Park admission is $25 per vehicle. The lodge and all services close from mid-October through mid-May.

 p73

The Drive » Follow Hwy 67 for 2.7 miles north from the lodge, passing the North Rim Campground. Continue about 1 mile west on the Point Sublime Access Rd.

- - - - - - - - - - - - - -

❿ Widforss Trail

Pick up a sack lunch ($12; order it the night before) at the Grand Canyon Lodge Dining Room (p73), then spend the morning hiking through meadows and aspen on this 10-mile round-trip trail. It follows the edge of a forested plateau, a pleasant walk in the shade with great rim-side views. It ends at 7811ft-high Widforss Point with expansive canyon views. It's a particularly pretty hike in September and October when leaves are golden.

The Drive » Drive north 0.25 miles on Hwy 67 to Cape Royal Rd. Turn right.

- - - - - - - - - - - - - -

⓫ Point Imperial

Point Imperial is the highest overlook on the North Rim at 8803ft. Soak up the view of Nankoweap, the Vermilion Cliffs, Marble Canyon and the Painted Desert.

The Drive » Return to Cape Royal Rd, passing viewpoints at Vista Encantada, Roosevelt Point and Walhalla Overlook.

- - - - - - - - - - - - - -

TRIP HIGHLIGHT

⓬ Cape Royal

At the end of the road follow the 0.6-mile paved trail which passes Angel's Window, a natural arch, before ending at Cape Royal Point and its stupendous views of the canyon.

Eating & Sleeping

Page ❷

✖ Bonkers
American; Italian $$

(www.bonkerspagaz.com; 810 N Navajo Dr; mains $ 9-22; ☺ from 4pm Mon-Sat) The murals of local landscapes are inspiring at this unfortunately named restaurant, which serves satisfying steaks, seafood, and pasta to appreciative crowds. Burgers and sandwiches also on the menu.

✖ Ranch House Grille
Diner $

(www.ranchhousegrille.com; 819 N Navajo Dr; mains $7-16; ☺6am-3pm) There's not much ambiance but the food is good, the portions huge and the service fast. This is your best bet for breakfast.

▣ Lake Powell Motel
Motel $$

(☎928-645-3919; www.powellmotel.com; 750 S Navajo Dr; r $69-159; ☺Apr-Oct) Formerly Bashful Bob's, this revamped motel was originally constructed to house Glen Canyon Dam builders. Four units have kitchens and they book-up quickly. A fifth, smaller room is typically held for walk-ups unless specifically requested.

Lees Ferry ❺

▣ Lees Ferry
Camping $

(www.nps.gov/glca; tent & RV sites $12) Flanked by red rocks, this hilltop campground is stunningly pretty. It has 54 river-view sites along with drinking water and toilets, but no hookups.

Lees Ferry Lodge ❻

▣ Lees Ferry Lodge
Motel $

(☎928-355-2231; www.vermilioncliffs.com; Hwy 89A; r $74; ▣) At the foot of the burnt-orange Vermilion Cliffs, the cobblestone Lees Ferry Lodge is appealingly unfussy, with porch chairs providing front-row seats for stargazing. Its 10 cosy, occasionally snug, rooms include a Cowboy Room. 3.5 miles west of Navajo Bridge.

Jacob Lake ❽

✖ Jacob Lake Inn & Restaurant
American $$

(☎928-643-7232; www.jacoblake.com; r $89-117, cabins $121-139; ☺6:30am-9pm, hours vary seasonally;) The inn offers rustic cabins, basic motel rooms and more stylish hotel rooms. For a quick meal, order hamburgers and sandwiches and sit at the diner-stye counter. The dinner specialty in the dining room is the Kaibab Jagerschnitzel. Reduced hours in winter.

Grand Canyon Lodge ❾

✖ Grand Canyon Lodge Dining Room
American $$

(☎928-638-2611, 928-645-6865 call Jan 1-Apr 15 for next season; www.grandcanyonlodgenorth.com; breakfast $7-12, lunch & dinner $12-30; ☺6:30-10am, 11:30am-2:30pm & 4:45-9:45pm, mid-May–mid-Oct) What comes with the big view? Rainbow trout, bison flank steak, several vegetarian dishes and Arizona-crafted microbrews. Dinner reservations are required.

▣ Grand Canyon Lodge
Lodge $$

(☎advance reservations 877-386-4383, reservations outside USA 480-337-1320, same-day reservations 928-638-2611; www.grandcanyonlodgenorth.com; r $124, 2-person cabins $124-192, extra guest over 15yr $10; ☺mid-May–mid-Oct; ☎) Rustic yet modern cabins are the bulk of the accommodations, with motel rooms also available. The most expensive cabins offer two rooms, a porch and beautiful rim views. There are no rooms in the lodge itself. Reserve far in advance.

▣ North Rim Campground
Campground $

(☎928-638-7814, 877-444-6777; www.recreation.gov; tent sites $6-18, RV sites $18-25; ☺mid-May–Oct; ☒) Has a general store, water, showers, a coin-operated laundry and ponderosa-shaded campsites. Sites 11, 14, 15, 16 and 18 have views of a side canyon. By reservation only from mid-May to mid-October.

Jerome 'The Wickedest Town in the West' in its mining heyday

Classic Trip

Fantastic Canyon Voyage

5

Old West meets New West on this scenic route to the Grand Canyon, climbing from cowboy country to mining towns, stylish wineries and red rocks, with a grand finale at the Big Ditch.

TRIP HIGHLIGHTS

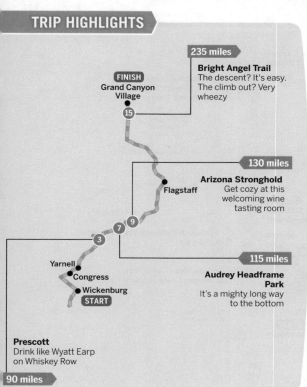

235 miles
Bright Angel Trail
The descent? It's easy. The climb out? Very wheezy

FINISH
Grand Canyon Village
15

130 miles
Arizona Stronghold
Get cozy at this welcoming wine tasting room
Flagstaff

9
7
3

115 miles
Audrey Headframe Park
It's a mighty long way to the bottom

Yarnell
●**Congress**
●**Wickenburg**
START

Prescott
Drink like Wyatt Earp on Whiskey Row
90 miles

4–5 DAYS
285 MILES / 459KM

GREAT FOR...

BEST TIME TO GO
Visit in fall and spring, to beat the heat and summer crowds.

ESSENTIAL PHOTO
The Grand Canyon from Mather Point.

✔ BEST FOR HISTORY & CULTURE
Push through the swinging doors of history in Wickenburg, Prescott and Jerome.

75

Classic Trip

5 Fantastic Canyon Voyage

This road trip wins Best All Around. It's pretty, it's wild and it embraces Arizona's rough-and-tumble history. Scenic trails wind past sandstone buttes, ponderosa pines and canyon views. Wild West adventures include horseback rides, saloon crawls and taking a stand atop a 1910ft mine shaft. But the route's not stuck in the past. A burgeoning wine scene and a new ale trail add 21st-century sparkle.

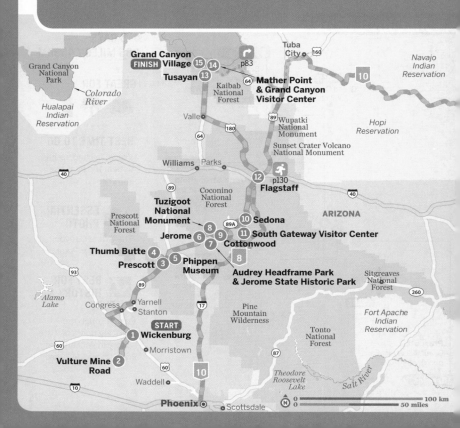

❶ Wickenburg

With its saddle shops and Old West storefronts, Wickenburg looks like it fell out of the sky – directly from the 1890s. At the newly expanded **Desert Caballeros Western Museum** (☎928-684-2272; www.westernmuseum. org; 21 N Frontier St; adult/ child/senior $9/free/7; ⏰10am-5pm Mon-Sat, noon-4pm Sun, closed Mon Jun-Aug), the artwork celebrates the West. The *Spirit of the Cowboy* collection examines the raw materials behind the cowboy myth, showcasing rifles, ropes and saddles. The *Cowgirl Up!* exhibit and sale in March and April is a fun and impressive tribute to an eclectic array of Western women artists.

LINK YOUR TRIP

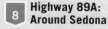

8 Highway 89A: Around Sedona

For close-up views of sandstone scenery, explore Sedona along Hwy 89A.

10 Tribal Trails

From Grand Canyon National Park, follow Hwy 64 east to Wupatki National Monument to learn about early residents.

Scattered across downtown are statues of the town's founders and colorful characters. One of the latter was George Sayers, a 'bibulous reprobate' who was chained to the **Jail Tree** on Tegner St in the late 1800s. Press the button to hear his tale then walk next door to the beloved **Chapparal** (45 N Tegner St; 1 scoop $3.50; ⏰11am-7pm Tue-Sat, noon-5pm Sun & Mon) for a scoop of homemade ice cream.

Wickenburg is pleasant anytime but summer, when temperatures can top 110°F (43°C).

The Drive ≫ Head west on Hwy 60, turn left onto Vulture Mine Rd. It's 12 miles to the mine. Saguaros and cattle guards mark the lonely drive.

---

❷ Vulture Mine Road

At the remote and dusty **Vulture Mine** (www. vultureminetours.com; 36610 N 355th St, off Vulture Mine Rd; donation $10; ⏰ tour 8:30am-10:30am Sat early May–mid-Oct, 10am-noon rest of year), Austrian immigrant Henry Wickenburg staked his claim and made his fortune. The site holds the main shaft, where $30 million worth of gold was mined, the blacksmith shop and other decrepit old buildings, and the Hanging Tree. Under new ownership, you can

visit by guided tour on Saturday mornings.

On the way back into town, consider spending the night at rustically posh **Rancho de Los Caballeros** (☎928-684-5484; www. ranchodeloscaballeros.com; 1551 S Vulture Mine Rd; r incl 3 meals $485-660; ⏰Oct–mid-May; ❄☎), where guests can sign up for a trail ride (half-day ride $50 to $60).

The Drive ≫ From downtown Wickenburg, pick up Hwy 93 north and drive 5 miles to 89N. Continuing north, the route leaves the Sonoran Desert and tackles the Weaver Mountains, climbing 2500ft in 4 miles. On top, tiny Yarnell was the site of a devastating forest fire in June 2013, when 19 members of the Granite Mountain Hotshots were killed while battling the blaze.

TRIP HIGHLIGHT

❸ Prescott

Fire raged through Whiskey Row in downtown Prescott ('press-kit') on July 14, 1900. Quick-thinking locals saved the town's most prized possession: the 24ft-long Brunswick Bar that anchored the Palace Saloon. After lugging the solid oak bar onto Courthouse Plaza, they grabbed their drinks and continued the party. Prescott's cooperative spirit lives on, infusing the city with a welcoming vibe.

The columned County Courthouse, situated in

Classic Trip

an elm-shaded plaza, anchors the **Historic Downtown**. Just west is Whiskey Row, where 40 drinking establishments once supplied suds to rough-hewn cowboys, miners and wastrels. The fire in 1900 destroyed 25 saloons, five hotels and the red-light district, but several early buildings remain. Stroll through the **Palace Saloon**, rebuilt in 1901, which displays photographs and artifacts (including the still-in-use Brunswick Bar). Wyatt Earp and Doc Holliday drank here back in the day.

To learn more about Prescott, which was Arizona's first territorial capital, visit the engaging **Sharlot Hall Museum** (☎928-445-3122; www.sharlot.org; 415 W Gurley St; adult/child $7/3; ⏰10am-5pm Mon-Sat, noon-4pm Sun May-Sep,

10am-4pm Mon-Sat, noon-4pm Sun Oct-Apr), named for its 1928 founder, pioneer woman Sharlot Hall. The city is also home to the **World's Oldest Rodeo**, (www.worldsoldestrodeo.com) which dates to 1888 and is held the week before July 4th.

🍴 🛏 p85

The Drive » From the County Courthouse downtown, drive west on Gurley St, which turns into Thumb Butte Rd, for 3.5 miles.

- - - - - - - - - - -

④ Thumb Butte

Prescott sits in the middle of the Prescott National Forest, a 1.2 million-acre playground well stocked with mountains, lakes and ponderosa pines. The **Prescott National Forest Office** (☎928-443-8000; www.fs.fed.us/r3/prescott; 344 S Cortez St; ⏰8am-4:30pm Mon-Fri) has information about local hikes, drives, picnic areas and campgrounds. A $5 day-use fee is required – and payable – at many area trailheads.

Intra-agency passes, including the America the Beautiful pass, cover this fee.

For a short hike, head to the hard-to-miss Thumb Butte. The 1.75-mile **Thumb Butte Trail #33** (⏰7am-7pm) is a moderate workout and offers nice views of the town and mountains. Leashed dogs are OK.

The Drive » Follow Hwy 89N out of Prescott, passing the Granite Dells rock formations on the 7-mile drive. Granite Dells Rd leads to a trail through the granite boulders on the **Mile High Trail System** (http://cityofprescott.net/services/parks/trails).

- - - - - - - - - - -

⑤ Phippen Museum

Strutting its stuff like a rodeo champ, the recently expanded **Phippen Museum** (☎928-778-1385; www.phippenartmuseum.org; 4701 Hwy 89N; adult/child $7/free; ⏰10am-4pm Tue-Sat, 1-4pm Sun) ropes in visitors with an entertaining mix of special exhibits spotlighting cowboy and Western art. Named for the late George Phippen, a local self-taught artist who helped put Western art on the map, it's worth a stop to see what's brewing. As you'll discover, Western art is broader than oil paintings of weather-beaten faces under broad hat brims – although you might see some of that too.

LOCAL KNOWLEDGE: THE GREEN FROG

Perhaps this box should be called Local Pranksters. You'll see what we mean as you leave the village of Congress, which sits at the junction of Hwy 71 and Hwy 89N. Look left for the **big green frog**; this painted rock was created in 1928 and has been maintained by locals ever since.

The Drive » Just north, leave Hwy 89 for Hwy 89A. This serpentine road brooks no distraction as it approaches hillside Jerome, tucked in the Mingus Mountains. If you dare, glance east for stunning glimpses of the Verde Valley.

6 Jerome

As the road snakes down steep Cleopatra Hill, it can be hard to tell whether the buildings are winning or losing their battle with gravity. Just look for the **Sliding Jail** – it's waaaay down there at the bottom of town.

Shabbily chic, this resurrected ghost town was known as the 'Wickedest Town in the West' during its late-1800s copper mining heyday. In those days it teemed with brothels, saloons and opium dens. When the mines petered out in 1953, Jerome's population plummeted. Then came the '60s, when scores of hippies snapped up crumbling buildings for pennies, more or less restored them and injected the town with a groovy *joie de vivre*.

Join the party with a stroll past the galleries, indie shops, old buildings and wine-tasting rooms that are scattered up and down the hillside. Local artists sell their work at the **Jerome Artists Cooperative Gallery**

(☎928-639-4276; www. jeromeartistscoop.com; 502 N Main St; ⏱10am-6pm) while burly but friendly-enough bikers gather at the **Spirit Room Bar** (☎928-634-8809; www. spiritroom.com; 166 Main St; ⏱10:30am-1am).

✕ 🛏 p85

The Drive » Follow Main St/ Hwy 89A out of downtown then turn left onto Douglas Rd.

TRIP HIGHLIGHT

7 Audrey Headframe Park & Jerome State Historic Park

Holy moly! Wow! That's no joke! I'm not stepping on that! Yep, the glass platform covering the mining shaft at **Audrey Headframe Park** (55 Douglas Rd; admission free; ⏱8am-5pm) isn't your everyday roadside attraction. It's death staring you in the face. If the cover shattered, the drop is 1910ft – which is 650ft longer than the Empire State Building!

Sufficiently disturbed? Chill out next door at the excellent **Jerome State Historic Park** (☎928-634-5381; www.azstateparks.com; adult/child $5/2; ⏱8:30am-5pm), which explores the town's mining past. The museum is inside the 1916 mansion of eccentric mining mogul Jimmy 'Rawhide' Douglas. The folksy video is worth watching

before you explore the museum.

The Drive » Hwy 89A drops to tiny Clarkdale. At the traffic circle, take the second exit onto the Clarkdale Parkway and into town. Follow Main St east to S Broadway then turn left onto Tuzigoot Rd.

8 Tuzigoot National Monument

Squatting atop a ridge, **Tuzigoot National Monument** (☎928-634-5564; www.nps.gov/tuzi; adult/child $5/free, combination ticket with Montezuma Castle National Monument $8/free; ⏱8am-5pm), a Sinaguan pueblo like nearby Montezuma, is believed to have been inhabited from AD 1000 to 1400. At its peak as many as 225 people lived in its 110 rooms. Stop by the revamped visitor center to examine tools, pottery and arrowheads then climb a short, steep trail (not suitable for wheelchairs) for memorable views of the Verde River Valley.

The Drive » Return to S Broadway and follow it south just over 1.5 miles into Old Town Cottonwood.

TRIP HIGHLIGHT

9 Cottonwood

Cottonwood has kicked up its cool quotient, particularly in its pedestrian-friendly Old Town District. On this low-key strip

RICHARD CUMMINS/ROBERT HARDING WORLD IMAGERY/CORBIS ©

WHY THIS IS A CLASSIC TRIP
AMY BALFOUR, AUTHOR

You know you're on a good road trip when you see a horde of motorcyclists roaring up in your rearview mirror. That happens all the time on Hwy 89/89A. I love it. The red rock and Verde Valley views are superb, plus the route ends at the best show in the Southwest: the Grand Canyon. Along the way, every stop is loaded with possibilities for adventure.

Top: Desert View Watchtower
Left: Welcome sign, Cottonwood
Right: Jerome

there are loads of good restaurants and several interesting indie stores. The inviting **Arizona Stronghold** (www.azstronghold.com; 1023 N Main St; tastings $9; ⏰ noon-7pm Sun-Thu, to 9pm Fri & Sat) tasting room has welcoming staff, comfy couches, and live music on Friday nights. Enjoy a few more wine samples across the street at the chocolate-and-wine pairing **Pillsbury Wine Company** (www.pillsburywine.com; 1012 N Main St; ⏰ 11am-6pm Sun-Thu, 11am-8pm Fri). For wet-and-wild wine tasting in Cottonwood, join a Water to Wine kayak tour ($97.25) with **Sedona Adventure Tours** (📞 928-204-6440; www.sedonaadventuretours.com; 2020 Contractors Rd; 🚐) on the Verde River to Alcantara Vineyards.

The Drive » Follow Main St south to reconnect with Hwy 89A N. Follow it into Sedona. At the roundabout at the junction of Hwy 89A and Hwy 179, called the Y, continue into Uptown Sedona. The visitor center (p105) sits at the junction of Hwy 89A and Forest Rd.

⑩ Sedona

The stunning red rocks here have an intensely spiritual pull for many visitors. Some New Age believers even think that the sandstone formations hold vortices that exude high-octane spiritual energy. See for

Classic Trip

yourself atop **Airport Mesa**, the vortex closest to downtown. Here, a short scramble leads to a lofty view of the surrounding sandstone monoliths, which blaze a psychedelic red and orange at sunset. To get to the viewpoint, drive up Airport Rd for 0.5 miles and look for a small parking area on the left.

Another pretty site is the **Chapel of the Holy Cross** (☎928-282-4069; www.chapeloftheholycross. com; 780 Chapel Rd; ◷9am-5pm Mon-Sat, 10am-5pm Sun), a church tucked between spectacular red-rock columns 3 miles south of town. This modern, non-denominational chapel was built by Marguerite Brunwig Staude in the tradition of Frank Lloyd Wright.

The Drive » Follow Hwy 179 south past Bell Rock, passing the Village of Oak Creek.

---

⑪ South Gateway Visitor Center

Outdoor adventurers love the super-scenic hiking and biking trails in and around Sedona. The US Forest Service provides the helpful and free *Recreation Guide to Your National Forest*, which has brief descriptions of popular trails and a map pinpointing routes and trailheads. Pick one up at the **USFS South Gateway Visitor Center** (☎928-203-2900; www. redrockcountry.org; 8375

STEVE RABIN/GETTY IMAGES ©

Sedona Red rocks at sunset

Hwy 179; ☻8am-5pm) just south of the Village of Oak Creek. Staff can guide you to trails suited to your interests.

The Drive » Hwy 89A rolls north through the riparian greenery of scenic Oak Creek Canyon, where red cliffs flank the drive. North of the canyon pick-up I-17 north. Sedona is 30 miles from Flagstaff.

⑫ Flagstaff

From its pedestrian-friendly historic downtown to its high-altitude pursuits like skiing and hiking, Flagstaff's charms are countless. Humphrey's Peak, the highest point in Arizona, provides an inspiring backdrop. Start at the **visitor center** (☎800-842-7293; flagstaffarizona.org; 1 E Rte 66; ☻8am-5pm Mon-Sat, 9am-4pm Sun), which has free brochures for walking tours, including a guide to Flagstaff's haunted places, or try our walking tour, p130.

The interesting **Lowell Observatory** (☎928-233-3212; www.lowell.edu; 1400 W Mars Hill Rd; adult/child $12/5; ☻9am-10pm Jun-Aug, shorter hours Sep-May), built in 1894, sits on a hill just outside downtown. It witnessed the first sighting of Pluto in 1920. During the day, take a guided tour. At night, weather permitting, try stargazing. Flagstaff's microbreweries are the stars on the one-mile

DETOUR: DESERT VIEW DRIVE

Start: ⑭ Mather Point & Grand Canyon Visitor Center

This scenic road meanders 25 miles to the East Entrance on Hwy 64, passing some of the park's finest viewpoints, picnic areas and historic sites. **Grand View Point** marks the trailhead where miner Peter Berry opened his Grand View Hotel in 1897. Views are indeed spectacular. Another stunning view awaits at **Moran Point**, named for Thomas Moran, a landscape painter whose work aided in designating the Grand Canyon as a national monument in 1908. Further along is **Tusayan Ruin & Museum**, where you can walk around the remains of an excavated Puebloan village dating to 1185. At the end of the road is the **Watchtower**, designed by Mary Colter and inspired by ancient Puebloan watchtowers. The terrace gives panoramic views of the canyon and river. The circular staircase inside leads past Hopi murals to 360-degree views on the top floor.

Flagstaff Ale Trail (www.flagstaffaletrail.com). Or hop on the **Alpine Pedaler** (☎928-213-9233; www.alpinepedaler.com; per person $25), a 15-passenger 'party on wheels' that stops at bars and breweries.

✕ ⊨ p85

The Drive » The next morning – and mornings are best for the 90-mile trip – take Hwy 180 west and enjoy the views of the San Francisco Peaks through the treetops. When you reach Hwy 64 at the town of Valle, turn right and drive north on the big flat of the Coconino Plateau.

⑬ Tusayan

This little town sits 1 mile south of the Grand Canyon's South Entrance, along Hwy 64. It's basically a half-mile strip of hotels and restaurants. Stop at the **National Geographic Visitor Center & IMAX** (☎928-638-2468; www.explorethecanyon.com; 450 Hwy 64; adult/child $13.72/10.42; ☻8am-10pm Mar-Oct, 10:30am-6:30pm Nov-Feb) to pre-pay the $25 per-vehicle park fee and save yourself what could be a long wait at the entrance. Currently screening in the IMAX theater is the terrific 34-minute film *Grand Canyon – The Hidden Secrets*. With exhilarating river-running scenes and

Classic Trip

virtual-reality drops off canyon rims, the film plunges you into the history and geology of the canyon through the eyes of ancient Native Americans, John Wesley Powell and a soaring eagle.

In summer, you can leave your car here and catch the Tusayan shuttle into the park.

The Drive » Follow Hwy 64 1 mile north to the park entrance. Admission to the national park is $25 per vehicle or $12 for someone entering by foot, bicycle or motorcycle, and is good for 7 days.

TRIP HIGHLIGHT

14 Mather Point & Grand Canyon Visitor Center

Park at the visitor center but don't go inside. Not yet. Walk, or run, directly to **Mather Point**, the first overlook after the South Entrance. It's usually packed elbow-to-elbow with a global array of tourists, all taking photos, but even with the crowds there's a sense of communal wonder that keeps the scene polite. You'll see – the sheer immensity of the canyon

just grabs you, then pulls you in for a look at the gorgeous details – rugged plateaus, crumbly spires and colorful ridges.

Three hundred yards behind Mather Point is the main **visitor center** (www.nps.gov/grca; ☺8am-5pm), with a theater and a bookstore. On the plaza, bulletin boards and kiosks display information about ranger programs, the weather, tours and hikes. Inside is a ranger-staffed information desk and a lecture hall, where rangers offer daily talks on a variety of subjects. The theater screens a 20-minute movie, *Grand Canyon: A Journey of Wonder*, on the hour and half-hour.

From here, explore the park via park shuttle, rent a **bike** (☎928-638-3055; www.bikegrandcanyon.com; 10 S Entrance Rd, Grand Canyon Visitor Center; full-day adult/child $40/30; ☺8am-6pm May-Oct, 10am-4pm Mar, Apr, Oct & Nov), or your own four wheels. In summer, parking can be a challenge in Grand Canyon Village.

The Drive » The Village Loop Rd leads into Grand Canyon Village. Pass El Tovar, Kachina and Thunderbird lodges and Bright Angel Lodge. The Bright Angel Trailhead is just west of Bright Angel Lodge.

15 Grand Canyon Village

In 2013 the park opened a new plaza and parking area beside the Bright Angel Trailhead. The **Bright Angel** is the most popular of the corridor trails, and its steep and scenic 8-mile descent to the Colorado River has four logical turn-around points: Mile-and-a-half Resthouse, Three Mile Resthouse, Indian Garden and Plateau Point. Summer heat can be crippling and the climb is steep. Day hikers should turn around at one of the two resthouses (a 3- to 6-mile roundtip).

If you're more interested in history and geography than strenuous hiking, follow the easy **Rim Trail** east from here (see p43). Heading west, the Rim Trail passes every overlook on the way to **Hermits Rest**, offering spectacular views. The Hermits Rest shuttle runs parallel to the trail, so hike until you're tired then hop on the shuttle to continue or return. But be sure to hop off for the sunset, which is best at Hopi Point (which draws crowds) or Pima Point.

🛏 p85

Eating & Sleeping

Prescott ❸

✘ Iron Springs Cafe   Cafe $$

(📞928-443-8848; www.ironspringscafe.com;
1501 Iron Springs Rd; mains brunch $10-13, lunch
$10-15, dinner $10-21; ⊘8am-8pm Wed-Sat,
9am-2pm Sun) Savory Cajun and Southwestern
specialties, often spicy, are highlights at this
cafe inside a former train station.

✘ Lone Spur Cafe   Breakfast $

(📞928-445-8202; www.thelonespur.com; 106 W
Gurley St; breakfast & lunch $8-17, dinner $14-24;
⊘8am-2pm daily, 4:30-8pm Fri) Portions are
huge, and the sausage gravy will knock your hat
off. Decor includes stuffed mounts, cowboy gear
and an antler chandelier.

🛏 Motor Lodge   Bungalow $$

(📞928-717-0157; www.themotorlodge.com;
503 S Montezuma St; r $99-119, ste $149, apt
$159; ✻🛜) Rooms in the 12 snazzy bungalows
at this welcoming place come with whimsical
prints and stylish but comfy bedding.

Jerome ❻

✘ Grapes   American $$

(📞928-639-8477; www.grapesjerome.com;
111 Main St; lunch & dinner $9-17; ⊘11am-9pm)
Everything on the menu has a wine pairing
suggestion. Top-drawer pizza, pasta and steak
in a classy but lively environment.

🛏 Jerome Grand Hotel   Hotel $$

(📞928-634-8200; www.jeromegrandhotel.
com; 200 Hill St; r $120-205, ste $270-460;
✻🛜) Built in 1926 as a hospital for the mining
community, this sturdy fortress plays up its
unusual history with relics of the past, from
incinerator chutes to patient call lights. For
$20 hotel guests can join the evening ghost
tour. Enjoy fine dining and and a dazzling

valley panorama at the attached **Asylum
Restaurant** (lunch $10 to $16, dinner $20
to $32).

Flagstaff ❿❷

✘ Beaver Street Brewery   Brewpub $$

(www.beaverstreetbrewery.com; 11 S Beaver
St; lunch $8-13, dinner $10-20; ⊘11am-11pm
Sun-Thu, to midnight Fri & Sat; 🚼) This place
packs in families, river guides, ski bums and
businesspeople. The menu is typical brewpub
fare, with delicious pizzas, burgers and salads,
and there's usually five handmade beers on tap.

🛏 Hotel Monte Vista   Hotel $$

(📞928-779-6971; www.hotelmontevista.com;
100 N San Francisco St; d $65-110, ste $120-140;
🛜) In downtown Flagstaff. Ask for a quiet room
if you think the live music at the downstairs bar
will irritate. Wi-fi and ghosts are free.

Grand Canyon Village ❿❺

🛏 Bright Angel Lodge   Lodge $$

(www.grandcanyonlodges.com; r with/without
private bath $94/83, suites $185-362, cabins
$120-340; ⊘year-round; ✻@🛜) The cabins
are most coveted, but lodge rooms (some with
shared shower) are cozy and immaculate. The
Bright Angel Bar is perfect for those who
want to unwind with a burger and a beer without
cleaning up too much.

🛏 El Tovar   Lodge $$$

(www.grandcanyonlodges.com; d $178-273, ste
$335-426; ⊘year-round; ✻🛜) The rugged
yet elegant (it's possible!) El Tovar remains a
grande dame of national park lodges. Standard
rooms can be small, so go for deluxe if you
need elbow room. At the stone-and-oak **dining
room** enjoy a steak beside the best views in
the state.

Superstition Mountains *A surreal massif dominating the landscape*

Mogollon Rim Country

6

Natural wonders and quirky towns dot the Mogollon Rim, a 200-mile swath of forested cliffs at the southern edge of the Colorado Plateau. The Salt River crashes past with a dramatic flourish.

TRIP HIGHLIGHTS

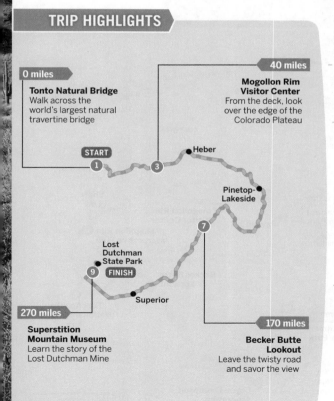

0 miles

Tonto Natural Bridge
Walk across the world's largest natural travertine bridge

START ① ③ Heber

40 miles

Mogollon Rim Visitor Center
From the deck, look over the edge of the Colorado Plateau

Pinetop-Lakeside

⑦

Lost Dutchman State Park
⑨ **FINISH**

Superior

270 miles

Superstition Mountain Museum
Learn the story of the Lost Dutchman Mine

170 miles

Becker Butte Lookout
Leave the twisty road and savor the view

3–5 DAYS
285 MILES / 460KM

GREAT FOR...

BEST TIME TO GO

Spring for wildflowers and fall for the colorful cottonwoods and aspens.

 ESSENTIAL PHOTO

The grandeur of the Salt River Canyon from along Hwy 60.

BEST FOR HISTORY

Learn about the 1800s Indian Wars at Fort Apache National Historic Park.

6 Mogollon Rim Country

I will keep my eyes on the road. I will keep my eyes on – zoinks! Is that a canyon? Where did those buttes come from? Why is the road dropping so fast? What's happening?! Yep, after the womb-like safety of the pines atop the Mogollon Rim (pronounced 'muggy-own'), the stark, twisting drop into Salt River Canyon is a shocker. But the dramatic changes also make this trip fun. Plus the rumors of buried treasure.

TRIP HIGHLIGHT

❶ Tonto Natural Bridge State Park

The drive from Flagstaff to Hwy 87 on S Lake Mary Rd is gorgeous, passing pine trees and lakes on its climb along the Mogollon Rim. When you reach Hwy 87, turn right and continue to **Tonto Natural Bridge State Park** (928-476-4202; www.azstateparks.com; off Hwy 87; adult/child $5/2; 8am-6pm daily Jun-Aug, 9am-5pm Thu-Mon Sep-May). The park's precipitous

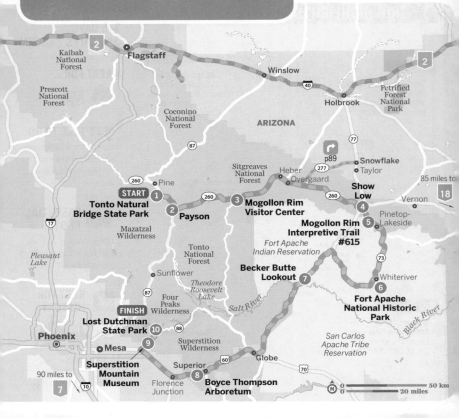

entrance road ends at the world's largest natural travertine bridge, which is 183ft high and spans a 150ft-wide canyon. You can view it from multiple angles, and steep trails descend into the canyon for close-ups. The bridge formed because Pine Creek, which flowed downhill, ran smack into a massive dam of calcium carbonate. It gradually cut its way through.

The Drive » Continue east 10 miles on Hwy 87 to Payson.

2 Payson

Founded by gold miners in 1882, Payson's real riches turned out to be above ground. Vast pine forests fed a booming timber industry; ranchers ran cattle along the Mogollon Rim and down to the Tonto Basin; and wild game was plentiful. Today, Payson

LINK YOUR TRIP

2 **Route 66: The Southwest**

From Payson, follow Hwy 87 north to Take-It-Easy Corner in Winslow.

18 **Into the Gila**

Hankerin' for pie? Drive east on Hwy 60 to Pie Town, NM

DETOUR: SNOWFLAKE

Start ❸ Mogollon Rim Visitor Centre

Snowflake is the northernmost city of Rim Country. It gets an occasional light dusting of snow but the town is really named after the founders, a Mr Snow and a Mr Flake – seriously. Settled by Mormon pioneers in the late 1800s, there are more than 100 historic homes, many with red brick and white trim. From Heber-Overgaard, take Hwy 277 east.

is a recreational and retirement destination for Phoenix citizens, with hunting and fishing in the nearby forests, lakes and streams.

Exhibits at the **Rim Country Museum** (928-474-3483; www.rimcountrymuseums.com; 700 S Green Valley Pkwy; adult/student/senior/child $5/3/4/free; 10am-4pm Wed-Mon, 1-4pm Sun), which are viewed on a 75-minute docent-led tour, illustrate the native, pioneer and mining history of the region. Highlights include a replica of a blacksmith shop and a walk-through of the Zane Grey Cabin, faithfully rebuilt here after the author's original homestead burned in the 1990 Dude Fire. Docents can shorten the tour if you have limited time.

 p93

The Drive » Heading east, Hwy 260 cuts through a vast blanket of lofty pines, where 'Elk Crossing' and 'Watch for Elk' signs will keep you on your toes.

There may be patches of snow in these parts in April.

TRIP HIGHLIGHT

❸ Mogollon Rim Visitor Center

For expansive views of southern forests and lakes, stop at this **visitor center** (ranger 928-535-7300; Hwy 260; 9:30am-3:30pm Thu-Sun mid-May–Sep, Fri & Sat only late fall), 32 miles east of Payson. Its deck looks over the Mogollon Rim, a dramatic geological break a couple of thousand feet between the high desert of the Colorado Plateau and the low desert to the south. The Rim contains the world's largest stand of ponderosa pine.

Inside the visitor center you'll find information about local flora, fauna and recreation. There are also animal mounts, including a full-size bear. Several trails leave from the Rim Top Trailhead across Hwy 260. Of these, the Rim Lakes Vista Trail crosses back over the highway and travels along the rim for 3 miles to the Woods Canyon Vista.

The Drive >> Continue east on Hwy 260. Look south after passing Forest Lakes to see a fire scar from the 2002 Rodeo-Chediski fire, one of the largest fires in Arizona history. After the town of Heber, stay right to follow Hwy 260 to Show Low.

④ Show Low

Back in 1876, a 100,000-acre ranch was at stake in a marathon card game. As daybreak approached, the players agreed that whoever could 'show low' would take the prize. One player flipped over the deuce of clubs. The town that arose here took the name Show Low and its main drag was named Deuce of Clubs St. A life-size **statue** memorializing the players and the card game sits on a small plaza on the south side

of E Deuce of Clubs St. To park, continue past the Thunderbird Motel to Hwy 260. Turn right, then take a right onto E Cooley St. Pull over just ahead.

The Drive >> Drive east on Hwy 260. About 6 miles ahead, look for the pull-off for the Mogollon Rim Interpretive Trail, before mile marker 348. It's just within the city limits for Pinetop-Lakeside, where there are restaurants and hotels (p93).

⑤ Mogollon Rim Interpretive Trail #615

This easy 1-mile trail meanders through ponderosa pines in the Apache-Sitgreaves National Forest along the edge of the Mogollon Rim. The rim was named for Don Juan Ignacio Flores Mogollon, a Spanish governor of the province of New Mexico in the 1700s. The trail passes an unusual site: a Douglas fir beside an alligator juniper,

LYNN GAIL/GETTY IMAGES ©

two plants rarely seen together because they have different climatic requirements. And the view from the rim? Picture rolling waves of trees. Or as one ranger explained, 'It's not the Grand Canyon, but it's nice!' The first half mile of the trail is paved and wheelchair accessible.

The Drive >> Follow Hwy 260 east to Hon-Dah Resort-Casino on the northern edge of the White Mountain Apache Indian Reservation. Turn right onto Hwy 73, driving south past pine trees and mountain meadows. The view opens up at Whiteriver. About 5 miles south of Whiteriver, turn left onto Indian Route 46.

THE TRUTH IS OUT THERE

One Rim Country resident who claims interstellar travel is Travis Walton, a logger who says he was abducted near Snowflake by an alien craft in 1975. What makes his story interesting is that there were eyewitnesses and a police manhunt failed to turn up Walton for two days – time on the mother ship, he says. According to the Forest Service, the telephone booth is still there and makes a nice photo op. For more details, visit Walton's website: www.travis-walton.com. The 1993 movie *Fire in the Sky* is based on his experience.

Goldfield Ghost Town

⑥ Fort Apache National Historic Park

Bounded by the Mogollon Rim to the north and the Salt River to the South, the White Mountain Apache Tribe Reservation covers 1.6 million acres, mostly forest. There's a cultural center and museum at **Fort Apache Historic Park** (☏information 928-338-4525, museum 928-338-4625; www.wmat. nsn.us; Whiteriver; adult/ senior/child $5/3/free; ☼park 7am-sunset, cultural center & museum 8am-5pm Mon-Sat

summer, closed Sat winter), an Army post between 1870 and 1922. Here you'll find a concise introduction to the White Mountain Apache world as well as some of the tribe's talented handiwork.

A self-guided tour leads to the fort's historic buildings. An exhibit inside an 1871 officers' quarters highlights Apache scouts and explains why tribal members helped the US Army subdue other native tribes. An Indian boarding school was established here in 1923 and is still in operation.

Admission includes entry to the **Kinishba Ruins**, a pre-Columbian stone pueblo that once had hundreds of rooms. At the museum, pick up a guide to the ruins, which are at the end of a well-graded dirt road that begins 4 miles west off Hwy 73. Worth a stop.

The Drive ≫ From the ruins, turn right onto Hwy 73 and drive to US 60. Turn left for a twisting descent through the stunning Salt River Canyon. As you drop into the canyon, watch for the overlook parking lot between mile marker 298 and 297.

TRIP HIGHLIGHT

❼ Becker Butte Lookout

Pullover, pullover, pullover! You've got to see the view from this stone-walled overlook, which is perched above the majestic Salt River Canyon, a 2000ft gash carving its way through the imposing landscape. The river, unhampered by dams, runs wild below the juniper-covered buttes. Hwy 60 runs through the White Mountain Apache Tribe Reservation north of the Salt River. A recreational permit is required to explore beyond the overlooks. For permit information, visit www.wmatoutdoors. org. South of the river, the highway runs through the San Carlos Apache Reservation. For recreational permit information see www. scatrw.com.

The Drive » Hwy 60 passes more viewpoints as it drops to the Salt River. After crossing the river the highway climbs out of the canyon. Continue west through Globe, which makes a good lunch stop (p93), and Superior, where copper country rises toward rim country.

❽ Boyce Thompson Arboretum

This lovely **arboretum** (📞520-689-2811; http:// ag.arizona.edu/bta; 37615 US Hwy 60, Superior; adult/child $10/5; ⏱8am-5pm Sep-Apr, 6am-3pm May-Aug) is a 323-acre living museum with more than 3,000 species of flora from arid regions around the world. During the spring bloom, which peaks March though early May, the park is vibrant with color and smells as sweet as a candy factory. Saguaros bloom in May and June. Leashed pets welcome.

The Drive » Follow US 60 west almost 24 miles to W Mountain View Rd. Turn right and drive north about 4.5 miles to North Apache Trail/AZ 88 and turn right.

TRIP HIGHLIGHT

❾ Superstition Mountain Museum

The thoroughly delightful **Superstition Mountain Museum** (📞480-983-4888; www. superstitionmountainmuseum. org; 4087 N Apache Trail, Apache Junction; adult/senior/ child $5/4/ free; ⏱9am-4pm) welcomes guests with mesmerizing dioramas of wild animals trying to kill each other – again. But most impressive is the wall of treasure maps, all purporting to lead to the Lost Dutchman Mine, where German prospector Jacob Waltz, the Dutchman, allegedly struck gold. On his deathbed, Waltz supposedly revealed the whereabouts of the source of ore, but it's never been found – despite the efforts of thousands to find it.

Outside, you'll find the Elvis Memorial Chapel from the Elvis movie *Charro*. It was moved here after surviving a devastating fire at Apacheland Movie Ranch.

The Drive » Drive 1 mile northeast on N Apache Trail, passing the Goldfield Ghost Town (www.goldfieldghosttown), an unabashed tourist trap that is also, well, kind of fun.

❿ Lost Dutchman State Park

Any **state park** (📞480-982-4485; www.azstateparks. com; 6109 N Apache Trail, Apache Junction; per vehicle $7; ⏱sunrise-10pm) named for a legendary lost gold mine qualifies as a must-visit in our book, and this striking place is a treasure itself, with a surreal massif of the Superstition Mountains dominating the terrain. Enjoy trails and a very pretty campground. Look for vast blooms of desert wildflowers here, especially after a wet winter.

🛏 p93

Eating & Sleeping

Payson ❷

✕ Ayothaya Thai Cafe   Thai $$
(404 E Hwy 60; mains $8-13; ⏱11am-9pm
Mon-Thu, later Fri & Sat) Service may not always
be king, but you won't really mind once your
spicy green curry arrives at this bright and airy
eatery. The owner and chef worked as a chef in
Thailand.

✕ Beeline Cafe   Diner $
(☎928-474-9960; 815 S Beeline Hwy; mains
$6-13; ⏱5am-9pm) This home-style restaurant
could be called the beehive, mornings are
so busy with locals swarming in for massive
breakfasts. Cash only.

⊨ Majestic Mountain Inn   Motel $$
(☎928-474-0185; www.majesticmountaininn.
com; 602 E Hwy 260; r incl breakfast $90-136;
🅿❄@🛜🏊) This two-story property, set
amongst landscaped pines and grassy lawns,
is more of a motel than a lodge-like inn, but the
luxury rooms have double-sided gas fireplaces,
sloped wooden ceilings and spa tubs.

⊨ Ponderosa Campground   Campground $
(☎877-444-6777; www.recreation.gov; Hwy
260; sites $14; ⏱mid-Apr–Oct) This site in
Tonto National Forest is 12 miles northeast of
Payson on Hwy 260 and has 48 tent and RV
sites, as well as drinking water and toilets (but
no showers).

Pinetop-Lakeside

✕ Darbi's Cafe   American $
(☎928-367-6556; 235 E White Mountain
Blvd; breakfast $6-12, lunch & dinner $8-16;
⏱6am-2pm Sun-Tue, to 8pm Wed-Sat) This
might be the most popular restaurant along the
Mogollon Rim. It's hard to tell what locals love
more, the yummy, stylized American food or the
owner, Darbi Massey, who grew up around here.
Breakfast gets especially fervent raves.

⊨ Nine Pines Motel   Motel $
(☎928-367-2999; www.ninepinesmotel.com;
2089 E White Mountain Blvd; r $77-110; 🅿🛜🏊)
Beds in these cozy rooms are set in natural
pine frames and the decor is tastefully homey.
Larger rooms have fireplaces and foldout futon
couches. All have refrigerators and microwaves.
Pets are $10. Welcoming owner.

Globe

✕ La Luz Del Dia Cafe   Cafe $
(304 N Broad St; mains $5-10; ⏱6:30am-
2:30pm Mon-Sat) This real locals' diner, run by
the same family for decades, has six tables and
a counter with stools. Regulars sip coffee while
browsing the newspaper and chatting with the
cook.

⊨ Quality Inn Globe   Hotel $
(☎928-425-7575; www.qualityinn.com; 1565
E South St; r incl breakfast $80-110, ste $130;
🅿❄@🛜🏊) Yep, it's a cookie cutter Quality
Inn, but it looks to be the nicest digs in town.
Rooms are fresh and modern, with nice staff.
Pets are $15 per night.

Lost Dutchman State Park ❿

⊨ Lost Dutchman State Park   Campground $
(☎520-586-2283; www.azstateparks.com;
6109 N Apache Trail, Apache Junction; tent
sites $15-17, RV sites $25-30) With saguaros up
close and a craggy offshoot of the Superstition
Mountains on the horizon, this is one of the
prettiest campgrounds in eastern Arizona. Has
104 campsites.

Saguaro National Monument *An army of majestic cacti*

Southern Desert Wanderings

7

You'll swoosh past saguaros on this loop through the Sonoran desert, where Spanish missions flank a missile site, wineries share their best elixirs and a lofty observatory looks to the stars.

TRIP HIGHLIGHTS

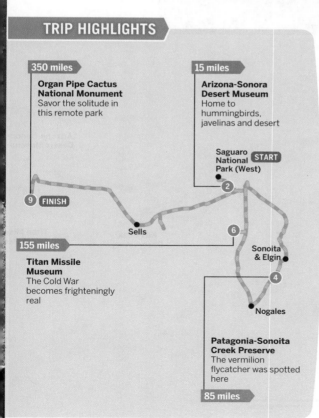

350 miles

Organ Pipe Cactus National Monument
Savor the solitude in this remote park

9 FINISH

Sells

155 miles

Titan Missile Museum
The Cold War becomes frighteningly real

15 miles

Arizona-Sonora Desert Museum
Home to hummingbirds, javelinas and desert

Saguaro National Park (West) **START**
2

6

Sonoita & Elgin

4

Nogales

Patagonia-Sonoita Creek Preserve
The vermilion flycatcher was spotted here

85 miles

3–4 DAYS
350 MILES / 563KM

GREAT FOR...

BEST TIME TO GO
October to March to avoid the desert heat.

 ESSENTIAL PHOTO
Frame a towering saguaro cactus against the sky in its namesake park.

☑ **BEST FOR FLORA & FAUNA**
Wander past coyotes and cacti at the Arizona-Sonora Desert Museum.

95

Southern Desert Wanderings

7

The urban legend is true. In 1982 two men decided to shoot at a saguaro cactus – which is illegal. After felling a 10ft saguaro with gunshots, they went after bigger game – a towering 27-footer. One shot took off the saguaro's giant, prickly arm. It promptly fell on the shooter and crushed him to death. The moral? Don't mess with these majestic plants. Saguaros grow slowly, taking 50 years to reach 7ft.

❶ Saguaro National Park (West)

If you're standing beside a docent at this cacti-filled **park** (📞Tucson Mountain District 520-733-5158, headquarters 520-733-5100; www.nps.gov/sagu; 2700 N Kinney Rd, western district; 7-day pass per vehicle/bicycle $10/5; ⊙ vehicles sunrise-sunset, walkers & cyclists 24hr), do not refer to the limbs of of the saguaro (sah-wah-ro) as branches. As you'll quickly learn, a saguaro has 'arms,' not lowly branches – a

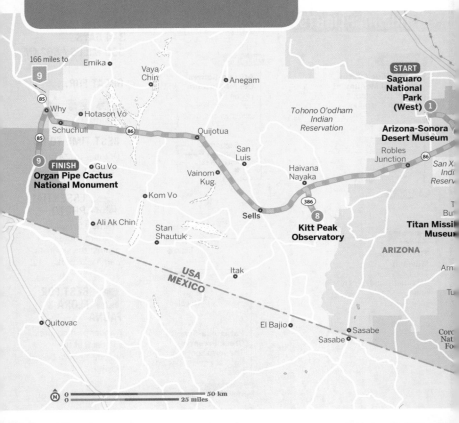

distinction that makes sense when you consider its human-like features. An entire army of these majestic ribbed sentinels is protected by the park.

The park is divided into two units separated by 30 miles and the city of Tucson. In the western Tucson Mountain District, the **Red Hills Visitor Center** (📞520-733-5158; 2700 N Kinney Rd; 🕑9am-5pm) sits beside the short **Cactus Garden Trail** where signage identifies desert plants. The nearby **Scenic Bajada Loop Drive** is a 6-mile graded dirt road through cactus forest.

The Drive » Watch for cyclists on N Kinney Rd as you drive 2 miles south.

TRIP HIGHLIGHT

2 Arizona-Sonora Desert Museum

Home to cacti, coyotes and tiny hummingbirds, this fascinating place is one part zoo, one part botanical garden and one part museum – a trifecta that'll keep young and old entertained for easily half a day. All sorts of desert denizens, from precocious coatis to playful prairie dogs, make their home in natural enclosures hemmed in by invisible fences. The grounds are thick with desert plants, and docents are on hand to answer questions and give demonstrations.

Wear a hat and walking shoes, and remember that the big cats are most active in the morning.

The Drive » Continue south to Hwy 86. Drive east to I-19, taking it north to I-10 east. Leave I-10 east at exit 281 for Hwy 83 south to Sonoita at Hwy 82. To get to Elgin, cross Hwy 82 and continue on Hwy 83 to Elgin Rd.

3 Sonoita & Elgin

Ah, what a view: long vistas of lush, windswept upland grassland; dark, knobby forest mountains; and a crinkle of slow streams. Sonoita and tiny Elgin, in the northern grasslands, were once important railway stops, but since the line closed in 1962 tourism and the arts have been their bread and butter.

The valleys here occupy a special microclimate amenable to wine grapes, making the region a center for Arizona's burgeoning wine industry. For tastings, start at **Callaghan Vineyards** (📞520-455-5322; www.callaghanvineyards.com; 336 Elgin Rd; tasting $10; 🕑11am-4pm Thu-Sun) in Elgin, traditionally one of the

Pusch Ridge Wilderness

Tucson

Saguaro National Park (East)

Mission San Xavier del Bac

(10) Vail

Continental

(83)

Sonoita & Elgin

Mt. Wrightson Wilderness

3

3

Elgin

Tumacacori National Historic Park

(82)

4 Patagonia

Washington

Nogales

7 SOUTHERN DESERT WANDERINGS

LINK YOUR TRIP

3 A Taste of the Old West

Follow Hwy 82 east to a ghost town and the OK Corral.

9 Highway 95 Yuma to Lake Mead

Looking for water? Take Hwy 85 north to I-10 then head west to Yuma and the Colorado River.

most highly regarded wineries in the state. Return to Sonoita for **Dos Cabezas** (☎520-455-5141; www.doscabezas winery.com; 3248 Hwy 82; tasting $15; ◷10:30am-4:30pm Thu-Sun), a rustically pretty, family-run operation near the crossroads of Hwys 82 and 83.

The Drive ≫ Return to Hwy 82 and follow it west to Patagonia, which is sandwiched between the Mexican border, the Santa Rita Mountains and the Patagonia Mountains.

TRIP HIGHLIGHT

❹ Patagonia

Sitting almost 5000ft above sea level, Patagonia is cool and breezy. The town borders Sonoita Creek, part of a riparian green zone that draws migrating birds and sharp-eyed birders.

A few gentle trails meander through the **Patagonia-Sonoita Creek Preserve** (☎520-394-2400; www.nature.org/arizona; 150 Blue Heaven Rd; admission $6; ◷6:30am-4pm Wed-Sun Apr-Sep, 7:30am-

4pm Wed-Sun Oct-Mar), an enchanting riparian willow and cottonwood forest managed by the Nature Conservancy. It supports seven distinct vegetative ecosystems, four endangered species of native fish and more than 300 species of birds, including rarities from Mexico. The peak migratory seasons are April and May, and late August to September. Join guided nature walks on Saturday mornings at 9am.

✗ ⇇ p101

The Drive ≫ Follow Hwy 82 southwest, passing Patagonia Lake State Park, to the border town of Nogales. Pick up I-19 north.

❺ Tumacacori National Historic Park

This pink-and-cream **edifice** (☎520-398-2341; www.nps.gov/tuma; I-19 exit 29; adult/child $3/free; ◷9am-5pm) shimmers on the desert like a conquistador's dream. In

1691 Father Eusebio Kino and his cohort arrived at the Tumacácori settlement and quickly founded a mission to convert the local Native Americans. However, repeated Apache raids and the harsh winter of 1848 drove the priests out, leaving the complex to crumble for decades. Start self-guided tours of the hauntingly beautiful ruins at the visitor center.

Just south, pick up spices, salsa and fantastic homemade chile paste, at **Santa Cruz Chili & Spice** (☎520-398-2591; www.santacruzchili.com; 1868 E Frontage Rd; ◷8am-5pm Mon-Fri, from 10am Sat, 1-3pm Sat), in business for more than 60 years.

The Drive ≫ Continue north on I-19. Exit 34 leads to Tubac, a cluster of 100 or so galleries and shops selling art and high-end crafts. Continue north to exit 69.

TRIP HIGHLIGHT

❻ Titan Missile Museum

The **Titan Missile Museum** (☎520-625-7736; www.titanmissilemuseum.org; 1580 W Duval Mine Rd, Sahuarita; adult/child/senior $9.50/6/8.50; ◷8:45am-5pm) is where the obliteration of humanity becomes frighteningly real. At this original Titan II missile site, a crew stood ready 24/7 to launch a nuclear warhead within seconds of receiving a presidential order. The Titan II was the first liquid-propelled

TELLES FAMILY SHRINE

On Hwy 82 south of Patagonia, just beyond mile marker 16, look east for a pull-off and historic plaque. The latter spotlights John Ward's Ranch, established here in 1858. Behind the plaque, stairs climb to a protected shrine built inside a rock face. The shrine was created in the 1940s by Juanita and Juan Telles, who promised to keep its candles burning if their sons returned safely from WWII. Their sons came home, and the candles still burn.

Arizona-Sonora Desert Museum Ibex

Intercontinental Ballistic Missile (ICBM) that could be fired from below ground and could reach its target – halfway around the world – in 30 minutes or less. It was on alert from 1963 to 1986. The one-hour tours are both creepy and fascinating.

The Drive >> Hop back on I-19 north and drive to exit 92.

⑦ Mission San Xavier del Bac

The dazzling white towers of this **mission** (📞520-294-2624; www.patronatosanxavier.org; 1950 W San Xavier Rd; donations appreciated; 🕐museum 8:30am-5pm, church 7am-5pm) bring an otherworldly glow to the desert. Nicknamed 'White Dove of the Desert,' the original mission was founded by Jesuit missionary Father Eusebio Kino in 1700 but was mostly destroyed in the Pima uprising of 1751. Its successor was gracefully rebuilt in the late 1700s in a harmonious blend of Moorish, Byzantine and Mexican Renaissance styles. Carefully restored in the 1990s and still religiously active, it's one of the best-preserved and most beautiful Spanish missions in the country.

The wall-sized carved, painted and gilded retable behind the altar, in the moody, candlelit interior, tells the story of creation in dizzying detail. The faithful line up to pray to a reclining wooden figure of St Francis, the mission's patron saint.

The Drive >> Return to Tucson on I-19 north, where there are plenty of restaurants and hotels (p101), or follow San Xavier Rd west to S Mission Rd. Take it north to W Valencia Rd. Drive west 9 miles to Hwy 86 south. Continue just over 25 miles. Turn left onto Hwy 386 and drive almost 12 miles to the top of Kitt Peak – a twisty climb!

⑧ Kitt Peak Observatory

Dark and clear night skies make **Kitt Peak** (📞520-318-8726; www.noao.edu/kpno; Hwy 86; visitor center by donation; 🕐9am-4pm) a perfect site for one of the world's largest observatories. Just west of Sells, this 6875ft-high mountaintop is stacked with two radio and 23 optical telescopes. Guided tours (adult/child $4/2.50; at 10am, 11:30am and 1:30pm) last about an hour. Make reservations two to four weeks in advance for the worthwhile nightly observing program (adult/child $46/41; no programs from July 1 to September 15 because of monsoon season). The small visitor center has exhibits and a gift shop, but no food.

The Drive >> Take Hwy 386 north back to Hwy 86. Drive west on Hwy 86 to Hwy 85. Follow Hwy 85 south. It's 22 miles to the Organ Pipe National Monument visitor center.

TRIP HIGHLIGHT

⑨ Organ Pipe Cactus National Monument

Along the Mexican border, this remote **national monument** (📞520-387-6849; www.nps.gov/orpi; Hwy 85; per vehicle $8; 🕐visitor center 8:30am-4:30pm) is a gorgeous, forbidding land. It's home to an astonishing number of animals and plants, including 28 species of cacti, first and foremost its namesake organ-pipe. A giant columnar cactus, it differs from the more prevalent saguaro in that its branches radiate from the base. Organ-pipes are common in Mexico but very rare north of the border. Animals here include bighorn sheep, coyotes, kangaroo rats, mountain lions and the piglike javelina.

Winter and early spring, when Mexican gold poppies and purple lupines blanket the barren ground, are the most pleasant seasons to visit. Summers are shimmering hot (above 100°F, or 38°C) and bring monsoon rains between July and September.

The 21-mile **Ajo Mountain Drive** leads through a spectacular landscape of steep-sided jagged cliffs and burnt-red rocks.

🛏 p101

Eating & Sleeping

Tucson

🍴 Cafe Poca Cosa   South American $$

(📞520-622-6400; www.cafepocacosatucson.
com; 110 E Pennington St; lunch $12-15, dinner
$18-26; 🕙11am-9pm Tue-Thu, to 10pm Fri & Sat)
The food here's all freshly prepared, innovative
and beautifully presented. And it serves the
best margaritas in town.

🍴 Tania's   Mexican $

(www.tanias33.com; 614 N Grande Ave; dishes
$2-8; 🕙7am-6pm Mon-Sat, to 3pm Sun) Stop
here in the morning on the way to Saguaro
National Park. The breakfast burritos are tightly
stuffed and delicious, and you can get 'em to go.
The tortillas are made daily on-site.

🛏 Catalina Park Inn   B&B $$

(📞520-792-4541; www.catalinaparkinn.com;
309 E 1st St; r $140-170; 🕙closed Jul & Aug;
❄@🛜) This 1927 Mediterranean-style villa
has six rooms, which range from the oversized
and over-the-top peacock-blue-and-gold
Catalina Room to the white and uncluttered
East Room with iron canopy bed. There's also a
cacti-and-desert garden.

🛏 Gilbert Ray Campground   Campground $

(📞520-877-6000; www.pima.gov/nrpr/
camping; Kinney Rd; tent/RV sites $10/20)
Camp amongst the saguaros at this Pima
County campground 13 miles west of downtown
Tucson. It has 130 first-come, first-served sites
along with water, but no showers. There are five
tent-only sites. No credit cards.

Patagonia ❹

🍴 Velvet Elvis   Pizzeria $$

(📞520-394-2102; www.velvetelvispizza.com;
292 Naugle Ave; mains $10-26; 🕙11:30am-
8:30pm Thu-Sat, to 7:30pm Sun) Motorcyclists,
foreign visitors, and date-night couples –
everybody rolls in at some point for one of the
14 designer pies. These diet-spoilers will make
you feel like Elvis in Vegas: fat and happy.

🍴 Wagon Wheel Saloon   Burgers $

(400 Naugle Ave; mains $8-9; 🕙noon-8pm
Mon-Sat, 11am-8pm Sun) Kick it cowboy-style at
the Wagon Wheel, where the bar is big, the 'art'
is taxidermied and the pool table is ready for
action. Burgers and tacos on the menu.

🛏 Duquesne House   B&B $$

(📞520-394-2732; www.theduquesnehouse.
com; 357 Duquesne Ave; r incl breakfast $125;
@) This photogenic, ranch-style B&B has
three spacious, eclectically appointed suites
with their own garden areas. On Tuesday and
Wednesday the B&B offers a 'Bed, No Bread'
special – $110 per night with no breakfast.

🛏 Stage Stop Inn   Inn $

(📞520-394-2211; www.stagestophotel
patagonia.com; 303 McKeown; s $79, d $89-99,
ste $109; 🛜🐾🐾) Salute the Old West and
its simple charms at this two-story inn, once a
stage coach stop on the Butterfield Trail. Rooms
surround a central courtyard and pool.

Organ Pipe Cactus National Monument ❾

🛏 Twin Peaks Campground   Campground $

(www.nps.gov/orpi; tent & RV sites $12) These
208 first-come, first-served sites by the visitor
center are often full by noon from mid-January
through March. Offers drinking water, toilets
and three solar-heated showers, but no
hookups. You can call 📞520-387-6849 ext
7302 on your day of travel to confirm campsite
availability.

Cathedral Rock Visit at sunset for a dramatic light show

Highway 89A: Around Sedona

8

This gorgeous drive is a glide through a landscape painting, from the lush greenery of Oak Creek to the fiery brilliance of the Red Rock Scenic Byway.

TRIP HIGHLIGHTS

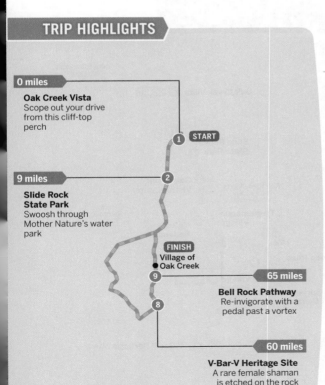

0 miles

Oak Creek Vista
Scope out your drive from this cliff-top perch

1 START

2

9 miles

Slide Rock State Park
Swoosh through Mother Nature's water park

FINISH
Village of Oak Creek

9

65 miles

Bell Rock Pathway
Re-invigorate with a pedal past a vortex

8

60 miles

V-Bar-V Heritage Site
A rare female shaman is etched on the rock

**2 DAYS
75 MILES / 120KM**

GREAT FOR...

BEST TIME TO GO
Temperatures are most pleasant fall through spring.

 ESSENTIAL PHOTO
Cathedral Rock looks mighty majestic from Red Rock Crossing.

 BEST FOR OUTDOORS
Wheee! Whoosh over red rocks at Slide Rock State Park.

103

8 Highway 89A: Around Sedona

Sunday drivers, this trip is for you. A 75-mile lasso loop, it was designed to maximize gaping, with just a few easy stops that will quickly get you close to the red rocks. And there's shopping and dining along the way. Once you've driven the main loop, choose a path, a pink jeep or another petroglyph site for further exploring.

TRIP HIGHLIGHT

❶ Oak Creek Vista

With its dramatic canyon walls and riparian lushness, Oak Creek Canyon is certainly stunning, but what makes this 14-mile stretch of Hwy 89A really special is the hint of the untamed, the lure of nature's bounty not yet captured and commodified. See for yourself at Oak Creek Vista, about 9 miles south of Flagstaff's airport. From this

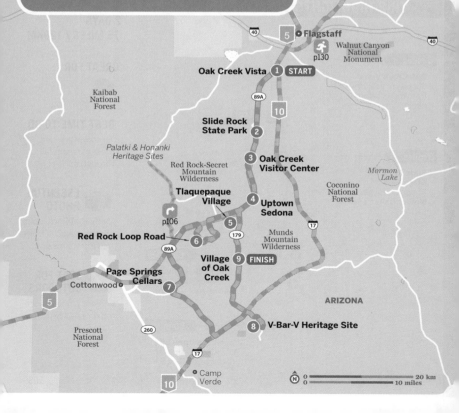

towering perch, the pine-draped canyon whooshes ahead like an unruly child just released from Mother Nature's time out.

Native American vendors sell jewelry beside the parking lot. There's also a small **visitor center** (⊘8am-4:30pm, closed winter).

📷 p109

The Drive » Hwy 89A twists into the canyon then rolls along Oak Creek past Pine Flat and Cave Springs campgrounds in the Coconino National Forest. The trailhead for the popular West Fork Trail, which follows the creek for 7 miles, soon beckons on the right.

TRIP HIGHLIGHT

② Slide Rock State Park

On a hot summer day you're likely to get caught in a traffic slowdown at

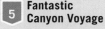

LINK YOUR TRIP

5 Fantastic Canyon Voyage

Continue north on Hwy 89A from Oak Creek Vista to easygoing Flagstaff.

10 Tribal Trails

From V-Bar-V drive north on I-17 to the cliff dwellings at Walnut Canyon National Monument.

Slide Rock State Park

(📞928-282-3034; www.azstateparks.com/Parks/SLRO; 6871 N Hwy 89A; per car Memorial Day-Labor Day $20, Sep-May $10, individual & bicycle $3; ⊘8am-7pm Memorial Day-Labor Day, 8am-5pm Sep-May) where swimmers swoosh down the creek on rock-lined chutes and watery slides. Come early or late in the day to avoid the worst congestion. Unfortunately, water quality can be an issue, and it's tested daily; call 📞602-542-0202.

The Drive » Continue south past Manzanita Campground to mile marker 378.2.

③ Oak Creek Visitor Center

The pull-off for this small **visitor center** (📞928-203-0624; ⊘8am-4:30pm Apr-Sep) is a nice place to stretch your legs. A good coffee and sandwich shop, **Indian Gardens Cafe & Market** (www.indiangardens.com; 3951 N 89A; breakfast $5-7, lunch $6-10; ⊘7am-7pm) is here, and the long-established **Garland's Indian Jewelry** (www.garlandsjewelry.com; ⊘10am-5pm) sells jewelry, kachinas, baskets, and pottery.

The Drive » Continue south on Hwy 89A, passing a great swimming hole, Grasshopper Point (day use $8), before rolling into Sedona's city center, called Uptown.

④ Uptown Sedona

Compact and busy, Uptown is where you'll find guide companies serving Sedona.

Jeep tours are a fun, bumpy way to see the sights, but it can be hard to distinguish the companies. Check backcountry accessibility; companies have permits for different routes, so if there's a specific formation you want to see, check around. The hard-to-miss **Pink Jeep Tours** (📞928-282-5000; www.pinkjeeptours.com; 204 N Hwy 89A) runs 13 thrilling and funny off-road and hiking tours lasting from about two hours (adult/child $89/67) to four hours ($110/83).

The **visitor center** (📞800-288-7336; www.visitsedona.com; 331 Forest Rd; ⊘8:30am-5pm Mon-Sat, 9am-3pm Sun) is at the corner of Hwy 89A and Forest Rd.

🍴📷 p109

The Drive » Take Hwy 89A a short distance south to the roundabout at the junction of Hwy 89A and Hwy 179, known as the Y. Take Hwy 179 south and turn right almost immediately.

⑤ Tlaquepaque Village

This shopping **village** (📞928-282-4838; www.tlaq.com; 336 Hwy 179; ⊘10am-5pm) is a series of Mexican-style interconnected plazas that are home to dozens of high-end art galleries, shops and restaurants. It's easy to lose a couple of hours meandering the lovely maze here. Directly across the highway is the **Center for the New Age** (☑928-282-2085; 313 Hwy 179; ⏱8:30am-8:30pm), an interesting purveyor of crystals and New Age books and gifts. Come here for a vortex guide.

The Drive » Return to the Y and pick up Hwy 89A south. Chimney Rock and Coffee Pot Rock glow to the north, above the sprawl. After passing Arroyo Pinon Dr, turn left onto upper Red Rock Loop Rd. It's 4 miles west of the Y.

 Red Rock Loop Road

Any time is a good time to drive the winding 7-mile **Red Rock Loop Rd**, which is paved except for one short section. If you're in a mood to take photographs, turn left after 1.5 miles for the **Red Rock Crossing/ Crescent Moon Picnic Area** (day-use per vehicle $9; ⏱9am-dusk). A small army of photographers usually gathers at sunset to record the dramatic light show unfolding on iconic Cathedral Rock.

Continue driving through the blaze of sandstone glory to the aptly named **Red Rock State Park** (☑928-282-6907; www.azstateparks.com/Parks/RERO; 4050 Red Rock Loop Rd; per car/bicycle or pedestrian $10/3; ⏱8am-5pm, visitor center 9am-4:30pm). Not to be confused with Slide Rock State Park, this low-key place includes an environmental education center, a visitor center, picnic areas and 5 miles of well-marked trails in a riparian habitat amid gorgeous scenery. Ranger-led activities include nature walks, bird walks and full-moon hikes during warmer months.

The Drive » Turn left onto Red Rock Loop Rd and drive to Hwy 89A. Turn left and drive almost six miles to N Page Springs Rd.

7 Page Springs Cellars

New vineyards, wineries and tasting rooms along Hwy 89A and I-17 are bringing a dash of energy and style to central Arizona. Several wineries with tasting rooms hug a scrubby stretch of Page Springs Rd east of Cornville. For an extended stop, try **Page Springs Cellars** (www.pagespringscellars.com; 1500 N Page Springs Rd; wine tasting $10; ⏱11am-7pm Mon-Wed, to 9pm Thu-Sun). This busy spot has welcoming, knowledgeable staff and a cozy back porch overlooking Oak Creek. It's a nice place to savor the bruschetta and Rhone-style Arizona wines.

The Drive » Turn right onto Page Springs Rd and drive south to Cornville Rd. Follow it south 8 miles to I-17. Drive

DETOUR:
PALATKI & HONANKI HERITAGE SITES

Start 4 Uptown Sedona
Thousand-year old Sinaguan cliff dwellings and rock art are great reasons to brave a 9-mile dirt road leading to two archaeological sites on the edge of the wilderness. At **Palatki** (☑reservations 928-282-3854; http://www.redrockcountry.org/recreation/cultural.shtml; admission free, Red Rock Pass required; ⏱9:30am-3pm) there's a small visitor center and three easy trails (not suitable for wheelchairs). To manage crowds, reservations are required. True ruin groupies should ask here about the ruins at **Honanki** (⏱9:30am-4pm), north another three miles. To get to Palatki, follow Hwy 89A west 10 miles from the Y then turn right onto FR 525 (Red Canyon Rd, dirt) and follow it about 6 miles to FR 795. Take FR 795 for 1.5 miles. Both sites require a Red Rock Pass.

V-Bar-V Heritage SIte Sinagua petroglyph

TOP TIP: RED ROCK PASSES

To park at many trailheads and recreational areas in the Coconino National Forest, you'll need to buy a **Red Rock Pass** (www.redrockcountry.org; per day/week $5/15) from visitor centers, ranger stations or vending machines at some trailheads and picnic areas. Passes go on your dashboard. Federal Interagency passes are valid. Applicable areas are plastered with signs, which you can ignore if stopping briefly for a photograph. Check the *Recreation Guide to Your National Forest*, available at the National Forest visitor centers or online, to determine where the passes are required. Currently, passes are required at most recreational sites beside Hwy 89A in Oak Creek Canyon and beside Hwy 179 between Chapel Rd and the Bell Rock Pathway trailhead in the Village of Oak Creek.

north to exit 298 and Hwy 179. Take Hwy 179 east about 2.8 miles, passing Beaver Creek Campground.

- - - - - - - - - - - -

TRIP HIGHLIGHT

8 V-Bar-V Heritage Site

More than 1000 petroglyphs have been identified at this well-protected Forest Service **site** (http://www.redrockcountry.org/recreation/cultural.shtml; 🕘9:30am-3pm Fri-Mon). A short trail from the visitor center to the rock site runs parallel to a tributary of the Verde River. Many of the etchings appear unique to the Southern Sinaguan who lived

here between AD 1150 and 1400. The site was probably used by shamans and in part as a solar calendar. See if you can find the depiction of a female shaman. And the embracing stick-figure couple? Not dancing. Red Rock Pass required.

The Drive » Follow Hwy 179 west, crossing I-17. The Red Rock Scenic Byway begins three miles north and continues for 7.5 miles. Enjoy the show.

- - - - - - - - - - - -

TRIP HIGHLIGHT

9 Village of Oak Creek

Now that the scenic driving is done, stop at the **Red Rock Ranger**

District Visitor Center (📞928-282-4119, 928-203-2900; www.redrockcountry.org; 8375 Hwy 179, mile marker 304.7; 🕘8am-5pm), just south of the Village of Oak Creek, for more information about places you want to further explore. Pick up the free *Recreation Guide to Your National Forest*, which has a great map of hiking and biking trails in greater Sedona and along Oak Creek. The map also shows camping spots and picnic areas.

A great ride for cyclists is the easy but beautiful **Bell Rock Pathway** just north on Hwy 179. The Pathway is across the street from **Sedona Bike & Bean** (📞928-284-0210; www.bike-bean.com; 75 Bell Rock Plaza; 2hr/half-/full day from $30/40/50), a blissful combo of coffee bar and bike-rental place. The 7-mile round-trip crosses lots of other hiking and biking paths, and it's easy to spend a day exploring. Follow Hwy 179 north to return to Uptown Sedona.

✕ 🛏 p109

Eating & Sleeping

Oak Creek Canyon ❶

Dispersed camping is not permitted along Hwy 89A in Oak Creek Canyon.

🏕 USFS Campground $

(📞877-444-6777; www.recreation.gov; campsites $18) Operates four campgrounds along N Hwy 89A: Cave Springs, Manzanita, Pine Flat East and Pine Flat West. Some campsites are first-come, first-serve, and others are available by reservation.

Sedona ❹

✕ Coffee Pot Restaurant Breakfast $

(📞928-282-6626; www.coffeepotsedona.com; 2050 W Hwy Alt 89; mains $6-14; ⊙6am-2pm; 👶) This go-to breakfast and lunch joint is always busy and service can be slow, but it's friendly, reasonably priced and the selection is huge – 101 types of omelets, for a start.

✕ Elote Cafe Mexican $$$

(📞928-203-0105; www.elotecafe.com; King's Ransom Hotel, 771 Hwy 179; mains $17-26; ⊙5pm-late Tue-Sat) Some of the best, most authentic Mexican food in the region. Serves traditional dishes you won't find elsewhere, like fire-roasted corn with lime and cotija cheese, and tender, smoky pork cheeks. Reservations are not accepted, so arrive early.

✕ Picazzo's Pizzeria $$

(📞928-282-4140; 1855 W Hwy 89A; slices $4, pizzas $13-17; ⊙11am-9pm Sun-Thu, to 10 pm Fri & Sat) Pizza purists might shudder at the unorthodox toppings, but clued-in devotees gobble 'em up. If fig and gorgonzola or Indian chicken curry pizzas don't sound good, you can design your own.

✕ Rene at Tlaquepaque Restaurant $$$

(📞928-282-9225; www.renerestaurantsedona. com; Tlaquepaque Arts & Crafts Village, Hwy 179; lunch $9-22, dinner $19-48; ⊙11:30am-2:30pm daily, 5:30-8:30pm Mon-Thu, to 9pm Fri & Sat) A sentimental favorite with locals and repeat visitors, romantic Rene infuses classic French cuisine with Southwestern touches. It does meat best (lamb is a specialty).

🏕 Lantern Light Inn B&B $$$

(📞928-282-3419; www.lanternlightinn.com; 3085 W Hwy Alt 89; r $139-195, ste $195-309; @🛜) The lovely couple running this small inn in West Sedona put you right at ease in their comfortable antique-filled rooms. Credit cards not accepted.

🏕 Star Motel Motel $

(📞928-282-3641; www.starmotelsedona.com; 295 Jordan Rd; r $80-100) At these prices you won't find candy on your pillow, but who cares so long as the bed is clean, the shower strong and the refrigerator handy for chilling sunset beers. Uptown eateries are a few steps away.

Village of Oak Creek ❾

✕ Red Rock Cafe Cafe $

(www.facebook.com/theredrockcafe; 100 Verde Valley School Rd; mains under $11; ⊙6:30am-3pm) Look for the kokopelli on the window and nab a seat quickly if it's Sunday morning, when the place bustles with locals squeezing in breakfast before church. Come here for a solid meal before hitting Bell Rock Pathway.

🏕 Cozy Cactus B&B $$$

(📞928-284-0082; www.cozycactus.com; 80 Canyon Circle Dr; r incl breakfast $190-290; ❄@🛜) This recently revamped five-room B&B works well for adventure-loving types. The Southwest-style abode is beside a National Forest trail and is just around the bend from cyclist-friendly Bell Rock Pathway.

CELLS LOCKED AT NIGHT
PRISONERS HAD DAILY WORK DETAILS

These details included rock quarry, kitchen, sewing shop, adobe yard, wood yard, and prison construction. After work and on Sunday prisoners had time for reading, arts and crafts, education or relaxing.

Yuma Territorial Prison Notorious lock-up for the West's worst

Highway 95: Yuma to Lake Mead

9

In western Arizona the scenery comes with a few quirky sides: a notorious prison, a tiny chapel, a lonely ghost town and London Bridge.

TRIP HIGHLIGHTS

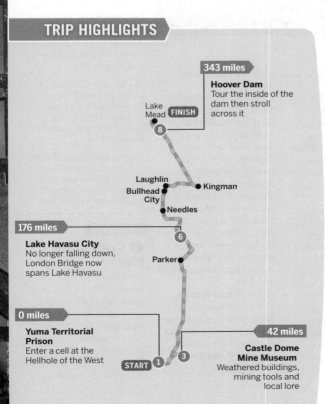

343 miles

Hoover Dam
Tour the inside of the dam then stroll across it

Lake Mead **FINISH**
8

Laughlin
Bullhead City
Needles
● Kingman

6

176 miles

Lake Havasu City
No longer falling down, London Bridge now spans Lake Havasu

Parker●

0 miles

Yuma Territorial Prison
Enter a cell at the Hellhole of the West

START 1   3

42 miles

Castle Dome Mine Museum
Weathered buildings, mining tools and local lore

3 DAYS
350 MILES / 563KM

GREAT FOR...

BEST TIME TO GO

Fall to spring for gem shows and to avoid the searing summer heat.

 ESSENTIAL PHOTO

The Hoover Dam from the Mike O'Callahan-Pat Tillman Memorial Bridge.

 BEST FOR HISTORY & CULTURE

Drop deep into Hoover Dam to learn how it was built.

Highway 95: Yuma to Lake Mead

9

The driving gets weird in western Arizona. Consider the trek to the Castle Dome Mining Museum in a remote corner of Kofa National Wildlife Refuge. As you rattle east for seven unpaved miles, the craggy mountains ahead take on a menacing snarl. To the north, a mysterious, grounded aircraft might appear, shimmering on the Yuma Proving Ground. And then it hits: there's nary a soul to hear you scream. It's eerie, and completely invigorating.

 p117

The Drive ›› Jump onto US 95 north, following the railroad tracks and sandy hills.

➋ The Pause-Rest-Worship Church

Fourteen miles northeast of Yuma, a tiny white-and-blue chapel – and we mean tiny – sits lightly on a patch of farmland. A local farmer built the original in 1995 as a memorial to his wife. A freak storm destroyed the church in 2011, but the community helped rebuild it. The 8ft-by-12ft structure seats about 12 and has stained-glass windows. If you're feeling contemplative, pull over and step inside.

The Drive ›› Continue north on Hwy 95. Turn right onto Castle Dome Rd at mile marker 55 and drive 10 miles, the last seven of which are unpaved but well maintained.

The drive takes you south of the Yuma Proving Ground, where the Army tests weapon systems and munitions, and then into the Kofa National Wildlife Refuge.

➊ Yuma

This sprawling city at the confluence of the Gila and Colorado Rivers was home to Arizona's notorious **territorial prison** ([☎]928-783-4771; www.azstateparks.com; 1 Prison Hill Rd; adult/child/under 7yr $6/$3/free; ⊙9am-5pm daily, closed Tue & Wed Jun-Sep), which was nicknamed the Hellhole of the West, in part because of the city's blazing temperatures. Between 1876 and 1909, 3069 convicts were incarcerated here for crimes ranging from murder to 'seduction under the promise of marriage.'

Today, the prison is Yuma's star attraction. Walking around the yard, behind iron-grille doors and into cells crowded with stacked bunks, you might get retroactively scared straight. And that's without mentioning the Dark Cell, a cave-like room where troublesome prisoners were locked together in a 5ft-high metal cage. Step inside, if you dare.

A new **trail system** along the adjacent Colorado River links the prison with downtown's Gateway Park and the restored **Yuma East Wetlands**.

TRIP HIGHLIGHT

➌ Castle Dome Mine

Meticulously reconstructed using as many original artifacts as possible, this remote **museum** ([☎]928-920-3062; www.castledomemuseum.com; adult/child $10/5; ⊙10am-5pm daily Nov-Apr, 10am-5pm Tue-Sun Oct) is an impressively

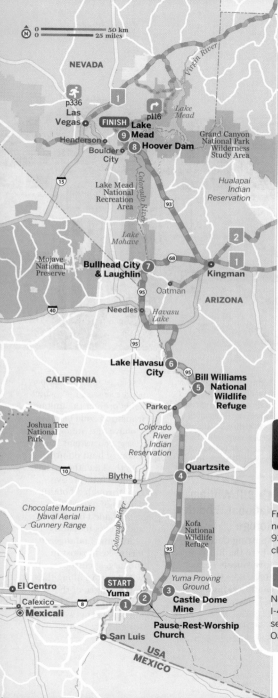

reconstructed mining town that was founded in 1864 during a silver boom.

There are about 50 buildings in all, many of them retrieved from nearby mines. As you walk from the saloon to the blacksmith shop you can read about the people who used to live here. Also displayed is the world's oldest pair of Levis, dating from 1890. A separate walking tour passes mine shafts and an old cemetery. Cash or check only.

The Drive » Continue north 50 miles on Hwy 95. Cross the I-10 then turn left on W Main St and follow it about 1 mile.

❹ Quartzsite

The desert here floods with RVs in January and February, when visitors arrive for rock

LINK YOUR TRIP

1 Four Corners Cruise

From Hoover Dam, drive northwest 30 miles on Hwy 93 to Sin City to kick off a classic southwest loop.

2 Route 66: The Southwest

North of Lake Havasu, leave I-40W at exit 1 then climb to see the begging burros of Oatman.

and mineral shows. Quartzsite's most curious monument is a small stone pyramid topped by a metal camel in the town graveyard. This memorial is for Haiji Ali, a Syrian camel driver who arrived in 1856 to help with a US army experiment using camels to transport goods across the desert. The experiment didn't work but Ali, nicknamed Hi Jolly, became a prospector. He died here in 1902.

The Drive >> Hwy 95N enters the Colorado River Indian Reservation 25 miles north of Quartzsite. Buy gas and fast food in Parker. To drive over Parker Dam, which formed Lake Havasu, turn left onto Parker Dam Rd about 15 miles north of town. It's the world's deepest dam, with 73% of its 320ft height buried beneath the riverbed. Return to Hwy 95 N.

- - - - - - - - - - - -

5 Bill Williams National Wildlife Refuge

Abutting Cattail Cove, where the Bill Williams River meets Lake Havasu, is this calm **wildlife refuge** (☎928-667-4144; www.fws.gov/refuge/Bill_Williams_River/; 60911 Hwy 95; admission free; ☺visitor center 8am-4pm Mon-Fri, 10am-2pm Sat & Sun, refuge sunrise-sunset), which helps protect the unique transition zone between Mohave and Sonoran desert ecosystems. On a finger of land pointing into the lake, there's a 1.4-mile interpretive trail through a botanic garden of native flora, with shaded benches and access to fishing platforms. Endangered birds like to roost in the largest cottonwood/willow grove along the entire length of the Colorado River. The entrance is between mile 161 and 162.

Hoover Dam

The Drive » With Lake Havasu to the west, drive north 20 miles to Lake Havasu City.

TRIP HIGHLIGHT

6 Lake Havasu City

Gracefully arched **London Bridge** may be one of Arizona's most incongruous tourist sites, but it's also among its most popular. And yes, it's the original bridge, having spanned the Thames from 1831 to 1967, when it was, quite literally falling down (as predicted in the nursery rhyme). The bridge was purchased by a developer, dismantled, and reassembled in the Arizona desert. Daytrippers come by the busload to walk across it and soak up faux British heritage in the kitschy-quaint **English Village**.

The lake is the other major draw. Formed in 1938 by the construction of Parker Dam, it's beloved by water rats, especially students on spring break (roughly March to May) and summer-heat refugees from Phoenix and beyond.

The **visitor center** (☎928-855-5655; www.golakehavasu.com; 422 English Village; ⊙9am-5pm; 🛜) is near the bridge.

✕ 🛏 p117

The Drive » Drive north to I-40 W/Hwy 95 N. From I-40, either continue north on Hwy 95 through Needles, passing Boundary Cone Rd to Route 66 and Oatman, or take River Rd/Needles Hwy, north out of Needles, which has less suburban sprawl.

----

7 Bullhead City & Laughlin

Named for a rock that resembled the head of a snoozing bull (now under Lake Mojave), Bullhead City began as a construction camp for Davis Dam, built in the 1940s. The town survives today, primarily because of the casinos across the Colorado River in Laughlin, which has a little more sizzle. The town was founded in 1964 by gaming impresario Don Laughlin, a high-school dropout from Minnesota. Stop here for gambling and cheap sleeps.

✕ 🛏 p117

The Drive » Follow Hwy 95N to Hwy 68E. It's not the quickest route but does swing by Route 66 hotspot Kingman. From Kingman, take Hwy 93 north. After crossing into Nevada, take exit 2 for NV 172, the dam access road.

TRIP HIGHLIGHT

8 Hoover Dam

Completed in 1936, this mighty dam (☎866-730-9097, 702-494-2517; www.usbr.gov/lc/hooverdam; Hwy 93; visitor center $8, incl powerplant tour adult/child $11/9, all-inclusive tour $30; ☻9am-6pm, last ticket sold 5:15pm) on the Arizona–Nevada border created Lake Mead, which has 700 miles of shoreline. The 726ft concrete structure was the Colorado River's first major dam. Its graceful curve and art-deco style contrasts superbly with the stark landscape.

Guided tour options include the 30-minute power plant tour or the more in-depth, one-hour Hoover Dam tour. Tickets for both are sold at the visitor center. If you're interested in history and construction facts, spring for the longer tour. Tickets for the power plant tour can also be purchased online. Parking at the site is an additional $7.

The nearby **Mike O'Callaghan-Pat Tillman Memorial Bridge** features a pedestrian walkway with perfect views upstream of Hoover Dam. Nearby Boulder City (p117) is a pleasant place to spend the night.

The Drive » Return to Hwy 93 W. Drive about a mile and a half to Lakeshore Dr. Turn right.

9 Lake Mead

Lake Mead and Hoover Dam are the most-visited sites within the **Lake Mead National Recreation Area** (☎park information desk 702-293-8906, visitor center 702-293-8990; www.nps.gov/lake; car/bicycle $10/5; ☻24hr, visitor center 9am-4:30pm Wed-Sun), which encompasses 110-mile-long Lake Mead, 67-mile-long Lake Mohave and many miles of desert around the lakes. The excellent **Alan Bible Visitor Center**, on Hwy 93 halfway between Boulder City and Hoover Dam, has information on recreation and desert life. Here, hikers and cyclists can pick up a map of the **River Mountains Loop Trail** (www.rivermountainstrail.com), which offers 32 miles of trails around the lake. From there, North Shore Rd winds around the lake and makes a great scenic drive.

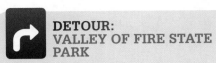

DETOUR: VALLEY OF FIRE STATE PARK

Start: 9 Lake Mead

For a scenic drive with an even more scenic end point, follow Lakeshore Scenic Dr northwest from the Alan Bible Visitor Center to Northshore Rd, heading northeast along Lake Mead.

At Hwy 169, turn left for **Valley of Fire State Park** (☎702-397-2088; www.parks.nv.gov/parks/valley-of-fire-state-park; per vehicle $10; ☻visitor center 8:30am-4:30pm), a fantasyland of wondrous shapes carved in vibrant red sandstone by the erosive forces of wind and water. Hwy 169 runs past the visitor center, which offers excellent desert-life exhibits, sells books and maps, and has information about hikes and ranger-led activities.

Eating & Sleeping

Yuma ❶

✕ Lutes Casino   American $

(☎928-782-2192; www.lutescasino.com; 221 S
Main St; mains under $8; ⏱10am-8pm Mon-Thu,
to 9pm Fri & Sat, to 6pm Sun) What's inside this
1940s-era hang-out (it's not a casino)? Attic-like
treasures hanging from the ceiling, old-school
domino players, movie memorabilia, a dude
playing the piano and a cross-section of the
town. The 'especial' is a burger topped with a
sliced hot dog.

⌂ La Fuente Inn & Suites   Inn $

(☎928-329-1814, 800-841-1814; www.
lafuenteinn.com; 1513 E 16th St; r incl breakfast
$89-109; P ❄ 🛜 🏊 🐾) Pretty gardens wrap
around a modern, Spanish Colonial–style
building. The evening social hour includes free
beer and wine. It has a $25 one-time pet fee.

Lake Havasu City ❻

✕ Barley Brothers   Pub $$

(☎928-505-7837; www.barleybrothers.com;
1425 N McCulloch Blvd; mains $9-24; ⏱11am-
9pm Sun-Thu, to 10pm Fri & Sat) It's brews and
views at this busy microbrewery overlooking
London Bridge. Steaks, burgers and salads
are on the menu, but the place is known for its
wood-fired pizzas. Beer drinkers can choose
from six microbrews.

✕ Red Onion   American $

(☎928-505-0302; www.redonionhavasu.com;
2013 N McCulloch Blvd; mains $7-12; ⏱7am-
2pm) A step above a diner, a step below a bistro,
the dining room here opens onto Havasu's
'uptown district.' Try the omelets for a hearty
start to your day. Service is friendly, if a bit
disorganized.

⌂ Heat   Boutique Hotel $$$

(☎928-854-2833; www.heathotel.com; 1420
N McCulloch Blvd; r $209-299, ste $249-439;
❄ 🛜) Rooms are hip and contemporary, and
most have private patios with views of London
Bridge. In the 'inferno' rooms, bathtubs fill from
the ceiling!

Bullhead City & Laughlin ❼

✕ Laughlin Ranch Grill   Eating $$

(☎928-754-1322; www.laughlinranch.com/grill;
1360 William Hardy Dr; lunch $8-10, dinner $8-28;
⏱10am-9pm Mon-Sat, 9am-6pm Sun) Part of
the Laughlin Ranch Golf Club, the grill looks like
a chic mountain lodge, with stone walls, high
ceilings and a fireplace. Serves burgers, wraps
and pizza, plus steaks and pasta at night.

⌂ Aquarius Casino Resort   Hotel $$

(☎702-298-5111; www.aquariuscasinoresort.
com; 1900 S Casino Dr, Laughlin; r $80-120, ste
$219-340; ❄ @ 🛜 🏊) The Aquarius is stylish,
welcoming and budget friendly. The lobby has
art-deco touches, while rooms are modern with
big windows and flat-screen TVs.

Boulder City

✕ Milo's   Wine Bar $$

(www.miloswinebar.com; 538 Nevada Hwy; mains
$9-13; ⏱11am-10pm Sun-Thu, to midnight Fri
& Sat) In downtown Boulder City, Milo's serves
fresh sandwiches, salads and gourmet cheese
plates at sidewalk tables outside the wine bar.

⌂ Boulder Dam Hotel   Hotel $

(☎702-293-3510; www.boulderdamhotel.com;
1305 Arizona St; r incl breakfast $72-89, ste
$99; ❄ 🛜) This simple and gracious Dutch
Colonial–style hotel has welcomed illustrious
guests since 1933. Rate includes made-to-order
breakfast and entry to the on-site Boulder City/
Hoover Dam Museum.

Montezuma Castle National Monument *Ancient cliffside perch*

Tribal Trails

10

Native American history is the draw on this busy trip that rolls north from Phoenix to cliff dwellings, a lava field and trading posts before ending at remote but beautiful Canyon de Chelly.

TRIP HIGHLIGHTS

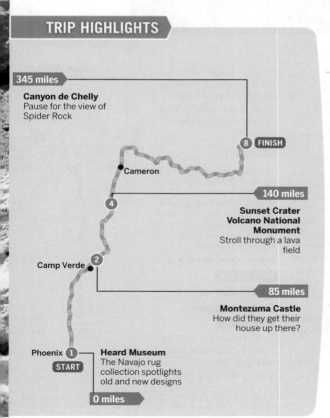

345 miles

Canyon de Chelly
Pause for the view of Spider Rock

8 FINISH

Cameron

140 miles

Sunset Crater Volcano National Monument
Stroll through a lava field

Camp Verde **2**

85 miles

Montezuma Castle
How did they get their house up there?

Phoenix **1**
START

Heard Museum
The Navajo rug collection spotlights old and new designs

0 miles

**4–5 DAYS
425 MILES / 684KM**

GREAT FOR...

BEST TIME TO GO

Navajo rodeos are held most weekends May through September, the Navajo Nation Fair is in September.

 ESSENTIAL PHOTO

The improbably perched Montezuma's Castle.

 BEST FOR HISTORY

The Boarding School Experience at the Heard Museum.

119

10 | Tribal Trails

Dominant cultures in the Arizona region between AD 100 and 1400 included the Hohokam, Sinaguan, Mogollon and Ancestral Puebloans. Their cliff dwellings, irrigation canals and petroglyphs stretch from the Phoenix area north into the Navajo Nation. It's not entirely clear why these ancient peoples abandoned their settlements, but it's generally accepted that some of the communities may have assimilated, becoming the forebears of the Hopi and New Mexico's Puebloans.

TRIP HIGHLIGHT

1 Phoenix

For an engaging introduction to Native American tribes in the Southwest, visit the **Heard Museum** (☎602-252-8848; www.heard.org; 2301 N Central Ave; adult/ senior/ child 6-12 & student $18/13.50/ 7.50; ⏰9:30am-5pm Mon-Sat, 11am-5pm Sun; 👪) downtown. The eye-catching kachina (Hopi spirit doll) collection is particularly memorable as is the 'Boarding School Experience' gallery, a moving look at the controversial Federal policy of removing Native American children from their families and sending them to remote boarding schools to Americanize them. For a walking tour of downtown Scottsdale, see p126.

🍴 🛏 p125

The Drive » Take I-17 north. Fort Verde State Historic Park at exit 287 is the site of an 1873 US Army fort built during the Indian Wars. Further north, take exit 289 and follow W Middle Verde Rd half a mile east to Montezuma Castle Rd.

TRIP HIGHLIGHT

2 Montezuma Castle National Monument

This stunningly well-preserved Sinagua **cliff dwelling** (☎928-567-3322; www.nps.gov/moca; adult/

child $5/free; ⊘8am-5pm)
dates back 1000 years.
The name refers to its
castle-like location
high on a cliff; early
explorers thought the
five-story-high pueblo
was Aztec and hence
dubbed it Montezuma. A
museum interprets the
archaeology of the site,
which is visible from
a short, wheelchair-
accessible trail. Entry
into the 'castle' itself is
prohibited.

If you're interested
in prehistoric irrigation
techniques, drive
north to exit 293 to see
Montezuma Well (☎928-
567-4521; admission free;
⊘8am-5pm), a 470ft-wide
sinkhole surrounded by
Sinaguan and Hohokam
dwellings.

The Drive » Return to I-17
and drive north. At exit 298 Hwy
179 leads east to petroglyphs
at V-Bar-V Heritage Site (p108).
Just south of Flagstaff, on the
cool and wooded Colorado

LINK YOUR TRIP

1 Four Corners Cruise

On the Navajo reservation,
take Hwy 160 east from
Tuba City to link to the
majestic Monument Valley.

5 Fantastic Canyon Voyage

From Cameron, Hwy 64 rolls
west to the South Rim of the
Grand Canyon.

Plateau, turn right onto I-40 and drive to exit 204. Follow Walnut Canyon Rd 3 miles.

---

❸ Walnut Canyon National Monument

With so many big-name attractions nearby, the beautiful and strangely peaceful **Walnut Canyon** (☎928-526-3367; www.nps.gov/waca; 7-day admission adult/child $5/ free; ☺8am-5pm May-Oct, 9am-5pm Nov-Apr) doesn't get the appreciation it deserves. The Sinaguan cliff dwellings here are set in the nearly vertical walls of a small limestone butte amid the forested canyon. The mile-long **Island Trail** steeply descends 185ft (more than 200 stairs) and passes 25 rooms built under the natural overhangs of the curvaceous butte. The shorter, wheelchair-accessible **Rim Trail** affords several views of the cliff dwellings from across the canyon.

The Drive ≫ Follow Walnut Canyon Rd across I-40 and turn left onto Route 66. Follow Route 66 west to Hwy 89. From here it's about 12 miles to Park Loop Rd.

TRIP HIGHLIGHT

❹ Sunset Crater Volcano National Monument

In AD 1064 a volcano erupted here, spewing ash over 800 sq miles,

spawning the Kana-A lava flow and leaving behind 8029ft Sunset Crater. The eruption forced farmers to vacate lands they had cultivated for 400 years; subsequent eruptions continued for more than 200 years.

Covered by a single $5 entrance fee (valid for seven days), both **Sunset Crater Volcano** (☎928-526-0502; www.nps.gov/sucr; adult/child $5/free; ☺visitor center 8am-5pm May-Oct, 9am-5pm Nov-Apr, monument sunrise-sunset) and Wupatki National Monument lie along Park Loop Rd, a well-marked 35-mile byway east of Hwy 89.

The **visitor center** houses a seismograph and other exhibits pertaining to volcanology. Viewpoints and a 1-mile interpretive trail through the **Bonito lava flow** (formed c 1180) spotlight volcanic features; a 0.3-mile loop is wheelchair accessible.

🛏 p125

The Drive ≫ Continue north on Park Loop Rd, passing through the Bonito lava flow, to the Wupatki visitor center.

---

❺ Wupatki National Monument

The first eruptions here enriched the soil, and ancestors of today's Hopi and Zuni people returned to farm the land in the early 1100s. By 1180, thousands were living here in advanced

FRANK STAUB/GETTY IMAGES ©

multistory buildings, but by 1250 their pueblos stood abandoned.

About 2700 of these structures lie within **Wupatki** (☎928-679-2365; www.nps.gov/wupa; 7-day admission adult/child $5/ free; ☺9am-5pm), though only a few are open to the public. A short self-guided tour of the largest dwelling, Wupatki Pueblo, begins behind the visitor center.

The Drive ≫ Return to Hwy 89N. The highway enters the Navajo Nation just beyond Gray Mountain. Cameron Trading Post, which has a large selection of Native American crafts, is just north of Hwy 64. Continue on

Hopi dancers

Hwy 89 N for almost 16 miles. Turn right onto Hwy 160 and drive 10 miles to Tuba City.

- - - - - - - - - -

⑥ Tuba City & Moenkopi

Tuba City is the largest single community in the Navajo Nation. To the southeast is the village of Moenkopi, a small Hopi enclave surrounded by Navajo land. For details about cultural protocol, visit www.explorenavajo. com. Alcohol is not permitted on the reservation.

Tuba City, named for 19th-century Hopi chief Tuve (or Toova), is home to the interesting **Explore Navajo Interactive Museum** (☎928-640-0684; www.explorenavajo.com/go2/ navajo_museum.cfm; cnr Main St & Moenave Rd; adult/senior/ child $9/7/6; ⏰10am-6pm Mon-Sat, noon-6pm Sun), where you'll discover why the Navajo call themselves the 'People of the Fourth World,' and learn about the tragic Long Walk. Aspects of contemporary life are also addressed.

Next door, and included in your entry fee, is a small **museum** about the Navajo Code Talkers. Visits wrap up in the historic **Tuba Trading Post**, which dates to the 1880s. For more information about exploring the Navajo Nation and obtaining the permits required for hiking and camping, visit www. navajonationparks.org.

✖ 🛏 p125

The Drive ≫ Drive east 62 miles on Hwy 264 to Second Mesa.

- - - - - - - - -

⑦ Hopi Nation

Three rocky, buff-colored mesas, named First, Second and Third Mesa, form the heart of the Hopi Nation, which is

DETOUR: NAVAJO NATIONAL MONUMENT

Start: 6 Tuba City & Moenkopi

The sublimely well-preserved Ancestral Puebloan cliff dwellings of Betatkin and Keet Seel are protected at the **Navajo National Monument** (☎928-672-2700; www.nps.gov/nava; Hwy 564; admission free; ☺visitor center 8am-5:30pm Jun–mid-Sep, 9am-5pm mid-Sep–May) and can only be reached on foot. The site, administered by the National Park Service, is 9 miles north of Hwy 160 at the end of paved Hwy 564.

For a distant glimpse of Betatkin follow the easy **Sandal Trail** about half a mile from the center. Betatkin is reached on a ranger-led 3-mile round-trip hike from the visitor center daily at 8:15am and 10am (June to early September; follows Mountain Standard Time March to November). Carry plenty of water. The 17-mile round-trip hike to the beautiful Keet Seel is steep and strenuous. The trail, open late May to early September, is limited to 20 people daily and requires a backcountry permit. Make reservations starting in late January.

There are two free campgrounds with first-come, first-served sites, and water nearby.

completely surrounded by the Navajo Nation. Descendants of the Ancestral Puebloans, the Hopi are one of the most untouched tribes in the US. Their village of Old Oraibi may be the oldest continuously inhabited settlement in North America.

On Second Mesa, the Hopi Cultural Center (p125) provides food and lodging, and is the home of the small **Hopi Museum** (☎928-734-6650; adult/child $3/1; ☺8am-5pm Mon-Fri, 9am-3pm Sat), with walls full of historic photographs and cultural exhibits. The Hopi are extremely accomplished artists and craftspeople. For a list of galleries and artists, visit www.hopiartstrail.com.

An eclectic mix of music plays on KUYI 88.1, Hopi's radio station. Photographs, sketching and recording are not allowed on the reservation.

🛏 p125

The Drive » Drive 57 miles east on Hwy 264 to Hwy 191. The Navajo Nation Fair (www.navajonationfair.com) is held the first week of September just east in Window Rock. For Canyon de Chelly, turn left and follow Hwy 191 north to Chinle. Turn right onto Indian Route 7.

TRIP HIGHLIGHT

8 Canyon de Chelly National Monument

Inhabited for 5000 years, the remote and beautiful **Canyon de Chelly** (☎928-674-5500; www.nps.gov/cach; Chinle; admission free; ☺visitor center 8am-5pm) – pronounced d-shay – shelters prehistoric rock art and 1000-year-old Ancestral Puebloan dwellings. Families still farm the land and raise animals here.

The national monument is on private Navajo land but is run by the National Park Service. The 16-mile **South Rim Drive** runs along the main canyon and has the most dramatic viewpoints. It dead-ends at the spectacular **Spider Rock Overlook**. For the most part **North Rim Drive** follows a side canyon called **Canyon del Muerto**. Viewpoints at the **Antelope House Overlook** offer lofty clifftop views of a natural rock fortress and cliff dwellings.

Only enter hogans (traditional homes) with a guide and don't take photographs without permission. To travel inside the canyon, choose a guide from the list provided by the Visitor Center and found on the park website.

🛏 p125

Eating & Sleeping

Phoenix ❶

✕ Fry Bread House   Native American $

(📞602-351-2345; 4140 N 7th Ave; mains $5-8; ⏰10am-8pm Mon-Thu, to 9pm Fri & Sat) The Native American treat known as an elephant ear or Navajo taco is a flat piece of fried dough topped with meat, beans and veggies. For dessert it's smeared with honey. Office workers crowd in at lunchtime. At press time, Fry Bread House was planning to move to 1003 E Indian School Rd, a larger location.

🛏 Sheraton Wild Horse Pass Resort & Spa   Resort $$$

(📞602-225-0100; www.wildhorsepassresort. com; 5594 W Wild Horse Pass Blvd, Chandler; r $209-279, ste $284-520, mains $44-54; 🅿❄@🛜🏊) Owned by the Gila River tribe and nestled on its sweeping reservation south of Tempe, this 500-room resort is a stunning alchemy of luxury and Native American traditions. Rooms reflect the traditions of local tribes. The award-winning **Kai Restaurant** serves indigenous Southwestern cuisine.

Sunset Crater Volcano National Monument ❹

🛏 Bonito Campground   Campground $

(📞928-526-0866; www.fs.usda.gov/recarea/ coconino/recreation; tent & RV sites $18; ⏰May– mid-Oct) Across from the visitor center, this USFS-run campground provides running water and restrooms, but no showers or hook-ups.

Tuba City & Moenkopi ❻

✕ Tuuvi Cafe   Native American, American $

(www.experiencehopi.com; cnr Hwys 160 & 264; breakfast $7-10, lunch & dinner $7-13; ⏰6am-9pm) Inside the travel center across from the Moenkopi Legacy, this casual Hopi eatery is a good place to refuel after a day of exploring. Enjoy omelets for breakfast, and burgers,

fry-bread tacos and daily stews for lunch and dinner.

🛏 Moenkopi Legacy Inn & Suites   Hotel $$

(📞928-283-4500; www.experiencehopi.com; cnr Hwys 160 & 264; r incl breakfast $145, ste $165-195; ❄@🛜🏊) The exterior is a stylized version of traditional Hopi village architecture, and the lobby, with a soaring ceiling supported by pine pillars, is stunning. Rooms have marble and granite baths and reproductions of historic photographs from the Hopi archives at Northern Arizona University.

Hopi Reservation ❼

🛏 Hopi Cultural Center Restaurant & Inn   Hotel $

(📞928-734-2401; www.hopiculturalcenter. com; Hwy 264; r $95-110, breakfast $5-15, lunch $8-20, dinner $13-20; ⏰breakfast, lunch & dinner) Reservations are essential for the hotel, especially in summer when its 33 modern, if bland, rooms usually book out. The **restaurant** serves tasty Hopi dishes such as *noqkwivi* (lamb and hominy stew) served with blue-corn fry bread. There's also American fare.

Canyon de Chelly National Monument ❽

🛏 Canyon de Chelly Campground   Campground $

(sites $10) The Navajo-run campground near the Sacred Canyon Lodge has about 90 sites on a first-come, first served basis with water but no showers.

🛏 Sacred Canyon Lodge   Motel $$

(📞800-679-2473; www.scacredcanyonlodge. com; r /ste$122-129/178, cafeteria mains $5-17; ⏰cafeteria breakfast, lunch & dinner; ❄@🛜🐾) Formerly Thunderbord Lodge, this Navajo-owned and run property is the only lodging in the park. It has 70 comfortable rooms and an inexpensive cafeteria serving Navajo and American meals ($5 to $17). Wi-fi is best in the rooms near the lobby.

STRETCH
YOUR LEGS
PHOENIX

Start/Finish: Scottsdale Visitor Center

Distance: 2 miles/3.2km

Duration: Three hours

History and art are highlights on this stroll through the heart of downtown Scottsdale, which swings from the Wild West rah-rah of Old Town to the chic galleries and upscale eateries of the Arts District and Southbridge.

Take this walk on Trip

Scottsdale Visitor Center

The helpful staff at this **visitor center** (📞800-782-1117, 480-421-1004; www.experiencescottsdale.com; Suite 170, 4343 N Scottsdale Rd; 🕐8am-5pm Mon-Fri) will have you headed in the right direction in no time. The Historic Old Town Scottsdale brochure has details about nearby historic buildings.

The Walk ❯❯ Turn right out of the building and walk to Scottsdale Rd. Turn left and continue south, crossing Indian School Rd then 1st Ave. On your left is the Sugar Bowl, a popular ice-cream parlor that opened in 1958. Take your next left onto Main St.

Old Town Scottsdale

This tiny, Wild West–themed enclave is filled with cutesy buildings, covered sidewalks and stores hawking mass-produced Indian jewelry and Western art. But it's not all bad. There are usually some fun-loving folks kicking back in the **Rusty Spur Saloon** (📞480-425-7787; 7245 E Main St; 🕐10am-1am Sun-Thu, to 2am Fri & Sat), a pack-em-in-tight country bar where the grizzled Budweiser crowd gathers for cheap drinks and twangy country bands. It's in an old bank that closed during the Depression. The vault now holds liquor instead of greenbacks, although you'll see lots of dollar bills hanging from the ceiling.

The Walk ❯❯ Walk east on Main St, crossing Brown Ave, and continue east a short distance on the plaza.

Scottsdale Civic Center Mall

Old school meets new school in the blocks near the Civic Center. Learn about Scottsdale's first settlers while wandering past artifacts and old photographs at the **Scottsdale Historical Museum** (📞480-945-4499; www.scottsdalemuseum.com; 7333 E Scottsdale Mall; admission free; 🕐10am-5pm Wed-Sun Oct-May, to 2pm Wed-Sun Jun & Sep) inside the Little Red Schoolhouse, built in 1909. Things turn contemporary just south at the **Scottsdale Museum of Contemporary Arts** (📞480-874-4666;

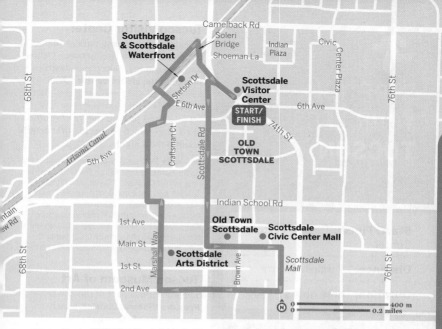

www.smoca.org; 7374 E 2nd St; adult/student / child $7/5/free, Thu free; ☺noon-5pm Sun, Tue & Wed, noon-9pm Thu-Sat), which sits inside a cleverly adapted ex-movie theater and showcases global art, architecture and design.

The Walk » Turn right out of the museum and take an immediate right onto 2nd Ave. Cross Brown Ave and Scottsdale Rd. Turn right at Marshall Way. To reach Main St, walk two blocks north.

Scottsdale Arts District

The Arts District teems with galleries laden with everything from epic Western oil paintings to cutting-edge sculpture and moody Southwestern landscapes. Every Thursday evening art lovers descend for the **Art Walk** (www. scottsdalegalleries.com; ☺7-9pm Thu), which centers on Marshall Way and Main St. It's been going strong for 30 years.

The Walk » Continue north on Marshall Way, crossing Indian School Rd. At the Horse Fountain, turn right onto 5th Ave, which is lined with boutiques and eateries.

Southbridge & Scottsdale Waterfront

Restaurants with nice patios border the **Arizona Canal**, which separates Southbridge from the Waterfront District to the north. Enjoy lunch and the nice weather at the **Herb Box** (📞480-289-6160; www.theherbbox.com; 7134 E Stetson Dr; lunch $10-19, dinner $15-28; ☺lunch daily, dinner Tue-Sat), a chichi bistro focused on fresh, regional ingredients, artful presentation and attentive service. From here, cross the Marshall Way bridge and follow the pedestrian walkway east to the 100ft-long **Soleri Bridge**, a stainless-steel wonder by artist and architect Paolo Soleri, who died in 2013. The bridge is also a solar calendar. Walk north for the upscale **Fashion Square** (www.fashionsquare.com; 7014 E Camelback, at Scottsdale Rd; ☺10am-9pm Mon-Sat, 11am-6pm Sun).

The Walk » Cross Scottsdale Rd to return to the Visitor Center.

STRETCH YOUR LEGS
TUCSON

Start/Finish: Tucson Visitor Center

Distance: 1.7 miles/2.7km

Duration: Three hours

Set in a flat valley hemmed in by craggy, odd-shaped mountains, Arizona's second-largest city smoothly blends Native American, Spanish, Mexican and Anglo traditions. Western art sets an inspirational tone for this stroll through downtown Tucson. The walk winds through the city's oldest neighborhood, site of a 1770s Spanish fort, then heads to the Congress Hotel — once a hideout for bank robber John Dillinger.

Take this walk on Trips

Tucson Visitor Center

To explore downtown, park at the garage on Church Ave, between Ochoa and Jackson Sts. Take the pedestrian bridge to the **visitor center** (📞800-638-8350, 520-624-1817; www.visittucson.org; 100 S Church Ave; ⏰9am-5pm Mon-Fri, to 4pm Sat & Sun) and pick up the free *Presidio Trail* map, which shares historic details about nearby sights.

The Walk » Cross Broadway and Congress Sts via the Garcés Bridge. Father Francisco Garcés rode with Lt Col Hugh O'Conor, an Irishman in the Spanish Army, to establish the Tucson Presidio. A second footbridge crosses Pennington St then passes the Mormon Battalion sculpture dedicated to the Mormon soldiers who passed through in 1846 on their way to California to fight in the Mexican War. Continue north across Alameda St.

Tucson Museum of Art

The museum is part of the low-key **Presidio Historic District**, which was the site of the original Spanish fort and a ritzy residential area once nicknamed 'Snob Hollow.' For a small city, the art **museum** (📞520-624-2333; www.tucsonmuseumofart.org; 140 N Main Ave; adult/child/student/senior $10/free/5/8; ⏰10am-5pm Wed, Fri & Sat, 10am-8pm Thu, noon-5pm Sun) is impressive. There's a respectable collection of Western and contemporary art, and the permanent exhibition of pre-Columbian artifacts will awaken your inner Indiana Jones. The special exhibits can shine too. A superb gift shop rounds out the works. First Sunday of the month is free.

The Walk » Walk east across Meyer Ave.

Old Town Artisans

The Presidio Historic District, bounded by W Alameda St, N Stone Ave, W 6th St and Granada Ave, teems with adobe townhouses and restored 19th-century mansions. Per current historical knowledge, this is one of the oldest inhabited places in North America. **Old Town Artisans** (www.oldtownartisans.com; 201 N Court

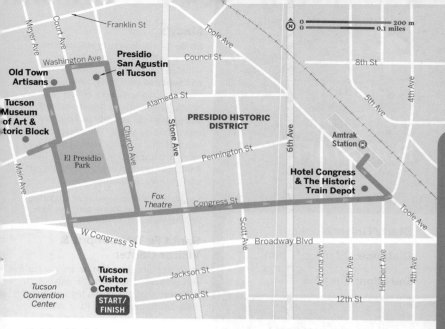

Ave) is a block-long warren of adobe apartments filled with galleries and crafts stores set around a lush and lovely courtyard cafe. It's a good destination for quality arts and crafts produced in the Southwest and Mexico.

The Walk » Walk east on Washington St to reach the fort, which borders Church Ave.

Presidio San Agustin del Tucson

The Spanish Presidio del San Augustín del Tucson dates back to 1775, but the fort itself was built over a Hohokam site that has been dated to AD 700–900. The original fort is completely gone, although there's a small reconstructed section at the corner of Church Ave and Washington St.

The Walk » Follow Church Ave south to Congress St. Turn left and walk east passing the 1930s Fox Theatre, a renovated art-deco theater with fluted golden columns, water fountains and a giant sunburst mural radiating from the ceiling.

Hotel Congress & Historic Train Depot

This beautifully restored 1919 hotel is a bohemian vintage beauty and a beehive of activity, mostly because of its popular cafe, bar and club. Infamous bank robber John Dillinger and his gang were captured here during their 1934 stay when a fire broke out at the hotel. Off the lobby, peruse newspaper clippings and photos about Dillinger's capture. The popular **Cup Cafe** (☎520-798-1618; www.hotelcongress.com/food; 311 E Congress St; breakfast $7-12, lunch $10-12, dinner $13-23; ☑) serves a global array of dishes, with a decent selection of vegetarian mains.

The train depot just across Toole Ave has a small **transportation museum**. On the train platform are statues of Wyatt Earp and Doc Holliday. The pair shot Frank Stilwell here in 1882.

The Walk » Follow Congress St back to the visitor center, or walk south for more stops along the Presidio Trail.

STRETCH YOUR LEGS
FLAGSTAFF

Start/Finish: Macy's

Distance: 0.7 miles/1.1km

Duration: One hour

Tales of ghosts and Old West artists keep this walk rooted in the past as its winds through Flagstaff's downtown, passing buildings dating back to the early days of the 1900s.

Take this walk on Trips

Macy's

Students, outdoorsy types, caffeine lovers – all hunker down at the wooden tables at this beloved **coffeehouse** (www.macyscoffee.net; 14 S Beaver St; mains under $8; ⊘6am-8pm; 🛜🖉). The delicious house-roasted coffee has kept the city buzzing for more than 30 years. The vegetarian menu includes many vegan choices, along with traditional cafe grub like pastries, steamed eggs, bagels, yogurt and granola, and sandwiches.

The Walk ≫ Walk north on Beaver St, crossing Phoenix Ave and then the railroad tracks. Turn right into the train station parking lot.

Santa Fe Train Depot & Visitor Center

At some point during your walk, a train will probably glide through downtown. For more than 125 years, beginning in 1882, trains announced their presence with loud blasts – ruining a good night's sleep for travelers on their way to the Grand Canyon. At one point, up to 125 trains passed through daily. After years of wrangling, city officials finally established quiet zones, and on March 2, 2010 a final symbolic blare blasted across Flagstaff. The train depot houses the Amtrak station and the **visitor center** (📞800-842-7293, 928-774-9541; www.flagstaffarizona.org; 1 E Rte 66; ⊘8am-5pm Mon-Sat, 9am-4pm Sun), which has free downtown walking tour guides for Route 66 and haunted sites.

The Walk ≫ From the depot, turn right and walk to San Francisco St. Turn left and follow San Francisco St across Route 66. Walk one block north and cross Aspen St.

Hotel Monte Vista

An old-fashioned neon sign towers over this allegedly haunted 1926 hotel (p85), and hints at what's inside: feather lampshades, vintage furniture, bold colors and eclectic decor. Rooms are named for the movie stars and musicians who slept in them.

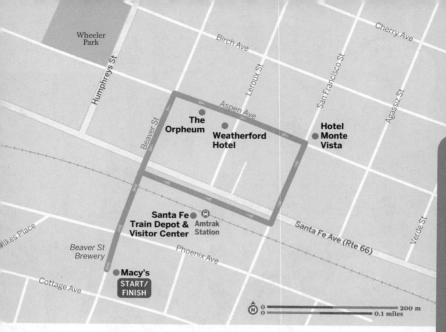

The hotel is perhaps best known for its ghosts, and the front desk keeps a list of resident spirits. According to one story, in the late 1970s a woman died in the rocking chair of the Jon Bon Jovi Room and is said to haunt the room. Creepier still is the Gary Cooper Room, supposedly haunted by two prostitutes who were stabbed and thrown out the window in the 1930s. And if you're in room 210, listen out for the Phantom Bellboy.

The Walk » Cross San Francisco St and walk northwest on Aspen Ave passing Heritage Sq. Cross Leroux St and turn left.

Weatherford Hotel

There's something undeniably appealing about this Old West **hotel** (☏928-779-1919; www.weatherfordhotel.com; 23 N Leroux St; ❀ ☏), which opened on new year's day in 1900. Maybe it's the fact that this not-so-big place has three bars, two on the 1st floor and one on the 3rd. It's also cool that two icons of the west, artist Thomas Moran and

author Zane Grey, were guests. Moran drew sketches of the Western landscape while staying here, and Zane Grey worked on his book *Call of the Canyon*.

An illuminated, 6ft-tall pine cone drops here twice on new year's eve, at 10pm EST and midnight Mountain Time.

The Walk » Head back to W Aspen Ave, turn left and walk a half block.

The Orpheum

John Weatherford, the original owner of the Weatherford Hotel, also built this **theater** (☏928-556-1580; www.orpheumpresents.com; 15 W Aspen St; tickets from $15), which opened as a movie house in 1911. The theater closed in 1915 after the roof collapsed following a snowstorm. It reopened in 1917. Today the Orpheum is a concert hall showcasing regional and indie bands.

The Walk » Continue to Beaver St and turn left, crossing Route 66 and Phoenix Ave. Wrap up with a microbrew at Beaver St Brewery or cross Beaver St to return to Macy's.

New Mexico Trips

NEW MEXICO IS CALLED THE LAND OF ENCHANTMENT for a reason, and you'll find out why as you drive through the Technicolor landscapes that inspired Georgia O'Keeffe, past traditional adobe villages tucked beneath the 13,000ft Sangre de Cristo range, and over juniper-speckled plains that seem to roll to infinity. You'll stop at old mud-brick *santuarios* filled with sacred folk art, visit ancient and living Indian pueblos, explore surreal underground caverns, and soak in hot springs. You'll travel what might be the oldest road in America and follow in the footsteps of Geronimo and Billy the Kid. And you're never far from great hiking and camping – or platters of local cuisine smothered in the state's signature green or red chile sauce.

Albuquerque International Balloon Fiesta (Trips 12 & 14)
BILL HEINSOHN/GETTY IMAGES ©

New Mexico Trips

COLORADO

San Isabel National Forest

Manitou Springs
Colorado Springs

Florence
Pueblo

Rio Grande National Forest

Great Sand Dunes National Park

La Junta

Walsenburg

Alamosa

Comanche National Grassla

South San Juan Wilderness

Trinidad

Ute Mountain Indian Reservation

Chama

Latir Peak Wilderness

Raton

Capulin Volcano National Monument
Des Moines

Shiprock
Farmington

Gorbernador

Carson National Forest

Taos

Maxwell

Clayton

Rita Blanca National Grassland

Navajo Indian Reservation

Newcomb

15

Springer

Naschitti

13

Cuba

Los Alamos

11

Santa Fe National Forest

15

Kiowa National Grassland

Wagon Mound

Chaco Culture National Historical Park

Gallup

14

Santa Fe

Las Vegas

Thoreau

San Ysidro

12

Variadero

Logan

Zuni
Zuni Indian Reservation

Ramah

El Morro

19

Laguna Indian Reservation

Albuquerque

Tijeras
Isleta Indian Reservation

Santa Rosa

Cuervo

Tucumcari

San Jon

ARIZONA

Correo

Acoma Indian Reservation

Belen

Vaughn

Fort Summer

Clovis

Quemado

Cibola National Forest

12

NEW MEXICO

Mesa

Portales

Datil

18

Socorro

Kenna

Luna

17

Apache Kid Wilderness

Carrizozo

Capitan

Lincoln

Tatum

Gila National Forest

Chloride

Elephant Butte Reservoir

Ruidoso

20

Roswell

Gila Wilderness

18

Silver City

17

Truth or Consequences

Tularosa

Lincoln National Forest

Lovingston

Hope

Artesia

Hobbs

Hatch

White Sands National Mounument

Alamogordo

16

Carlsbad

Eunice

Lordsburg

12

16

Las Cruces

Orogrande

Whites City

Carlsbad Caverns National Park

Malaga

Deming

Animas

Rodeo

USA

MEXICO

El Paso

Ciudad Juarez

Guadalupe Mountains National Park

Kermit

Coronado National Forest

TEXAS

Pecos

Van Horn

Aguas Temales

134

N   0   100 km
     0   50 miles

Classic Trip

11 **High & Low Roads to Taos 2–4 days**
Take the mountains up and the canyons down, looping between iconic destinations. (p137)

12 **El Camino Real & Turquoise Trail 3–4 days**
Follow the 400-year-old Royal Road up the Rio Grande valley. (p147)

13 **Georgia O'Keeffe Country 2–3 days**
Enter a world of vibrant color and raw elemental force. (p155)

14 **Highway 4: Jemez Mountains 2 days**
Hot springs, hiking, ancient cave dwellings and the birthplace of 'The Bomb'. (p163)

15 **Enchanted Circle & Eastern Sangres 2 days**
From high mountains to grassy prairies, with canyon hikes and haunted hotels. (p171)

16 **Las Cruces to Carlsbad Caverns 2–3 days**
Pure white sand dunes and surreal caves dazzle the eye – and the mind. (p179)

17 **Geronimo Trail 2–3 days**
Mountain roads twist past restored mining towns in Geronimo's old stomping grounds. (p187)

18 **Into The Gila 2 days**
Cruise from high-tech telescopes into a wild range of elk, bear and mountain lions. (p195)

19 **Highway 53 to Acoma 2 days**
Explore Indian pueblos and lava fields – and meet the wolves! (p203)

20 **Billy the Kid Trail 2 days**
See where the Kid escaped, Smokey Bear was found and aliens (maybe) landed. (p211)

 DON'T MISS

Lincoln

The entire town is a historical monument, including the courthouse from which Billy the Kid shot his way to freedom; on Trip **20**

Ghost Ranch

Hike, ride horseback, or take a van tour through the colorful terrain immortalized in the paintings of Georgia O'Keeffe, on Trip **13**

Santuario de Chimayó

This 1816 adobe church is home to miracle healings and is the site of the largest Catholic pilgrimage in the US. Find it on Trip **11**

Canyon Road

The heart of the Santa Fe art scene, with over 100 galleries plus fine dining and the oldest tavern in town (El Farol). Dive in on Trips **11** **12**

Indian Pueblos

Find some of the oldest continuously inhabited places in North America, rich in culture, on Trips **11** **15** **19**

Taos Pueblo
Visit in July for the summer pow-wow

Classic Trip

High & Low Roads to Taos

11

Santa Fe. Taos. The Rio Grande. The Sangre de Cristos. And all the adobe villages, art galleries, Spanish-colonial churches and burrito stands in between make this loop a classic.

TRIP HIGHLIGHTS

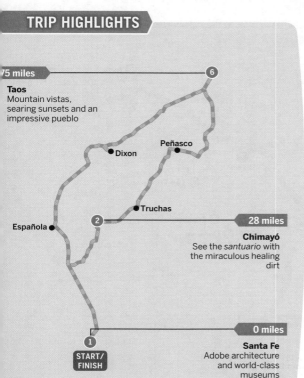

75 miles ──────────────── 6

Taos
Mountain vistas, searing sunsets and an impressive pueblo

Peñasco

● Dixon

● Truchas

2 ──────── **28 miles**

Española ●

Chimayó
See the *santuario* with the miraculous healing dirt

──────── **0 miles**

1
START/
FINISH

Santa Fe
Adobe architecture and world-class museums

**2–4 DAYS
150 MILES / 241KM**

GREAT FOR...

BEST TIME TO GO
June to March.

 ESSENTIAL PHOTO

Get the gorge and mountains at once, from Hwy 68 near Taos.

 BEST FOR CULTURE

The 'miracle church' – and the chile – in Chimayó.

137

Classic Trip

11 High & Low Roads to Taos

Starting in hip, historic Santa Fe, you'll rise from scrub-and-sandstone desert into ponderosa forests, snaking between the villages at the base of the 13,000ft Sangre de Cristos, until you reach the Taos plateau. After checking out this little place that's lured artists, writers and hippies for the past century, head back south through the ruggedly sculpted Rio Grande gorge, with the river coursing alongside you.

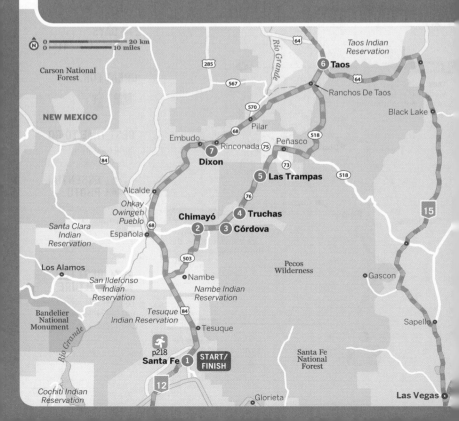

TRIP HIGHLIGHT

❶ Santa Fe

Walking among the historic adobe neighborhoods, and even around the tourist-filled plaza, there's no denying that 400-year-old Santa Fe has a timeless, earthy soul. Known as 'the city different,' it seamlessly blends historical and contemporary styles and casts a spell that's hard to resist: it's the second-oldest city in the US, the oldest state capital, and throws the oldest annual party (Fiesta) while boasting the second-largest art market in the nation, plus gourmet restaurants, world-class museums, opera, spas and more. At 7000ft above sea level, Santa Fe is also the highest US state capital, and

LOCAL KNOWLEDGE: NATURE CALLS

Want to see the scenery without a pane of glass in front of your face? Off the High Road, take a stroll on the **Santa Barbara Trail**, which follows a trout-filled creek through mixed forest into the Pecos Wilderness; it's pretty flat and easygoing. To reach the trailhead, take Hwy 73 from Peñasco and follow the signs.

Off the Low Road, turn onto Hwy 570 at Pilar and check out the **Orilla Verde Recreation Area** (day-use $3, tent/RV sites $7/15), where you can hang out or camp along the Rio Grande (or tube on it or fish in it). Hike up to the rim on Old 570, a dirt road blocked by a landslide, with expansive vistas of the Taos Plateau and the Sangre de Cristos.

Some of the best views in the state are from the top of **Lake Peak** (12,409ft), which can be reached on a day hike starting at the Santa Fe Ski Basin.

From Taos Ski Valley, you can day hike to the top of **Wheeler Peak** (13,161ft), New Mexico's highest summit (the views are pretty good up there, too). For trail maps and more information, go to the **Travel Bug** (www.mapsofnewmexico.com; 839 Paseo de Peralta; 🕐7:30am-5:30pm Mon-Sat, 11am-4pm Sun; 📶) bookshop in Santa Fe or the Taos **visitor center** (📞575-758-3873; Paseo del Pueblo Sur, Paseo del Cañon; 🕐9am-5pm; 📶).

LINK YOUR TRIP

12 **El Camino Real & Turquoise Trail**

A natural segue south from Santa Fe along the historic Rio Grande road.

15 **Enchanted Circle & Eastern Sangres**

Loop north from Taos, over the mountains and back again.

a fantastic base for hiking, mountain biking, backpacking and skiing. The plaza area has the highest concentration of sights (see p218) but it's also worth a trip to Museum Hill for the fantastical **Museum of International Folk Art** (www.internationalfolkart.org; 706 Camino Lejo; NM resident/nonresident/child $6/9/free, free 5-8pm Fri summer; 🕐10am-5pm, closed Mon Sep-May) and the excellent (and free) **Wheelwright Museum**

of the American Indian (www.wheelwright.org; 704 Camino Lejo; 🕐10am-5pm Mon-Sat, 1-5pm Sun), among others.

🍴 🛏 p145

The Drive » For this 27-mile leg, take Hwy 84/285 north, then exit right onto Hwy 503 towards Nambé. Turn left onto Juan Medina Rd, toward the Santuario de Chimayó.

TRIP HIGHLIGHT

❷ Chimayó

Tucked into this little village is the so-called

Classic Trip

'Lourdes of America,' **El Santuario de Chimayó** (www.elsantuariodechimayo. us; ⏱9am-5pm Oct-Apr, to 6pm May-Sep), one of the most important cultural sites in New Mexico. In 1816, this two-towered adobe chapel was built over a spot of earth said to have miraculous healing properties. Even today, the faithful come to rub the *tierra bendita* – holy dirt – from a small pit inside the church on whatever hurts; some mix it with water and drink it. The walls of the dirt room are covered with crutches, left behind by those healed by the dirt. During Holy Week, about 30,000 pilgrims walk to Chimayó from Santa Fe, Albuquerque and beyond in the largest Catholic pilgrimage in the US. The artwork in the *santuario* is worth a trip on its own.

Chimayó also has a centuries-old tradition of producing some of the finest weavings in the area and has a handful of family-run galleries. Irvin Trujillo, a seventh-generation weaver, whose carpets are in collections at the Smithsonian in Washington DC and the Museum of Fine Arts in Santa Fe, works out of his gallery **Centinela Traditional Arts** (www. chimayoweavers.com; NM 76; ⏱9am-6pm Mon-Sat, 10am-5pm Sun). Naturally dyed blankets, vests and pillows are sold, and you can watch the artists weaving on handlooms.

🍴 p145

The Drive » Follow Hwy 76 north for a few miles, and take the right-side turn off to Córdova.

WINTER THRILLS

One of the biggest winter draws to this part of New Mexico is the skiing and snowboarding, and **Taos Ski Valley** (www.skitaos.org; half-/full-day lift ticket $64/77) is the premier place to hit the slopes. There's just something about the snow, challenging terrain and laid-back atmosphere that makes this mountain a wintery heaven-on-earth – that is, if heaven has a 3275ft vertical drop.

Offering some of the most difficult terrain in the USA, it's a fantastic place to zip down steep tree glades into untouched powder bowls. Seasoned skiers luck out, with more than half of the 70-plus trails at the Taos Ski Valley ranked expert; but there's also an award-winning ski school, so complete beginners thrive here too. The valley has a peak elevation of 11,819ft and gets an average of more than 300in of all-natural powder annually – but some seasons are much better than others. The resort also has a skier-cross obstacle course at its popular terrain park.

That said, **Ski Santa Fe** (☎505-982-4429, snow report 505-983-9155; www.skisantafe.com; lift ticket adult/child $66/46; ⏱9am-4pm late Nov-Apr) is no slouch. Less than 30 minutes from the Santa Fe plaza, it boasts the same fluffy powder (though usually a little less of it), with an even higher base elevation (10,350ft) and higher chairlift service (12,075ft). Briefly admire the awesome desert and mountain vistas, then fly down powder glade shoots, steep bump runs or long groomers. The resort caters to families and expert skiers alike with its varied terrain. The quality and length of the ski season can vary wildly from year to year depending on how much snow the mountain gets, and when it falls (you can almost always count on a good storm in late March).

3 Córdova

Down in the Rio Quemado Valley, this little town is best known for its unpainted, austere *santos* (saint) carvings created by local masters like George Lopez, Jose Delores Lopez, and Sabinita Lopez Ortiz – all members of the same artistic family. Stop and see their work at the **Sabinita Lopez Ortiz shop** (☎505-351-4572; County Rd 9; ⊙variable) – one of a few galleries in town.

The Drive » Hop back on Hwy 76 north, and climb higher into the Sangre de Cristo Mountains, about 4 miles.

4 Truchas

Rural New Mexico at its most sincere is showcased in Truchas, originally settled by the Spaniards in the 18th century. Robert Redford's *The Milagro Beanfield War* was filmed here (but don't bother with the movie – the book it's based on, by John Nichols, is waaaay better). Narrow roads, many unpaved, wend between century-old adobes. Fields of grass and alfalfa spread toward the sheer walls and plunging ridges that define the western flank of the Truchas Peaks. Between the run-down homes are some wonderful art galleries, which double as workshops for local weavers, painters, sculptors and other artists. The best place to get an overview of who's painting/sculpting/carving/weaving what, is the **High Road Marketplace** (www.highroadnewmexico.com; 1642 Hwy 76; ⊙10am-5pm, to 4pm winter), a cooperative art gallery with a huge variety of work by area artists.

The Drive » Continue north on Hwy 76 for around 8 miles, transecting the little valleys of Ojo Sarco and Cañada de los Alamos.

HIGH/LOW ROAD FESTIVALS

Try to catch – or avoid, if you hate crowds – some of the highlights from around the year on the High and Low Roads. Check websites for exact dates each year:

» **Easter** (Chimayo) – March/April

» **Taos Solar Music Festival** (www.solarmusicfest. com) – June

» **Taos Pueblo Pow-Wow** (www.taospueblopowwow. com; adult/child $10/free) – July

» **International Folk Art Market** (www.folkartmarket. org; Santa Fe) – July

» **Spanish Market** (www.spanishcolonial.org; Santa Fe) – July

» **Indian Market** (www.swaia.org; Santa Fe) – August

» **Santa Fe Fiesta** (www.santafefiesta.org) – September

» **High Road Art Tour** (www.highroadnewmexico.com; Hwy 76 to Peñasco) – September

» **Dixon Studio Tour** (www.dixonarts.org) – November

» **Christmas on Canyon Rd** (Santa Fe) – December

5 Las Trampas

Completed in 1780 and constantly defended against Apache raids, the **Church of San José de Gracia** (Hwy 76; ⊙9am-5pm Fri & Sat) is considered one of the finest surviving 18th-century churches in the USA and is a National Historic Landmark. Original paintings and carvings remain in excellent condition, and self-flagellation bloodstains from Los Hermanos Penitentes (a 19th-century religious order with a strong following in the northern

KERRICK JAMES/CORBIS ©

COLLEEN MINIUK-SPERRY/ALAMY ©

WHY THIS IS A CLASSIC TRIP
MICHAEL BENANAV, AUTHOR

In this one loop, you delve into the enchanted essence of New Mexico: its oldest settlement, its most sacred sight, its highest peaks, its biggest river, its best food. From top art galleries and museums to rural villages where horse pastures and orchards are laced together by *acequias* (irrigation ditches), this is the state as you most imagined it might be. And more.

Above: Church at Taos Pueblo
Left: Wood crafts by Gloria Lopez Cordova at the Santa Fe Spanish Market
Right: Chili ristras and dried flowers

ANN CECIL/GETTY IMAGES ©

mountains of New
Mexico) are still visible.
On your way out of
town, look right to see
the amazing irrigation
aqueduct, carved from
tree trunks!

The Drive » Continue north
on Hwy 76, through lovely
Chamisal. At the T, turn right
onto Hwy 75 and stay on it
through Peñasco and Vadito. At
Hwy 518, turn left towards Taos.
At the end of the road, turn right
on Paseo del Pueblo Sur/Hwy
68 and take it on into Taos –
around 32 miles in total.

TRIP HIGHLIGHT

6 Taos

Taos is a place
undeniably dominated
by the power of its
landscape: 12,300ft
often-snowcapped
peaks rise behind
town, a sage-speckled
plateau unrolls to the
west before plunging
800ft straight down
into the Rio Grande
Gorge. The sky can be
a searing sapphire blue
or an ominous parade of
rumbling thunderheads.
And then there are the
sunsets...

The pueblo here
is one of the oldest
continuously inhabited
communities in the
United States and it
roots the town in a
long history with a
rich cultural legacy –
including conquistadors,
Catholicism, and
cowboys. Taos remains
a relaxed and eccentric

Classic Trip

place, with classic mud-brick buildings, quirky cafes and excellent restaurants. It's both rural and worldly, and a little bit otherworldly.

The best thing to do is walk around the plaza area soaking in the aura of the place. But you also won't want to miss **Taos Pueblo** (☎505-758-1028; www.taospueblo.com; Taos Pueblo Rd; adult/child $10/free, photography or video permit $6; ◎8am-4:30pm). Built around 1450 and continuously inhabited ever since, it's the largest existing multistoried pueblo structure in the USA and one of the best surviving examples of traditional adobe construction. Also well worth a visit is the **Millicent Rogers Museum** (www.millicentrogers.org; 1504 Millicent Rogers Rd; adult/child $10/2; ◎10am-5pm, closed Mon Nov-Mar), filled with pottery, jewelry, baskets and textiles from the private collection of a model and oil heiress who moved to Taos in 1947 and acquired one of the best collections of Indian and Spanish colonial art in the USA.

 p145

The Drive ≫ On this 26-mile leg, cruise the Low Road back to Santa Fe by taking Hwy 68 South. Just before the road drops downhill, there's a large pullout with huge views, so hop out and see what you're leaving behind. Then head down into the Rio Grande gorge. Go left on Hwy 75 to Dixon.

---

⑦ Dixon

This small agricultural and artistic community is spread along the gorgeous Rio Embudo valley. It's famous for its apples but plenty of other crops are grown here too, including some of the grapes used by two award-winning local wineries, **Vivac** (www.vivacwinery.com; ◎10am-6pm Mon-Sat, from noon Sun) and **La Chiripada** (www.lachiripada.com; NM 75; ◎11am-6pm Mon-Sat, from noon Sun), both of which have tasting rooms. In summer and fall, there's a farmers market on Wednesday afternoons, with food fresh from the fields. Our favorite art gallery is actually on Hwy 68, in Rinconada, just north of Hwy 75; **Rift Gallery** (www.saxstonecarving.com; Hwy 68; ◎10am-5pm Wed-Sun) features masterful ceramics and stonework. On the first weekend in November, local artists open their homes and studios to the public in New Mexico's oldest studio tour. In summer, ask at the local food co-op and some kind soul might point you to the waterfalls, up a nearby dirt road.

p145

The Drive ≫ Back on Hwy 68, head south along the river, through Embudo and out of the gorge. Continue through Española, where you'll meet Hwy 84/285, and can take it back to Santa Fe. Both these towns are great lunch stops (p145). This leg is around 47 miles.

Eating & Sleeping

Santa Fe ①

🍴 Harry's Roadhouse
American, New Mexican $

(📞505-989-4629; www.harrysroadhouse-santafe.com; 96 Old Las Vegas Hwy; mains breakfast $5-8, lunch $7-11, dinner $9-16; ⏰7am-10pm; 👶) This longtime favorite on the southern edge of town feels like a rambling cottage. And, seriously, *everything* is good here. Especially dessert! The mood is casual and there's a full bar.

🛏 El Paradero
B&B $$

(📞505-988-1177; www.elparadero.com; 220 W Manhattan Ave; r $110-200; 🅿️❄️@📶) Just a few blocks from the Plaza, this 200-year-old adobe B&B is one of Santa Fe's oldest inns. Each room is unique and loaded with character; our favorite is No 6.

Chimayó ②

🍴 Rancho de Chimayo
New Mexican $$

(📞505-984-2100; www.ranchodechimayo.com; County Rd 98; mains $8-18; ⏰8:30-10:30am Sat & Sun, 11:30am-9pm daily, closed Mon Nov-Apr) Classic New Mexican home cooking and the perfect margarita in atmospheric Southwestern ambiance.

Taos ⑥

🍴 El Gamal
Middle Eastern $

(www.elgamaltaos.com; 12 Doña Luz St; mains $7-12; ⏰9am-5pm Sun-Wed, to 9pm Thu-Sat; 📶🍴👶) We're not sure the falafel at this vegetarian Middle Eastern place quite achieves its goal to 'promote peace...through evolving people's consciousness and taste buds,' but it just might. There's a kids' playroom in the back, plus a pool table and free wi-fi.

🍴 Michael's Kitchen
New Mexican $

(www.michaelskitchen.com; 304C Paseo del Pueblo Norte; mains $7-16; ⏰7am-2:30pm

Mon-Thu, to 8pm Fri-Sun; 👶) Locals and tourists converge on this old favorite because the menu is long, the food's reliably good, and it's an easy place for kids. Plus, it serves the best damn breakfast in town. The fresh pastries fly out the door.

🛏 Historic Taos Inn
Historic Hotel $$

(📞575-758-2233; www.taosinn.com; 125 Paseo del Pueblo Norte; r $75-275; 🅿️❄️📶) With a cozy lobby, a top-notch restaurant, a sunken fireplace, a prime location, and lots of live local music at its famed Adobe Bar, the Taos Inn is more than the sum of its parts. The older rooms, some from the 19th century, are the nicest.

Dixon ⑦

🍴 Zuly's Cafe
Cafe $

(www.zulyscafe.org; 234 Hwy 75; mains $5-11; ⏰7:30am-3pm Tue-Thu, 7:30am-8pm Fri, 9am-8pm Sat) Scarf down a burrito, enchilada or buffalo burger at this excellent local cafe that surprises with some of the best green and red chile anywhere in the state. Seriously.

Embudo

🍴 Sugar's BBQ
BBQ $

(1799 Hwy 68; mains $5-12; ⏰11am-6pm Thu-Sun) This bustling roadside stand serves up juicy burgers and succulent barbeque. Brisket burritos = mmmmmm.

Española

🍴 El Parasol
New Mexican $

(📞www.elparasol.com; 603 Santa Cruz Rd; mains $2-5; ⏰7am-9pm) As local as it gets. Line up outside of this tiny trailer for the greasy-good chicken-guacamole tacos (order at least two) or the *carne adovada* (pork in red chile) burrito. Eat at a shaded picnic table.

2024

Albuquerque *Old Town charm*

El Camino Real & Turquoise Trail

12

Historic sights, hot springs, wildlife sanctuaries, and well-known cities line this route first established over 400 years ago – the Royal Road, which linked Mexico City to Santa Fe.

TRIP HIGHLIGHTS

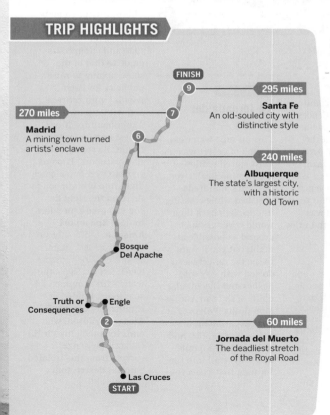

FINISH

9

295 miles

Santa Fe
An old-souled city with distinctive style

270 miles

7

Madrid
A mining town turned artists' enclave

6

240 miles

Albuquerque
The state's largest city, with a historic Old Town

Bosque Del Apache

Truth or Consequences ● **Engle**

2

60 miles

Jornada del Muerto
The deadliest stretch of the Royal Road

● **Las Cruces**
START

3–4 DAYS
295 MILES / 475KM

GREAT FOR...

BEST TIME TO GO
September until December is best for festivals.

 ESSENTIAL PHOTO
Late afternoon glow on an adobe wall in Santa Fe.

BEST FOR BIRDERS
Cranes and more at Bosque del Apache.

12 El Camino Real & Turquoise Trail

Leaving Las Cruces, this trip mostly follows New Mexico's main arteries – the Rio Grande and Interstate 25 – north. Except when you're driving a dirt road through a section of desert called the Jornada del Muerto (Journey of Death). Or meandering through a bird sanctuary. Or winding past the Ortiz Mountains and through old mining towns along the legendary Turquoise Trail on your way into Santa Fe.

❶ Las Cruces

New Mexico's second-largest city, Las Cruces isn't much of a charmer, but before you hit the road take a stroll around the **Old Mesilla plaza**, which still exudes a sense of history even though it's *only* 160 years old. Billy the Kid was sentenced to death in the courthouse here.

🛏 p153

The Drive » Take I-25 north to exit 32, then turn right onto dirt County Road 71/72 and follow it – staying on the main road – for 5.2 miles, Then, turn left at an intersection, heading north on CR E 070 toward Engle. Go 14 miles, driving around the aptly-named Point of Rocks, to Yost Escarpment.

TRIP HIGHLIGHT
❷ Jornada del Muerto

This 90-mile waterless stretch of desert was the most feared section of the Camino Real. Over the years, hundreds perished while crossing it. Travelers back then would cover as much ground as possible at night, but you'll want to see the desert basin dotted with creosote bushes and the angular uplift of the San Andres Mountains. Pull over at **Yost Escarpment** (www.nps.gov/elca; CR A013) and walk an easy 1.5 mile (one-way) trail into the Jornada that takes you

along the actual Camino Real route. There are interpretive signs along the way. In summer, try to avoid midday.

The Drive » Continue north – you'll hit pavement in 4 miles – to Engle. Along the way you'll pass Spaceport America (p148), but you can't just drop by – guided tours are the only way to visit. At Engle, turn left to Truth or Consequences on Hwy 51 – which curves around 300ft-high Elephant Butte Dam and the drought-shrunken lake behind it.

- - - - - - - - - - - - -

❸ Truth or Consequences

This quirky town met a challenge posed by a radio game show in 1950 and changed its name to that of the show, hoping to raise publicity for itself. Popular with retirees and with a growing New Age subculture, T or C is best known for two things: its springs and the Spaceport. Though you can't yet hop a quick flight into orbit, if you're there on the right day you can take a 'preview tour' of **Spaceport America** (📞575-740-6894; www.ftstours.com; adult/under 12yr $59/29; ⏰9am & 1pm Fri-Sat, 9am Sun) – the world's first commercial spaceport, funded in significant part by Sir Richard Branson, who aims to launch his Virgin Galactic passenger rockets from this isolated patch of desert; tours

leave from T or C and the round trip takes about three hours.

✕ 🛏 p153

The Drive >> Take I-25 north for 35 miles to exit 115, then turn right into Hwy 1 and follow the signs to 'El Camino Real IHC'.

- - - - - - - - - - - - - - - - -

❹ El Camino Real International Heritage Center

Put your trip in context at this modern **museum** (www.caminorealheritage.org; I-25 exit 115; adult/child $5/free; ⏰8:30am-5pm Wed-Sun) dedicated to the history of the original American highway. It's in the middle of nowhere, but a worthwhile stop for adults and kids.

The Drive >> Take Hwy 1 north for 20 hilly miles (don't get on the interstate).

LINK YOUR TRIP

11 **High & Low Roads to Taos**

Continue north from Santa Fe on this classic route into the soul of New Mexico.

13 **Georgia O'Keeffe Country**

From Santa Fe, head 48 miles northwest on Hwy 84 to Abiquiu for the state's most colorful trip.

149

⑤ Bosque del Apache National Wildlife Refuge

A surprising oasis of water and wildlife, the **Bosque del Apache** (www.fws.gov/southwest/refuges/newmex/bosque; per vehicle $5; ☺dawn-dusk) covers over 57,000 acres along the Rio Grande, with forested wetlands at its heart. Though a menagerie of mammals, reptiles, and amphibians can be spotted, birds are the big draw: 371 species that roost here by the tens of thousands, mainly from November to February. The stars of the avian show are the sandhill cranes, who even get their own festival (mid-November). Its worth driving the 15-mile loop through the refuge any time of year.

🛏 p153

The Drive » Head north on Hwy 1 to San Antonio, then west on Hwy 380, then north on I-25, 98 miles in total.

DETOUR: HATCH

Start: ❶ Las Cruces

The town of Hatch, 40 miles north of Las Cruces up I-25, is known as the 'Chile Capital of the World,' sitting at the heart of New Mexico's chile-growing country. New Mexican chiles didn't originate here – most have centuries-old roots in the northern farming villages around Chimayó and Española – but the earth and irrigation in these parts proved perfect for mass production. Recent harvests have declined sharply, as imported chile is encroaching on the market, but the town still clings to its title. Even if you miss the Labor Day Weekend **Chile Festival** (www.hatchchilefest.com; per vehicle $5), pull off the interstate at exit 41 and pop into **Sparky's Burgers** (www.sparkysburgers.com; 115 Franklin St; mains $4-10; ☺10:30am-7pm Thu-Mon, to 7:30 Fri & Sat) for what might be the best green chile cheeseburger in the state (*New Mexico Magazine* thinks so), served with casual pride.

To get there, when driving north from Las Cruces, skip exit 32 to the Jornada del Muerto and continue another 8.5 miles on I-25 to Hatch. Then, after getting your chile fix, head back to the Jornada exit and continue along the route – or blow off the desert road and continue on I-25 to re-join the drive in T or C.

TRIP HIGHLIGHT

⑥ Albuquerque

New Mexico's largest city was founded in 1706 and for centuries centered on the Old Town Plaza, which is where you'll find many of Albuquerque's sights and attractions (see p220). Though its gritty charm can sometimes be hard to spot, the neighborhoods around the University of New Mexico and Nob Hill are hipper than ever. And some fantastic museums can be found here, including the **National Museum of Nuclear Science & History** (www.nuclearmuseum.org; 601 Eubank Blvd SE; adult/child & senior $8/7; ☺9am-5pm; ♿), with engaging exhibits on the development of nuclear weapons, energy, medical technology and more.

✕ 🛏 p153

The Drive » On this 43-mile leg we diverge from the Camino Real to hop on the more scenic Turquoise Trail. Take I-40 east to exit 175, where you'll take Hwy 14 north.

TRIP HIGHLIGHT

⑦ Madrid

This former company-owned mining village has transformed into a quirky gallery town that looks cute on the surface

Bosque del Apache National Wildlife Refuge Snow geese in flight

LOCAL KNOWLEDGE: TURQUOISE TRAIL GEMS

Along with the main stops on the Turquoise Trail, you won't want to miss the **Tinkertown Museum** (www. tinkertown.com; 121 Sandia Crest Rd; adult/child $3/1; ⏱9am-5:30pm Apr-Nov; 🚹) – one of the weirdest in the state. Huge, detailed hand-carved dioramas of Western towns, circuses and other bizarre scenes come alive with a quarter and signs encourage visitors to 'eat more mangoes naked.' It's just outside of Cedar Crest on Hwy 536.

But wait, there's more: one of our favorite restaurants ever. The **San Marcos Cafe** (☎505-471-9298; www.sanmarcosfeed.com; 3877 Hwy 14; mains $7-10; ⏱8am-2pm; 🚹), south of Santa Fe, feels like a country home. Aside from some of the best red chile you'll ever taste, turkeys strut and squabble outside and the whole place is connected to a feed store, giving it genuine Western soul.

but still has an unruly edge underneath. Hop out and browse a while.

✖ p153

The Drive » Continue north on Hwy 14 for 3 miles, then turn left into Cerrillos.

- - - - - - - - - - - - - -

⑧ Cerrillos

This little village was at the center of the turquoise trade in Spanish colonial times. To see an erratic display of historical memorabilia, stop into the **Turquoise Mining Museum** (17 Waldo St; admission $3; ⏱9am-sunset); but the town's real gem

is the **Thomas Morin Studio** (☎505-474-3147; 8 First St; ⏱10am-4pm Mon-Sat Apr-Nov), where you can see the master sculptor creating exquisite artwork out of his current medium of choice: used sandpaper belts.

The Drive » Continue north on Hwy 14, which will turn into one of Santa Fe's main commercial drags, Cerrillos Rd.

- - - - - - - - - - - - - -

TRIP HIGHLIGHT

⑨ Santa Fe

Though spurs of El Camino Real continued on up to Taos and

beyond, the main trail ended here, at the Santa Fe plaza, once the Spanish chose this spot as the capital of New Mexico in 1610. For a walking tour of the plaza, see p218. To get the best sense of what life might have been like during the days when El Camino Real was the main route into the city, head to Santa Fe's southern outskirts, where you'll find **El Rancho de las Golondrinas** (www. golondrinas.org; 334 Los Pinos Rd, La Cienega; adult/child $6/free; ⏱10am-4pm Wed-Sun Jun-Sep; 🚹). Once an overnight stopping place on the trail, it's now a 200-acre living museum, carefully reconstructed and populated with historical re-enactors. You can watch bread baking in an *horno* (traditional adobe oven), visit the blacksmith, the molasses mill or traditional crafts workshops. There are orchards, vineyards and livestock. Festivals are held throughout the summer. It's fascinating for adults, and kids love it too. To get there, take I-25 south to exit 276, then follow the signs.

✖ 🛏 p153

Eating & Sleeping

Las Cruces ❶

🛏 Lundeen Inn of the Arts   B&B $$

(📞505-526-3326; www.innofthearts.com;
618 S Alameda Blvd; r incl breakfast $80-125,
ste $99-155; 🅿❄🛜) This large, turn-of-the-
19th-century Mexican Territorial–style inn has
20 thoughtfully decorated guest rooms, each
unique and named for – and decorated in the
style of – New Mexico artists. The breakfast
spread, served in the high-ceilinged Great
Room, is itself great.

Truth or Consequences ❸

🍴 Café Bellaluca   Italian $$

(www.cafebellaluca.com; 303 Jones St; lunch
mains $8-15, dinner mains $13-38; ⏰11am-9pm
Mon, Wed & Thu, to 10pm Fri & Sat, to 8pm Sun)
Earns raves for its Italian specialties; pizzas
are amazing and the spacious dining room is a
pitch-perfect blend of classy and funky.

🛏 Blackstone
Hotsprings   Boutique Hotel $

(📞575-894-0894; www.blackstonehotsprings.
com; 410 Austin St; r $75-135; 🅿❄🛜)
Blackstone embraces the T or C spirit with
an upscale wink, decorating each of its seven
rooms in the style of a classic TV show, from the
Jetsons to the *Golden Girls* to *I Love Lucy*. Best
part? Each room comes with its own hot spring
tub or waterfall.

Bosque del Apache National Wildlife Refuge ❺

🛏 Casa Blanca Bed & Breakfast   B&B $

(📞575-835-3027; www.casablancabed-
andbreakfast.com; San Antonio; r $80-100)
Devoted birders will want to stay close to the
wildlife refuge at this homey place.

Albuquerque ❻

🍴 Frontier   New Mexican $

(www.frontierrestaurant.com; 2400 Central
Ave SE; mains $3-11; ⏰5am-1am; 🅿🛜) Get
in line for enormous cinnamon rolls and some
of the best huevos rancheros in town at this
outstanding place, a favorite of UNM students.

🛏 Hotel Blue   Hotel $

(📞877-878-4868; www.thehotelblue.com;
717 Central Ave NW; r incl breakfast $60-99;
🅿❄@🛜🏊) Well positioned on the western
edge of downtown, the Hotel Blue is a great
value, with Tempur-Pedic beds, a swimming
pool, and flat-screen TVs.

Madrid ❼

🍴 Mine Shaft Tavern   Tavern $

(www.themineshafttavern.com; 2846 NM 14; mains
$8-12; ⏰11:30am-7:30pm Sun-Thu, to 9pm Fri &
Sat, bar open late daily; 🛜) Drop into the Mine
Shaft Tavern to meet locals, listen to live music on
weekends and experience the 'longest stand-up
bar in New Mexico.' Cowboys and bikers welcome.

Santa Fe ❾

🍴 Tune-Up Café   International $$

(www.tuneupsantafe.com; 1115 Hickox St; mains
$7-14; ⏰7am-10pm Mon-Fri, from 8am Sat & Sun;
🛜) The casual, busy Tune-Up is a local favorite.
The chef, from El Salvador, adds twists to classic
New Mexican and American dishes while also
serving fantastic Salvadoran *pupusas* (stuffed
corn tortillas) and huevos. The *molé colorado*
enchiladas and fish tacos are exceptional.

🛏 Silver Saddle Motel   Motel $

(📞505-471-7663; www.santafesilversaddlemotel.
com; 2810 Cerrillos Rd; r winter/summer from
$45/62; 🅿❄@🛜🏊) Rooms have shady
wooden arcades outside and cowboy-inspired
decor. For a bit of kitsch, request the Kenny
Rogers or Wyatt Earp rooms. This is great
budget value; continental breakfast included.

Abiquiú *Sandstone landscapes that inspired Georgia O'Keeffe*

Georgia O'Keeffe Country

13

From the multicolor cliffs that inspired O'Keeffe, to Chaco Canyon's Anasazi architecture, to the intricate textiles of Navajo weavers, topography and creativity seem inseparable here.

TRIP HIGHLIGHTS

15 miles

Ghost Ranch
Hike or ride horseback among colorful cliffs

Shiprock •   • Aztec

FINISH
Toadlena •

Nageezi •

2 **START**
1

3

Chaco Canyon
Ancient Anasazi architecture wows with its rockwork

150 miles

Abiquiú
Tour the former home of artist Georgia O'Keeffe

0 miles

2–3 DAYS
327 MILES / 526KM

GREAT FOR...

BEST TIME TO GO
May to October.

ESSENTIAL PHOTO

Capture the perspective of doorways and stonework at Chaco.

BEST FOR DRIVERS

Hwy 96 is one of the most beautiful roads in the state.

Georgia O'Keeffe Country

13

The first part of this trip just might cover our favorite stretches of road in the state, around Abiquiú Lake, up the Chama River, through a rainbow-hued gap in the Jemez Mountains – the colors and the light blend into pure eye-candy. Then you strike out through the badlands of the Navajo Nation, across barren desert flats, and under the shadow of Shiprock, where the earth and sky converge with raw, elemental intensity.

TRIP HIGHLIGHT

❶ Abiquiú

Founded in 1754 through a Spanish land grant, the tiny town of Abiquiú near the Chama River has a few galleries and a lovely church, but is most famous as the home of the painter Georgia O'Keeffe. After returning to the area many times in the 1930s and '40s, she bought an old adobe fixer-upper in 1945, restored it, and moved into it in 1949. She lived between there

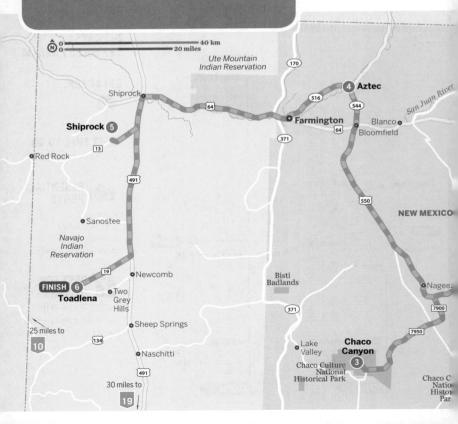

and her place up the road at Ghost Ranch for the next 35 years. You can visit her Abiquiú house on the **Georgia O'Keeffe Home & Studio Tour** (📞505-685-4539; shuttle from Abiquiú Inn; 1hr tour $35-50; 🕙varied). Enclosed by a mudbrick wall, this Spanish colonial hacienda blends into the landscape and remains much as it was when she lived here. You must make reservations for the tour, and of course also check out the Georgia O'Keeffe Museum (p42) in Santa Fe.

 p161

The Drive » Taking Hwy 84 north, force yourself to keep your eyes on the road as you drive around the jewel-like Abiquiu Lake ringed by multicolored cliffs. Turn right at the sign for Ghost Ranch.

TRIP HIGHLIGHT

2 Ghost Ranch

If you're familiar with O'Keeffe's work, you may feel like you've been here before. Some of her

LINK YOUR TRIP

19 Highway 53 to Acoma

From Toadlena, head south to Gallup on Hwy 491 to check out ancient pueblos, lava flows and wolves!

10 Tribal Trails

From Toadlena, skip state lines to check out more of the Navajo Nation, crossing the Chuska Mountains via Hwy 134.

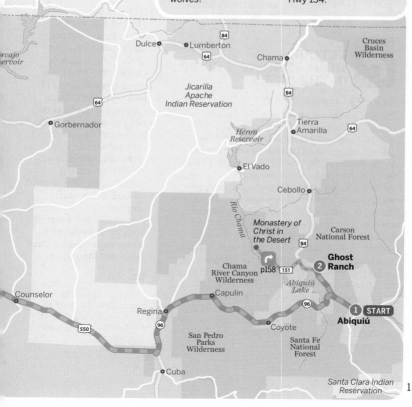

most celebrated pieces were inspired by the sensual forms and colors of the cliffs, canyons, and mesalands around **Ghost Ranch** (📞505-685-4333; www.ghostranch.org; US Hwy 84; admission $3; 🚻). Though her home here is closed to the public, you can explore the area on hiking trails, guided horseback adventures, or a van tour that includes stops at vistas immortalized in O'Keeffe's paintings. There are also anthropology and paleontology museums and a massage studio, and various lodging options.

🛏 p161

The Drive » Backtrack 6 miles south on Hwy 84, then turn right onto Hwy 96, which takes you through a pastel geological wonderland. When you reach Hwy 550, near Cuba, turn right (north); before Nageezi turn left onto County Rd 7900, then right onto County Rd 7950 (rough dirt), following signs for Chaco Culture National Historical Park.

- - - - - - - - - - - -

❸ Chaco Canyon

About 1000 years ago, Chaco Canyon was the center of an Anasazi (Ancient Puebloan) civilization that spread across the San Juan Basin and beyond,

linked together by a carefully engineered network of 30ft-wide roads. Today, Chacoan culture is famed for the impressive architecture it left behind: the Great Houses intricately pieced together, stone by stone, and oriented with remarkable accuracy to solar and lunar events as well as the cardinal directions.

You can walk through some Great Houses and other structures at **Chaco Culture National Historical Park** (www.nps.gov/chcu; per vehicle/bike $8/4; 🕑7am-sunset). The biggest attraction is Pueblo Bonito, which towered four stories tall and may have had 600 to 800 rooms and kivas. Though none of Chaco's sites have been reconstructed, plenty of rockwork is still intact. A loop road connects the main archaeological sites, hiking trails head off into the surrounding area, there's an informative visitor center and a campground. But there's no food, gas or other supplies (water is available only at the visitor center). The closest towns with accommodations are Cuba (p161) and Bloomfield.

🛏 p161

The Drive » Head back to Hwy 550 and head north. At Bloomfield, turn right onto Hwy 64, then make a pretty quick left onto Hwy 544.

DETOUR:
MONASTERY OF CHRIST IN THE DESERT

Start: ❷ Ghost Ranch

It's hard to imagine a more peaceful place for spiritual contemplation. Set 13 miles down a dirt road, surrounded by the majestic Chama River Wilderness, you'll find the **Monastery of Christ in the Desert** (📞505-990-8581; www.christdesert.org; 🕑9:15am-5pm). This Benedictine Abbey welcomes visitors as day or overnight guests; you can go into the unique church that combines elements of Japanese and New Mexican design, attend prayer services, or stay in the small, simple guesthouse (p161). In tune with the aura of the place, quiet is requested. With an advance appointment, you can tour the on-site brewery that produces Monk's Ale. To get here from Ghost Ranch, head north on Hwy 84 for 2.5 miles, then turn left onto Forest Rd 151. The drive is spectacular: some of the cliffs are purple! There are plenty of places to hang out by the river, and a few campsites (p161). When you're done with this detour, retrace your steps back to Hwy 96 and pick up the drive there.

Navajo textiles

---

④ Aztec

Although little Aztec has a handful of interesting turn-of-the-19th-century buildings on the National Register of Historic Places, the town's main draw is the 27-acre **Aztec Ruins National Monument** (www.nps.gov/azru; adult/child $5/free; ⊙8am-5pm Sep-May, to 6pm Jun-Aug).

This ancient Anasazi settlement features the largest reconstructed kiva in the country, with an internal diameter of almost 50ft, originally built around AD 1100. Though the site itself isn't as amazing or extensive as Chaco, the Great Kiva is pretty impressive. During summer, rangers give early-afternoon

talks about ancient architecture, trade routes and astronomy.

If you're into river sports, check out the seconds at **Jack's Plastic Welding** (www.jpwinc.com; 115 S Main Ave) for good deals on slightly imperfect dry bags and Paco Pads (camping mattresses).

🛏 p161

LOCAL KNOWLEDGE: BISTI BADLANDS

One of the weirdest micro-environments in New Mexico is 38 miles south of Farmington, off Hwy 371. The Bisti Badlands, part of the Bisti/De-Na-Zin Wilderness Area, is an undeveloped realm of multicolored hoodoos, sculpted cliffs and balancing rocks. From the parking area, you have to follow the unmaintained path for at least a mile before getting to the heart of the formations, then wander as you will, taking care not to damage the fragile geology. The hours just after sunrise and before sunset are most spectacular. Overnight camping is allowed, but you have to haul in all your water. The **Farmington Bureau of Land Management office** (☎505-564-7600; www.nm.blm.gov; 6251 College Blvd; ⏰7:45am-4:30pm Mon-Fri) has information.

The Drive » Take Hwy 516 to Farmington, which makes a good lunch stop (p161), then Hwy 64 west to the town of Shiprock. Cross the San Juan River and continue straight ahead on Hwy 491 (formerly Hwy 666, nicknamed the Devil's Highway). At mile marker 85, turn right onto Indian Route 13.

- - - - - - - - - - - - -

❺ Shiprock

The most striking sight in New Mexico's northwestern corner is Shiprock, a 1700ft volcanic plug that is eerily eroded into what looks like a schooner – at least to white people. The Navajo name for it – Tsé Bit'a'i – means 'rock with wings.' According to one Navajo history, the tribe had been under attack in a place far to the north when the ground beneath them became a giant bird that flew them to safety, delivering them to their homeland; the bird then turned back into earth, but kept its shape. It's also said that for some time, Navajos dwelt atop the great rock, coming down to farm and tend sheep, but that one day the trail to the desert floor was destroyed by lightning; those up at the summit couldn't descend and died there. Climbing Shiprock is strictly forbidden (yes, illegal), in part for fear that the spirits of the dead will be disturbed. Unfortunately, you can't even hike over to it, but there are some great views about 5 miles west along Indian Route 13.

The Drive » Head back to Hwy 491 and turn right, heading south. When you reach the Shell station at mile marker 61, turn right onto Indian Route 19 and go about 12 miles.

- - - - - - - - - - - - -

❻ Toadlena

Tucked against the Chuska Mountains, Toadlena and neighboring Two Grey Hills are renowned as the sources of the finest rugs anywhere in Navajo country. Some weavers from this area continue to reject commercially produced wool and synthetic dyes, preferring the wool of their own churro sheep in its natural hues. They card white, brown, grey and black hairs together, blending the colors to the desired effect, then they spin and weave the wool – tightly – into mesmerizing geometric patterns. The **Toadlena Trading Post** (☎888-420-0005; www.toadlenatradingpost.com), run by textile expert Mark Winter, is the local market where many of these world-class artisans sell their work. Prices range from about $125 to $7000 or more. The Trading Post has a small museum with extraordinarily fine exhibits.

Eating & Sleeping

Abiquiú ❶

✖ Bode's General Store   Deli $

(www.bodes.com; US Hwy 84; mains $5-12; ⏱6:30am-7pm Mon-Sat, to 6pm Sun; 🛜) The hub of Abiquiú, Bode's (pronounced Boh-dees) has been around since 1919. This is the place to buy everything from artsy postcards to fishing lures to saddle blankets. Grab a sandwich or tamale at the deli.

🛏 Abiquiú Inn   Hotel $$

(☎888-735-2902, 505-685-4378; www.abiquiuinn.com; US Hwy 84; RV sites $18, r $110-150, casitas from $179; Ⓟ🛜) An area institution, this sprawling collection of shaded faux-dobes is peaceful and lovely; some spacious rooms have kitchenettes. The on-site **Cafe Abiquiú** (breakfast mains under $10, lunch & dinner mains $10-20; ⏱7am-9pm) is the best restaurant around. Specialties include chipotle honey-glazed salmon and fresh trout tacos.

Ghost Ranch ❷

🛏 Ghost Ranch   Hostel $

(☎505-685-4333; www.ghostranch.org; US Hwy 84; tent/RV sites $19/22, dm incl board $50, r without/with bathroom incl breakfast from $50/80; Ⓟ) A friendly place to stay in an unbeatable setting, with easy access to hikes, horseback riding, and massage therapy.

Monastery in the Desert

🛏 Christ in the Desert Monastery   Monastery $

(www.christdesert.org; off US Rte 84; r incl board suggested donation $50-75; Ⓟ) At the monastery along the Chama River, simple rooms include vegetarian meals served in silence. Chores are requested (not required) and include minding the gift shop or tending the garden. The location is incredible.

🛏 Rio Chama Campground   Campground $

(FR 151, NM; tent site free; ⏱mid-Apr–Nov 15; 🐾) Riverside camping 1 mile from the monastery, with 11 sites surrounded by brilliant colored cliffs, birds and the silence of the Chama River Canyon Wilderness. There's no drinking water available.

Cuba

🛏 Frontier Motel   Motel $

(☎575-289-3474; 6474 Main St; r from $60; Ⓟ❄🛜) No frills but not bad, the best feature of the Frontier is that it's within striking distance of Chaco Canyon.

Chaco Canyon ❸

🛏 Gallo Campground   Campground $

(campsites $10) Gallo Campground is 1 mile east of the visitor center; no RV sites. Campsites are first-come, first-served; bring your own drinking water.

Aztec ❹

🛏 Step Back Inn   Hotel $

(☎505-334-1200; www.stepbackinn.com; 123 W Aztec Blvd; r from $72; ❄🛜) Aztec's finest hotel has tidy, Victorian-style rooms; next door to a popular Chinese restaurant.

Farmington

✖ Three Rivers Eatery & Brewhouse   American $$

(www.threeriversbrewery.com; 101 E Main St; mains $8-26; ⏱11am-9pm; 👶) Managing to be both trendy *and* kid-friendly, this almost hip spot has good food and its own microbrews. Try the homemade potato skins or artichoke and spinach dip, but keep in mind that the steaks are substantial. Plenty of spiffy sandwiches (like a Thai turkey wrap) and soups (broccoli cheddar) are served at lunchtime.

Bandelier National Monument
Explore ancient cliff dwellings

Highway 4: Jemez Mountains **14**

One minute you're in the cutting-edge scientific community where the atomic bomb was built; then you're exploring ancient cave dwellings; and by day's end, you're soaking in a hot spring.

TRIP HIGHLIGHTS

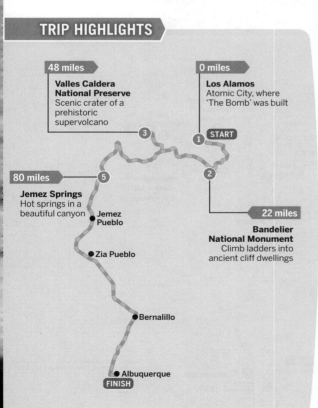

48 miles
Valles Caldera National Preserve
Scenic crater of a prehistoric supervolcano

0 miles
Los Alamos
Atomic City, where 'The Bomb' was built

START ①

②

③

80 miles ⑤
Jemez Springs
Hot springs in a beautiful canyon

● Jemez Pueblo

22 miles
Bandelier National Monument
Climb ladders into ancient cliff dwellings

● Zia Pueblo

● Bernalillo

● Albuquerque
FINISH

2 DAYS
80 MILES / 129KM

GREAT FOR...

BEST TIME TO GO
May to October.

 ESSENTIAL PHOTO
Climbing a ladder to a cave dwelling in Bandelier National Monument.

✔ **BEST FOR RELAXING**
Soak up the waters in Jemez Springs.

14 Highway 4: Jemez Mountains

From Los Alamos, this route takes you across the finger-like mesas to Bandelier National Monument, where cave dwellings line beautiful Frijoles Canyon. Then wend your way into the heart of the Jemez Mountains, passing through the caldera of an ancient supervolcano that's now home to huge herds of elk. Descend through the red-walled Jemez River canyon, where hot springs abound, then into the horse pastures of Albuquerque's north valley.

TRIP HIGHLIGHT

1 Los Alamos

The top-secret Manhattan Project sprang to life in Los Alamos in 1943, turning a sleepy mesa-top village into a laboratory of secluded geniuses busy developing the first atomic bomb. Los Alamos National Laboratory still develops weapons, but it's also been at the cutting edge of other scientific advances, including mapping

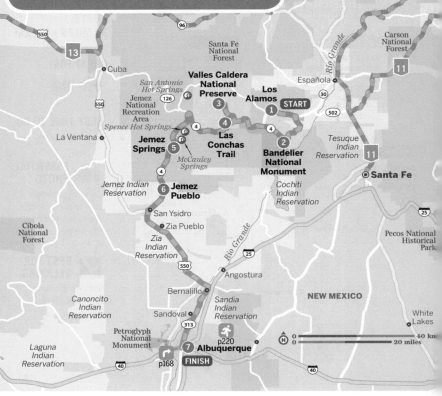

the human genome and supercomputing. The Lab dominates everything here and gives Los Alamos County the highest concentration of PhDs per capita in the US, along with the highest per-capita income in the state. It's set atop a series of mesas and hugged by national forest, much of which unfortunately burned in the 48,000-acre Cerro Grande fire of 2000, leaving the hills behind town eerily barren. More of the surrounding forest was ablaze in 2011, as the fire around Las Conchas scorched over 150,000 acres – the largest ever recorded in New Mexico. Fortunately, it narrowly missed the Lab.

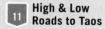

LINK YOUR TRIP

11 High & Low Roads to Taos

While driving the Low Road south from Taos, take Hwy 30 to Hwy 502 to Los Alamos to start your Jemez trip.

13 Georgia O'Keeffe Country

Take Hwy 550 north to join this colorful route near Chaco Canyon.

The **Los Alamos Historical Museum** (www.losalamoshistory.org; 1050 Bathtub Row; ⊙10am-4pm Mon-Fri, from 11am Sat, from 1pm Sun) has interesting exhibits on what daily life was like in 'the town that didn't exist' during the Manhattan Project era. The **Bradbury Science Museum** (www.lanl.gov/museum; 1350 Central Ave; admission free; ⊙10am-5pm Tue-Sat, 1-5pm Sun & Mon) has replicas of the original bombs, displays devoted to atomic science and history (and ethics), plus a new exhibit on emerging security technologies.

✗ p169

The Drive » Take East Jemez Rd to Hwy 4 W, which curves around finger-like mesas. Turn left onto the entrance road for Bandelier.

- - - - - - - - - - -

TRIP HIGHLIGHT

❷ Bandelier National Monument

The sublime, peach-colored cliffs of Frijoles Canyon are pocked with caves and alcoves that were home to Ancestral Puebloans until the mid-1500s. Today, they're the main attraction at **Bandelier National Monument** (www.nps.gov/band; per vehicle $12; ⊙visitor center 9am-4:30pm, park to dusk; ⊕) – a rewarding stop whether you're interested in ancient Southwestern cultures or just want to walk

among pines and watch the light glowing off the canyon walls. The **Ceremonial Cave**, 140ft above the ground and reached by climbing four ladders, is a highlight (though it was closed for restoration on our most recent visit). The more adventurous can strike out on rugged trails that traverse 50 sq miles of canyon and mesa wilderness dotted with archaeological sites; backpackers should pick up a free backcountry permit from the visitor center. Kids love it here.

🛏 p169

The Drive » Head back out of Bandelier and turn left on Hwy 4, heading west as the road twists its way into the heart of the Jemez.

- - - - - - - - - - -

TRIP HIGHLIGHT

❸ Valles Caldera National Preserve

Ever wonder what the crater of a dormant supervolcano looks like 1,250,000 years after it first blows? Just check out **Valles Caldera National Preserve** (☎866-382-5537; www.vallescaldera.gov; permits adult/child $10/5) – the prehistoric explosion here was so massive that chunks were thrown as far away as Kansas. The 89,000-acre bowl – home to New Mexico's largest elk herd – is simply breathtaking, with vast meadows from which hills rise like pine-covered islands. Though there are two trails on the edge of the preserve with free, open hiking, you should make reservations for the limited number of permits given out to hike within the caldera on any given day. Access to those trailheads is only possible by shuttle bus from the visitor center. If you want to gape at the lay of the land but aren't up for high-altitude exertion, take a van tour. It's also possible to bike, ride horseback, fish, hunt, and cross-country ski here. There's an information center in Jemez Springs.

The Drive » Continue on Hwy 4 West, until you come to the trailhead for Las Conchas – about 0.25 miles past the fishing/picnic area of the same name – between mile markers 36 and 37.

- - - - - - - - - - -

④ Las Conchas Trail

A perfect spot to get out of the car and stretch your legs, the Las Conchas Trail follows the East Fork of the Jemez River as it meanders through grassy meadows and rocky canyons. For the first couple of miles, it's a blissful, easy hike. Las Conchas is also a popular climbing area, with a number of routes bolted into the volcanic rhyolite. Note that the weather can change quickly here, especially during the summer monsoon season.

The Drive » There's only one road here – so keep heading west on Hwy 4, as it descends into the tight Jemez River Canyon.

- - - - - - - - - - -

TRIP HIGHLIGHT

⑤ Jemez Springs

The little village of Jemez Springs was built around a cluster of hot springs, as was the ruined pueblo that's preserved at **Jemez State Monument** (www.nmmonuments. org; NM 4; adult/child $3/free; ⊙8:30am-5pm Wed-Sun). Today, most visitors come for the waters, which you can experience yourself at the rustic **Jemez Springs Bath House** (☏575-829-3303; 62 Jemez Springs Plaza; per hr $17; ⊙10am-7pm), which has private tubs, massages and more. There's also the friendly, outdoor **Giggling Springs** (☏575-829-9175; www. gigglingsprings.com; 40 Abousleman Loop; per hr/day $15/35; ⊙11am-midnight Wed-Sun). In winter, bliss out in the huge, shared, feng-shui'd hot-spring pools – bathing suits required – at **Bodhi Manda Zen Center** (☏575-829-3854; www.bmzc. org; suggested donation $10; ⊙9am-5pm Tue-Sat). At other times the center runs intensive Zen meditation programs – see the website for details.

 ✕ ⮕ p169

The Drive » Keep heading down canyon on Hwy 4, between the red rock walls and past popular fishing pull-outs.

- - - - - - - - - - -

⑥ Jemez Pueblo

Ten miles south of Jemez Springs, in a Martian-red landscape, the **Walatowa Visitor Center**

LOCAL KNOWLEDGE: MORE HOT SPRINGS

Along Hwy 4 just north of Jemez Springs, there are a number of natural hot springs that you can hike into. One of the most accessible is **Spence Hot Springs**, between miles 24 and 25. The temperature's about perfect, and the inevitable weird naked guy adds authenticity to the experience. The nearby **McCauley Springs**, with a trailhead at Battleship Rock Picnic Area, is pretty lukewarm. For something more ambitious, seek out **San Antonio Hot Springs** – it's a 5-mile hike in to the pools – but worth it! From Hwy 4, take Hwy 126, then Forest Rd. 376 for a rough 5 miles or so to the trailhead.

Jemez Mountains

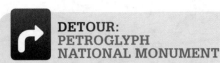

DETOUR: PETROGLYPH NATIONAL MONUMENT

Start: ❼ Albuquerque

Along the edge of an ancient lava field on Albuquerque's west side, more than 20,000 petroglyphs are etched on basalt slabs – hence, **Petroglyph National Monument** (www.nps.gov/petr; ⊙visitor center 8am-5pm). It's easy to spot the rock art in the park's three viewing areas: **Rinconada Canyon** has the longest trail (2.2 miles round-trip) and is best if you want some solitude; **Boca Negra Canyon** features three short trails; **Piedras Marcadas** has 300 petroglyphs along a 1.5-mile trail. For powerful views but no rock art, hit the **Volcanoes Trail**, where you'll hike among cinder cones. Note: smash-and-grab thefts have been reported at some trailhead parking lots, so don't leave valuables in your vehicle. The visitor center, on Western Trail at Unser Blvd, is 7.5 miles north of Old Town; head west on I-40 across the Rio Grande and take exit 154 north.

(7413 Hwy 4; ⊙8am-5pm) at Jemez Pueblo houses the small, sort-of-interesting Museum of Pueblo Culture. The gift shop sells the pottery for which the pueblo's artisans are renowned.

The Drive » Follow Hwy 4 to the end, turn left on Hwy 550 south, then right onto Hwy 313. After 8 miles, at the roundabout, take 4th St, then go right on Hwy 528. Turn left on S Rio Grande Blvd, through surprisingly rural North Valley horse country as you head downtown.

❼ Albuquerque

As the largest city in the only state other than Hawaii in which white people are not the majority (at least at the time of writing), Albuquerque offers some unique introductions to Hispanic and Native American culture. The **Indian Pueblo Cultural Center** (IPCC; ☎505-843-7270; www.indianpueblo.org; 2401 12th St NW; adult/child $6/3; ⊙9am-5pm) is a must-see even on the shortest of Albuquerque itineraries. The history exhibits are fascinating, and the arts wing features the finest examples of each pueblo's work. The IPCC also houses a large gift shop and retail gallery. Along with serving Pueblo-style cuisine, the on-site **Pueblo Harvest Café** (mains $5-8; ⊙8am-3pm Mon-Fri, to 5pm Sat & Sun; 🖉🐾) holds weekend art demonstrations, bread-baking demos and dances. For more Albuquerque museums, see p220.

South of downtown, the **National Hispanic Cultural Center** (www.nhccnm.org; 1701 4th St SW; adult/child $3/free, Sun free; ⊙10am-5pm Tue-Sun) for visual, performing and literary arts has three galleries and the nation's premier Hispanic genealogy library. The work in the permanent collection is exciting and provocative, with many pieces by Albuquerque-based artists. Each June the center hosts the **Festival Flamenco**.

✕ ⊨ p169

Eating & Sleeping

Los Alamos ❶

✘ Coffee House Cafe — Cafe $$

(www.thecoffeebooth.com; 723 Central Ave; mains $6-12, pizzas $21-30; ⏱6am-8pm Tue-Fri, 7am-3pm Sat, 8am-3pm Sun, 6am-3pm Mon) The hippest space in Los Alamos boasts a long list of breakfasts and grilled sandwiches, five kinds of quiche, and pizza and pasta dinners. Trusted sources from the Lab have leaked to us that this is the best spot in town.

✘ Pyramid Cafe — Mediterranean $$

(www.pyramidcafesf.com; 751 Central Ave; mains $8-22; ⏱11am-2:30pm & 4:30-8pm Mon-Fri; from noon Sat & Sun) A new branch of the popular Santa Fe restaurant, the gyros, felafel, shwarma, and moussaka bring in the crowds.

Bandelier National Monument ❷

🛏 Juniper Campground — Campground $

(campsites $12) Set among the pines near Bandelier's entrance, Juniper Campground offers about 100 campsites, drinking water, toilets, picnic tables and fire grates, but no showers or hookups.

Jemez Springs ❺

✘ Hwy 4 Coffee — Cafe $

(www.hwy4coffee.com; 17502 Hwy 4; mains $6-12; ⏱8am-3pm Mon, Tue, Thu & Fri, to 7pm Sat, to 5pm Sun) Locals rave about this little spot that specializes in sandwiches, pizzas and pastries. Breakfast choices include oatmeal and breakfast burritos. And espresso!

✘ Los Ojos Restaurant & Saloon — Restaurant $

(www.losojossaloon.com; Hwy 4; mains $5-11; ⏱11am-9:30pm Mon-Fri, from 8am Sat & Sun,

bar open late; 🍴) An atmospheric saloon with a surprising variety of vegetarian fare considering the number of animal heads on the walls.

🛏 Cañon del Rio B&B — B&B $$

(☎575-829-4377; www.canondelrio.com; r $140-150; 🏊🖥) If you're looking for gorgeous canyon views, a pool, hot tub and day spa, killer breakfasts and terrific hosts, this is your place.

🛏 Jemez Mountain Inn — Inn $

(☎575-829-3926; www.jemezmtninn.com; 17555 Hwy 4; r $85-105; 🅿🛜) Each room at this peaceful place has a different New Mexican theme and all are comfortably appointed – but no kids and no pets allowed.

🛏 Laughing Lizard Inn — Motel $

(☎575-829-3410; www.thelaughinglizard.com; 17526 Hwy 4; r $70) This simple four-room motel is nuthin' fancy, but has been renovated with care and has a real homey feel. Mattresses are new, and each room is unique. (We like No 3 best). All open onto a covered porch.

Albuquerque ❼

✘ Garcia's Kitchen — New Mexican $

(1736 Central Ave SW; mains $6-8; ⏱7am-9pm Sun-Thu, to 10pm Fri & Sat) Part of a small local chain, this place just east of Old Town has some of the best New Mexican food in Albuquerque. The red vinyl booths and eclectic crowd give it a pure local feel.

🛏 Cinnamon Morning B&B — B&B $$

(☎800-214-9481; www.cinnamonmorning. com; 2700 Rio Grande Blvd NW; r $109-129, casita $139-225; 🅿🛜🖥) This wired B&B near Old Town has four rooms, a two-bedroom guesthouse and an outdoor hot tub. Lots of Southwest charm and common areas make it a relaxing and homey place to slumber.

St James Hotel
Cimarron's icon is full of ghosts

Enchanted Circle & Eastern Sangres

15

Hike the Rio Grande gorge, stay at a haunted hotel, hit some hot springs, spot pronghorns and feed alpacas on this scenic trip up and over the Sangre de Cristos.

TRIP HIGHLIGHTS

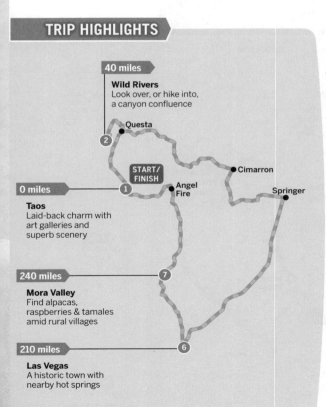

40 miles

Wild Rivers
Look over, or hike into, a canyon confluence

Questa

2

START/FINISH

1

Angel Fire

Cimarron

Springer

0 miles

Taos
Laid-back charm with art galleries and superb scenery

240 miles

7

Mora Valley
Find alpacas, raspberries & tamales amid rural villages

210 miles

6

Las Vegas
A historic town with nearby hot springs

2 DAYS
320 MILES / 515KM

GREAT FOR...

BEST TIME TO GO
August to October: after monsoon season, before winter.

 ESSENTIAL PHOTO

Capture the confluence of the Red River and the Rio Grande from above.

 BEST FOR SEANCES

Cimarron's Hotel St James.

171

DANITA DELIMONT/ALAMY ©

Enchanted Circle & Eastern Sangres

This loop links canyons to forests to mountains to prairies. You'll catch views of 13,107ft Wheeler Peak (the state's highest) and pass through gorgeous valleys with classic New Mexican villages where century-old adobes sit beside modern mobile homes. You'll probably see plenty of wildlife – from elk and antelope to bighorn sheep. Hiking and fishing opportunities abound; and if you're into meditating, we've got the spot for you!

TRIP HIGHLIGHT

① Taos

For over 100 years, Taos has been a magnet for artists, writers and creative thinkers of all types. Painters were entranced by the light here in 1898 and established an art colony; DH Lawrence hoped to build a utopia outside of town; Carl Jung was deeply affected by visiting Taos Pueblo, the place that also inspired Aldous Huxley's *Brave New World*; Georgia O'Keeffe

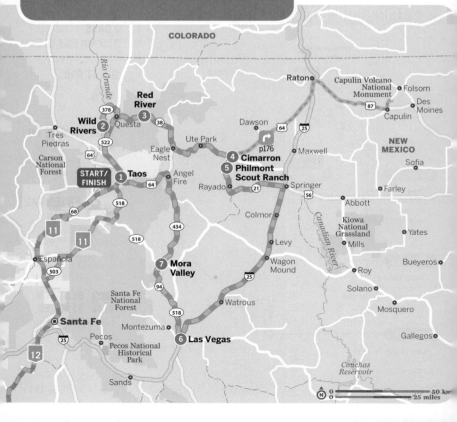

and Ansel Adams were here; Dennis Hopper shot key scenes from *Easy Rider* around Taos, then moved here himself. It's easy to see why.

Innovators today include architect Michael Reynolds, designer of Earthships – self-sustaining, environmentally savvy houses built with recycled materials like used automobile tires and cans. Earthships heat and cool themselves, make their own electricity and catch their own water. You can visit one Earthship community by heading 1.5 miles past the **Rio Grande Gorge Bridge** – itself well worth seeing – on US Hwy 64 W. Granted, the **Earthship 'tour'** (www.earthship.com; US Hwy 64; self-guided tours $7; ☉10am-4pm) is a little disappointing – you basically watch a short DVD and check out

LINK YOUR TRIP

11 High & Low Roads to Taos

Join these two loops at Taos to cover both sides of the Sangre de Cristos.

12 El Camino Real & Turquoise Trail

From Las Vegas, continue south on I-25 to hop on these historic routes.

LOCAL KNOWLEDGE: KTAO: SOLAR-POWERED RADIO

When in Taos, unplug your iPod and turn on your radio! Set the dial to 101.9 KTAO, which claims to be 'the world's largest solar-powered radio station.' The real live DJs play whatever they feel like playing and daily features include horoscope readings (at 10am and 6pm) by local astrologer Josseph the Starwatcher and 'Trash and Treasures' (an on-air flea market, 10:10am). Weekly shows include 'Moccasin Wire' (7pm to 10pm Monday), devoted to Native American music, and 'Listen Up' (7pm to 8pm Thursday), a talk show by and for Taos teens.

Attached to the station is the **KTAO Solar Center,** (www.ktao.com; 9 Ski Valley Rd; ☉bar from 4pm) one of the best places in town to see concerts or just have a drink and a meal in the bar/restaurant. It's family friendly, with a playground on the lawn for kids.

the visitor center. Actually staying in an **Earthship Rental** (☎505-751-0462; www.earthship.com; US Hwy 64; earthship $145-305; 🛜🐾) overnight is way better.

To see some choice works of the original Taos Society of Artists, visit the **Blumenschein Home & Museum** (www.taoshistoricmuseums.org; 222 Ledoux St; adult/child $8/4; ☉10am-5pm Mon-Sat, noon-5pm Sun).

 p177

The Drive » Take Hwy 522 North just past Questa, then turn left onto Hwy 378.

TRIP HIGHLIGHT

② Wild Rivers

One of the most impressive stretches of the Rio Grande gorge is where it meets the Red River. At **Wild Rivers**

Recreation Area (day use $3; ☉6am-10pm), some trails plunge 800ft down into the canyon while others meander along the mesa. If you don't feel like a hike, drive the scenic 13-mile Wild Rivers Backcountry Byway loop, and stop at La Junta, the perfect spot for a picnic overlooking the twin gorges. The waters are popular with trout fishermen.

p177

The Drive » Backtrack to Questa, then take Hwy 38 east.

③ Red River

A blend of Bavaria and the Old West, Red River brings people in with festivals and events year-round – except mid-March to mid-May, when the town is dead. In summer, kids love **Frye's Old Town Shootout** (Main St; 🕓4pm Tue, Thu & Sat Jun-Sep; 🚻), a Wild-Western drama.

🍴 p177

The Drive » Continue east on Hwy 38, over Bobcat Pass (9820ft) and down through the little lakeside village of Eagle Nest. Drive Hwy 64 east through curvaceous Cimarron Canyon, where there's good fishing, camping, and rock climbing.

- - - - - - - - - - - - - - -

4 Cimarron

Cimarron has a wild past. It once served as a stop on the Santa Fe Trail, and a hangout for gunslingers, train robbers, desperadoes, lawmen and other Wild West figures like Kit Carson, Buffalo Bill Cody, Annie Oakley, Wyatt Earp, Jesse James and Doc Holliday. The old **St James Hotel** alone saw the deaths of 26 men within its walls. Today, the restored hotel is said to be so haunted that one of its rooms is never rented out. It's really the main reason for stopping in Cimarron, either for the night or a bite to eat.

🛏 p177

The Drive » Head south on Hwy 21. You might see herds of Boy Scout burros here!

- - - - - - - - - - - - - - -

5 Philmont Scout Ranch

The largest Boy Scout camp in the country,

Philmont Scout Ranch covers 137,000 acres along the breathtaking eastern slope of the Sangre de Cristos. While you need to be a Scout to trek the trails, anyone can drop into the **Philmont Museum** (admission free; 🕓8am-5pm Mon-Sat) or tour **Villa Philmonte** (📞575-376-1136; suggested donation $5; 🕓10:30am & 2:30pm Mon-Fri Apr-Oct), a Spanish Mediterranean mansion built in 1927 by Waite Phillips, the oil baron who was Philmont's original benefactor. Pick up high-quality outdoor gear and all sorts of Philmont-related souvenirs at **Tooth of Time Traders** (🕓7:30am-6:30pm Jun-Aug, 8am-5pm Sep-May).

The Drive » Continue south, then east, on Hwy 21. Look out for antelope! At Springer, pick up I-25 South. Before long, you'll see why Wagon Mound is so-named. Get off the interstate at exit 345.

- - - - - - - - - - - - - - -

TRIP HIGHLIGHT

6 Las Vegas

Once a major stop along the Santa Fe Trail and later the Santa Fe Railroad, 19th century Las Vegas was one of the biggest, baddest boomtowns in the West. Billy the Kid held court here with his pal Vicente Silva (leader of the Society of Bandits – the roughest, toughest gang in New Mexico) and Doc Holliday owned a saloon (although ultimately his

TIM FITZHARRIS/GETTY IMAGES ©

Sangre de Cristo Mountains Aspen forest

175

DETOUR: CAPULIN VOLCANO NATIONAL MONUMENT

Start: ❹ Cimarron

Rising 1300ft above the surrounding plains, Capulin is the most accessible of several volcanoes in the area. From the visitor center at **Capulin Volcano National Monument** (www.nps.gov/cavo; admission per vehicle $5; ⊙8am-4pm), a 2-mile road spirals up the mountain to a parking lot at the crater rim (8182ft), where trails lead around and into the crater. From Cimarron, take Hwy 64 N, hop on I-25 for 5 miles, take exit 451, and head east on Hwy 87/64. The park entrance is 3 miles north of Capulin village, off Hwy 325.

business failed because he kept shooting at the customers.

Today, aside from strolling around the plaza, the best reasons to visit Las Vegas are 5 miles northwest of town on Hwy 65, near Montezuma Castle (you'll know it when you see it), which is part of the United World College of the West. Along the road in front of the castle, you can soak in a series of natural **hot spring pools** (Hwy 65; admission free; ⊙5am-midnight). Bring a swimsuit and test the water – some are scalding hot! And don't miss the **Dwan Light Sanctuary** (admission free; ⊙6am-10pm) on the school campus, a meditation chamber where prisms in the walls cast rainbows inside.

✗ 🏠 p177

The Drive ❯❯ Head north on Hwy 518; at mile marker 12, turn left onto Hwy 94, which you will take you all the way to Mora – but pay attention, as a couple of turns are required. Between mile markers 4 and 5, look south for great views of Hermit Peak.

TRIP HIGHLIGHT

❼ Mora Valley

This scenic agricultural valley, whose hub is the town of Mora, is known throughout northern New Mexico as an enclave where traditional Hispanic ways still remain strong. In 2013, Mora County became the first in the nation to ban fracking for oil and gas.

At **Tapetes de Lana Weaving Center** (www.tapetesdelana.com; Hwy 518, at Hwy 434; ⊙9am-4pm, closed Sat in winter), you can see handlooms in action, browse for handmade rugs and buy yarns that are spun and dyed on site, and tour one of the few active wool mills in the US.

At the **Victory Ranch** (📞575-387-2254; www.victoryranch.com; Hwy 434; adult/child $5/3; ⊙10am-4pm, closed Jan-Mar 15; 🚻), 1 mile north of Mora, hand-feed the cute and fluffy alpacas and shop for alpaca wool gifts.

Two miles west of Mora is the **Cleveland Roller Mill Historical Museum** (www.clevelandrollermillmuseum.com; adult/child $2/1; ⊙10am-3pm Sat & Sun summer), housed in a functional 19th-century adobe-and-stone flour mill, with gears and cogs and pulleys inside.

Five miles east of Mora, the **Salman Ranch** (📞866-281-1515; Hwy 518 at Hwy 442; ⊙10am-4pm Tue-Sun in season; 🚻) is famous for its pesticide-free raspberry fields, where you pick your own from mid-August to mid-October. Off-season, stop by the ranch store and La Cueva Mill, one of New Mexico's best-preserved 19th-century industrial adobe buildings.

✗ p177

The Drive ❯❯ Take Hwy 434 north, through Guadalupita and the ski-resort town of Angel Fire. Turn left on Hwy 64 W, which will take you back into Taos. Watch for elk – sometimes in the middle of the road!

Eating & Sleeping

Taos ①

✕ Taos Diner   Diner $

(www.taosdiner.com; 908 Paseo del Pueblo
Norte; mains $4-14; ⏰7am-2:30pm; 🖱) Diner
grub at its finest, prepared with a Southwestern,
organic spin. Mountain men, scruffy jocks, solo
diners and happy tourists – everyone's welcome
here. The breakfast burritos rock.

✕ Taos Pizza Out Back   Pizza $

(www.taospizzaoutback.com; 712 Paseo del
Pueblo Norte; slices $4-8, whole pies $13-29;
⏰11am-10pm May-Sep, to 9pm Oct-Apr; 🖊🖱)
Pizza dreams come true with every possible
ingredient under the sun at Taos' top pizza
palace. Slices are enormous, and crusts are
made with organic flour.

🛏 American Artists
Gallery House B&B   B&B $$

(☎800-532-2041; www.taosbedandbreakfast.
com; 132 Frontier Lane; r $99-219; ❄@🛜)
George the peacock and lots of cats will be your
inn-mates, while Jacuzzi suites will blow your
mind. All rooms have wood-burning fireplaces.
The creative breakfasts are legendary.

🛏 El Pueblo Lodge   Hotel $

(☎800-433-9612; www.elpueblolodge.com; 412
Paseo del Pueblo Norte; r from $89; ❄🛜🏊)
This standard hotel is right downtown, with
big, clean rooms, some with kitchenettes and/
or fireplaces, a pool, hot tub and fresh pastries
in the morning. Discounts are offered when it's
slow.

Wild Rivers ②

🛏 Wild Rivers Recreation Area

(campsite $5-7) Five small campgrounds dot
the scenic drive that loops through the sage-
speckled recreation area.

Red River ③

✕ Shotgun Willie's   Diner $

(cnr Main St & Pioneer Rd; mains $6-12; ⏰7am-
2pm) Locals love this artery-clogging place.
The true house specialty is the barbecue.
Mmmmm... brisket.

Cimarron ④

🛏 St James Hotel   Hotel $$

(☎888-376-2664; www.exstjames.com; 617
Collison St; r $85-135; ❄🛜) Sleep here... if the
ghosts will let you. The 10 modern rooms are
nice, but it's the period rooms that make this
one of the most authentic-feeling historic hotels
in New Mexico. Count the bullet holes in the
original ceiling. There's a restaurant/bar too.

Las Vegas ⑥

✕ World Treasures
Traveler's Café   Cafe $

(1814 Plaza St; snacks $3-6; ⏰7:30am-4:30pm
Mon-Sat; 🛜) This coffee-and-sandwich
shop housed in a weaving gallery appeals to
international travelers and locals alike, with wi-
fi, a book exchange, board games and couches.

🛏 Plaza Hotel   Hotel $

(☎800-328-1882, 505-425-3591; www.
plazahotel-nm.com; 230 Old Town Plaza; r incl
breakfast from $89; P❄@🛜🖱) This is Las
Vegas' most celebrated and historic lodging, and
it's also decent value. It was opened in 1882 and
carefully remodeled a century later; architectural
details abound. It offers 72 comfortable rooms,
as well as the best restaurant and bar in town.

Mora Valley ⑦

✕ Casa de Teresa's Tamales

(Hwy 518; mains $5-7; ⏰8am-5pm Mon-Sat,
Sun in summer) A few miles west of Mora on
Hwy 518, this super-friendly local joint turns out
top-notch tamales.

White Sands National Monument Ethereal dunes

Las Cruces to Carlsbad Caverns

16

Crossing the southern swath of the state, you can sled down gleaming white sand dunes, walk through stalagmite-columned caves, and swim in a waterfall in the desert. It's no mirage...

TRIP HIGHLIGHTS

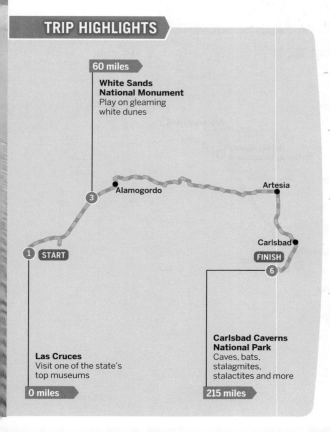

60 miles

White Sands National Monument
Play on gleaming white dunes

3 Alamogordo

Artesia

Carlsbad
FINISH
6

1 START

Las Cruces
Visit one of the state's top museums

0 miles

Carlsbad Caverns National Park
Caves, bats, stalagmites, stalactites and more

215 miles

2–3 DAYS
215 MILES

GREAT FOR...

BEST TIME TO GO
September till November offers the best weather.

 ESSENTIAL PHOTO
The play of shadow on wind-sculpted dunes at White Sands National Monument.

 BEST NATURAL SIGHT
Carlsbad Caverns is like nothing else in the Southwest.

179

16 Las Cruces to Carlsbad Caverns

White Sands means two things in these parts: the national monument where you can frolic in dunes that look like giant snowdrifts, and the missile range surrounding it that's the largest military installation in the US — within which the first atomic blast ever was unleashed. From this sandy basin, the route climbs into pine-clad forests and, ultimately, descends 755ft underground into the trippy subterranean world of Carlsbad Caverns.

TRIP HIGHLIGHT

① Las Cruces

Though this city at the southern crossroads of I-25 and I-10 doesn't have a wealth of attractions, it does have one museum you won't want to miss. The **New Mexico Farm & Ranch Heritage Museum** (www.nmfarmandranchmuseum.org; 4100 Dripping Springs Rd; adult/child $5/2; ☾9am-5pm Mon-Sat, noon-5pm Sun; 🚹) has more than just engaging displays about the agricultural history

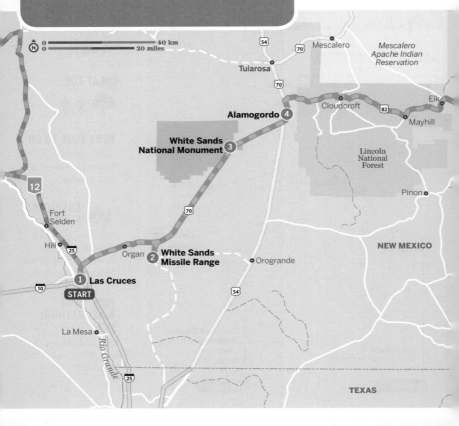

of the state – it's got livestock! There are daily milking demonstrations and an occasional 'parade of breeds' of cattle, along with stalls of horses, donkeys, sheep and goats. Other demonstrations include blacksmithing (Friday to Sunday), spinning and weaving (Wednesday), and heritage cooking (call for times). You'll understand much more about New Mexican life and culture after a visit here.

✗ ⌂ p185

The Drive ›› Take I-25 North to Hwy 70 E. Pass through a notch in the Organ Mountains and drop into the Tularosa Valley. Between mile markers 169 and 170, exit at White Sands Missile Range.

----

② White Sands Missle Range

If it flies and explodes and was made in America, there's a good chance it was tested here. (Occasionally, Hwy 70 closes to prevent 'collateral damage' during launches). The **White Sands Missile Test Center Museum** (www. wsmr-history.org; Bldg 200, Headquarters Ave; ⏰8am-4pm Mon-Fri, 10am-3pm Sat) features an outdoor missile garden, a real V-2 rocket and exhibits with lots of defense-related artifacts. Park outside the Test Center gate and check in at the office before walking to the museum.

The Drive ›› Continue on Hwy 70 E. Be prepared to stop along the way at a border inspection checkpoint sometimes manned with drug-sniffing dogs.

TRIP HIGHLIGHT

③ White Sands National Monument

Undulating through the Tularosa Basin like something straight out of a dream, these ethereal dunes at **White Sands National Monument**

LINK YOUR TRIP

12 El Camino Real & Turquoise Trail

From Las Cruces, head north up the Rio Grande Valley along the 400-year-old route that links Mexico City to Santa Fe.

20 Billy the Kid Trail

From Artesia, drive 30 miles north on US 285 to Roswell, for a trip that covers UFOs, outlaws and Smokey Bear.

MIKE THEISS/GETTY IMAGES ©

(www.nps.gov/whsa; adult/child under 16yr $3/free; ⊙7am-9pm Jun-Aug, to sunset Sep-May) are a highlight of any trip to New Mexico and a must on every landscape photographer's itinerary. Try to time a visit to White Sands with sunrise or sunset (or both), when it's at its most magical. From the visitor center drive the 16-mile scenic loop into the heart of the dazzlingly white sea of sand that is the world's largest gypsum dune field, covering 275 sq miles. Along the way, get out of the car and romp around a bit. Hike the **Alkali Flat**, a 4.5-mile (round-trip) backcountry trail through the heart of the dunes, or the simple 1-mile loop nature trail. Don't forget your sunglasses – the sand is as bright as snow!

Spring for a $17 plastic saucer at the visitor center gift shop then **sled** one of the back dunes. It's fun, and you can sell the disc back for $5 at day's end (no rentals to avoid liability). Check the park calendar for **sunset strolls** and occasional moonlight **bicycle rides** (adult/child $5/2.50), the latter best reserved in advance.

Backcountry campsites, with no water or toilet facilities, are a mile from the scenic drive. Pick up one of the limited permits ($3, issued first-come, first-served) in person at the visitor center at least one hour before sunset.

The Drive » Keep heading east on Hwy 70.

---

4 Alamogordo

Alamogordo (Spanish for 'fat cottonwood') might not be laden with charm, but it's super convenient to White Sands.

The main attraction is the four-story **New Mexico Museum of Space History**

CHEAP SLEEPS

The least expensive lodging on this route is just west of Cloudcroft: the **Cloudcroft Mountain Park Hostel** (✆575-682-0555; www.cloudcrofthostel.com; 1049 Hwy 82; dm $17, r without bathroom $30-50; 🛜) offers dorm, family, and private rooms, with a common kitchen and hang out space – plus hiking trails through its 28 acres. For primitive dispersed camping near Carlsbad, go west on Jones St and just keep going, onto the dirt roads on public lands.

(www.nmspacemuseum. org; Hwy 2001; adult/child $6/4; ☉9am-5pm; 🚻). Nicknamed 'the golden cube,' it looms over town and has excellent exhibits on space research and flight. Its **Tombaugh IMAX Theater & Planetarium** (adult/ child $6/4.50; 🚻) shows films on everything from the Grand Canyon to the dark side of the moon, as well as laser shows and multimedia presentations on a huge wraparound screen.

Railroad buffs and kids flock to the **Toy Train Depot** (www.toytraindepot. homestead.com; 1991 N White Sands Blvd; admission $4; ☉noon-4:30pm Wed-Sun; 🚻), an 1898 railway depot with five rooms of train memorabilia and toy trains, and a 2.5-mile narrow-gauge mini-train you can ride through Alameda Park.

✗ 🛏 p185

The Drive » Take Hwy 82 E, and you'll soon find yourself rising from the Chihuahuan Desert into the forested Sacramento Mountains. Pass Cloudcroft – maybe stop to grab a bite or stay overnight (p185) – and continue on, downhill and across open plains. At Artesia, turn right onto Hwy 285 S.

⑤ **Carlsbad**

Carlsbad is a convenient base from which to visit the famous caverns south of town, as well as **Guadalupe Mountains National Park** just across state lines in Texas. There's not a whole lot to see in Carlsbad itself, but **Living Desert State Park** (www.nmparks.com; 1504 Miehls Dr, off Hwy 285; adult/child $5/3; ☉8am-5pm Jun-Aug, 9am-5pm Sep-May) is worth a gander. It is a great place to see and learn about roadrunners, wolves and antelopes, along with desert plants like agave, ocotillo

DETOUR:
SITTING BULL FALLS

Start: 5 Carlsbad

An oasis in the desert, **Sitting Bull Falls** (per vehicle $5; ⏱noon-6pm Fri-Mon Apr-Sep, to 5pm Oct-Mar) is tucked among the burly canyons of the Guadalupe Mountains, 30 miles southwest of Carlsbad. A spring-fed creek pours 150ft over a limestone cliff, with natural pools below and above the falls that are big enough to splash around in. There are a series of caves behind the waterfalls, which can be explored with a ranger. Twenty-six miles of trails around the falls offer the best hiking anywhere near Carlsbad. Though there's no camping in the designated recreation area right around the falls, backpackers may hike in and camp further up Sitting Bull Canyon, or up Last Chance Canyon, where you should also find water flowing. It can get brutally hot here in summer, so hiking is generally best from late fall to early spring. Arrange cave walks and pick up trail maps and other info – including a pamphlet about what to do if you encounter a mountain lion – at the **Lincoln National Forest office** (📞575-885-4181; 114 S Halagueno; ⏱7:30am-4:30pm Mon-Fri) in Carlsbad. To get there, turn west on NM 137 (also called the 'Queen Hwy') from US 285 just north of Carlsbad, or turn west on County Road 408 (the Dark Canyon Road) from US 180/62 just south of Carlsbad, and follow the signs to Sitting Bull Falls.

and yucca. The park has a good 1.3-mile trail that showcases different habitats of the Chihuahuan Desert, plus a reptile house.

For primitive dispersed camping near Carlsbad, go west on Jones St and just keep going, onto the dirt roads on public lands.

✖ 🛏 p185

The Drive » Take Hwy 62/180 South to White's City, then Hwy 7 into Carlsbad Caverns National Park.

TRIP HIGHLIGHT

6 Carlsbad Caverns National Park

Huge caves hide under the hills at **Carlsbad Caverns National Park** (📞575-785-2232, bat info 505-785-3012; www.nps.gov/cave; 3225 National Parks Hwy; adult/child $6/free; ⏱caves 8:30am-5pm late May-early Sep, 8:30am-3:30pm early Sep-late May, visitor center 8am-5pm, to 7pm late May-early Sep; 👶), where you can walk through a weird subterranean

wonderland that's covered in stalactites, stalagmites and other fantastical geological features. Ride an elevator from the visitor center (which descends the length of the Empire State Building in under a minute) to the Big Room, an underground chamber 1800ft long, 255ft high and over 800ft below the surface. You can also hike in 2 miles from the cave mouth. If you've got kids (or are just feeling goofy), plastic caving helmets with headlamps are sold in the gift shop. Bring long sleeves and closed shoes: it gets chilly.

The cave's other claim to fame is the 300,000-plus Mexican free-tailed bat colony that roosts here from mid-May to mid-October. Be here by sunset, when they cyclone out for an all-evening insect feast.

Guided tours of **additional caves** (📞877-444-6777; www.recreation.gov; adult $7-20, child $3.50-10) are available, and should be reserved well in advance.

Wilderness backpacking – above ground, in the desert – requires a permit (free); the visitor center sells topographical maps of the hiking trails. November to March is the best time (no rattlesnakes, better temperatures). To get up close to the desert in air-conditioned comfort, take the 9-mile gravel **Walnut Canyon Desert Drive**.

Eating & Sleeping

Las Cruces ❶

🍴 Nellie's Café — New Mexican $

(1226 W Hadley Ave; mains $5-8; ⏰8am-2pm Tue-Sun) A favorite of locals, Nellie's has been serving homemade burritos, *chile rellenos* (stuffed chiles) and tamales for decades now. It's humble in decor, but big in taste.

🛏 Royal Host Motel — Motel $

(📞575-524-8536; 2146 W Picacho Ave; r $45-65; ❄🤖🐾) Pets are welcome (extra $10) at this basic budget motel, which is clean and friendly with an on-site restaurant.

Alamogordo ❹

🍴 Pizza Patio & Pub — Italian $$

(2203 E 1st St; mains $7-15; ⏰11am-8pm Mon-Thu & Sat, to 9pm Fri; 🐕) This is the best something-for-everyone place in Alamogordo, with an outdoor patio and casual indoor dining room. Pizzas and pastas are good, salads are big, and pitchers or pints of beer are on tap.

🛏 Best Western Desert Aire Hotel — Hotel $$

(📞575-437-2110; www.bestwestern.com; 1021 S White Sands Blvd; r from $78; ❄@🛜🤖) Recently remodeled, this chain hotel has standard-issue rooms and suites. In summer, the swimming pool is a cool sanctuary.

🛏 Oliver Lee State Park — Campground $

(www.nmparks.com; 409 Dog Canyon Rd; tent/RV sites $8/14) Twelve miles south of Alamogordo, this park is set in a spring-fed canyon where you might see ferns and flowers growing in the desert. From the campground, Dog Canyon National Recreational Trail climbs some 2000ft over 5.5 miles, featuring terrific views of the Tularosa Basin.

Cloudcroft

🛏 Lodge Resort & Spa — Lodge $$

(📞888-395-6343; www.thelodgeresort.com; 601 Corona Pl; r from $125; @🛜🤖) A grand old lodge built in 1899 as a vacation getaway for railroad employees, today it is a full-scale resort, with a pampering spa, a wonderful restaurant, a golf course and beautifully maintained grounds.

Carlsbad ❺

🍴 Blue House Bakery & Café — Breakfast $

(609 N Canyon St; mains $4-8; ⏰6am-noon Mon-Sat) This sweet Queen Anne house perks the best coffee and espresso in this quadrant of New Mexico.

🍴 Red Chimney Pit Barbecue — Barbecue $$

(www.redchimneypitbarbecue.com; 817 N Canal St; mains $7-15; ⏰11am-2pm & 4:30-8:30pm Mon-Fri) Quality meats with tasty sauce. You'll leave full.

🛏 Stagecoach Inn — Motel $

(📞575-887-1148; 1819 S Canal St; r from $50; ❄🛜🤖) One of the best values in town, the Stagecoach has clean rooms, a swimming pool and an on-site playground for kids.

🛏 Trinity Hotel — Boutique Hotel $$

(📞575-234-9891; www.thetrinityhotel.com; 201 S Canal St; r from $169-219; ❄🛜) This luxurious new place is Carlsbad's best hotel. It's not exactly 'new' – it's in a renovated building that was once the First National Bank. The sitting room of one suite is inside the old vault! Family-run, it's friendly, and the restaurant is easily Carlsbad's classiest.

Silver City Apache heritage and coffee culture

Geronimo Trail

17

Follow the trail of this legendary Apache chief, through old mining towns, over serpentine passes, and into the box canyon where he ultimately surrendered.

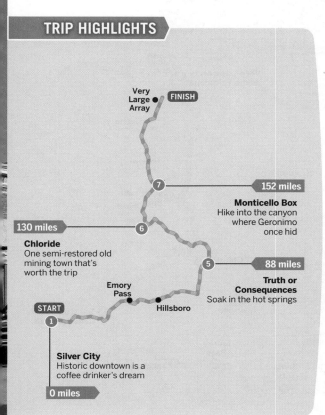

TRIP HIGHLIGHTS

Very Large Array ● **FINISH**

7 ────── **152 miles**

Monticello Box
Hike into the canyon where Geronimo once hid

130 miles ────── **6**

Chloride
One semi-restored old mining town that's worth the trip

5 ────── **88 miles**

Truth or Consequences
Soak in the hot springs

Emory Pass ●
Hillsboro ●

START
1

Silver City
Historic downtown is a coffee drinker's dream

0 miles

2–3 DAYS
190 MILES / 306KM

GREAT FOR...

BEST TIME TO GO
May to October, for warm days that linger into evening.

ESSENTIAL PHOTO

Frame an antique at Chloride's Pioneer Store.

BEST FOR VIEWS

Emory Pass: gape at the Rio Grande Basin panorama and beyond.

187

17 Geronimo Trail

From the former boom town of Silver City – which is now rich with great cafes – you'll snake your way over precipitous Emory Pass and out to the Rio Grande valley. Like Geronimo himself, you can soak in the healing mineral springs at Truth or Consequences before heading for the eastern flank of the Gila's Black Range and north to the sublime Plains of San Agustin.

TRIP HIGHLIGHT

❶ Silver City

Way back in the day, the site of Silver City was settled by Apaches. When the Spanish came to the area to mine copper, they opted to set up residence outside this little valley. Less tactful were the American prospectors who arrived in the late 1860s – and flooded in following the silver strike in 1870. They established the town and conflict with the Indians erupted. Silver City's founder,

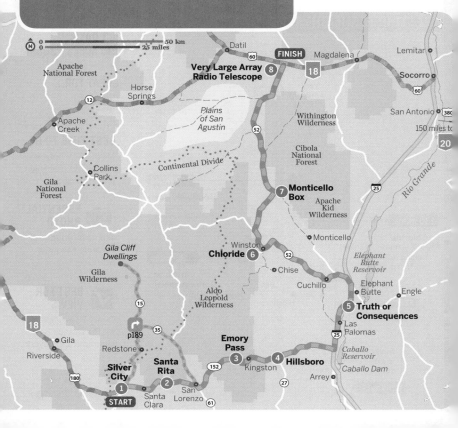

John Bullard, was killed by Apaches in 1871. Since then, the fortunes of the town have risen and fallen a few times. Today, the economy is largely based on copper mining from the nearby Santa Rita mine, though you couldn't be faulted for thinking it's based on caffeine consumption; there seem to be more coffee houses per capita here than anywhere else in New Mexico.

These days, Silver City is a pretty lively place. The town attracts adventure addicts, who come to work and play in the nearby mountains and rivers. It's also home to a healthy student population – Western New Mexico University is based here. The **Western New Mexico University Museum** (www.wnmu.edu/univ/museum.shtml; 1000 W College Ave; admission free; ⏰9am-4:30pm Mon-Fri, 10am-

DETOUR:
GILA CLIFF DWELLINGS

Start: ❶ Silver City

It's easy to imagine how the mysterious, relatively isolated and easily accessible **Gila Cliff Dwellings National Monument** (www.nps.gov/gicl; admission $3; ⏰trail 9am-4pm, visitor center to 4:30pm) might have looked at the turn of the first century. Here, the influence of the Ancestral Puebloans on the Mogollon culture is writ large. Take the 1-mile round-trip self-guided trail that climbs 180ft to the dwellings, overlooking a lovely forested canyon. Parts of the trail are steep and involve ladders. The trail begins at the end of Hwy 15, 2 miles beyond the visitor center. To get here, take twisting Hwy 15 north from Silver City. Heading back from the cliff dwellings, take Hwy 35 down the pleasant Mimbres Valley for a change of scenery, or to skip onwards to stop 3 on this Trip.

4pm Sat & Sun) boasts the world's largest collection of Mimbres pottery, though the displays are desperately in need of some modernization.

 p193

The Drive » Take Hwy 180 E, then at Santa Clara turn left onto Hwy 152 E. After about 5.5 miles, look for the Chino Mine Observation Point on your right.

- - - - - - - - - - - - -

❷ Santa Rita Chino Open Pit Copper Mine Observation Point

Worked by Native Americans and Spanish and Anglo settlers, this is the oldest active mine in the Southwest. From the observation point along Hwy 152, you can get an eyeful of it. A

staggering 1.5 miles wide, the open pit is 1800ft deep, and produces 300 million pounds of copper annually.

The Drive » Continue east on Hwy 152. After San Lorenzo, the road becomes increasingly serpentine as you climb over the Black Range. There are a number of Forest Service campgrounds along this section.

- - - - - - - - - - - - -

❸ Emory Pass

Your journey over the Black Range tops out at the 8228ft Emory Pass. The lookout point offers expansive views of the Rio Grande basin to the east and the rows of craggy peaks that jut from it like sharp teeth. There's a hiking trailhead here that leads north along the spine of the Black Range.

LINK YOUR TRIP

18 Into the Gila
Check out the west side of the range on this trip, which connects at Silver City.

20 Billy the Kid Trail
Take Hwy 60 east, I-25 South, then Hwy 380 east to hitch up with this outlaw's route.

The Drive » You're not done with the curves yet – you've still got to go down the other side of the pass!

JILL FROMER/GETTY IMAGES ©

❹ Hillsboro

Precious ore, including gold, silver and copper, was discovered around Hillsboro in the mid-1800s, but the boom didn't last long. When the silver market crashed in 1893 so did most of the towns. Today, Hillsboro is one of the largest ones left, with a population of around 300. It's best known for its Apple Festival on the Labor Day weekend (early September), featuring everything apple, including freshly baked pies and delicious cider. See some historical miscellany at the **Black Range Museum** (Hwy 152; admission by donation; ⏰ 11am-5pm Fri-Mon); if it's closed, go around back and yell for Jim and he'll likely open up.

 p193

The Drive » Continue east, out of the foothills and into the Rio Grande Valley. Take the I-25 North.

TRIP HIGHLIGHT

❺ Truth or Consequences

According to local lore, Geronimo himself came to this place to partake of the healing hot waters – and you should too. Long said to have therapeutic

properties, the waters range in temperature from 98°F to 115°F (36°C to 46°C) and have a pH of 7 (neutral). Our favorite spot to soak is **Riverbend Hot Springs** (www. riverbendhotsprings.com; 100 Austin St; shared/private per hr $10/15; ⏰ 8am-10pm), which has shared and private tubs overlooking a – wait for it – bend in the river. For something

more spa-tastic, and way more expensive, hit the **Sierra Grande Lodge & Spa** (☎ 575-894-6976; www.sierragrandelodge. com; 501 McAdoo St), with posh private pools and a full menu of massages, facials, scrubs and even private yoga classes.

To engage your brain as well as your body, stop by the **Geronimo Springs Museum** (211

Chloride Tiny town of historic buildings

Main St; adult/student $6/3; ⊙9am-5pm Mon-Sat, noon-5pm Sun), an engaging mishmash of minerals, local art and historical artifacts ranging from prehistoric Mimbres pots to beautifully worked cowboy saddles.

 p193

The Drive » After filling up with gas, head north out of Truth or Consequences on Hwy 181, then turn left onto Hwy 52, bearing west, toward the Black Range. The road winds around Cuchillo Mountain, into the little town of Winston. At the T intersection, turn left and follow signs for 2.7 miles to Chloride.

- - - - - - - - - - - - -

TRIP HIGHLIGHT

6 Chloride

In the foothills of the Black Range, tiny Chloride (population 8) was abustle in the 19th century with enough silver miners to support eight saloons. By the end of the 20th century, the town was on the verge of disintegration. Fortunately, the historic buildings are being restored by Don and Dona Edmund, who began renovating the old **Pioneer Store** (☎575-743-2736; www. pioneerstoremuseum.com;

LOCAL KNOWLEDGE: KINGSTON

A blink-and-you'll-miss-it community of just 30 people (compared to 7000 in its heyday), Kingston is a small clutch of wooden buildings about a quarter mile off Hwy 152, between Emory Pass and Hillsboro. It's hard to believe this was one of the baddest cities in New Mexico, boasting 28 bars catering to everyone from Chinese fortune seekers to Billy the Kid, Butch Cassidy and Mark Twain. The only building that looks almost like it did during the 19th century is the beautifully restored **Percha Bank** (575-895-5032; Main St, Kingston; admission free; 11am-3pm Fri-Sun May-Sep), c 1884. Complete with an enormous working vault, the bank building is now a museum and art gallery. If no-one's there, ask over at the **Black Range Lodge** (575-895-5652; www.blackrangelodge.com; 119 Main St; r $80-115;), a comfortably rustic B&B that was once a casino and saloon.

10am-4pm) in 1994. Today, this general store from 1880 is a museum with a rich collection of miscellany from Chloride's heyday, including wooden dynamite detonators, farm implements, children's coffins, saddles and explosion-proof telephones used in mines. You can see the Hanging Tree to which rowdy drunks were tied until they sobered up; the Monte Cristo Saloon (now an artist co-op/gift shop); and a few other buildings in various stages of rehabilitation.

p193

The Drive » Backtrack to Winston and keep going straight, north on Hwy 52. After 9 miles, continue straight onto the dirt road, toward Dusty. After 9 more miles, turn right onto Forest Rd 140/CRE 14. Drive to the parking/turnaround area just before the track crosses the stream.

- - - - - - - - - - - - -

TRIP HIGHLIGHT

7 Monticello Box

This steep-walled canyon that rises abruptly along Alamosa Creek was frequented by Geronimo and his renegade Chiricahua Apache band during the mid-1870s, in part because of a sacred warm spring inside the gorge. Outside it, not far from the junction of Hwy 52 and Forest Rd 140, sat the headquarters of the Warm Springs Apache reservation. It was here, in April 1877, that Geronimo arrived for what he believed would be a peaceful meeting with Indian agent John Clum; instead, Geronimo was captured, shackled, and interned at the San Carlos reservation in Arizona (from which he would later escape).

Though the land surrounding the box is private, it's OK to respectfully explore inside the canyon. You'll want to wear water shoes or sandals, as you'll have to cross the stream a few times even if you're only hiking in a short distance.

The Drive » Heading north on Hwy 52, you'll traverse some of New Mexico's most subtly stunning terrain, up intermittent Alamosa Creek and out onto the undulating Plains of San Agustin. Bonus points if you can manage to time this around sunset. You'll hit the Very Large Array just before reaching Hwy 60.

- - - - - - - - - - - - -

8 Very Large Array Radio Telescope

If you make it to this literally otherworldly looking spread of massive antenna dishes before dark, check out the museum and take a walking tour of the facility (see p197). If you arrive too late, it's still worth the trip just to see the silhouettes against the twilight sky. For the museum, turn left on Hwy 166.

Eating & Sleeping

Silver City ①

✕ Diane's Restaurant & Bakery
American $$

(☎575-538-8722; www.dianesrestaurant.com; 510 N Bullard St; lunch $8-10, dinner $15-30; ⊙11am-2pm & 5:30-9pm Tue-Sat, 11am-2pm Sun) Diane's is the local restaurant of choice, especially for weekend breakfasts – though it's pretty busy for weekday lunch, too. The romantic appeal is upped at dinner, when there is dim lighting and white linen.

Javalina
Cafe $

(201 N Bullard St; pastries from $2; ⊙6am-9pm Mon-Thu, to 10pm Fri & Sat, to 7pm Sun; 🛜) This is a great coffee shop, with seating of all sizes and styles, from couches to love seats to wooden chairs. There are board games and reading material and a few computer terminals if you don't have your laptop with you.

✕ Peace Meal Cooperative
Vegetarian $

(www.peacemealcoop.com; 601 N Bullard St; mains $6-10; ⊙11am-7pm Wed-Mon; ✍) This build-your-own burrito bar dishes up fresh ingredients to order. Ask if the amazing tofu curry is on the menu.

🛏 Palace Hotel
Historic Hotel $

(☎575-388-1811; www.silvercitypalacehotel. com; 106 W Broadway; r from $51; ❋🛜) A restored 1882 hostelry, the Palace exudes a low-key turn-of-the-20th-century charm. The rooms range from small (with a double bed) to two-room suites outfitted with refrigerators, microwaves and TVs. All have old-fashioned decor.

Gila Cliff Dwellings National Monument

🛏 Gila Cliff Dwellings Campgrounds
Campground $

(www.nps.gov/gicl; Gila Cliff Dwellings National Monument; free) There are four campgrounds in and around Gila Cliff Dwellings National Monument; all have vault toilets but none have drinkable water. Check the website for details on each.

Hillsboro ④

✕ Hillsboro General Store Café
New Mexican $

(www.hillsborogeneralstore.com; 100 Main St; mains $8-12; ⊙8am-3pm Fri-Wed) Housed in Hillsboro's historic general store, this place is a surprise of the best kind. The New Mexican plates feature local chile, free-range locally raised meats, organic veggies – and the pies are so good they often sell out.

Truth or Consequences ⑤

✕ Happy Belly Deli
Deli $

(313 N Broadway; mains $2-8; ⊙7am-3pm Mon-Fri, 8am-3pm Sat, 8am-noon Sun) Draws the morning crowd with fresh breakfast burritos.

🛏 Riverbend Hot Springs
Boutique Hotel $

(☎575-894-7625; www.riverbendhotsprings. com; 100 Austin St; r from $70; ❋🛜) Former hostel Riverbend Hot Springs now offers more traditional motel-style accommodations – no more tipis – from its fantastic perch beside the Rio Grande. Rooms exude a bright, quirky charm, and several units work well for groups. Guests get discounts on the private hot spring tubs and soak for free in the public pools.

Chloride ⑥

🛏 Harry Pye Cabin
Cabin

(☎575-743-2736; cabin $100; 🐾) Stay in Chloride's oldest building – which has been renovated and modernized into comfortable two-bedroom accommodation. It's got a mini-kitchenette with a microwave.

Very Large Array Radio Telescope *Star gazing*

Into the Gila

18

From the other-worldly sight of the Very Large Array to the absolutely earthy experience of the burly Gila Mountains, take a trip into New Mexico's wild southwest.

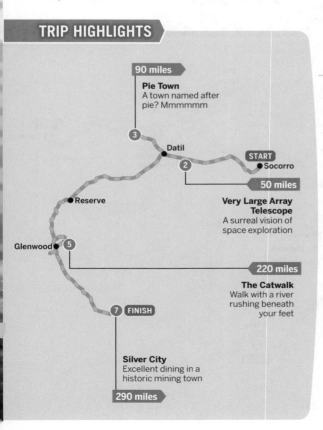

90 miles

Pie Town
A town named after pie? Mmmmmm

3

Datil

2

START
● Socorro

● Reserve

Glenwood ● **5**

50 miles

Very Large Array Telescope
A surreal vision of space exploration

220 miles

The Catwalk
Walk with a river rushing beneath your feet

7 FINISH

Silver City
Excellent dining in a historic mining town

290 miles

**2 DAYS
298 MILES / 479KM**

GREAT FOR...

BEST TIME TO GO
May to October, when's its warm enough to enjoy!

 ESSENTIAL PHOTO
Focus on the telescope that's the Very Large Array.

BEST FOR DESSERTS
Pie Town – c'mon, the town is named for its pie!

195

18 | Into the Gila

With its huge dish antennas spread across a swath of the Plains of San Agustin and pointing at the sky, the Very Large Array launches this trip to an out-of-this-world beginning. Highways 12 and 180 curve around the Gila massif, bringing you to the Catwalk trail, the San Francisco Hot Springs, and on into the historic Wild West town of Silver City, now bursting with art galleries.

❶ Socorro

Named in 1598 by conquistador Don Juan de Oñate after local Indians gave him and his men so much corn, Socorro (which means 'aid' or 'help') has a pleasant plaza, with a couple of good places to grab a bite nearby – but that's about it. The main sight in town is the **San Miguel Mission** (403 San Miguel Rd), sections of which date to the 1600s. It's been closed for a while for renovation but is expected to reopen

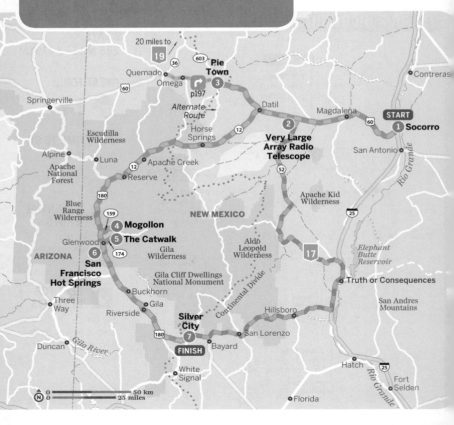

someday... Socorro is also close to the Bosque del Apache National Wildlife Refuge (p150).

 p201

The Drive » Head west on Hwy 60 for 45 miles, then turn left onto Hwy 52; go 2.3 miles and turn right on Hwy 166 to the Very Large Array Radio Telescope. Don't expect to have mobile phone service for most of this drive.

TRIP HIGHLIGHT

➋ Very Large Array Radio Telescope

Twenty-seven huge antenna dishes (each weighing 230 tons) together comprise a single superpowered telescope – the **Very Large Array Radio Telescope** (VLA; www.nrao.edu; off Hwy 52; admission free; ⏰8:30am-sunset), run by the National Radio Astronomy Observatory. They move

LINK YOUR TRIP

17 **Geronimo Trail**
At Silver City, just keep on going to follow the path of this Apache legend.

19 **Highway 53 to Acoma**
Take the scenic back roads north of Pie Town to check out lava flows, pueblos, and more.

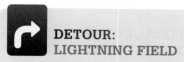

DETOUR: LIGHTNING FIELD

Start: ➌ Pie Town

Heading on toward the Arizona border on Hwy 60, out in the high desert plains around Quemado, gleams the **Lightning Field** (📞505-898-3336; www.diacenter.org/sites/main/lightningfield; Quemado; adult/child Jul-Aug $250/100, May, Jun, Sep & Oct $150/100), an art installation created by Walter de Maria in 1977. Four hundred polished steel poles stand in a giant grid, with each stainless rod about 20ft high – but the actual lengths vary so the tips are all level with each other. During summer monsoons, the poles seem to draw lightning out of hovering thunderheads. The effect is truly electrifying! You can only visit if you stay overnight in the simple on-site cabin, with only six visitors allowed per night. Advance reservations are required. Check out the website for more details.

along railroad tracks that crisscross the open plains, their layout reconfigured as needed to study the outer limits of the known universe. To match the resolving power of the VLA, a regular telescope would have to be 22 miles wide!

The VLA has increased our understanding of black holes, space gases and radio emissions, among other celestial phenomena. And it's had starring and cameo roles in Hollywood films, including *Contact*, *Armegeddon* and *Independence Day*. If none of that's enough to interest you, well, they are just unbelievably cool. There's a small museum at the visitor

center, where you can take a free, self-guided tour with a window peak into the control building.

The Drive » Head west on Hwy 60 for 35 miles; when you see the striking crags of the Sawtooth Mountains to the north, you're getting close. Hope you're hungry!

TRIP HIGHLIGHT

➌ Pie Town

Further west on Hwy 60, you'll pass through Pie Town. Yes, seriously, a town named after pie. And for good reason. They say you can find the best pies in the universe here (which makes you wonder what they've really been doing at the VLA). The **Pie-O-Neer Café** (📞575-772-2711; www.pie-o-neer.com; Hwy 60;

LOCAL KNOWLEDGE: HATE TO BACKTRACK?

If you're in Pie Town, you don't need to retrace your route to Datil to pick up Hwy 12. Instead, from Hwy 60, head south on the dirt road that's directly across from the junction with Hwy 603 N. Go straight on this for 6.2 miles, then take the left fork onto Green Gap Rd/A56. At the next fork 8.8 miles later, continue straight towards Horse Springs. Then 2 miles later, go left at an unsigned fork, down a hill (there's a mailbox at the fork). Stay on that for 28 miles, until you hit Hwy 12 at Horse Springs. (If you're trying to do this route backwards, there's no sign on Hwy 12 at Horse Springs, so look for the dirt road heading north at the windmill between mile markers 48 and 49.) In dry weather, two-wheel drive vehicles should be okay; in wet weather, you'd definitely want 4x4, if you attempt it at all.

slices $4.50; ⊙11am-4pm Thu-Sun) just might prove their case. The pies are dee-lish, the soups and stews are homemade, and you'll be hard pressed to find another host as welcoming as Kathy Knapp – who advises you to call in advance to make sure they won't run out of pie before you get there! Across the highway, there's also the **Good Pie Cafe** (☎575-772-2700; www.goodpie.com; ⊙8am-4pm Mon-Thu, 10am-6pm Fri). Opening hours for both places are flexible, so call before you drive out there!

On the 2nd Saturday of September, Pie Town holds its annual **Pie Festival** (www.pietownfestival.com), with baking and eating contests, the crowning of the Pie Queen, Wild West gunfight reenactments and horned toad races.

The Drive >> Backtrack 20 miles to Datil, then turn south on Hwy 12. Curve into the Gila, past Reserve, which is a good lunch stop (p201), and head south on Hwy 180. Turn left at Hwy 159 and follow it for nine vertiginous, slow-going miles on a route that's often impassible in winter. Let the carsick-prone ride shotgun!

- - - - - - - - - - - -

❹ Mogollon

Once an important mining town, Mogollon is now a semi-ghost town inhabited by only a few antique and knickknack shops and, as is typical for middle-of-nowhere New Mexico, one proud little restaurant. This one is called the **Purple Onion** (Main St; mains $5-10; ⊙9am-5pm Fri-Sun May-Oct), and it's as good as you'd hope after making the trip. You can poke around in spring and fall, but things here are mostly open on summer weekends.

The Drive >> Wind your way back to Hwy 180 and continue south for 3 miles, then turn left on Hwy 174 and follow signs for the Catwalk.

- - - - - - - -

TRIP HIGHLIGHT

❺ The Catwalk

Sixty-five miles northwest of Silver City, the Catwalk trail follows a suspended metal walkway through narrow Whitewater Canyon. You can see the creek rushing beneath your feet! The catwalk is wheelchair-accessible and great for kids. While some will find it disappointingly short, it offers a painless way to experience a bit of the Gila – and from the end of it you can continue forever into the mountains on dirt trails, if you like.

The Drive >> Back on Hwy 180, head south for about 7 miles to the turn off for San Francisco Hot Springs (between mile markers 59 and 58) and continue to the parking lot.

- - - - - - - - - -

❻ San Francisco Hot Springs

Down in the bottom of a cottonwood-shaded

The Catwalk Suspended walkway through Whitewater Canyon

oasis, right along the gently flowing San Francisco River, are a couple of hot-spring pools. To reach them you've got to hike about 2 miles, gradually descending until you reach the canyon's edge, when the trail becomes steeper – but from there it's only a hundred feet or so down to the bottom. You've got to wade across the river to reach the springs, but poke around a bit and you'll find them. In summer, it can be extremely hot at midday – and afternoon skies can suddenly brew with thunderstorms – so be sure to take drinking water and watch the weather.

🛏 p201

The Drive » Continue on Hwy 180 South, all the way into Silver City.

⑦ Silver City

The grand-daddy of New Mexico's boom-bust-boom town success

THE GILA

The 3.3 million acres of 'The Gila' (*hee*-lah) cover eight mountain ranges, including the Mogollon, Tularosa, Blue and Black. This rugged country is just right for black bears, mountain lions and the reintroduced Mexican grey wolves (despite what the billboards around Reserve may say...), plus four species of endangered fish including Gila trout. Really, it's no surprise that it was here that legendary conservationist Aldo Leopold spearheaded a movement to establish the world's first designated wilderness area, resulting in the creation of the Gila Wilderness in 1924; in 1980, the adjacent terrain to the east was also designated as wilderness and named after Leopold.

stories, Silver City's streets are dressed with a lovely mishmash of old brick and cast-iron Victorians and thick-walled red adobe buildings. The place still emits a Wild West air. Billy the Kid spent some of his childhood here, and a few of his haunts can still be found mixed in with the new gourmet coffee shops, quirky galleries and Italian ice-cream parlors gracing the historic downtown. Ensconced in an elegant house from 1881, the

Silver City Museum

(www.silvercitymuseum.org; 312 W Broadway; suggested donation $3; ⊙9am-4:30pm Tue-Fri, 10am-4pm Sat & Sun) features mining and household artifacts from Silver City's Victorian heyday, as well as stunning photographs of the aftermaths of some of the flash floods that ripped through town.

✗ 🛏 p201

Eating & Sleeping

Socorro ❶

✗ M Mountain Coffee Coffee Shop $
(110 Manzanares St W; ⏱7am-8pm; 🛜) A
casual, comfy-chair coffeeshop, with pastries,
hot breakfasts and fresh sandwiches.

🛏 Socorro Old Town B&B B&B $$
(📞575-838-2619; www.socorrobandb.com;
114 W Baca St; r $125; ❄🛜) In the Old Town
neighborhood, this B&B has a casual attitude –
and entering through the unkempt, screened-in
porch, you may wonder if this is just a private
home. Inside, that's what it feels like, with
easygoing hosts and clean, comfortable rooms.

Reserve

✗ Adobe Café & Bakery Bakery $
(www.theadobecafeandbakery.com; cnr Hwys
180 & 12; mains $8-12; ⏱7am-8pm Sun-Mon, to
3pm Wed-Fri; 🚶) A culinary oasis in the middle
of nowhere. Aside from creative renditions
of typical diner fare, the Adobe features
venison burgers, elk sausage – and some good
vegetarian options.

San Francisco Hot Springs ❻

🛏 San Francisco Hot Springs
Campground Campground $
(Hwy 180; camping free) There's free primitive
camping at the trailhead to the hot springs. The
forest service supplies the outhouse, you bring
everything else.

Silver City ❼

✗ Buckhorn
Saloon Steakhouse, Bar $$
(📞575-538-9911; www.buckhornsaloonand-
operahouse.com; Main St, Pinos Altos; mains

$10-39; ⏱5-9pm Mon-Sat) About 7 miles north
of Silver City, this restored adobe eatery offers
serious steaks (a house specialty) and seafood
amid 1860s Wild West decor – try the buffalo
burgers, they're fresh and tasty. Live country
music livens up the joint most nights. The
crowd ranges from Silver City gallery owners
to hard-core mountain men.

✗ Nancy's Silver Cafe Cafe $
(514 N Bullard; mains $4-10; ⏱7am-7:30pm
Mon-Sat) Slip into a red vinyl booth for your
morning – or afternoon, or evening – chile
fix, with some straight up, down home, New
Mexican grub. Helpings are hearty and most
customers are loyal locals.

✗ Tre Rosat Café Cafe $$
(www.trerosat.com; 304 N Bullard; mains $10-
25; ⏱11am-9pm Mon-Fri, from 5pm Sat; 🚶)
Popular for pizzas, Tre Rosat goes far beyond
that with stuffed burgers, elk ribs and seared
fish platters. The kids menu is a winner, too, but
best of all might be the chocolate mousse cake
with raspberry sauce, which is our new favorite
dessert anywhere in the state. Period.

🛏 KOA Campground $
(📞575-388-3351; www.campsilvercity.com;
11824 E Hwy 180; tent/RV sites $24/30, cabins
from $53; 🛜🍽🐾) Five miles east of town, this
campground franchise is a clean, child-friendly
option with a playground and coin laundry.
The 'kamping kabins' are compact but cute
and good value. Fills up in summer, so reserve
ahead.

🛏 The 400 B&B $$
(📞575-313-7015; www.gilahouse.com; 400
N Arizona St; r from $90; ❄🛜) Housed in an
adobe that's over 100 years old, this B&B has
preserved its character while upgrading to 21st-
century comforts. The common area doubles
as one of downtown Silver City's well-regarded
art galleries.

Zuni Pueblo *Famous jewelry, fascinating culture*

Highway 53 to Acoma **19**

Take the back road from Gallup to Acoma Pueblo, where you can meet wolves, explore lava caves and check out a mountain of old-school graffiti.

TRIP HIGHLIGHTS

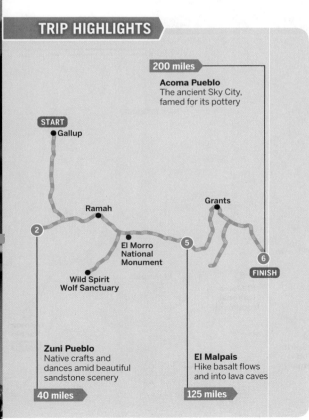

200 miles

Acoma Pueblo
The ancient Sky City, famed for its pottery

START
● Gallup

Ramah ●

Grants

2

El Morro National Monument

5

6

FINISH

Wild Spirit Wolf Sanctuary

Zuni Pueblo
Native crafts and dances amid beautiful sandstone scenery

40 miles

El Malpais
Hike basalt flows and into lava caves

125 miles

2 DAYS
200 MILES / 322KM

GREAT FOR...

BEST TIME TO GO
May to October, after the winds and before the snows.

 ESSENTIAL PHOTO
Shoot a howling wolf at Wild Spirit Wolf Sanctuary.

 BEST FOR CULTURE
Dances at Zuni Pueblo.

203

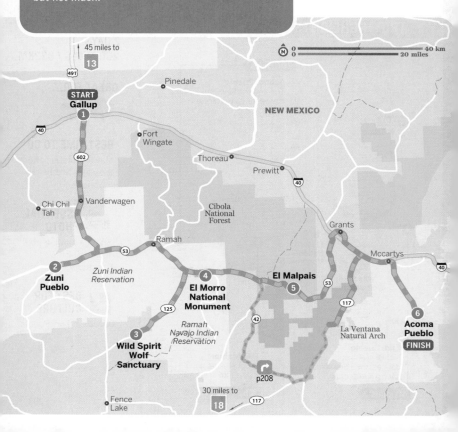

19 Highway 53 to Acoma

Your GPS may tell you that the best route from Gallup to Acoma is I-40, but humans are still (sometimes) smarter than their devices. Prove it by taking the back road, first to Zuni Pueblo, famous for its jewelry, then across rippling hills and alongside a massive lava field set against sandstone cliffs. Before hitting mesa-top Acoma Pueblo, you'll spend some time on the interstate — but not much.

❶ Gallup

The mother town on New Mexico's Mother Road seems stuck in time. Settled in 1881, when the railroad came through, Gallup had her heyday during the road-tripping 1950s, and many of the dilapidated old hotels, pawn shops and billboards, mixed in with today's galleries and trading posts, seem like they haven't changed much since the Eisenhower administration.

45 miles to 13

Pinedale

START Gallup ❶

NEW MEXICO

Fort Wingate

Thoreau
Prewitt

Chi Chil Tah · Vanderwagen

Cibola National Forest

Grants

Ramah

Mccartys

❷ Zuni Pueblo

Zuni Indian Reservation

❹ El Morro National Monument

El Malpais ❺

Ramah Navajo Indian Reservation

La Ventana Natural Arch

❸ Wild Spirit Wolf Sanctuary

p208

❻ Acoma Pueblo FINISH

Fence Lake

30 miles to 18

Modern-day Gallup is an interesting mix of Anglos and Native Americans; it's not unusual to hear people speaking Navajo on their cell phones while buying groceries at the local Walmart. Tourism is limited mostly to Route 66 road-trippers and those in search of Native American history and handicrafts: Route 66 runs straight through downtown Gallup's historic district and is lined with pretty, renovated light-red sandstone buildings housing dozens of kitschy souvenir shops as well as high-quality Indian art.

Downtown, stretch your legs and check out the murals – some from the 1930s – painted on numerous buildings. Then stop into the **Ellis Tanner Trading Company**

LINK YOUR TRIP

13 Georgia O'Keeffe Country

Head north from Gallup along Hwy 491 for Navajo culture and Anasazi ruins.

18 Into The Gila

Take small roads south from Hwy 53 to Hwy 60, for rugged mountains, high-tech telescopes – and pie!

(www.etanner.com; 1980 Hwy 602; ⊙8am-7pm Mon-Sat). The shop doubles as a sort of social gathering place for local Navajos and still operates a functional trade counter. If you don't have anything to swap, your dollar is good in the huge pawn room. Dig around for one of the unique pieces of turquoise jewelry tucked away behind a collection of vintage sheep-wool rugs in the massive pawn room.

🍴📖 p209

The Drive » Take Hwy 602 S, then fork right onto Indian Route 4. Turn right on Hwy 53, toward Zuni.

TRIP HIGHLIGHT

2 Zuni Pueblo

Zuni is the name given by the Spanish to the pueblo known to the tribe that dwells there as Halona-weh, meaning 'red ant hill' – which symbolizes the center of the universe. Its artisans are famed for their jewelry, and you can buy beautiful pieces at little shops throughout the town. For a good selection in one place, go to **Turquoise Village** (www.turquoisevillage.com; 1184 Hwy 53; ⊙10:30am-6pm Mon-Sat).

The **Ashiwi Awan Museum & Heritage Center** (www.ashiwi-museum.org; Ojo Caliente Rd; admission by donation; ⊙9am-5pm Mon-Fri) traces Zuni history with tribal artifacts and

early photos. Nearby, the massive **Our Lady of Guadalupe Mission** features impressive locally painted murals of about 30 life-size *kachinas* (ancestral spirits). The church dates from 1629, although it has been rebuilt twice since then. It can be visited on one of the walking tours offered by the **Zuni Tourism Office** (☎505-782-7238; www.zunitourism.com; ⊙8am-5:30pm Mon-Fri, 10am-4pm Sat, noon-4pm Sun), which is a good place to start your visit anyway.

The most famous ceremony at Zuni is the all-night **Shalak'o ceremonial dance**, held on the last weekend in December. The **Zuni Tribal Fair** (late August) features a powwow, local food, and arts-and-crafts stalls. To observe any ceremony in Zuni, you must attend an orientation; call the tourist office for more information.

📖 p209

The Drive » Take Hwy 53 east 8 miles past Ramah, which makes a good lunch stop (p209), turn right onto Indian Route 125, then go 7.8 miles and hang a right on Indian Route 120. Your next stop is 4 miles up, on your left.

3 Wild Spirit Wolf Sanctuary

Animal-lovers won't want to miss the **Wild Spirit Wolf Sanctuary**

(📞505-775-3304; www.
wildspiritwolfsanctuary.org; 378
Candy Kitchen Rd; tours adult/
child $7/4; ⊙10:30am-5pm Tue-
Sun; 🐾), a 20-mile detour
off Hwy 53, southeast of
Ramah. Home to rescued
captive-born wolves
and wolf-dog mixes, the
sanctuary offers four
interactive walking tours
per day, where you walk
with the wolves – and
get closer than you
imagined – that roam the
sanctuary's large natural-
habitat enclosures. On the
quarter-mile walk you'll
learn everything you ever
wanted to know about
wolves – from behavior
to what they like to eat to
why they make terrible
watchdogs. For a special
'photo tour' ($50 per
person per hour) – when
you can actually get inside
the wolves' pens – make
reservations two weeks
in advance. Primitive
camping is available for
$10 per night, with all
the wolf howling you ever
wanted to hear included.
There's also a guest cabin
with two bedrooms, a big
loft and full kitchen; call
for rates.

The Drive ≫ Having got your
wolf fix, get back on Hwy 53 and
head east for 3 miles.

- - - - - - - - - - - - - -

④ El Morro National Monument

**El Morro National
Monument** (www.nps.gov/
elmo; admission free; ⊙9am-
5pm, last trail entry 4pm), also
called 'Inscription Rock,'

has been autographed
by passers-by since 1250,
when the first pueblo
petroglyphs were etched
near the top of this
200ft hunk of sandstone
rising above a permanent
pool of water. Spanish
conquistadors, Anglo
pioneers and railway
surveyors all paused
to fill their canteens
at the 200,000-gallon
waterhole, and when they
stopped many couldn't
help leaving a record
of their visit behind.
It's quite a sight – more
than 2000 messages
were carved into the soft
rock before President
Teddy Roosevelt
turned El Morro into
America's second
national monument. Of
the two trails that leave
the visitor center, the
paved, half-mile loop
to **Inscription Rock** is
wheelchair accessible.
The unpaved, 2-mile
Mesa Top loop trail
requires a steep climb to
the pueblos. Trail access
ends one hour before
closing.

The Drive ≫ Continue east for
about 19 miles on Hwy 53, past
the Cimarron Rose (p209).

- - - - - - - - - - - - - -

TRIP HIGHLIGHT

⑤ El Malpais

New Mexico's most
recent volcanic eruption
happened here, about
3000 years ago. Now
117,200 sq meters of pure
chunky basalt covers
the plains known as El

Acoma Pueblo Kiva ladders

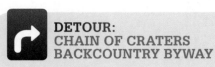

DETOUR:
CHAIN OF CRATERS
BACKCOUNTRY BYWAY

Start: ⑤ El Malpais

For a real backcountry adventure, follow the rugged Chain of Craters Backcountry Byway (aka County Rd 42) across the western and southern quadrants of the Malpais. The road connects with Hwy 53 a few miles west of El Malpais Information Center and bounces along for 33 miles until it hits Hwy 117, about 15 miles south of La Ventana arch. Along the way, it passes several craters, caves and lava tubes (reached by signed trails). Unless you paid for full-coverage on your rental car, a high-clearance vehicle is highly recommended, but 4WD isn't (usually) necessary; in wet weather, the road might be impassible.

Malpais – pronounced 'el mahl-pie-ees,' meaning 'bad land' in Spanish. The area is covered with cinder cones and spatter cones, smooth pahoehoe lava and jagged aa lava, while under the surface lurk ice caves and a 17-mile-long lava tube system. There are hiking trails across the flow, and at the time of writing it was possible to explore four of the lava caves (with a free permit).

Part of the area belongs to **El Malpais National Monument**, another part is **El Malpais National Conservation Area**, but they're well coordinated with each other, so you can stop at either the **El Malpais Information Center** (☎505-783-4774; www.nps.gov/elma; Hwy 53; ⊘8:30am-4:30pm) on Hwy 53 or the **BLM Ranger Station** (☎505-528-2918; Hwy 117; ⊘8:30am-4:30pm) on Hwy 117 for information, trail maps, and cave permits.

To get to the Hwy 117 side, take I-40 East for two exits. The scenic drive here includes a stop at the second-largest sandstone arch in New Mexico, **La Ventana**, plus trail access to the top of the mesa, which has commanding views of El Malpais.

🛏 p209

The Drive » Hop back on I-40 east to exit 96. Turn right on Hwy 124, then left on Indian Route 27. Go left again on Indian Route 30 (Pueblo Rd), then right on Indian Route 38 (Haaku Rd), and keep going for about 6 miles.

- - - - - - - - - - - - -

TRIP HIGHLIGHT

⑥ Acoma Pueblo

Journeying to the top of 'Sky City' is like climbing into another world. There are few more dramatic mesa-top locations – the village sits 7000ft above sea level and 367ft above the surrounding plateau. It's one of the oldest continuously inhabited settlements in North America; people have lived at Acoma since the 11th century. In addition to a singular history and a dramatic location, it's also justly famous for its pottery, which is sold by individual artists on the mesa. There is a distinction between 'traditional' pottery (made with clay dug on the reservation) and 'ceramic' pottery (made elsewhere with inferior clay and simply painted by the artist), so ask the vendor.

Visitors can only go to Sky City on **guided tours** (☎800-747-0180; www.acomaskycity.org; adult/child $20/10; ⊘hourly 9:30am-3:30pm daily Mar-Nov, Sat & Sun Dec-Feb), which leave from the visitor center at the bottom of the mesa. Check the website or phone to confirm that it'll be open. Note that between July 10 and July 13 and either the first or second weekend in October, the pueblo is closed to visitors. Though you must ride the shuttle to the top of the mesa, you can choose to walk down the rock path to the visitor center on your own.

✕ p209

Eating & Sleeping

Gallup ❶

✕ Earl's Family Restaurant Diner $$

(1400 E Hwy 66; mains $8-15; ⊘6am-9pm Mon-Sat, 7am-9pm Sun; ⓐ) The name says it all – Earl's is a great spot to bring the kids. It has also been serving tasty green chile and fried chicken since the late 1940s. And the locals know it; this diner-like place is packed on weekends.

✕ Genaro's Café New Mexican $

(600 W Hill Ave; mains $6-12; ⊘10:30am-7:30pm Tue-Sat) This small, out-of-the-way place serves large plates of New Mexican food. If you like your chile hot, you'll feel right at home here, just like the rest of Gallup – this place can get crowded.

⊨ El Rancho Historic Hotel $$

(☎505-863-9311; www.elranchohotel.com; 1000 E Hwy 66; r from $85; 🅿 ❄ 🛜 🛝) Gallup's best, and only, full-service historic lodging option. Opened in 1937, many of the great actors of the '40s and '50s stayed here, including Humphrey Bogart, Katharine Hepburn and John Wayne, when he was filming Westerns in the area. El Rancho features a superb two-story open lobby decorated in rustic old National Park lodge–style – which is substantially more impressive than the rooms, which are nothing special. There's also a **restaurant** and **bar**.

⊨ Red Rock Park Campground Campground $

(☎505-722-3839; Churchrock, off Hwy 66; tent/RV sites $15/18; 🛝) Pop your tent up in this beautiful setting with easy access to tons of hiking trails. Six miles east of town, it has showers, flush toilets, drinking water and a grocery store.

Zuni Pueblo ❷

⊨ Inn at Halona Inn $

(☎800-752-3278, 505-782-4547; www.halona.com; Halona Plaza; r from $79; 🅿 🛜) The charming eight-room Inn at Halona, decorated with local Zuni arts and crafts, is the only place to stay on the pueblo. Its breakfasts rank with the best of any B&B in the state.

Ramah

✕ Stage Coach Café Cafe $

(3370 Bond St/Hwy 53; mains $5-15; ⊘7am-9pm Mon-Sat) Friendly service, Mexican and American dishes and a big selection of pies.

Highway 53

⊨ Cimarron Rose B&B $$

(☎505-783-4770; www.cimarronrose.com; 689 Oso Ridge Rd; ste $110-185) Two Southwestern-style suites with tiles, pine walls and hardwood floors are offered at this eco-friendly B&B off Hwy 53 between El Morro and El Malpais National Monuments.

El Malpais ❺

⊨ Joe Skeen Campground Campground $

(Hwy 117; camping free) Eleven miles south of I-40 on Hwy 117, in El Malpais National Conservation Area, this small, peaceful campground offers vault toilets and picnic tables but no water.

Acoma Pueblo ❻

✕ Y'aak'a Cafe Native American $

(mains $6-9; ⊘9am-4pm) At the Sky City Cultural Center, grab a bite here before or after you take a tour of the pueblo. Try the Pueblo Taco, served on fresh fry bread.

Billy the Kid's grave Last resting place of the famous outlaw

Billy the Kid Trail 20

Walk in the bootprints of Billy the Kid, the pawprints of Smokey Bear, and the ET-prints (just roll with the metaphor...) of the Roswell aliens.

TRIP HIGHLIGHTS

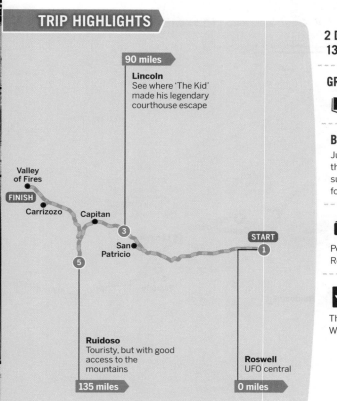

90 miles

Lincoln
See where 'The Kid' made his legendary courthouse escape

Valley of Fires

FINISH

Carrizozo   **Capitan**

San Patricio

START

Ruidoso
Touristy, but with good access to the mountains

135 miles

Roswell
UFO central

0 miles

2 DAYS
135 MILES / 217KM

GREAT FOR...

BEST TIME TO GO
July to October, for the UFO Festival, hot summer days and fall foliage.

ESSENTIAL PHOTO
Pose with aliens in Roswell.

 BEST FOR HISTORY
The legendary Wild West town, Lincoln.

211

Crisscross classic outlaw country in a section of New Mexico that's rife with mystery. Did aliens crash near Roswell? Did Pat Garrett kill Billy the Kid? And how did they get that bear into pants and a hat, anyway? Here, the Rio Hondo carves a sweet canyon through the foothills of the Capitan Mountains, Sierra Blanca Peak towers over the Tularosa Basin, and a lava field is open for exploration.

TRIP HIGHLIGHT

1 Roswell

Whether or not you're a true believer, a visit to Roswell is worthwhile to experience one of America's most enduring, eclectic and fanatical pop-culture phenomena. Sure it's about as cheesy as it gets for some, but conspiracy theorists and *X-Files* fanatics descend from other worlds into Roswell in real seriousness. Oddly famous as both

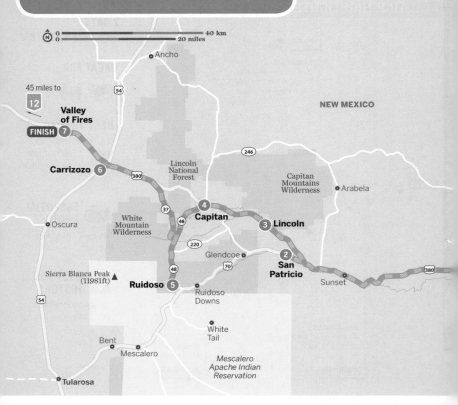

the country's largest producer of wool and its UFO capital, Roswell has built a tourist industry around the alleged July 1947 UFO crash, after which the military quickly closed the area and allowed no more information to filter out for several decades. Was it a flying saucer? The local convention and visitors bureau suggest that Roswell's special blend of climate and culture attracted touring space aliens who wanted a closer look. Decide for yourself at the **International UFO Museum & Research Center** (www. roswellufomuseum.com; 114 N Main St; adult/child $5/$2; ☺9am-5pm), where original photographs and witness statements form the 1947 Roswell Incident Timeline and explain the 'great cover-up.' The library claims to have the most comprehensive UFO-related materials in the world, and we have no reason to be skeptical.

✗ 🛏 p217

The Drive ≫ Take Hwy 70/380 W, across the plains and into the scenic Hondo Valley. At the fork where Hwys 70 and 380 split, go left onto Hwy 70 and travel about 4 miles.

② San Patricio

San Patricio, a tranquil country village along the Rio Ruidoso, boasts the kind of golden glow and gentle scenery that's been drawing artists to New Mexico for more than a century. Stop in at the **Hurd-La Rinconada Gallery** (☎800-658-6912; www.wyethartists.com; off Hwy 70; ☺9am-5pm Mon-Sat), set on a huge spread with an orchard and a polo field, to see (and buy) the work of classic New Mexican artist Peter Hurd and his son Michael, plus that of their relatives, the Wyeths. You can stay overnight here in one of five lovely casitas (from $140).

The Drive ≫ Backtrack to Hwy 380 and turn left at the fork, heading west.

TRIP HIGHLIGHT

③ Lincoln

More of a museum than a town, Lincoln is where the gun battle that turned Billy the Kid into a legend took place. Favoring authenticity over Hollywood stereotypes, Lincoln is about as close to 19th-century reality as it gets. Some say it's the best preserved Wild West town in America. Modern influences, such as souvenir stands, are

LINK YOUR TRIP

16 Las Cruces to Carlsbad Caverns

Connect Roswell and Carlsbad to see the caverns, White Sands, and more.

12 El Camino Real & Turquoise Trail

From Valley of Fires, continue west on Hwy 380 to hop on this historic route at Bosque del Apache National Wildlife Refuge.

(20)

(285)

p214

(70)

Pecos River

① Roswell
START

(285)

35 miles to

not allowed in town, and the main street has been designated the **Lincoln State Monument** (www.nmmonuments.org/lincoln; adult/child $5/free; ⏰8:30-am-4:30pm). It's a pretty cool place to get away from this century for an afternoon. Start at the **Anderson Freeman Visitor Center & Museum**, where exhibits on the Buffalo soldiers, Apaches and the Lincoln County War explain the town's history. Then stroll the main street to the **Tunstall Store** (with a remarkable display of late-19th-century merchandise), the **courthouse** where the Kid famously shot his way to freedom, and **Dr Wood's house**, an intact turn-of-the-century doctor's home and office.

 p217

The Drive » Continue west for 12 miles on Hwy 380.

- - - - - - - - - - - - - - -

4 Capitan

You've seen his likeness in state and national forests everywhere around the region. But did you know that Smokey Bear was also a real black bear? Once upon a time (back in 1950), a little cub was found clinging to a tree, paws charred from a 17,000-acre forest fire in the Capitan Mountains. What better name to give him than that of the famous cartoon bear

that had been the symbol of fire prevention since 1944? Nursed back to health, Smokey spent the rest of his days in the National Zoo in Washington, DC, and became a living mascot. At the 3-acre **Smokey Bear Historical State Park** (118 W Smokey Bear Blvd; adult/child $2/1; ⏰9am-5pm), in the village of Capitan, 12 miles west of Lincoln, you can see the bear's grave and learn tons about forest fires. Every Fourth of July, a **Smokey the Bear Stampede** features a parade, a rodeo, cookouts and other festivities. **Smokey Bear Days**, celebrated the first weekend in May, includes a street dance, wood-carving contest, and craft and antique-car shows.

The Drive » Head uphill on Hwy 48 S, which skirts the eastern edge of the million-acre Lincoln National Forest – this is the part of the drive that really

rocks in fall when the leaves put on a spectacular color show. The Sacramento Mountain range to the west of the highway adds to the scenic allure.

- - - - - - - - - - - - - - -

`TRIP HIGHLIGHT`

5 Ruidoso

You want lively in these parts? You want Ruidoso. Downright bustling in the summer and big with punters at the racetrack, resortlike Ruidoso has an utterly pleasant climate thanks to its lofty and forested perch near the Sierra Blanca (11,981ft). Neighboring Texans and local New Mexicans escaping the summer heat of Alamogordo and Roswell are happy campers here (or more precisely, happy cabiners). The lovely Rio Ruidoso, a small creek with good fishing, runs through town. Summer hiking and winter skiing at Ski Apache keep folks busy, as do a number of galleries.

DETOUR: BILLY'S GRAVE

Start: 1 Roswell

If you're driving this route as a pilgrimage to Billy, then you might want to make the 84-mile trek north from Roswell to **Fort Sumner**, where Sheriff Pat Garret shot and killed Billy the Kid on July 14, 1881 when the outlaw was just 21 years old. Billy's grave is behind the **Old Fort Sumner Museum** (Billy the Kid Rd; admission $5; ⏰10am-5pm). His tombstone is protected by an iron cage to keep 'souvenir hunters' from stealing it. Again.

International UFO Museum & Research Center

215

The **Hubbard Museum of the American West** (www.hubbardmuseum.org; 26301 Hwy 70; adult/child $6/2; ⊙10am-4:30pm; 🖐) displays more than 10,000 Western-related items including Old West stagecoaches and American Indian pottery, and works by Frederic Remington and Charles M Russell. An impressive array of horse-related displays, including a collection of saddles and the Racehorse Hall of Fame, lures horse-lovers.

Ruidoso Downs (www.raceruidoso.com; Hwy 70; grandstand seats free; ⊙Fri-Mon late May-early Sep) has weekend horse racing, including Labor Day's All American Futurity, the world's richest quarter-horse race, with a purse of $2.8 million. The Downs has recently been in the center of a horse-doping scandal, but track owners are promising a crackdown.

✕ 🛏 p217

The Drive » Take Hwy 48 N, then turn left onto Hwy 37 N. At Hwy 380, hang a left, then another left once you reach Hwy 54/Central Ave in Carrizozo.

- - - - - - - - - -

6 Carrizozo

Sitting where the Sacramento Mountains hit the Tularosa Basin, Carrizozo is worth a stop to peruse the art galleries and antiques shops that line historic 12th St, downtown's main axis. Take a look into **Gallery 408** (www.gallery408.com; 408 12th St; ⊙10am-5pm Mon, Fri & Sat, noon-5pm Sun). In addition to the work of a number of regional artists, you can see what remains of the herd of Painted Burros – a local public sculpture project similar to the Cow Parades of Chicago and New York, but on a slightly smaller scale. Some have pun-tastic names, like The Asstronomer, its body decorated with the night sky. Proceeds from donkey sales benefit the local animal shelter, Miracles Paws for Pets.

The Drive » Backtrack to Hwy 380 then head west a few miles to the sprawling slab of basalt. You can't miss it.

LOCAL KNOWLEDGE: BEST VISTAS

The best views for many miles are at the summit of Sierra Blanca Peak (11,981ft); to claim them, you'll have to leave the car and set out on foot for a day. Park in the smaller lot at Ski Apache, and set out on Trail 15. Follow signs west and south along Trails 25 and 78 to the top of Lookout Mountain (11,580ft). From there, an obvious beaten path continues due south for 1.25 miles up Sierra Blanca. On the way up you'll gain about 2000ft of elevation; the round-trip hike is just over 9 miles long. It's best done from June to October. The **ranger station** (☎575-257-4095; 901 Mechem Dr; ⊙7:30am-4:30pm Mon-Fri year-round, plus Sat in summer) in Ruidoso has more information.

- - - - - - - - - -

7 Valley of Fires

Four miles west of Carrizozo, explore the rocky blackness of a 125-sq-mile lava flow that's 160ft deep in the middle. A 0.6-mile nature trail at **Valley of Fires Recreation Area** (Hwy 380; vehicles $3, tent/RV sites $7/12) is well paved, easy for kids and marked with informative signs describing the geology of the volcanic remains. You're also allowed to hike off-trail, simply cutting cross-country over the flow as you like to create your own adventure. There are campsites and shaded picnic tables near the visitor center.

🛏 p217

Eating & Sleeping

Roswell ❶

✗ Cowboy Cafe
Diner $

(1120 E 2nd St; mains $4-10; ⏱6am-2pm Mon-Sat) One of the few truly local joints left in town, this friendly cowboy roost is the place to come for breakfast before hitting the UFO museum or the road.

🛏 Bottomless Lakes State Park
Campground $

(www.nmparks.com; Hwy 409; day-use per vehicle $5, tent/RV sites $10/14) This water-pocked park has a number of primitive camping areas; the Lea Lake campground has utilities including real bathrooms and showers, and the only lake you're allowed to swim in. To get here, drive 10 miles east of Roswell on Hwy 380, then 5 miles south on Hwy 409.

🛏 Sally Port Inn
Hotel $

(☎575-622-6430; www.bestwestern.com; 2000 N Main St; r from $89; P🛜❄) Yes, it's a Best Western, much like many other Best Westerns – which in Roswell, isn't a bad way to roll.

Lincoln ❸

✗ Laughing Sheep Farm and Ranch
American $$$

(☎575-653-4041; www.laughingsheepfarm. com; Hwy 380; mains $10-35; ⏱5-9pm Thu-Sat; 🚸) The friendly folks who run this working ranch raise cows, sheep, and bison – along with vegetables and fruits – then serve them up, farm-fresh, for dinner. There's usually live music and nightly specials, along with a play-dough table and easel for the kids. You can also stay here in a private modern cabin for $130.

🛏 Ellis Store Country Inn
B&B $$

(☎800-653-6460; www.ellisstore.com; Hwy 380; r incl breakfast $89-129) This historic,

160-or-so-year-old inn offers three antique-filled rooms (complete with wood stove) in the main house; five additional rooms are located in the adjoining Mill House. On weekends, the host – an award-winning chef – offers a six-course dinner ($75 per person), served in the lovely dining room – reservations required.

Ruidoso ❺

✗ Café Rio
Pizza $

(2547 Sudderth Dr; mains $8-25, cash only; ⏱11:30am-8pm, closed Wed off-season; 🍴🚸) The thick-crust pizza is deservedly popular here, but the stuffed calzones and Greek offerings are also decent for a small-town restaurant. Wash it down with a big selection of international and seasonal beer.

✗ Cornerstone Bakery
Breakfast $

(www.cornerstonebakerycafe.com; 359 Sudderth Dr; mains under $10; ⏱7am-2pm; 🍴) Stay around long enough and the Cornerstone may become your morning touchstone. Everything on the menu, from omelets to croissant sandwiches, is worthy. Locals are addicted.

🛏 Sitzmark Chalet
Hotel $

(☎800-658-9694; www.sitzmark-chalet.com; 627 Sudderth Dr; r from $60; ❄🛜) This ski-themed chalet offers 17 simple but nice rooms. Picnic tables, grills and an eight-person hot tub are welcome perks.

Valley of Fires ❼

🛏 Valley of Fires Campground
Campground $

(Hwy 380; tent/RV sites $7/18) Camp beside the lava flow, with easy access to hikes.

STRETCH YOUR LEGS
SANTA FE

Start/Finish: Santa Fe Plaza

Distance: 2.5 miles/4km

Duration: Two to four hours

The only way to see the best of Santa Fe is on foot, strolling through it's old adobe soul and into its renowned museums, churches, art galleries, and historic buildings.

Take this walk on Trips

New Mexico Museum of Art

At the plaza's northwest corner, the **Museum of Art** (www.nmartmuseum.org; 107 W Palace Ave; ⊘10am-5pm, closed Mon Sep-May) features collections of the Taos Society of Artists, Santa Fe Society of Artists and other legendary collectives – it's a who's who of the geniuses who put this dusty town on par with Paris and New York.

The Walk ›› Cross Lincoln Ave.

Palace of the Governors

Built in 1610, the **Palace of the Governors** (☏505-476-5100; www.palaceofthegovernors.org; 105 W Palace Ave; adult/child $9/free; ⊘10am-5pm, closed Mon Oct-May) is one of the oldest public buildings in the USA. It displays a handful of historic relics, but most of its holdings are now shown in an adjacent exhibition space called the **New Mexico History Museum** (113 Lincoln Ave), a glossy, 96,000-sq-ft expansion that opened in 2009.

The Walk ›› Browse the selection of Native American pottery and jewelry, talking to the artisans about their work. Then cross Palace Ave.

Shiprock

In a 2nd-floor loft at the northeast corner of the Plaza, **Shiprock** (www.shiprocktrading.com; 53 Old Santa Fe Trail, Plaza) has an extraordinary collection of Navajo rugs. Run by a fifth-generation Indian country trader, the vintage pieces are the real deal.

The Walk ›› Walk one block south, then turn left on E San Francisco St. If you're hungry, make a pit stop across the plaza at the casual Plaza Cafe.

St Francis Cathedral

Jean Baptiste Lamy was sent to Santa Fe by the pope with orders to tame the Wild Western outpost town through culture and religion. Convinced that the town needed a focal point for religious life, he began construction of **St Francis Cathedral** (www.cbsfa.org; 131 Cathedral Pl; ⊘8:30am-5pm) in 1869. Inside

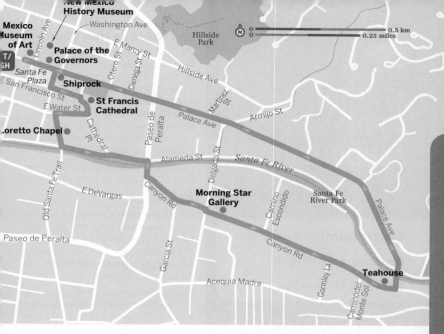

is a small chapel that houses the oldest Madonna statue in North America.

The Walk » Just south of the cathedral, turn right on Water St, to the corner with Old Santa Fe Trail.

Loretto Chapel

Modeled on Sainte Chapelle in Paris, **Loretto Chapel** (www.lorettochapel.com; 207 Old Santa Fe Trail; admission $3; ◷9am-5pm Mon-Sat, 10:30am-5pm Sun) was built between 1873 and 1878 for the Sisters of Loretto, the first nuns to come to New Mexico. Today it's a museum popular for **St Joseph's Miraculous Staircase** – which seems to defy the laws of physics by standing with no visible support.

The Walk » Walk south and turn left on E Alameda St. Turn right on Paseo de Peralta, then left onto Canyon Rd – the legendary heart of Santa Fe's gallery scene.

Morning Star Gallery

Of all the Canyon Rd shops dealing in Indian antiquities, **Morning Star** (www.morningstargallery.com; 513 Canyon Rd; ◷9am-5pm Mon-Sat) remains the best: weaving, jewelry, beadwork, *kachina* (Hopi spirit) dolls and even a few original ledger drawings are just some of the stars at this stunning gallery, which specializes in pre-WWII Plains Indian ephemera. Some artifacts here are finer than those in most museums and sell for hundreds of thousands of dollars.

The Walk » Meander on down Canyon Rd, stopping into whichever galleries catch your eye.

Teahouse

Prepare for a dilemma – at the **Teahouse** (www.teahousesantafe.com; 821 Canyon Rd; mains $8-17; ◷9am-7pm; 🛜), you'll be confronted with the list of 150 types of tea. There's coffee, too, and a great food menu, from baked polenta with poached eggs to wild mushroom porcini panini to grilled salmon salad. Oh, and freshly baked desserts. It's a perfect last stop on Canyon Rd.

The Walk » Turn left on Palace Ave and walk it back to the plaza.

STRETCH YOUR LEGS
ALBUQUERQUE

Start/Finish: Old Town Plaza

Distance: 1 mile/1.6km

Duration: Three hours

Albuquerque's Old Town Plaza is touristy for a reason: it's the one place in the city that's still got a historic ambiance, and it's easy to walk between its excellent museums and galleries (and cheesy souvenir shops, too).

Take this walk on Trips

San Felipe de Neri Church

The 1793 adobe **San Felipe de Neri Church** (www.sanfelipedeneri.org; Old Town Plaza; ⏰7am-5:30pm daily, museum 9:30am-4:30pm Mon-Sat) is Old Town's most famous photo op. Check out the pressed-tin ceiling inside. You can attend a Spanish-language mass at 8:30am on Sundays; weekday mass (in English) is at 7am, except Thursday.

The Walk » Stroll down the west side of the plaza to the southwestern corner with Romero St.

Romero St

Peruse the **galleries** that line both sides of the street, featuring arts and crafts by regional artists and southwestern Indian tribes. For creative ceramics, you can't beat **Romero St Gallery** (106 Romero St; ⏰10am-5pm).

The Walk » Head back to S Plaza St and turn right. You'll pass **Treasure House Books** (2102 S Plaza St NW; ⏰10am-6:30pm), with books on just about any subject related to New Mexico. Then turn right on San Felipe St.

American International Rattlesnake Museum

Probably the most interesting and unique museum in town, the **American International Rattlesnake Museum** (www.rattlesnakes.com; 202 San Felipe St NW; adult/child $5/3; ⏰10am-6pm Mon-Sat, 1-5pm Sun May-Sep, 11:30am-5:30pm Mon-Fri, 10am-6pm Sat, 1pm-5pm Sun Sep-May) hosts more species of rattlesnake than any other single place in the world. Looking at them up close, you may be surprised at how beautiful they are.

The Walk » Head north on San Felipe. Check out the work of the artisans under the portal opposite the plaza, then continue on and turn right into the alley at Old Town Antiques.

Our Lady of Guadalupe Chapel

Our Lady of Guadalupe Chapel (404 San Felipe NW) is small, and it's not historical, but it's worth going in anyway; the entries in the notebooks are moving

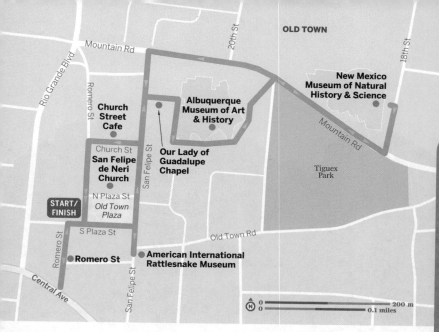

testimonies of faith in times of hardship. Some say a ghost or spirit resides here...

The Walk » Continue down the alley and turn right, circling around to the entrance of the Albuquerque Museum of Art & History.

Albuquerque Museum of Art & History

Conquistador armor and weaponry are highlights at the excellent **Albuquerque Museum of Art & History** (www.cabq.gov/museum; 2000 Mountain Rd NW; adult/child $4/1; ⏰9am-5pm Tue-Sun), where visitors can get a glimpse of the city's tricultural Native American, Hispanic and Anglo past. There's also an engaging gallery featuring the work of New Mexican artists. You can wander around the diverse array of sculptures outside.

The Walk » Walk across Mountain Rd.

New Mexico Natural History Museum

The **New Mexico Museum of Natural History & Science** (www.nmnaturalhistory. org; 1801 Mountain Rd NW; adult/child $7/4; ⏰9am-5pm; 👤) features an Evolator (evolution elevator), which transports visitors through 38 million years of New Mexico's geologic and evolutionary history. Best is the exhibit about the development of personal computing, focusing on the early days when Bill Gates operated out of Albuquerque – plus a room where you can play Pong projected on a big wall.

The Walk » Walk back across Mountain Rd and down San Felipe. Turn right on Church St.

Church Street Cafe

Grab a table at the **Church Street Cafe** (2111 Church St NW; mains $7-15; ⏰8am-4pm Sun-Wed, to 8pm Thu-Sat) and get your chile fix for the day. The food's the best around the plaza area, and the cafe is historic and huge, with a nice patio.

The Walk » The plaza is one block to the south.

Texas Trips

AS BIG AS TEXAS IS, the only way to truly appreciate it is to hit the road and find out what's out there in those wide, open spaces. The cities have tons to offer, but Texas does 'small town' like few other states, with friendly locals, historic buildings, quirky claims to fame, and an easygoing way of life everywhere you look.

So what's your pleasure? Fields of wildflowers and rolling hills in the land of Lady Bird Johnson? Beaches and seafood in towns along the Gulf? An epic journey from the Mexico border to the Texas panhandle? Or intriguing desert landscapes with surprising stops along the way, culminating in an enormous national park? Whatever route you choose, saddle up for adventure on a grand scale.

Big Bend National Park (Trip 22)
DENIS JR. TANGNEY/GETTY IMAGES ©

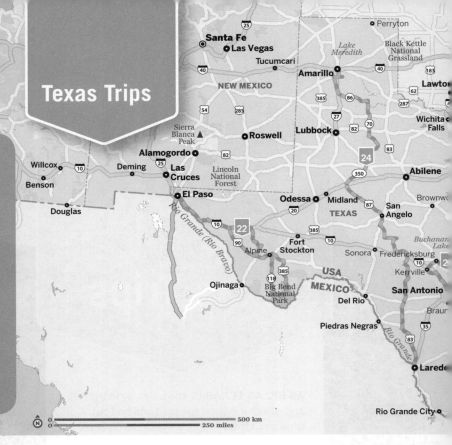

Texas Trips

DON'T MISS

Waring–Welfare Drive

When the wildflowers are in bloom, take this short but worthwhile detour on the way to Comfort, TX, in Trip 21

Marfa Prada

This roadside art installation is dramatically set against the backdrop of dusty West Texas; find it on Trip 22

Beer Drinking

Grab an ice-cold Shiner Bock and join the locals at Gruene Hall or on the Terlingua Porch in Trips 21 22

Goliad

Although not as well remembered as the Alamo, this fort has an equally important place in Texas history. See it in Trip 23

Miss Hattie's Bordello Museum

You can tell everyone you visited a notorious Texas brothel at this only slightly risqué stop on Trip 24

A porch in cowboy country

Wildflowers *Fields of bluebonnets show Texas' soft side*

Classic Trip

Hill Country

21

Take a drive through the countryside where gently rolling hills are blanketed with wildflowers, friendly folks enjoy an easy way of life, and there's plenty to do along the way.

TRIP HIGHLIGHTS

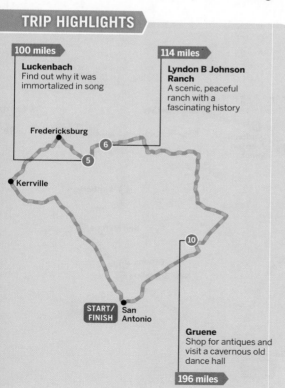

100 miles

Luckenbach
Find out why it was immortalized in song

114 miles

Lyndon B Johnson Ranch
A scenic, peaceful ranch with a fascinating history

Fredericksburg

Kerrville

START/FINISH San Antonio

Gruene
Shop for antiques and visit a cavernous old dance hall

196 miles

2–5 DAYS
229 MILES

GREAT FOR...

BEST TIME TO GO
In March and April for wildflower season.

 ESSENTIAL PHOTO

Bluebonnets – pose your kids or yourself in a field full of wildflowers.

 BEST FOR CULTURE

Two-stepping at Texas' oldest dance hall in Gruene.

Classic Trip

21 Hill Country

In March and early April when wildflowers are blooming, this is one of the prettiest drives in all of Texas — perfect for a day trip or a lazy, meandering vacation. Along this route, you can rummage through antique stores, listen to live music, dig in to a plate of barbecue, and learn about the president who called this area home.

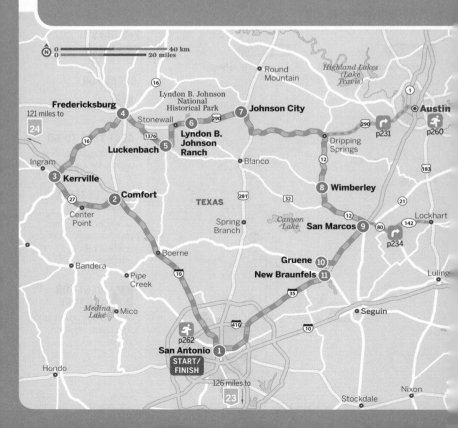

1 San Antonio

While sprawling San Antonio isn't part of the Hill Country, it's a great launching point for your trip. Don't miss the lovely, European-style River Walk, a paved canal that winds its way through downtown and is lined with colorful cafes, hotel gardens and stone footbridges. For the best overview, hop on a Rio San Antonio **river cruise** (📞800-417-4139; www.riosanantonio.com; adult/child under 5yr $8.25/2; 🕘9am-9pm), a 40-minute ride that loops through downtown, or take our walking tour, p262.

Pay your respects at the **Alamo** (📞210-225-1391; www.thealamo.org; 300 Alamo Plaza; 🕘9am-5:30pm Mon-Sat, from 10am Sun), where revolutionaries fought for Texas' independence from Mexico.

LINK YOUR TRIP

23 Texas Gulf Coast

From San Antonio, drive 143 miles south along Hwy 37 to reach the coastal town of Corpus Christi.

24 Heart of Texas

From Kerrville, travel 149 miles northwest to San Angelo.

The Drive ≫ Head northwest on I-10 to get to Comfort, less than an hour from downtown San Antonio. When the wildflowers are blooming, detour north on Waring-Welfare Rd then back on TX-27.

2 Comfort

Remarkably under the tourist radar, Comfort is a 19th-century German settlement and perhaps the most idyllic of the Hill Country bunch, with rough-hewn limestone homes from the late 1800s and a beautifully restored historic center in the area around High and 8th Sts.

Shopping for antiques is the number-one activity, but you'll also find a few good restaurants, a winery and, as the town's name suggests, an easy way of life. Start at the **Comfort Antique Mall** (📞830-995-4678; 734 High St; 🕘10am-5pm Sun-Fri, to 6pm Sat) where you can pick up a map of antique stores, or go to the **Comfort Chamber of Commerce** (www.comfort-texas.com) website for options.

🛏 p235

The Drive ≫ The interstate is a straight shot, but we prefer the back road of TX-27 west to Kerrville that takes you through serene farmland.

3 Kerrville

The Hill Country can feel a bit fussy at times, but not Kerrville. What it lacks in historic charm, it makes up for in size, offering plenty of services for travelers, as well as easy access to kayaking, canoeing and swimming on the Guadalupe River. The best place to hop in the water is **Kerrville-Schreiner Park** (2385 Bandera Hwy; day-use adult/child/senior $4/1/2; 🕘8am-10pm).

While you're in town, check out one of the world's best collections of cowboy art at the **Museum of Western Art** (📞830-896-2553; www.museumofwesternart.com; 1550 Bandera Hwy; adult/student/under 8yr $7/5/free; 🕘10am-4pm Tue-Sat). The building itself is beautiful, with hand-made mesquite parquet floors and unique vaulted domes overhead, and it's chock-full of paintings and sculptures depicting scenes from the Old West.

 p235

The Drive ≫ Take TX-16 northeast of town for half an hour to get to Fredericksburg.

4 Fredericksburg

The unofficial capital of the Hill Country, Fredericksburg is a 19th-century German settlement that specializes in 'quaint.' The town packs a lot of charm into a relatively small amount of space, with a boggling array of welcoming inns and B&Bs and a main street lined with historic buildings housing German restaurants, biergartens, antique stores and shops.

Many of the shops are typical tourist-town offerings, but there are enough interesting stores to make it fun to wander. Plus, the town is a great base for checking out the surrounding peach orchards and vineyards. Just a few miles east of town, **Wildseed Farms** (www.wildseedfarms.com; 100 Legacy Dr; ⏰9:30am-6:30pm) has cultivated fields of wildflowers and sells seed packets along with just about every wildflower-related gift you can imagine.

SCENIC DRIVE: WILDFLOWER TRAILS

You know spring has arrived in Texas when you see cars pulling up roadside and families climbing out to take the requisite picture of their kids surrounded by bluebonnets – Texas' state flower. From March to April in Hill Country, Indian paintbrushes, winecups and bluebonnets are at their peak.

Check the **Wildflower Hotline** (☎800-452-9292) to find out what's blooming where. Taking Rte 16 and FM 1323, north from Fredericksburg and east to Willow City, is usually a good route.

✗ 🛏 p235

The Drive » Five miles southeast of town on US 290, turn right on Ranch Rd 1376 and follow it 4.5 miles into Luckenbach. There are only a handful of buildings, so don't worry that the actual town is somewhere else.

TRIP HIGHLIGHT

5 Luckenbach

You won't find a more laid-back place than Luckenbach, where the main activity is sitting at a picnic table under an old oak tree with a cold bottle of Shiner Bock and listening to guitar pickers, who are often accompanied by roosters. Come prepared to relax, get to know some folks, and bask in the small-town atmosphere.

Start at the old trading post established back in 1849 – now the **Luckenbach General Store** (⏰10am-9pm Mon-Sat, noon-9pm Sun), which also serves as the local post office, saloon and community center. Out back you'll find the picking circle, and there's often live music on the weekends in the old dance hall; go online to check out the town's **music schedule** (www.luckenbachtexas.com).

The Drive » Take Luckenbach Rd back north to US 290. The LBJ Ranch is just 7 miles down and the entrance is right off the highway.

TRIP HIGHLIGHT

6 Lyndon B Johnson Ranch

You don't have to be a history buff to appreciate the family home of the 36th president of the United States. Now the **Lyndon Johnson National Historic Park** (www.nps.gov/lyjo; Hwy 290; park admission and driving tour free, house tour $3; ⏰9am-5:30pm, house tours 10am-4:30pm), this beautiful piece of Texas land is where Lyndon Johnson was born, lived and died.

The park includes the Johnson birthplace, the one-room schoolhouse where he briefly attended school and a neighboring farm that now serves as a living history museum. The centerpiece of the park is the ranch house where LBJ and Lady Bird lived and where he spent so much time during his presidency that it became known as the 'Texas White House.'

You can also see the airfield that he and other foreign dignitaries flew into, the private jet he used as president and the Johnson family cemetery, where LBJ and Lady Bird are both buried under sprawling oak trees.

Stop by the visitor center to get your free park permit, a map and a free CD audio tour.

The Drive ≫ LBJ's childhood home is just 15 minutes east on US 290.

❼ Johnson City

You might assume Johnson City was named after President Johnson, but the bragging rights go to James Polk Johnson, a town settler back in the late 1800s. The fact that James Johnson's grandson went on to become president of the United States was just pure luck.

Here you'll find **Lyndon Johnson's Boyhood Home** (100 E Ladybird Lane; ☺tours half hourly 9am-11:30 & 1-4:30pm), which Johnson himself had restored for personal posterity. Park rangers from the **Visitor Center** (Ladybird Ln & Ave G; ☺8:45am-5pm) – where you can also find local information and exhibits on the president

DETOUR: AUSTIN

Start: ❼ Johnson City

Since this trip is all about winding your way through the Hill Country, we didn't list Austin as a stop. After all, it warrants its own whole trip, which we hope your central Texas itinerary already includes.

However, we'd be remiss if we didn't mention that, when you get to Dripping Springs, you're only half an hour from the Texas state capital. If you go, check out the walking tour on p260.

and first lady – offer free guided tours every half hour that meet on the front porch. On the surface, it's just an old Texas house, but it's fascinating when you think about the boy who grew up here.

The Drive ≫ Follow US 290 south toward Blanco then east toward Dripping Springs. At Dripping Springs, turn right on Ranch Rd 12 towards Wimberley.

❽ Wimberley

A popular weekend spot for Austinites, this artists' community gets absolutely bonkers during summer weekends – especially on the first Saturday of each month from April to December, when local art galleries, shops and craftspeople set up booths for **Wimberley Market Days**, a bustling collection of live music, food and more than 400 vendors at Lion's Field on RR 2325.

For excellent scenic views of the surrounding limestone hills near Wimberley, take a drive on FM 32, also known as the Devil's Backbone. From Wimberley, head south on RR 12 to FM 32, then turn right toward Canyon Lake. The road gets steeper, then winds out onto a craggy ridge – the 'backbone' – with a 360-degree vista.

Afterwards, cool off at Wimberley's famous **Blue Hole** (☎512-847-9127; www.friendsofbluehole.org; 100 Blue Hole Lane, off CR 173; adult/child/under 4yr $8/4/ free; ☺10am-6pm Mon-Fri, to 8pm Sat, 11am-6pm Sun), one of the Hill Country's best swimming holes. It's a privately owned spot in the calm, shady and crystal-clear waters of Cypress Creek.

✕ p235

The Drive ≫ Keep going south on Ranch Rd 12; San Marcos is about 15 minutes southeast through some more (mostly) undeveloped countryside.

Classic Trip

WHY THIS IS A CLASSIC TRIP
MARIELLA KRAUSE, AUTHOR

Easily accessed from both San Antonio and Austin (my home town), the Hill Country is a popular getaway for both its natural beauty and easygoing nature. You can drive this entire loop in under five hours, but what's the rush? There are so many great little towns and interesting things to do, you'll be glad you decided to linger.

Above: Luckenbach General Store
Left: Lyndon Johnson National Historic Park
Right: Oak tree in Hill Country

NK8IMAGES/GETTY IMAGES ©

9 San Marcos

Around central Texas, 'San Marcos' is practically synonymous with 'outlet malls,' and bargain shoppers can make a full day of it at two side-by-side shopping meccas. It's not exactly in keeping with the spirit of the Hill Country, but it's a popular enough activity we had to point it out.

The fashion-oriented **San Marcos Premium Outlets** (📞512-396-2200; www.premiumoutlets.com; 3939 S IH-35, exit 200; 🕙10am-9pm Mon-Sat, to 7pm Sun) is enormous – and enormously popular – with 140 name-brand outlets. Across the street, **Tanger Outlets** (📞512-396-7446; www.tangeroutlet.com/sanmarcos; 4015 S IH-35; 🕙9am-9pm Mon-Sat, 10am-7pm Sun) has more modest offerings with brands that aren't that expensive to start with, but it's still fun to hunt.

The Drive >> Shoot 12 miles down I-35 to the turnoff for Canyon Lake. Gruene is just a couple miles off the highway.

TRIP HIGHLIGHT

10 Gruene

Get a true taste of Texas at **Gruene Hall** (www.gruenehall.com; 1280 Gruene Rd; 🕙11am-midnight Mon-Fri, 10am-1am Sat, 10am-9pm Sun), a dance hall where folks have been

233

congregating since 1878, making it Texas' oldest. It opens early, so you can stop by anytime to toss back a longneck, two-step on the well-worn wooden dance floor, or play horseshoes out in the yard. There's only a cover on weekend nights and when big acts are playing, so at least stroll through and soak up the vibe.

The town is loaded with antique stores and shops selling housewares, gifts and souvenirs, and **Old Gruene Market Days** are held the third weekend of the month, February through November.

✕ ⊨ p235

The Drive » You don't even have to get back on the interstate; New Braunfels is just 3 miles south.

⑪ **New Braunfels**

The historic town of New Braunfels was the first German settlement in Texas. In summer, visitors flock

DETOUR: LOCKHART

Start: ⑨ San Marcos

People travel from all over the state to dig into brisket, sausage and ribs in Lockhart, officially designated in 1999 as the Barbecue Capital of Texas. Lucky for you, you only have to detour 18 miles to experience the smoky goodness. You can eat very well for under $10 at:

Black's Barbecue (215 N Main St; sandwiches $4-6, brisket per pound $11; ⊙10am-8pm Sun-Thu, to 8:30pm Fri & Sat) A longtime Lockhart favorite since 1932, with sausage so good Lyndon Johnson had them cater a party at the nation's capital.

Kreuz Market (☎512-398-2361; 619 N Colorado St; brisket per pound $11.90, sides extra; ⊙10:30am-8pm Mon-Sat) Serving Lockhart since 1900, the barn-like Kreuz Market uses a dry rub, which means you shouldn't insult them by asking for barbecue sauce; they don't serve it, and the meat doesn't need it.

Smitty's Market (208 S Commerce St; lunch plates $6, brisket per pound $11.90; ⊙7am-6pm Mon-Fri, 7am-6:30pm Sat, 9am-3pm Sun) The blackened pit room and homely dining room are all original (knives used to be chained to the tables). Ask them to trim off the fat on the brisket if you're particular about that.

here to float down the Guadalupe River in an inner tube – a Texas summer tradition. There are lots of outfitters in town, like **Rockin' R River Rides** (☎830-629-9999; www.rockinr.com; 1405 Gruene Rd; tubes $17). Its rental prices include shuttle service, and for

an additional fee it can also hook you up with an ice chest and a tube to float your ice chest on.

✕ p235

The Drive » From New Braunfels it's 32 miles on the I-35 back to San Antonio.

Eating & Sleeping

Comfort ❷

🛏 Hotel Faust — B&B $$

(☎830-995-3030; www.hotelfaust.com; 717
High St; d $110-160, 2-bedroom cottage $175-195;
🛌✳) For some true historic charm, spend the
night in one of the beautifully restored rooms
in this late-1800s hotel. Better yet, stay in the
1820s log cabin that was moved to its present
location from Kentucky.

Kerrville ❸

🍴 Grape Juice — American $$

(☎830-792-9463; www.grapejuiceonline.
com; 623 Water St; mains $10-15; 🕚11am-11pm
Tue-Sat) Calling it a 'wine bar' would be ignoring
our favorite thing about this place: the purely
awesome macaroni and cheese made with
smoked gouda.

🛏 Inn of the Hills Resort & Conference Center — Motel $

(☎830-895-5000, 800-292-5690; www.
innofthehills.com; 1001 Junction Hwy; d $77-104;
🛌✳🛜🏊) The lovely renovated rooms that
open onto the pool are done in soothing earth
tones with boutique-hotel flair, but the best
feature of all is the beautiful Olympic-style pool
that's surrounded by shade trees.

Fredericksburg ❹

🍴 Pink Pig — American $$

(☎830-990-8800; www.pinkpigtexas.com;
6266 E US Hwy 290; lunch $9-12, dinner $18-28;
🕚11am-2:30pm Tue & Wed, 11am-2:30pm &
5:30-9pm Thu-Sat, from 10am Sun) Pick up
baked goods or a boxed lunch from the bakery
counter, or enjoy a meal inside the historic log
building. And save room for dessert: the Pink
Pig was opened by Rebecca Rather, AKA The
Pastry Queen.

🛏 Gastehaus Schmidt — Accommodation Services

(☎830-997-5612, 866-427-8374; www.
fbglodging.com; 231 W Main St) Nearly 300
B&Bs do business around here; this reservation
service helps sort them out.

Wimberley ❽

🍴 Leaning Pear — American $

(☎512-847-7327; www.leaningpear.com; 111
River Rd; mains $7-9; 🕚11am-3pm Sun, Mon,
Wed & Thu, to 8pm Fri & Sat) This cafe exudes
Hill Country charm like a cool glass of iced tea,
serving salads and sandwiches in a restored
stone house outside of downtown.

Gruene ❿

🍴 Gristmill Restaurant — American $$

(www.gristmillrestaurant.com; 1287 Gruene Rd;
mains $7-20; 🕚11am-9pm Sun-Thu, to 10pm
Fri & Sat) Located within the brick remnants
of a long-gone gristmill, the Gristmill has
character to spare. Indoor seating affords a
rustic ambiance, and outdoor tables get a view
of the river.

🛏 Gruene Mansion Inn — Inn $$$

(☎830-629-2641; www.gruenemansioninn.
com; 1275 Gruene Rd; d $195-250) Choose from
rooms in the mansion, former carriage house or
old barns. All are richly decorated in a style the
owners call 'rustic Victorian elegance,' featuring
lots of wood, floral prints and pressed-tin ceiling
tiles.

New Braunfels ⓫

🍴 Naegelin's Bakery — Bakery $

(☎830-625-5722; www.naegelins.com; 129 S
Seguin Ave; 🕚6:30am-5:30pm Mon-Fri, to 5pm
Sat) More than just a great place to pick up
German strudels and Czech *kolaches*, Naegelin's
is also the oldest bakery in Texas, opened in
1868.

McDonald Observatory *A celestial show in clear, dark skies*

Big Bend Scenic Loop

22

Although it's known for wide open spaces, west Texas is packed with surprising experiences that makes this a supremely well-rounded drive.

TRIP HIGHLIGHTS

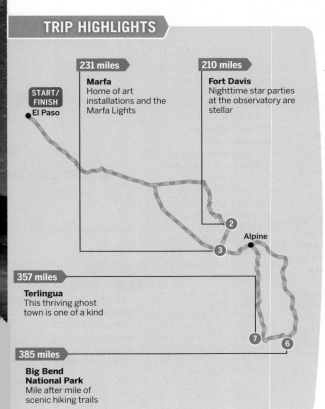

231 miles
Marfa
Home of art installations and the Marfa Lights

210 miles
Fort Davis
Nighttime star parties at the observatory are stellar

START/FINISH
El Paso

Alpine

2
3

357 miles
Terlingua
This thriving ghost town is one of a kind

7
6

385 miles
Big Bend National Park
Mile after mile of scenic hiking trails

5–7 DAYS
255 MILES / 410KM

GREAT FOR...

BEST TIME TO GO
Best between February and April – before the heat sets in.

 ### ESSENTIAL PHOTO
Prada Marfa, a quirky roadside art installation.

 ### BEST FOR OUTDOORS
McDonald Observatory's nighttime star parties.

237

22 Big Bend Scenic Loop

Getting to visit Big Bend National Park and experience the endless vistas straight out of an old Western are reason enough to make this trip. But you'll also get to have plenty of fun along the way, exploring the quirky small towns that are prime road trip material. West Texas offers an unforgettable set of experiences, including minimalist art installations, nighttime astronomy parties and thriving ghost towns.

❶ El Paso

Start your trip in El Paso, a border city that's wedged tightly into a remote corner of west Texas. Before you get out of town, take advantage of the great Mexican food you can find all over the city – it's right across the river from Mexico – and take time to enjoy some of El Paso's many free museums. Downtown, the **El Paso Museum of Art** (☎915-532-1707; www.elpasoartmuseum.org; 1 Arts Festival Plaza; special exhibits charge admission; ⏰9am-5pm Tue-Sat, to 9pm Thu, noon-5pm Sun) has a terrific Southwestern collection, and the

engaging modern pieces round out the display nicely.

Another one you shouldn't miss is the **El Paso Holocaust Museum** (www.elpasoholocaustmuseum.org; 715 N Oregon St; ⏰9am-4pm Tue-Fri, 1-5pm Sat & Sun). It may seem a little out of place in a predominately Hispanic town, but it hosts amazingly thoughtful and moving exhibits that are imaginatively presented for maximum impact.

The Drive » Head east on I-10 for two hours, then turn onto TX-118 towards Fort Davis. The area is part of both the Chihuahuan Desert and the Davis Mountains, giving it a unique setting where the endless horizons are suddenly interrupted by rock

formations springing from the earth.

TRIP HIGHLIGHT
❷ Fort Davis

Here's why you'll want to plan on being in Fort Davis on either a Tuesday, Friday or Saturday: to go to an evening star party at

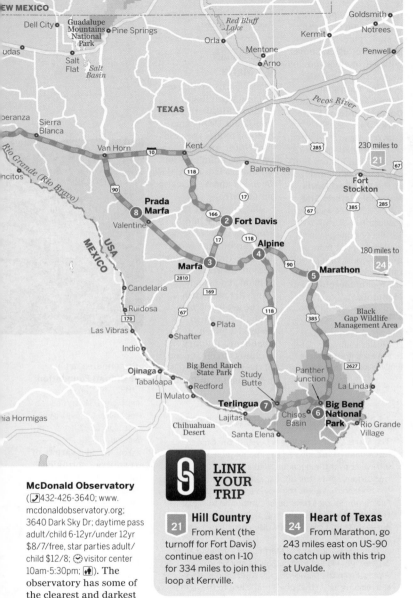

McDonald Observatory
(📞432-426-3640; www.
mcdonaldobservatory.org;
3640 Dark Sky Dr; daytime pass
adult/child 6-12yr/under 12yr
$8/7/free, star parties adult/
child $12/8; ⊙visitor center
10am-5:30pm; 🅿). The
observatory has some of
the clearest and darkest
skies in North America,
not to mention some
of the most powerful

🔗 LINK YOUR TRIP

21 **Hill Country**
From Kent (the
turnoff for Fort Davis)
continue east on I-10
for 334 miles to join this
loop at Kerrville.

24 **Heart of Texas**
From Marathon, go
243 miles east on US-90
to catch up with this trip
at Uvalde.

telescopes – a perfect combination for gazing at stars, planets and assorted celestial bodies with astronomers on hand to explain it all.

Other than that, nature lovers will enjoy **Davis Mountains State Park** (☏432-426-3337; http://www.tpwd.state.tx.us; Hwy 118; adult/child under 12yr $6/free), and history buffs can immerse themselves at the 1854 **Fort Davis National Historic Site** (☏432-426-3224; www.nps.gov/foda; Hwy 17; adult/child $3/free; ☺8am-5pm), a well-preserved frontier military post that's impressively situated at the foot of Sleeping Lion Mountain.

🛏 p243

The Drive » Marfa is just 20 minutes south on TX-17, a two-lane country road where tumbleweeds bounce slowly by and congregate around the barbed-wire fences.

TRIP HIGHLIGHT

3 Marfa

Marfa got its first taste of fame when Rock Hudson, Elizabeth Taylor and James Dean came to town to film the 1956 film *Giant*, and has served as a film location for movies like *There Will Be Blood* and *No Country for Old Men*.

But these days, this tiny town with one stoplight draws visitors from around the world for an entirely different reason: its art scene. Donald Judd single-handedly put Marfa on the art-world map in the 1980s when he used a bunch of abandoned military buildings to create one of the world's largest permanent installations

of minimalist art at the **Chinati Foundation** (☏432-729-4362; www.chinati.org; 1 Calvary Row; adult/student $25/10; ☺by guided tour only 10am & 2pm Wed-Sun).

You'll find a variety of art galleries sprinkled around town exploring everything from photography to sculpture to modern art. **Ballroom Marfa** (☏432-729-3600; www.ballroommarfa.org; 108 E San Antonio; ☺10am-6pm Wed-Sat, to 3pm Sun) is a great gallery to catch the vibe.

🍽 🛏 p243

MARFA LIGHTS VIEWING AREA

The Marfa Lights that flicker beneath the Chinati Mountains have captured the imagination of many a traveler over the decades, with accounts of mysterious lights that appear and disappear on the horizon that go all the way back to the 1800s. Numerous studies have been conducted to explain the phenomenon, but the only thing scientists all agree on is that they have no idea what causes the apparition.

Catch the show at the Marfa Lights Viewing Area, on the right side of the road between Marfa and Alpine. From the platform, look south and find the red blinking light (that one's real). Just to the right is where you will (or won't) see the Marfa Lights doing their ghostly thing.

WITOLD SKRYPCZAK/GETTY IMAGES ©

Terlingua Historic cemetery

The Drive » Alpine is about half an hour east of Marfa on Hwy 90/67.

- - - - - - - - - - - -

④ Alpine

The biggest little town in the area, Alpine is the county seat, a college town (Sul Ross University is here) and the best place to stock up on whatever you need before you head down into the Chihuahuan Desert.

Stop by the **Museum of the Big Bend** (☏432-837-8143; www.sulross.edu/museum; 400 N Harrison St; donations accepted; ⊙9am-5pm Tue-Sat, 1-5pm

Sun) to brush up on the history of the Big Bend region. But don't expect it to be dry and dusty. A renovation in 2006 added spiffy new exhibits, and reading is kept to a minimum. Most impressive? The enormous wing bone of the Texas pterosaur found in Big Bend – the largest flying creature ever found, with an estimated wing span of more than 50ft – along with the intimidatingly large re-creation of the whole bird that's big enough to snatch up a fully grown human and carry him off for dinner.

✕ ⊨ p243

The Drive » Keep heading east – half an hour later you'll reach the seriously tiny town of Marathon (pronounced mar-a-thun). The views aren't much during this stretch of the drive, but Big Bend will make up for all that.

- - - - - - - - - - - -

⑤ Marathon

This tiny railroad town has two claims to fame: it's the closest town to Big Bend's north entrance, providing a last chance to fill up your car and your stomach. And it's got the **Gage Hotel** (☏432-386-4205; www.gagehotel.com; 102 NW 1st

St/Hwy 90), a true Texas treasure that's worth a peek if not an overnight stay.

The Drive >> Heading south on US 385, it's 40 miles to the northern edge of Big Bend, and 40 more to get to the Chisos Basin, the heart of the park. The flat road affords miles and miles of views for most of the drive.

TRIP HIGHLIGHT

6 Big Bend National Park

Talk about big. At 1252 sq miles, this national park is almost as big as the state of Rhode Island. Some people duck in for an afternoon, hike a quick trail and head back out, but we recommend staying at least two nights to hit the highlights.

With over 200 miles of trails to explore, it's no wonder hiking is one of the most popular activities, with many of the best hikes leaving from the Chisos Basin. Hit the short, paved **Window View Trail** at sunset, then hike the 4.4-mile **Window Trail** the next morning before it gets too hot. Spend the afternoon hiking the shady 4.8-mile **Lost Mine Trail**, or take a scenic drive to see the eerily abandoned **Sam Nail Ranch** or the scenic **Santa Elena Canyon**.

Another great morning hike is the **Grapevine Hills Trail**, where a much-photographed formation of three acrobatic boulders form an inverted-triangle 'window.'

The visitor centers have tons of information and great maps. Pick up the *Hiker's Guide to Trails of Big Bend National Park* ($1.95 at park visitor centers) to learn about all your options.

🛏 p243

The Drive >> From the west park entrance, turn left after 3 miles then follow the signs for Terlingua Ghost Town, just past Terlingua proper. It's about a 45-minute drive from the middle of the park.

TRIP HIGHLIGHT

7 Terlingua

Quirky Terlingua is a unique combination: it's both a ghost town and a social hub. When the local cinnabar mines closed down in the 1940s, the town dried up and blew away like a tumbleweed, leaving buildings that fell into ruins.

But the area has slowly repopulated, businesses have been built on top of the ruins, and locals gather here for two daily rituals: in the late afternoon, everyone drinks beer on the porch of **Terlingua Trading Company** (☎432-371-2234; www.historic-terlingua.com;

100 Ivey Rd; ⊙10am-9pm). And after the sun goes down, the party moves next door to Starlight Theater (p243), where there's live music every night.

Come early enough to check out the fascinating **stone ruins** (from the road – they're private property) and the old **cemetery**, which you're welcome to explore.

✕ p243

The Drive >> Head north to Alpine, then cut west on US 90. It's a little over five hours back to El Paso, but there's one last stop on your way out that you can't miss.

8 Prada Marfa

So you're driving along a two-lane highway out in the middle of nowhere, when suddenly a small building appears in the distance like a mirage. You glance over and see...a Prada store? Known as the 'Prada Marfa' (although it's really closer to Valentine) this art installation set against the backdrop of dusty west Texas is a tongue-in cheek commentary on consumerism. You can't go in, but you're encouraged to window shop or snap a photo.

The Drive >> Take US 90 back to the I-10 and head west to El Paso.

Eating & Sleeping

Fort Davis ❷

🛏 Indian Lodge   Inn $$

(☏lodge 432-426-3254, reservations 512-389-8982; Hwy 118; d $95-125, ste $135-150; ❄🛜🐾) In Davis Mountains State Park, the surprisingly spacious and comfortable guest rooms in this historic, Spanish-style adobe lodge are a steal.

Marfa ❸

🍴 Cochineal   American $$$

(☏432-729-3300; 107 W San Antonio St; breakfast $4-10, small plates $5-15, dinner $24-28; ⏱9am-1pm Sat & Sun, 6-10pm Thu-Tue) This is where foodies get their fix, with a menu that changes regularly due to a focus on local, organic ingredients. Reservations recommended.

🍴 Future Shark   American $

(☏432-729-4278; www.foodsharkmarfa.com; 120 N Highland Ave; mains $7-13; ⏱11am-7pm Mon-Fri) Hooray! The Food Shark truck finally has a brick-and-mortar restaurant serving up similarly awesome fare as the popular truck, but cafeteria style.

🛏 El Cosmico   Campground $$

(☏432-729-1950; www.elcosmico.com; 802 S Highland Ave; tent camping per person $12, safari tents $65, teepees $80, trailers $110-180; 🛜) Sleep in an Airstream, a teepee or a safari tent at one of the funkiest choices in all of Texas. The cool lounge and hammock grove make particularly pleasant common areas.

Alpine ❹

🍴 Reata   Steakhouse $$

(☏432-837-9232; www.reata.net; 203 N 5th St; lunch $9-14, dinner $10-25; ⏱11:30am-2pm & 5-10pm Mon-Sat, 11:30am-2pm Sun) In the dining room, Reata turns on the upscale ranch-style charm. Step back into the lively bar or shady patio and it's a completely different vibe where you can nibble your way around the menu and enjoy a margarita.

🛏 Holland Hotel   Historic Hotel $$

(☏800-535-8040, 432-837-3844; www.thehollandhoteltexas.com; 209 W Holland Ave; d $99-120, ste $120-220; 😋❄🛜🐾) Built in 1928 and beautifully renovated in 2009, the Holland is a Spanish Colonial building furnished in an understated, hacienda-style decor that retains all of its 1930s charm.

Big Bend National Park ❻

🛏 Chisos Mountain Lodge & Dining Room   Lodge $$

(☏432-477-2291; http://chisosmountainslodge.com; lodge & motel r $123-127, cottages $150; ⏱restaurant 7-10am, 11am-4pm & 5-8pm) Decent accommodations and dining service within the park. You can do better outside Big Bend, but it's nice not to have to drive 45 minutes to rest up after your hike.

Terlingua ❼

🍴 Espresso...Y Poco Mas   Cafe $

(☏432-371-3044; 100 Milagro Rd; food $2.50-6.50; ⏱8am-2pm, to 1pm summer; 🛜) We love this friendly little walk-up counter at La Posada Milagro where you can find pastries, breakfast burritos, lunches and what might just be the best iced coffee in all of west Texas.

🍴 Starlight Theater   American $$

(☏432-371-2326; www.thestarlighttheatre.com; 631 Ivey St; mains $9-25; ⏱5pm-midnight) This former movie theater had fallen into roofless disrepair (thus the 'starlight' name) before being converted into a restaurant with nightly live music that makes it the center of Terlingua's nightlife.

Port Aransas *A mellow beach town overlooks the blue Gulf*

Texas Gulf Coast

23

Along more than 400 miles of coastline watch for endangered whooping cranes, explore miles of untouched stretches of sand and revel in great seafood and boozy fun.

TRIP HIGHLIGHTS

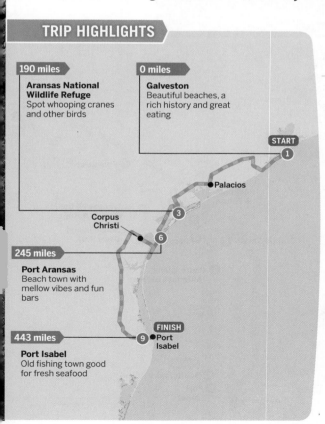

190 miles

Aransas National Wildlife Refuge
Spot whooping cranes and other birds

0 miles

Galveston
Beautiful beaches, a rich history and great eating

START
1

●Palacios

Corpus Christi
3

6
●

245 miles

Port Aransas
Beach town with mellow vibes and fun bars

FINISH
9 ●Port Isabel

443 miles

Port Isabel
Old fishing town good for fresh seafood

4 DAYS
443 MILES / 713KM

GREAT FOR...

BEST TIME TO GO
January to June and September to December, when it's not too hot.

 **ESSENTIAL PHOTO**
A whooping crane at Aransas National Wildlife Refuge.

 BEST FOR BEACHES
From Port Aransas to South Padre Island are miles and miles of white sand.

245

23 Texas Gulf Coast

The hard white sand forms a sharp contrast to the pure blue of the Gulf of Mexico. Follow this line right round the Texas coast south from the many diversions of Galveston to laid-back beach towns like Port Aransas and South Padre Island where you'll never quite get the sand out of your shorts — or want to. Natural and manmade surprises keep the ride interesting from start to finish.

TRIP HIGHLIGHT

❶ Galveston

Miles of sugary sand front the Galveston's Gulf Coast seawall. This island is part sunburned beach bum, part genteel Southern lady, with sizable Victorian districts that date to the city's heyday as a port of entry for immigrants heading west. Look into the history of the port and its storm-tossed times at the **Texas Seaport Museum** (www. galvestonhistory.org; cnr

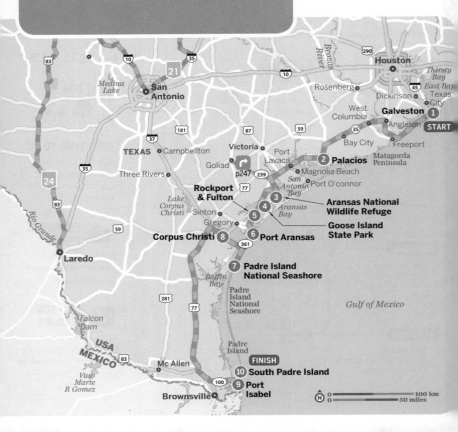

Harborside Dr & 21st St; adult/
child $8/5; ◷10am-4:30pm).

The historic **Strand**
commercial district
surrounding the
Mechanic and 22nd Sts
intersection shouldn't be
missed. Old-fashioned
brick-front buildings
are spiffily refurbished,
and there are boutiques,
ice-cream parlors and
general stores filled with
curiosities.

 p251

The Drive » Cross the San
Luis pass bridge to Follets
Island. At Surfside Beach, 13.5
miles southeast, go 30 miles
inland on TX 332 via Lake
Jackson to TX 35. Head south
through lush lands laced with
rivers for 45 miles.

❷ Palacios

At a pleasant bend in
TX 35, this somewhat
frayed small town
overlooks an inlet off
Matagorda Bay. It's a
town with, a realtor
would say, a lot of
potential, including

LINK YOUR TRIP

24 Heart of Texas
It's 224 miles west
of US 77 to Laredo.

21 Hill Country
Head north on I-37
from Corpus Christi to
link with this trip in San
Antonio.

DETOUR: HISTORIC GOLIAD

Start: ❷ Palacios

'Remember the Alamo!' is the verbal icon of the Texas
revolution, but it should also be 'Remember Goliad!'
where, on Palm Sunday, March 27, 1836, Mexican
general Antonio López de Santa Anna ordered 350
Texian prisoners shot. The death toll was double that
at the Alamo and helped inspire the Texians in their
victory over Santa Anna at San Jacinto the following
month.

There is a wealth of historic sites in and around
the lovely town of Goliad. Start at the 1749 church
and fort **Presidio la Bahia** (📞361-645-3752; www.
presidiolabahia.org; US 183; adult/child $4/1; ◷9am-4:45pm).
It's 36 miles each way from Tivoli.

that found at its small
waterfront. Stop into the
once-grand waterfront
Luther Hotel (📞361-
972-2312; www.facebook.
com/lutherhotel; 408 S Bay
Blvd) and check out the
memorabilia from a time
when it was an escape for
out-sized Texas pols like
Lyndon Johnson.

The Drive » Continue on
TX 35 for 50 miles through Port
Lavaca (avoiding any temptation
to detour to uninteresting Port
O'Connor) until just past tiny
Tivoli, where you turn southeast
on TX 239. Follow the signs for
18 miles through corn farms
until you reach Aransas National
Wildlife Refuge.

TRIP HIGHLIGHT

❸ Aransas National Wildlife Refuge

**Aransas National
Wildlife Refuge** (www.
fws.gov/refuge/aransas; FM
2040; per person/carload

$3/5; ◷6am-dusk, visitor
center 8:30am-4:30pm) is
a 115,000-acre wetland
park that protects the
wintering ground of
240 or so whoopers,
the most endangered
of the planet's cranes.
All 500 of the majestic
white birds living in
the wild or captivity
are descendents of the
15 that remained in
the 1940s. Standing
nearly 5ft tall, with a
7ft wingspan, whooping
cranes are an impressive
sight. Easy hiking
trails and observation
platforms let you spot
the birds from November
through March.

To get thrilling close-
up views from out on
the water, take a tour
with Captain Tommy's
**Rockport Birding &
Kayak Adventures**
(📞877-892-4737; www.
whoopingcranetours.com;

202 N Fulton Beach Rd, Fulton Habor; 3½hr tours $50; ◷7:30am & 1pm). His boats are custom made for whooper-spotting in the shallows outside the refuge. It's not uncommon to spot 60 bird species on a half-day excursion by boat or kayak.

The Drive » Take FM 774 through a series of turns 12 miles west to TX 35. Turn south and go 13.5 miles to Lamar and turn east.

4 Goose Island State Park

The main part of **Goose Island State Park** (☎361-729-2858; www.tpwd. state.tx.us; adult/child $5/ free; ◷8am-10pm), where admission is charged, is right on Aransas Bay (although there's no swimming). The busiest times at the park are during the summer and whooping crane season (November to March).

The oldest tree on the coast is an oak in excess of 1000 years near the main part of the park. The **'big tree'** (the trunk is more than 35ft in diameter) is in an idyllic spot amid a sea of wildflowers and surrounded by panels with poetry. It's near 12th St and outside of the gated park area.

The Drive » It's only 6 miles south on TX 35 to the fun twin coastal towns of Fulton and Rockport.

ROBBIE GEORGE/GETTY IMAGES ©

5 Rockport & Fulton

A pedestrian-friendly waterfront, numerous worthy attractions, fishing boats plying their trade and the cute little downtown of Rockport make the adjoining towns of Rockport and Fulton an enjoyable stop.

The side streets between TX 35 and Aransas Bay are dotted with numerous art galleries, especially in the center of Rockport; the towns claim to be home to the state's highest percentage of artists. Commune with crabs and other gulf critters at the small **Aquarium at Rockport Harbor** (☎361-727-0016; www. rockportaquarium.com; 702

Aransas National Wildlife Refuge Whooping crane and white-tailed deer

Navigation Circle; admission free; ⌚1-4pm Thu-Mon).

The Drive ›› Head 8 miles south on TX 35 to Aransas Pass, turn east on TX 361 for 6.5 miles until you reach the constantly running free ferries for the 10-minute ride to Port Aransas.

TRIP HIGHLIGHT

6 Port Aransas

Port Aransas (ah-ran-ziss), or Port A, on the northern tip of Mustang Island, is in many ways the most appealing beach town on the Texas coast. It is small enough that you can ride a bike or walk anywhere, but large enough that it has lots of activities and nightlife. The pace is very relaxed, and activities are dominated by hanging out on the beach, fishing and doing nothing. Stop by the **Tarpon Ice House** (☎361-749-2337; 321 N Allister St; ⌚around 4pm-late), a top local choice for drinking, carousing, mellowing out on the terrace or bursting into song. It's kind of the prototypical beach town bar.

✕ 🛏 p251

The Drive ›› Head south 31 miles on what starts as TX 361 to Padre Island National Seashore. It's all beaches along the way and places like Mustang Island State Park make good stops.

- - - - - - - - - -

❼ Padre Island National Seashore

If you're looking for more solitude, **Padre Island National Seashore** (www. nps.gov/pais; Park Rd 22; 7-day pass per car $10; ☺ visitor center 9am-5pm) fits the bill. Here the tidal flats, shifting dunes and shallow waters provide endless opportunities for hiking, swimming and windsurfing. Most of the 70 miles of this island refuge are accessible by 4WD only along the continuous beach. Hike a mile or two and you'll likely have the place to yourself.

The Drive ❯❯ Drive 15 miles back north to TX 358 and cross the John F Kennedy Causeway and after another 21 miles you are in the heart of downtown Corpus Christi.

- - - - - - - - - -

❽ Corpus Christi

In addition to a large marina and strollable waterfront with *miradores* (observation pavilions), the 'City By the Sea' has a small downtown strand and several good museums nearby. Anchored at bay, in front of beach-bum restaurants and t-shirt shops, is the **USS Lexington Museum** (www. usslexington.com; 2914 N Shoreline Blvd; adult/child $14/9; ☺9am-5pm, to 6pm

Jun-Aug). The 900ft naval carrier, the 'Blue Ghost,' is outfitted much as it would have been during its nearly 50 years at sea (it sailed from 1943 to 1991). Explore what's under the waves next door at the **Texas State Aquarium** (☎361-881-1200; www.texasstateaquarium.org; 2710 N Shoreline Blvd; adult/child $18/13; ☺9am-5pm, to 6pm summer; 👪). The jellyfish in the huge tank look ethereal and poetic.

✗ p251

The Drive ❯❯ Drive 15 miles west to US 77. Turn south and go 30 miles south to Kingsville. Here you can tour the world's largest ranch, King Ranch. Otherwise, continue on US 77 for another 102 miles through dry brushland to TX 100, turn east and drive 24 miles to the coast.

- - - - - - - - - -

TRIP HIGHLIGHT

❾ Port Isabel

Built in 1852, the atmospheric **lighthouse** (☎956-943-7602; www. portisabelmuseums.com; TX 100 & Tarnava St; adult/child $3/1; ☺9am-5pm) sets the small-town vibe in Port Isabel. It has the best restaurants in the area and is a delightful place for a waterfront stroll. Fantasize about sunken booty at the **Treasures of the Gulf Museum** (☎956-943-7602; www. portisabelmuseums.com; 317 Railroad Ave; adult/child $3/1; ☺10am-4pm Tue-Sat).

✗ p251

The Drive ❯❯ A mere 5-mile jaunt over the Queen Isabella Causeway and you're on South Padre Island.

- - - - - - - - - -

❿ South Padre Island

The town of South Padre Island (SPI) works hard to exploit its sunny climate and beaches. For most of the year utterly mellow bars on the beach and waterfront let you lounge away the day. But for a couple weeks in March SPI becomes a frenetic madhouse during spring break.

Wave-runner rental and parasailing opportunities abound and there are bird-watching trails. You can learn about the slowest moving coastal denizens at **Sea Turtle Inc** (www. seaturtleinc.com; 6617 Padre Blvd; suggested donation adult/child $3/2; ☺10am-4pm Tue-Sun), a rescue facility that offers tours and feeding presentations every half hour. For a drink, try **Boomerang Billy's Beach Bar & Grill** (☎956-761-2420; www. boomerangbillysbeachbar.com; 2612 Gulf Blvd; ☺11am-late), one of the few bars right on the sand on the gulf side. Mellow sounds a bit too energetic for this ultimate crash pad. And as you go north up the 34-mile-long island, the beach becomes ever more quiet and remote.

🛏 p251

Eating & Sleeping

Galveston ❶

✕ Farley Girls American $$
(www.farleygirls.com; 901 Post Office St; dishes $9-13; 🕐10:30am-3:30pm Mon-Fri, from 8:30am Sat & Sun) The historic building, with fern-studded colonnade and high wood ceilings, may be elegant, but the tasty comfort food and counter service are down-home casual.

🛏 Harbor House Boutique Hotel $$
(☎409-763-3321; www.harborhousepier21. com; Pier 21, off Harborside Dr; r incl breakfast $90-270; ❄️🛜🚲) Stay among the shops and museums in the heart of the historic Strand District. Rustic touches accent the 42 large, comfy rooms occupying a re-created, wharfside warehouse.

Port Aransas ❻

✕ The Gaff Bar $
(☎361-749-5970; 323 Beach St; mains from $8; 🕐11am-late) Out by the beach, this shacky bar is perfect for one aspiring to arrested development. Fun includes belt sander races and chicken poop bingo (come on bird, come on!). There's decent pizza and subs plus live music that includes blues and country. Most days are 'talk like a pirate day' here.

🛏 Tarpon Inn Historic Hotel $$
(☎361-749-5555, 800-365-6784; www. thetarponinn.com; 200 E Cotter Ave; r $90-220; ❄️🛜) Dating from 1900, this charming, rickety place has been rebuilt several times after hurricanes, most extensively after the 1919 big blow. The lobby has more than 7000 of the huge silver scales that come from tarpon, the 6ft-long namesake fish. Most of the 24 rooms are small but have lots of character and rocking chairs on the verandah.

Corpus Christi ❽

✕ Blackbeard's Tex-Mex $
(☎361-884-1030; 3117 Surfside Blvd; meals from $8; 🕐11am-10pm Sun-Thu, to 11pm Fri & Sat) Near North Beach plus the aquarium and the Lexington, this rollicking place serves up tasty Mexican and American cuisine. Wash it down with cheap margaritas while sitting back for the live music.

Port Isabel ❾

✕ Joe's Oyster Bar Restaurant Seafood $$
(☎956-943-4501; 207 Maxan St; mains from $8; 🕐11am-7pm) Delight in seafood direct off the boats at this simple joint. It makes a mean crab cake and the oysters are renowned.

South Padre Island ❿

🛏 Palms Resort Motel $$
(☎800-466-1316, 956-761-1316; www. palmsresortcafe.com; 3616 Gulf Blvd; r $70-200; 🛜🚲) This tidy two-story motel looks right over the grass-covered dune to the gulf. Units are large and have fridges and microwaves. The beachfront cafe-bar is fun.

Palo Duro Canyon *Walls of color among the plains*

Heart of Texas

24

From the Mexican border to the panhandle city of Laredo you'll cross the the rural length and breadth of a timeless Texas.

TRIP HIGHLIGHTS

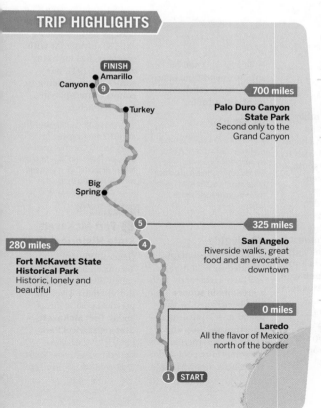

FINISH
Amarillo
Canyon ● ⑨

● Turkey

700 miles

Palo Duro Canyon State Park
Second only to the Grand Canyon

Big Spring ●

⑤ **325 miles**

④

San Angelo
Riverside walks, great food and an evocative downtown

280 miles

Fort McKavett State Historical Park
Historic, lonely and beautiful

0 miles

Laredo
All the flavor of Mexico north of the border

① **START**

4 DAYS
754 MILES /
1213KM

GREAT FOR...

BEST TIME TO GO

March–June and September–November to avoid scorching heat but enjoy wildflowers.

 ESSENTIAL PHOTO

Palo Duro Canyon glowing in a rainbow of colors.

☑ **BEST FOR WIDE OPEN SPACES**

The view-filling horizon of the plains.

253

24 Heart of Texas

The big city sprawls of Houston, Dallas or San Antonio seem very far away as you pass through hundreds of miles of open lands barely touched by humans. By the time you reach Fort McKavett you may even wonder what century you're in as this old outpost still seems to guard a wild and untamed frontier. At Palo Duro Canyon you'll travel back countless millenia.

TRIP HIGHLIGHT

❶ Laredo

Even more than other Texas border towns, Laredo has always been tightly entwined with its sister city to the south, the fittingly named Nuevo Laredo.

While the border situation remains unsettled, Laredo's historic old downtown is evocative. Start at leafy **San Agustín Plaza** and stop into the **Republic of the Rio Grande Museum** (☏956-727-3480; www.webbheritage.org; 1005 Zaragoza St; admission $2; ⏱9am-4pm Tue-Sat) and grand **San Agustín Church** (San Agustín Plaza;

⏱hours vary). Then be sure to spend time at any of the many excellent local restaurants.

🍴 🛏 p259

The Drive » Drive 112 miles north on US 83. The first 60 are through minimalist arid south Texas country, then it becomes more fecund as the road begins following rivers and fertile valleys.

❷ Uvalde

A pioneer town that was founded in 1853, Uvalde is a busy crossroads with a great **main square** that is crowned by the grand neoclassical 1928 **courthouse**. Stop and stroll the square, pausing for something cool and refreshing along Main St.

The Drive » Continue 40 miles north on US 83 through country that rivals the Hill Country in its oak-tree-dotted beauty.

❸ Leakey

Since prehistoric times, humans have been enjoying the beauty of the Frio River and its lovely canyon and valley. Tiny Leakey is little more than a crossroads, but what a crossroads! US 83 follows the river north and south, while FM 337 runs east and west through wooded hills and secluded little valleys.

Just 10 miles south of town, **Garner State Park** (www.garnerstatepark.com; off US 83) is popular with campers, has kayaking and, since 1941, has summertime dancing to country tunes playing from a jukebox.

The Drive » Go 57 miles north on US 83, then jog west for 18 miles on I-10. Continue north 25 miles on Ranch Rd 1674 through hilly uninhabited land textured with shrubs and trees.

TRIP HIGHLIGHT

❹ Fort McKavett State Historical Park

General William Tecumseh Sherman once called this fort along the San Saba River 'the prettiest post in Texas.' Today, **Fort McKavett State Historical Park** (☏325-396-2358; www.visitfortmckavett.com; FM 864; adult/child $4/3; ⏱8am-5pm)

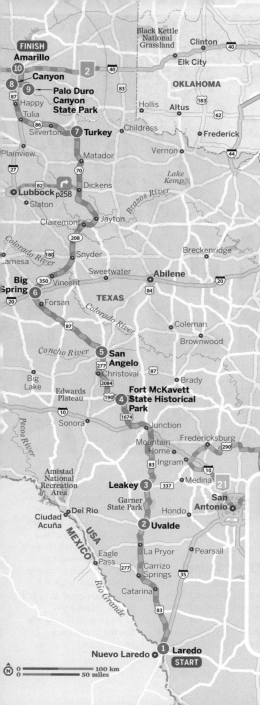

preserves the striking ruins of a once-important fort. It is a beautiful, evocative and remote spot.

Some of the 25 buildings have been restored; the grounds are alive with wildflowers for much of the year. Check out the boiled turnips recipe in the excellent museum.

The Drive » Jog east on FM 864, then head west 17 miles on US 190. Turn north on the wonderfully named Toe Nail Trail/Ranch Rd 2084 (it got its name from the toll it took on the feet of the first soldiers to march the route) and drive 27.5 miles north to US 277, where San Angelo is another 19 miles north.

- - - - - - - - - - - - - - - -

TRIP HIGHLIGHT

❺ San Angelo

Situated on the fringes of the Hill Country, San Angelo is the kind of place where nonposer men in suits ride motorcycles, while women in pickups look like they could wrestle a bull and then hit the

LINK YOUR TRIP

2 **Route 66**
The Mother Road passes right through Amarillo.

21 **Hill Country**
Out of Junction, head southwest on the I-10 to link to Kerrville, 54 miles away.

255

catwalk. The Concho River, which scenically runs through the town, offers **walks** along its wild, lush banks.

Fort Concho National Historic Landmark (☎325-481-2646; www. fortconcho.com; 630 S Oakes St; adult/child $3/1.50; ☻9am-5pm Mon-Sat, 1-5pm Sun) may be the best-preserved Western frontier fort in the US. Designed to protect settlers and people moving west on the overland trails, the fort went up in 1867 on the fringes of the Texas frontier.

At the heart of not-to-be-missed downtown, the **Concho Avenue Historic District** is a good place to stroll – be sure to pick up a historic walking tour brochure at the **Visitors Center** (☎325-655-4136, 800-375-1206; www.visitsanangelo. org; 418 W Ave B; ☻9am-5pm Mon-Sat, noon-4pm Sun). The most interesting section, known as Historic Block One, is between Chadbourne and Oakes Sts. Stop into **Miss Hattie's Bordello Museum** (☎325-653-0112; 18 E Concho Ave; admission free, tours $5; ☻10am-4pm Tue-Sat, tours 1-4pm Thu-Sat) which recalls the town's wilder days.

At night you can find great food, beer and music.

✕ ⊨ p259

JEREMY WOODHOUSE/GETTY IMAGES ©

The Drive ≫ Follow the green ribbon of the North Concho River 87 miles northwest on US 87 through lands on the edge of oil country.

- - - - - - - - - - - - -

➏ Big Spring

West of Big Spring, the land is flat and brown for 40 miles to the Permian Basin, where the cities of Midland and Odessa are at the heart of the energy boom. But here, it's quiet and time moves slow. Everywhere that is except at the 15-story Hotel Settles (p259), a long-closed 1930s luxury hotel (the product of an oil boom) that reopened in 2013 after a local boy who made good gave it a lavish restoration.

Nearby, 380-acre **Big Spring State Park** (☎432-263-4931; www.tpwd.state.

Bona fide cowboy boots

tx.us; 1 Scenic Dr; admission free; ☺ dawn to dusk) has a fine nature trail. There are few west Texas dance halls more authentic than the **Stampede** (📞432-267-2060; 1610 E TX 350), a barebones, early 1950s affair 1.5 miles northeast of Big Spring. The schedules, however, are sporadic.

🛏 p259

The Drive » Drive 190 miles north through some of the most lonesome terrain in Texas via TX 350, TX 208 and finally TX 70. The latter is a scenic gem, running through towns otherwise bypassed by time. Be sure to keep the tank filled as even some county seats don't have gas stations anymore.

- - - - - - - - - - - -

❼ Turkey

Like the flight path of its namesake bird, minute Turkey has been descending for decades.

Bob Wills is one of Texas's most important musicians, and his life is recalled at the modest but worthwhile **Bob Wills Museum** (📞806-423-1146; www.turkeytexas. net; admission free; ☺9am-11:30am & 1-4:30pm Mon-Fri, 9am-noon Sat).

The Drive » It's 54 miles of flat Texas two-lane driving

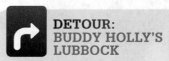

DETOUR: BUDDY HOLLY'S LUBBOCK

Start: ❻ Big Spring

The hub for the Western music that is emblematic of the Texas plains, Lubbock is the hometown of one of the genre's greatest legends: Buddy Holly. The town celebrates his legacy at the unmissable **Buddy Holly Center** (☎806-767-2686; www.buddyhollycenter.org; 1801 Crickets Ave; adult/child $5/2; ⏱10am-5pm Tue-Sat, from 1pm Sun). It's possible to still find the rockabilly sound that Holly made famous in the surrounding **Depot District** at venues like the legendary **Cactus Theater** (☎806-747-7047; www.cactustheater.com; 1812 Buddy Holly Ave). Be sure to listen to KDAV AM 1590, which stills plays the music of Holly's era.

See how people lived on the plains over the last 200 years at the excellent **National Ranching Heritage Center** (☎806-742-0498; www.nrhc.ttu.edu; 3121 4th St; ⏱10am-5pm Mon-Sat, 1-5pm Sun) with dozens of restored old structures in a park-like setting.

From TX 70, Lubbuck is 58 miles west on US 82.

west on TX 86. Then turn north, following the train tracks 32 miles north on US 87.

- - - - - - - - - - - - - - -

❽ Canyon

Georgia O'Keeffe once taught art at the West Texas A&M University in small yet cultured Canyon. Today's campus is home to what many people figure is the best history museum in Texas – the **Panhandle-Plains Historical Museum** (☎806-651-2244; www.panhandleplains.org; 2401 4th Ave; adult/child $10/5; ⏱9am-6pm Mon-Sat Jun-Aug, to 5pm Sep-May), where the many highlights include the myriad ways to skin a buffalo.

The Drive ❯❯ The geologic wonders of Palo Duro Canyon are a straight 15 miles east on TX 217.

- - - - - - - - - - - - - - -

TRIP HIGHLIGHT

❾ Palo Duro Canyon State Park

At 120 miles long and about 5 miles wide, Palo Duro Canyon is second in size in the USA only to the Grand Canyon. The cliffs striated in yellows, reds and oranges, rock towers and other geologic oddities are a refreshing surprise amongst the seemingly endless flatness of the plains, and are worth at least a gander.

Prehistoric Indians lived in the canyon 12,000 years ago. The more than 26,000 acres that make up the **park** (☎806-488-2227; www.tpwd.state.tx.us; 11450 Park Road 5; adult/child $5/free; ⏱main gate 6am-8pm Mon-Thu, to 10pm Fri & Sat, shorter hours winter) attract hikers, horseback riders and mountain bikers.

The Drive ❯❯ Retrace your drive 7 miles west on TX 217 and turn due north for 15 miles on FM1541 N/S Washington St.

- - - - - - - - - - - - - - -

❿ Amarillo

Although Amarillo may seem as featureless as the surrounding landscape, there's plenty here to sate even the most attention-challenged. Beef, the big local industry, is at the heart of Amarillo and it features in many of its attractions, including the moo-filled **Amarillo Livestock Auction** (☎806-373-7464; www.amarillolivestockauction.com; 100 S Manhattan St; ⏱10am Mon).

Don't miss the **San Jacinto District**, the strip between Georgia St and Western St was once part of Route 66 and is Amarillo's best shopping, dining and entertainment district.

✕ ⫴ p259

Eating & Sleeping

Laredo ❶

✕ El Meson De San Augustin   Mexican $

(www.elmesondesanagustin.com; 908 Grant
St; mains from $6; ⏱11am-4:30pm Mon-Sat)
Superb food issues forth at this tiny little, uber-
non-descript family-run restaurant. Seemingly
humdrum fare like enchiladas and chips and
salsa reach heights few thought possible.

✕ Palenque Grill   Mexican $$

(📞956-728-1272; www.palenquegrill.com; 7220
Bob Bullock Loop; mains $10-18; ⏱11am-11pm)
The upscale menu is ambitious and features
regional cuisine from around Mexico.

🛏 La Posada Hotel & Suites   Historic Hotel $$

(📞956-722-1701; www.laposada.com; 1000
Zaragoza St, San Agustín Plaza; r $110-200;
❄ @ 🛜 ✖ 🐾) This hacienda-style hotel
occupies a downtown complex of buildings
dating from 1916. The stylish rooms surround
two large pools and gardens.

San Angelo ❺

✕ Peasant Village Restaurant   Deli/Bistro $$

(📞325-655-4811; 23 S Park St; lunch mains
from $8, dinner mains $17-27; ⏱11am-1:30pm
Mon, 11am-1:30pm & 5-9pm Tue-Fri, 5-9pm
Sat) Located in a beautiful 1920s house near
downtown, creative mains of steak and seafood
plus seasonal specials highlight the menu. Enjoy
the best deli sandwiches, salads and desserts in
town at lunch.

🛏 Sealy Flats Blues Inn   Inn $$

(📞325-653-0437; www.sealyflats.com; 204 S
Oakes St; r $120-200; ❄🛜) Part of the excellent
downtown blues club and diner, this inn is
housed in a much-restored historic hotel. At the
popular bar, well-known blues musicians jam on
weekends. The back terrace is where it's at.

Big Spring ❻

🛏 Hotel Settles   Historic Hotel $$$

(📞432-267-7500; www.hotelsettles.com; 200 E
Third St; r $150-300; ❄🛜✖) While the public
areas have been restored to period glory, the
suites and smaller guest rooms are modern
and lavish. There's a top-end restaurant and a
sumptuous bar.

Amarillo ❿

✕ Big Texan Steak Ranch   Steakhouse $$

(www.bigtexan.com; 7701 I-40 E, exit 74; mains
$10-40; ⏱7am-10:30pm; 🚗) The legendary
come-on here: the 'free 72oz steak,' a devilish
offer as you either eat an insane amount of
food in an hour or you pay for the meal ($72).
Gimmicks aside, the steaks are excellent as is
the beer garden with 11 superb house-brewed
beers.

✕ Cowboy Gelato   American $

(📞806-376-5286; 2806 SW 6th Ave; treats from
$2; ⏱11am-8pm Mon-Sat) Escape the heat in
this cute little cafe which makes its own creamy
gelati.

✕ Golden Light Cafe & Cantina   Burgers $

(📞806-374-0097; 2908 SW 6th Ave; mains
$4-8; ⏱cafe 11am-10pm, bar 4pm-2am) Classic
cheeseburgers, home-cut fries and cold beer
have been sold at this modest brick dive since
1946. On most nights there's live country and
rock music next door.

🛏 Ambassador Hotel   Hotel $$

(📞800-817-0521, 806-358-6161; www.
ambassadoramarillo.com; 3100 I-40 W, near exit
68; r $100-160; ❄ @ 🛜 ✖ 🐾) The 263 rooms
over 10 stories have numerous plush touches.

STRETCH YOUR LEGS
AUSTIN

Start/Finish: Texas State Capitol

Distance: 4.1 miles/6.6km

Duration: Four to five hours

Get to the heart of this immensely popular city on this downtown walking tour. You'll get a peek at many of the things that have indelibly shaped Austin's character — everything from Texas politics to campus life to Mexican free-tailed bats.

Take this walk on Trip

Texas State Capitol

Built in 1888 from sunset-red granite, the Texas State Capitol is the largest in the US. Pick up a brochure outlining a self-guided tour of the capitol building and grounds inside the tour-guide office on the ground floor. If nothing else, take a peek at the lovely **rotunda** and try out the **whispering gallery** created by its curved ceiling.

The Walk >> Head up Congress Ave towards the University; it's just a few short blocks.

Bob Bullock Texas State History Museum

Big, glitzy and still relatively new, the **Bullock** (512-936-8746; www.thestoryoftexas.com; 1800 Congress Ave; adult/child 4-17yr $9/6, Texas Spirit film $5/4; 9am-6pm Mon-Sat, noon-6pm Sun) shows off the Lone Star State's history, from when it used to be part of Mexico up to the present, with high-tech interactive exhibits and fun theatrics. The museum's most famous resident is the grotesquely proportioned **Goddess of Liberty** that stood atop the capitol for nearly 100 years. Allow at least an hour or two if you stop in.

The Walk >> Go west one block up MLK Blvd, then turn right on University Ave and walk the two blocks to 21st St, where you'll find a postcard-perfect view of the University of Texas.

University of Texas

You could wander UT all day and still not see all of it, but this is probably the prettiest spot on campus and definitely the most iconic. **Littlefield Fountain** features a dramatic, European-style sculpture, and behind it stretches the gently sloping South Mall, a grassy lawn flanked by 80-year-old oak trees. Topping it off is the Main Building, whose tower is one of the most recognizable symbols of UT and Austin.

The Walk >> Stroll up the South Mall to the Main Building, then turn left and cross the West Mall to get to Guadalupe St.

The Drag

Running along the west side of campus, Guadalupe St – aka 'The Drag' – is a bustling corridor lined with restaurants and shops. Join the pedestrians streaming up and down the west side of the street and grab a snack at one of the cheap eateries located along this stretch. Stock up on Longhorn souvenirs at the **University Co-op** (📞512-476-7211; 2246 Guadalupe St; 🕐8:30am-7:30pm Mon-Fri, 9:30am-6pm Sat, 11am-5pm Sun), selling a huge quantity of objects in burnt orange and white.

The Walk ›› Walk down Guadalupe St to MLK, then jog over one block to Lavaca. At the corner of 11th and Lavaca Sts, notice the Texas Governor's Mansion (and try not to get jumped by Secret Service). Continue south and turn right on 7th St.

Bremond Block

Part of the National Register of Historic Places, the Bremond Block preserves a concentration of elegant Victorian mansions with sprawling lawns and mature live oak trees. On the corner of Guadalupe, the 1886 **John Bremond House** is the most impressive example. Take the right fork of 7th St and circle the block clockwise to see them all.

The Walk ›› Walk east to Congress Ave and head south to the Colorado River.

Congress Ave Bridge

If you can time your last stop right – dusk, between late March and early November – you'll see the world's largest urban bat colony making their nightly exodus from under the bridge.

The Walk ›› Stroll back up Congress Ave (which is well lit, well populated and completely safe at night) to return to the starting point. Sixth St east of Congress is lined with bars, making it party central come nightfall.

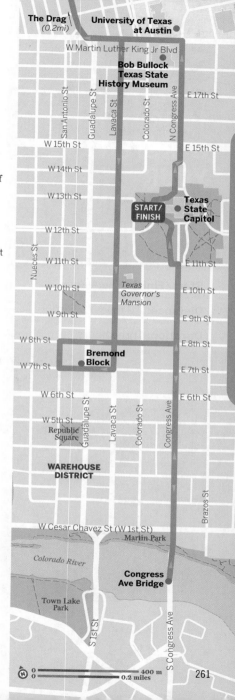

STRETCH YOUR LEGS

STRETCH YOUR LEGS SAN ANTONIO

Start/Finish: The Alamo

Distance: 2.2 miles/3.5km

Duration: Three hours

Sprawling San Antonio has lots to offer, but it packs its best attractions into a relatively small area – perfect for exploring on foot. Head downtown to hit the highlights, including the Alamo and the River Walk.

Take this walk on Trip

The Alamo

Snap an iconic picture of the most cherished monument in all of Texas. If you have time, go inside and learn how the former mission became a famous **military fort** (☏210-225-1391; www.thealamo.org; 300 Alamo Plaza; ☉9am-5:30pm Mon-Sat, from 10am Sun). For many, it's not so much a tourist attraction as a pilgrimage, and you might see visitors getting downright dewy-eyed at the description of how a few hundred revolutionaries died defending the fort against thousands of Mexican troops.

The Walk ≫ Go west two blocks on Houston St.

Buckhorn Saloon & Museum

Enjoy a beverage amidst an impressive number of mounted animals, including a giraffe, a bear and all manner of horn-wielding mammals. If that doesn't quench your thirst for taxidermy, pony up for a kitsch adventure at the **Buckhorn Museum** (☏210-247-4000; www.buckhornmuseum.com; 318 E Houston St; adult/child 3-11yr $19/15; ☉10am-5pm, to 8pm summer) that includes wildlife from all over the world, as well as oddities like a two-headed cow and eight-legged lamb.

The Walk ≫ Turn right on Presa St. Right before the bridge, you'll find a set of stairs leading down to the River Walk. At the bottom, turn right.

River Walk

Another of San Antonio's star attractions, the River Walk is a charming European-style canal that sits below street level. It gets mighty crowded, but it takes you past colorful cafes, landscaped hotel gardens and stone footbridges that stretch over the water. For the best overview, hop on a 40-minute **Rio San Antonio Cruise** (☏800-417-4139; www.riosanantonio.com; adult/child under 5yr $8.25/2; ☉9am-9pm).

The Walk ≫ Past St Marys St, turn left then take the Drury footbridge over the water. Ascend to Market St, then turn right. Take a moment to notice the imposing red-granite Bexar County Courthouse on the left.

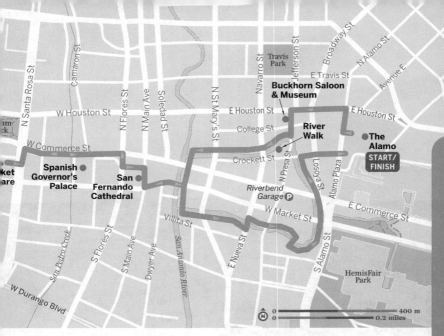

San Fernando Cathedral

San Fernando Cathedral (www.
sfcathedral.org; 115 Main Plaza; donations
welcome; ⏰9am-5pm Tue-Fri, to 6:30pm Sat,
8:30-5pm Sun) became an important
landmark when Mexican General Santa
Ana took it over during the Battle of
the Alamo. A hundred years later, some
remains were uncovered that were
purported to be those of Davy Crockett,
William Travis and James Bowie.
Pay your respects to whoever they
are at the marble casket near the left
entrance, and don't miss the dazzling
gilt retablo behind the main altar.

The Walk ≫ Take the path to the right of the
cathedral. Cross Military Plaza, then walk around
the stately City Hall, built in 1892.

Spanish Governor's Palace

A National Historic Landmark, this
low-profile adobe building from the
1700s was neither a palace nor the
home of the Spanish governor, but the
residence of the presidio captain and

seat of Texas' colonial government.
During the 20th century, it held
businesses including a saloon and a
pawn shop, but the city finally realized
its significance, bought it back, and
restored it to its former state.

The Walk ≫ Take Commerce St two blocks west. A
sidewalk from Santa Rosa St leads into the square.

Market Square

Mexican food, mariachi bands and a
Mexican-style market await at Market
Sq, which is a fair approximation of a
trip south of the border. Wander the
booths of the *mercado* and stock up
on paper flowers, colorful pottery and
the Virgin Mary in every conceivable
medium. Grab some Mexican food and
margaritas at the sprawling **Mi Tierra**
(☎210-225-1262; www.mitierracafe.com; 218
Produce Row; mains $12-16; ⏰24hr).

The Walk ≫ Return to the River Walk. After
the Drury footbridge, go right then turn left to
continue your route along the serene southern
stretch. Emerge at Crockett St and turn right to
return to the start.

Utah, Colorado & Nevada Trips

FROM ROCKY MOUNTAIN HIGHS TO ZION CANYON LOWS, it's all about extremes in Utah, Colorado and Nevada. Here you can go from the sleepiest of rural towns to the hyperactivity of Sin City itself. Hike a six-mile trail and never see another soul, or queue up in a car line to gawk at brown bears.

This rugged country is so stunningly beautiful that much of it has been protected as public lands. In southern Utah alone, there are eight national parks and monuments. And the history and culture represented here stretches from the age of dinosaurs, through Ancestral Puebloan peoples and Old West mining towns, to today's Navajo Nation. Populated, unpopulated; ancient, modern; high elevations and low: you'll find it all here in one outdoorsy region.

Goosenecks State Park Carved by the San Juan River (Trip 28)
NEALE CLARK/GETTY IMAGES ©

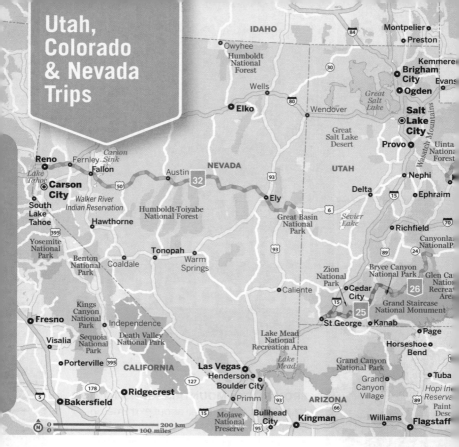

Utah, Colorado & Nevada Trips

DON'T MISS

Canyoneering

Rock-climb up then rappel down through narrow slot canyons on Trips 25 27

Montanya Rum Distillers

Enjoy gold-medal spirits at a welcoming plank bar in the tiny mining hamlet of Silverton on Trip 30

Ancient art appreciation

Ancestral Puebloan cultures left traces as rock art and ruins across the region. See for yourself on Trips 26 27 28

Independence Pass

Quaking aspens surround you as you navigate hairpin turns and experience craggy-rocked mountain-pass bliss on Trip 31

Digging dinosaurs

Visit three different working quarries and touch actual dinosaur bones in situ at several places along Trip 29

Bryce Canyon National Park
Sandcastle-like spires

Classic Trip

Zion & Bryce National Parks

25

From canyon floor to cliff-top perches, the red-rock country in southwestern Utah will delight your eyes and challenge your muscles.

TRIP HIGHLIGHTS

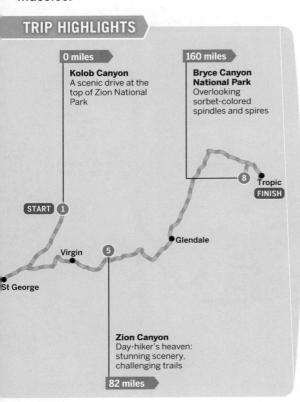

0 miles

Kolob Canyon
A scenic drive at the top of Zion National Park

160 miles

Bryce Canyon National Park
Overlooking sorbet-colored spindles and spires

 Tropic
FINISH

START 1

Virgin 5

Glendale

St George

Zion Canyon
Day-hiker's heaven: stunning scenery, challenging trails

82 miles

6 DAYS
178 MILES / 286KM

GREAT FOR...

BEST TIME TO GO

In April and September you'll likely have warm weather both at low and high elevations.

 ESSENTIAL PHOTO

The amphitheater's color at sunrise on Fairyland Point.

BEST FOR HIKING

Zion Canyon has easy river walks to strenuous, canyon-climbing hikes.

Classic Trip

25 Zion & Bryce National Parks

Standing in the umber earth atop Observation Point (6507ft), Zion Canyon spreads before you. The sinuous green river belt snakes through towering crimson cliffs, and hikers below on Angels Landing resemble ants. If you climbed the 4-mile trail up 2148ft from the canyon floor – *bravo*! But insiders know that the views look just as sweet if you hiked the backcountry East Mesa trail and descended to the point.

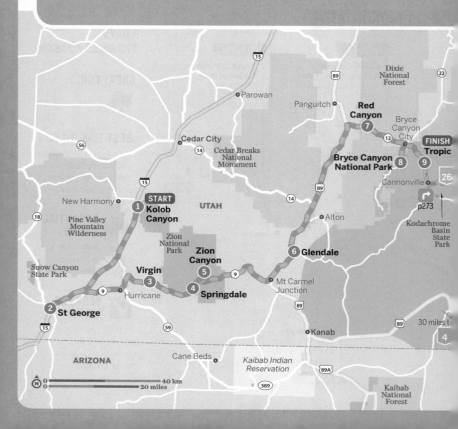

❶ Kolob Canyon

Start your visit at the **Kolob Canyons Visitor Center** (☎435-586-0895; www.nps.gov/zion; Kolob Canyons Rd, Zion National Park; 7-day vehicle pass $25; ⏱park 24hr, center 8am-6pm Jun-Sep, to 4:30pm Oct-May), gateway to the less-visited, higher elevation section of Zion National Park off I-15. Even in peak season you'll see relatively few cars on the scenic 5-mile **Kolob Canyon Rd**, a high-plateau route where striking canyon and rangeland views alternate. The road terminates at

LINK YOUR TRIP

26 Scenic Byway 12

From outside Bryce Canyon National Park, Scenic Byway 12 heads east through rugged and remote public lands and parks.

4 Grand Canyon North Rim & Lake Powell

Leaving Zion National Park, detour southeast down Hwy 89 for 115 miles to Page to start exploring northern Arizona.

Kolob Canyon Overlook (6200ft), from there the **Timber Creek Trail** (1-mile round-trip) follows a 100ft ascent to a small peak with great views of the Pine Valley Mountains beyond. In early summer the trail area is covered with wildflowers. Note that the upper section of the road may be closed due to snow from November through May.

The best longer hike in this section of the park is the **Taylor Creek Trail** (5-mile round-trip), which passes pioneer ruins and crisscrosses a creek, with little elevation change.

The Drive » Distant rock formations zoom by as you cruise along at 70-plus mph on I-15. St George is 41 miles south.

❷ St George

A spacious Mormon town with an eye-catching temple and a few pioneer buildings, St George sits about equidistant between the two halves of Zion. The **Chamber of Commerce** (☎435-628-1658; www.stgeorgechamber.com; 97 E St George Blvd; ⏱9am-5pm Mon-Fri) can provide information on the historic downtown. Otherwise, use this time to stock up on food and fuel in this trip's only real city (population 75,561). Eleven miles

north of town, **Snow Canyon State Park** (☎435-628-2255; http://stateparks.utah.gov; 1002 Snow Canyon Dr, Ivins; per vehicle $6; ⏱day use 6am-10pm; 🚻) is a 7400-acre sampler of southwest Utah's famous land features. Easy trails that are perfect for kids lead to tiny slot canyons, cinder cones, lava tubes and fields of undulating slickrock.

✖ ➡ p277

The Drive » Off the interstate, Hwy 9 leads you into canyon country. You'll pass the town of Hurricane before sweeping curves give way to tighter turns (and slower traffic). Virgin is 27 miles east of St George.

❸ Virgin

The tiny-tot town of Virgin, named after the river (what else?), has an odd claim to fame – in 2000 the city council passed a largely symbolic law requiring every resident (about 600 of them) to own a gun. You can't miss the **Virgin Trading Post** (☎435-635-3455; 1000 W Hwy 9; village $2; ⏱9am-7pm), which sells homemade fudge, ice cream and every Western knickknack known to man. Stop and have your picture taken in the 'Virgin Jail' or 'Wild Ass Saloon' in the replica Old West village

here. It's pure, kitschy fun.

The Drive » Springdale is 14 miles further along Hwy 9 (55 minutes from St George).

❹ Springdale

Stunning orangish-red mountains, including the **Watchman** (6555ft), form the backdrop for a perfect little park town. Here eclectic cafes and eateries are big on locally sourced ingredients. Galleries and artisan shops line

the long main drag, interspersed with indie motels, lodges and a few B&Bs. Make this your base for three nights exploring Zion Canyon and surrounds. Outfitters **Zion Rock & Mountain Guides** (☏435-772-3303; www. zionrockguides.com; 1458 Zion Park Blvd; ⏱8am-8pm Mar-Oct, hours vary Nov-Feb) and **Zion Adventure Company** (☏435-772-1001; www.zionadventures.com; 36 Lion Blvd; ⏱8am-8pm Mar-Oct, 9am-noon & 4-7pm Nov-Feb) lead canyoneering, climbing and 4WD trips outside the park; the latter has inner-tube rentals for summer float trips. They both outfit

for backcountry hikes through the Narrows.

Three times daily **Zion Canyon Giant Screen Theatre** (www. zioncanyontheatre.com; 145 Zion Park Blvd; adlut/child $8/6) shows the 40-minute *Zion Canyon: Treasure of the Gods*. The film's light on substance but long on beauty.

🍴 🛏 p277

The Drive » The entrance to the Zion Canyon section of Zion National Park is only 2 miles east of Springdale. Note that here you're at about 3900ft, the lowest (and hottest) part of your trip.

TRIP HIGHLIGHT

❺ Zion Canyon

More than 100 miles of trails cut through the surprisingly well-watered, deciduous tree-covered Virgin River canyon section of Zion National Park. Map out your routes at the **Zion Canyon Visitor Center** (☏435-772-3256; www.nps.gov/zion; Hwy 9, Zion National Park; 7-day vehicle pass $25; ⏱8am-7:30pm late May-early Sep, to 5pm late Sep-early May). Your first activity should be the 6-mile **Scenic Drive**, which pierces the heart of the park. From April through October, using the free shuttle is mandatory, but you can hop off and on at any of the scenic stops

---

LOCAL KNOWLEDGE: EAST MESA TRAIL

It feels deliciously like cheating to wander through open stands of tall ponderosa pines and then descend to Observation Point instead of hiking more than 2100ft uphill from the Zion Canyon floor. On **East Mesa Trail** (6.4 miles round-trip, moderate difficulty) you can do just that, because your vehicle does all the climbing. North Fork Rd is about 2.5 miles beyond the park's east entrance; follow it 5 miles north up Hwy 9 from there. Getting to the trailhead in some seasons requires 4WD; inquire about conditions and maps at the Zion Canyon Visitor Center (p272). Nearby **Zion Ponderosa Ranch Resort** (☏800-293-5444, 435-648-2700; www. zionponderosa.com; N Fork Rd, off Hwy 9; cabins $70-160, tent sites $10, RV sites with hookups $49; @🛜⛲), which also has accommodation and activities, can provide hiker shuttles. Note that at 6500ft, these roads and the trail may be closed due to snow November through May.

and trailheads along the way.

The paved, mile-long one-way **Riverside Walk** at the end of the road is an easy stroll. When the trail ends, you can continue hiking along in the Virgin River for 5 miles. Alternatively, a half-mile one-way trail leads up to the lower of the **Emerald Pools** where water tumbles from above a steep overhang stained by desert varnish.

The strenuous, 5.4-mile round-trip **Angels Landing Trail** (four hours, 1400ft elevation gain) is a vertigo-inducer with narrow ridges and 2000ft sheer drop-offs. Succeed and the exhilaration is unsurpassed. Canyon views are even more phenomenal from the top of the even higher **Observation Point** (8 miles round-trip; 2148ft elevation change).

For the 16-mile one-way trip down through the **Narrows**, spectacular slot canyons of the Virgin River, you need to plan ahead. An outfitter, shuttle and gear – see Springdale (p272) – plus a backcountry permit from the park are required; make advance reservations via the park website.

🛏 p277

DETOUR:
KODACHROME BASIN STATE PARK

Start: ❾ Tropic

Dozens of red, pink and white sandstone chimneys punctuate **Kodachrome Basin State Park** (☎435-679-8562; www.stateparks.utah.gov; off Cottonwood Canyon Rd; day-use per vehicle $6; ⏰day use 6am-10pm), named for its photogenic landscape by the National Geographic Society in 1948. The moderately easy, 3-mile round-trip **Panorama Trail** provides an overview of the otherworldly formations. Be sure to take the side trails to **Indian Cave**, where you can check out the handprints on the wall (cowboys' or Indians'?), and **Secret Passage**, a short spur through a narrow slot canyon. **Red Canyon Trail Rides** (☎800-892-7923; www.redcanyontrailrides.com; Kodachrome Basin State Park; 1-hr ride $40; ⏰Mar-Nov) offers horseback riding in Kodachrome.

The park lies 26 miles southeast of Bryce Canyon National Park, off Cottonwood Canyon Rd, south of Cannonville.

The Drive » Driving east, Hwy 9 undulates over bridges and up 3.5 miles of tight switchbacks before reaching the impressive gallery-dotted Zion–Mt Carmel Tunnel. From there until the east park entrance, the canyon walls are made of etched, light-colored slickrock, including Checkerboard Mesa. Glendale lies 32 miles (50 minutes) northwest of Zion Canyon.

- - - - - - - - - - - - - -

❻ Glendale

Several little towns line Hwy 89 north of the Hwy 9 junction. As you drive, look for little rock shops, art galleries and home-style cafes. Glendale is a small Mormon settlement founded in 1871. **Buffalo Bistro** (☎435-648-2778;

www.buffalobistro.net; 305 N Main St; burgers & mains $8-24; ⏰4-9:30pm Thu-Sun mid-Mar–mid-Oct) conjures a laid-back Western spirit with a breezy porch, sizzling grill and eclectic menu that includes wild boar ribs and elk burgers. Reservations recommended.

🛏 p277

The Drive » Hwy 89 is a fairly straight shot through pastoral lands; turn off from there onto Scenic Byway 12 where the red rock meets the road. Red Canyon is 41 miles northeast of Glendale.

- - - - - - - - - - - - - -

❼ Red Canyon

Impossibly red monoliths rise up

Classic Trip

RAUL TOUZON/GETTY IMAGES ©

LOCAL VOICE
LYMAN HAFEN,
DIRECTOR, ZION
NATURAL HISTORY
ASSOCIATION

My favorite time of year in Zion
is the first full week of November
when 24 amazing artists come
to paint in the Zion National Park
Plein Air Art Invitational. Cool but
bearable weather, fall colors, fewer
visitors, interaction with artists, and
a major art exhibition and sale, open
a new perspective on the magic of
Zion.

Above: Bridge across the Virgin River, Zion National
Park
Left: Rock tower, Kodachrome Basin State Park
Right: The Narrows, Zion National Park

RICHARD MASCHMEYER/GETTY IMAGES ©

roadside as you reach **Red Canyon** (📞435-676-2676; www.fs.usda.gov/recarea/dixie; Scenic Byway 12, Dixie National Forest; admission free; 🕐park 24hr, visitor center 9am-6pm Jun-Aug, 10am-4pm May & Sep). These parklands provide super-easy access to eerie, intensely colored formations. Check out the excellent geologic displays and pick up maps at the visitor center, where several moderate hiking trails begin. The 0.7-mile one-way **Arches Trail** passes 15 arches as it winds through a canyon. Legend has it that outlaw Butch Cassidy once rode in the area; a tough 8.9-mile hiking route, **Cassidy Trail**, bears his name.

25 ZION & BRYCE NATIONAL PARKS

The Drive » Stop to take the requisite photo before you drive through two blasted-rock arches to continue on. Bryce Canyon National Park is only 9 miles down the road.

BRENT WINEBRENNER/GETTY IMAGES ©

- - - - - - - - - - - -

8 Bryce Canyon National Park

The pastel-colored, sandcastle-like spires and hoodoos of **Bryce Canyon National Park** (📞435-834-5322; www.stateparks.utah.gov; Hwy 63; 7-day vehicle pass $25; 🕐24hr, visitor center 8am-8pm May-Sep, to 4:30pm Oct-Apr) look like something straight out of Dr Seuss' imagination.

275

The 'canyon' is actually an amphitheater of formations eroded from the cliffs. **Rim Road Scenic Drive** (18 miles one way), roughly follows the canyon rim past the visitor center (8000ft), the lodge, incredible overlooks and trailheads, ending at **Rainbow Point** (9115ft). From early May through early October, an optional free shuttle bus (8am until at least 5:30pm) departs from a staging area just north of the park

The easiest walk would be to follow the **Rim Trail** that outlines Bryce Amphitheater from Fairyland Point to Bryce Point (up to 5.5 miles one way). Several sections are paved and wheelchair accessible, the most level being the half mile between Sunrise and Sunset Points.

A number of moderate trails descend below the rim to the maze of fragrant juniper and undulating high-mountain desert. The **Navajo Loop** drops 521ft from Sunset Point. To avoid a super-steep ascent, follow the **Queen's Garden Trail** on the desert floor and hike up 320ft to Sunrise Point. From there take the shuttle, or follow the Rim Trail back to your car (2.9-mile round-trip).

Note that the high altitude means cooler temperatures – 80°F (27°C) average in July – here than at scorching Zion National Park.

p277

The Drive ≫ Only 11 miles east of Bryce Canyon, the town of Tropic is 2000ft lower in elevation – so expect it to be 10 degrees warmer there.

----

⑨ Tropic

A farming community at heart, Tropic does offer a few services for park goers. There's a grocery store, a couple of restaurants and several motels. Basing yourself here for two nights is definitely less expensive than staying in the park. Note that the town is entirely seasonal, many businesses shut their doors tight from October through March.

p277

Eating & Sleeping

St George ❷

✘ Painted Pony   Modern American $$$
(☎435-634-1700; www.painted-pony.com; 2 W
St George Blvd, Ancestor Sq; sandwiches $9-12,
dinner mains $24-35; ⊙11am-10pm) Expect
gourmet comfort food such as meatloaf with
a port wine reduction and rosemary mashed
potatoes.

⏝ Seven Wives Inn   B&B $$
(☎800-600-3737, 435-628-3737; www.
sevenwivesinn.com; 217 N 100 West; r & ste incl
breakfast $99-185; ❊@☎✖) Individually
furnished guest rooms occupy two 1800s
homes at this charming inn with a small pool.

Springdale ❹

✘ Bit & Spur Restaurant
& Saloon   Southwestern $$
(www.bitandspur.com; 1212 Zion Park Blvd;
mains $16-28; ⊙5-10pm daily Mar-Oct, 5-10pm
Thu-Sat Nov-Feb) Sweet-potato tamales and
chile-rubbed rib-eyes are two of the classics at
this Western-inspired eatery. Full bar.

⏝ Canyon Ranch Motel   Motel $$
(☎866-946-6276, 435-772-3357; www.
canyonranchmotel.com; 668 Zion Park Blvd; r $99-
119, apt $120-140; ❊☎✖) At this 1930s motor-
court motel the cottages that surround a shaded
lawn with redwood swings give the place a cool,
retro vibe but interiors are thoroughly updated.

⏝ Red Rock Inn   B&B $$
(☎435-772-3139; www.redrockinn.com; 998
Zion Park Blvd; cottages incl breakfast $127-132;
❊☎) Five romantic country-contemporary
cottages spill down a small desert hillside. Enjoy
the full hot breakfast on your private patio.

Zion Canyon ❺

⏝ Zion Lodge   Lodge $$
(☎435-772-7700, 888-297-2757; www.
zionlodge.com; Zion Canyon Scenic Dr; r $185,

cabins $195, ste $225; ❊@☎) Though not as
grand as some park lodges, the wooden cabins
and motels here are refined rustic. Here in the
middle of Zion Canyon you're surrounded by
stunning red-rock cliffs on all sides.

Glendale ❻

⏝ Historic Smith Hotel   B&B $$
(☎800-528-3558, 435-648-2156; http://
historicsmithhotel.com; 295 N Main St; r incl
breakfast $79-89; ❊) The seven-room Historic
Smith Hotel is more comfortable than a favorite
old sweater. Don't let the small rooms turn
you off. The proprietors are great and the big
breakfast table is a perfect place to meet other
intrepid travelers.

Bryce Canyon National Park ❽

⏝ Bryce Canyon Lodge   Lodge $$
(☎877-386-4383, 435-834-8700; www.
brycecanyonforever.com; Hwy 63; r & cabins
$175-200; ⊙Apr-Oct; @) The 1920s Bryce
park lodge exudes mountain charm with a large
stone fireplace and exposed timbers. Rooms
are in two-story wooden satellite buildings or
in cabins.

⏝ Ruby's Inn   Motel $$
(☎866-866-6616, 435-834-5341; www.
rubysinn.com; 1000 S Hwy 63; r $135-180;
❊@☎✖) More like a town than a resort
complex. Choose from several motel-hotel
lodging options, then take a helicopter ride,
watch a rodeo, shop for groceries and Western
art, fill up with gas, dine at one of several
restaurants and post a letter about it all.

Tropic ❾

⏝ Bryce Country Cabins   Cabins $$
(☎888-679-8643, 435-679-8643; www.
brycecountrycabins.com; 320 N Main St; cabins
$99-139; ⊙Feb-Oct; ❊☎) Knotty-pine walls
and log beds add charm to roomy one- and two-
bedroom cabins on the edge of town.

Scenic Byway 12 Travel one of the most remote regions in the US

Scenic Byway 12 | 26

Arguably Utah's most stunning drive, Scenic Byway 12 traverses moonscapes of sculpted slickrock, crosses razor-thin ridgebacks and climbs over an 11,000ft-tall mountain.

TRIP HIGHLIGHTS

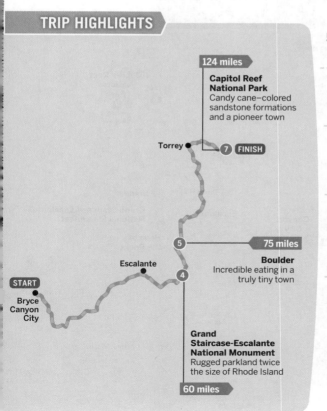

124 miles

Capitol Reef National Park
Candy cane–colored sandstone formations and a pioneer town

Torrey ● **7** FINISH

5 **75 miles**

Boulder
Incredible eating in a truly tiny town

Escalante ●

4

START
Bryce Canyon City

Grand Staircase-Escalante National Monument
Rugged parkland twice the size of Rhode Island

60 miles

5 DAYS
124 MILES / 200KM

GREAT FOR...

BEST TIME TO GO
June to August: the snow is gone and all attractions are open.

 ESSENTIAL PHOTO
Sandstone formations and distant mountains at Head of the Rocks.

 BEST FOR DRIVING
Tight swtichbacks and narrow Hogback Ridge rule the challenging road between Escalante and Boulder.

279

26 | Scenic Byway 12

Parts of this route are so remote that they were among the last to be mapped in the continental US. Until 1940 only wagon trails connected Escalante with Boulder and the mail was delivered by mule. That section of what would become Scenic Byway 12 wasn't fully paved until 1985. Few people live here even today: Escalante (population 792), Boulder (population 211), Torrey (population 362).

❶ Bryce Canyon City

What would a road trip be without kitchy roadside stops? **Bryce Museum** (www.brycewildlifeadventure.com; 1945 W Hwy 12; admission $8; ⏲9am-7pm Apr–mid-Nov), a barnlike natural history exhibit, contains more than 400 taxidermied animals, in addition to Native American artifacts, from one man's private collection. Out back, paid admission also allows you to visit the 60 or so exotic deer he raises. **Dixie National**

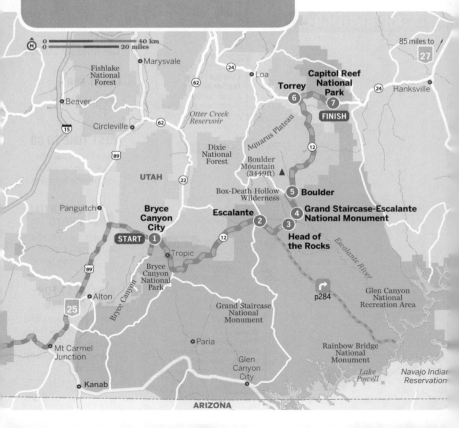

Forest (www.fs.usda.gov/dixie) surrounds Scenic Byway 12 here, just northeast of Bryce Canyon National Park. The museum and several other roadside stands rent ATVs (from $100 for three hours) and bicycles ($12 per hour) for exploring.

For more about places to stay and hiking in the national park, see p275.

 p285

The Drive » Past the town of Tropic, Byway 12 enters national monument park lands. A few grandfathered farming communities sit roadside as you wind your way the 41 miles (one hour) from Bryce City to Escalante.

❷ Escalante

Though hardly big enough to be called

LINK YOUR TRIP

25 **Zion & Bryce National Parks**

Scenic Byway 12 begins in Bryce, so you can just continue your exploration of Utah's national parks west from there.

27 **Moab & Southeastern National Parks**

From Capitol Reef, Moab is 145 miles to the northeast.

a town, Escalante does cater to visitors heading out into the rugged Grand Staircase-Escalante National Monument. The handful of restaurants and motels make this a good nighttime base for a day of hiking or driving in the monument.

Escalante Interagency Office (☎435-826-5499; www.ut.blm.gov/monument; 775 W Main St; ◷8am-4:30pm daily Apr-Sep, Mon-Fri Oct-Mar) has exhibits on area geography in addition to a gift shop and information.

Escalante Outfitters & Cafe (☎435-826-4266; www.escalanteoutfitters.com; 310 W Main St; ◷8am-9pm; 🛜) is a traveler's oasis. The large bookstore sells maps, guides, camping supplies and liquor; the cafe has breakfasts, pizza and much-coveted wi-fi. (Wireless phone and data signals are rare around here.) Long-time area outfitter **Excursions of Escalante** (☎800-839-7567; www.excursionsofescalante.com; 125 E Main St; full-day from $145; ◷8am-6pm) leads canyoneering, climbing and hiking trips into the monument.

 p285

The Drive » Monument country gets even more rough and rugged as you head further east. You'll find yourself driving up through canyons and down switchbacks to the overlook 8 miles away.

❸ Head of the Rocks

Don't miss the chance to pull off for one of the most arresting roadside viewpoints in Utah. Here atop the Aquarius Plateau you lord over giant mesas, towering domes, deep canyons and undulating slickrock unfurling in an explosion of color. In the far distance you can see Boulder Mountain to the northwest, the Henry Mountains to the east and Navajo Mountain to the southwest.

Continue 6 miles further east for coffee, a snack and more canyon views at **Kiva Koffeehouse** (☎435-826-4550; www.kivakoffeehouse.com; Mile 73, Hwy 12; dishes $2-8; ◷8am-4:30pm Wed-Mon Apr-Nov). Built to resemble a traditional Native American cliff dwelling, the semicircular building tucks into the hillside and has floor-to-ceiling glass walls supported by huge treelike timber. The Kiva also rents two cliffside cottages ($170).

The Drive » From the Koffeehouse, Lower Calf Creek is a 2-mile, downhill drive away.

TRIP HIGHLIGHT

❹ Grand Staircase-Escalante National Monument

At nearly 1.9 million acres, **Grand Staircase-Escalante National**

Monument (GSENM; 435-826-5499; www.ut.blm. gov/monument; PO Box 225, Escalante) is the largest park in the Southwest. Yet, it's one of the least visited. The harsh desert terrain *is* intimidating, but there are a few easy access points along Byway 12. The graded-dirt **Hole-in-the-Rock Rd** begins 5 miles east of Escalante; 12 miles down it is **Devils Garden**, a giant natural playground where rock fists, orbs, spires and fingers rise to 40ft above the desert floor.

Lower Calf Creek (Mile 75, Hwy 12; day use $2; ⏲ day use dawn-dusk) is the most popular recreation area in the park. From the picnic area and campground, a sandy, 3-mile one-way trail follows the creekside canyon to a 126ft **waterfall** – a joy on a hot day. Pick up the interpretive brochure at the payment kiosk to help you spot ancient granary ruins and pioneer relics along the trail.

The Drive ›› The next 16 miles are slow and windy ones as the road climbs from roughly 5300ft to 6700ft elevation in Boulder. That ridge your car is clinging to is called the 'Hogback.' Be sure to stop at the interpretive signs and the overlook of the valley just before Boulder.

- - - - - - - - - - - -

TRIP HIGHLIGHT

⑤ Boulder

Once primarily a ranching community, this frontier outpost

ALAN MAJCHROWICZ/GETTY IMAGES ©

has attracted a diverse population of down-to-earth folks that range from artists and ecologists to farmers and cowboys. One of the reasons is **Hell's Backbone Grill** (435-335-7464; http://hellsbackbonegrill.com; 20 N Hwy 12, Boulder Mountain Lodge; breakfast $8-12, lunch $12-18, dinner $18-27; ⏲7:30-11:30am & 5-9:30pm Mar-Oct),

at Boulder Lodge. Zen Buddhists Jen Castle and Blake Spalding have been feeding the community since they opened in 2000: training staff in mindfulness and inviting the whole town to celebrations like a July 4th ice-cream social and talent show.

Be sure to stop at **Anasazi State Park Museum** (www.stateparks.

Devils Garden Grand Staircase-Escalante National Monument

utah.gov; Main St/Hwy 12; admission $5; ☺8am-6pm Mar-Oct, 9am-5pm Nov-Apr), which protects an ancient site inhabited from AD 1130 to 1175 and excavated in the 1950s. The petite museum is well worth seeing for the re-created six-room pueblo and excellent exhibits on the Ancestral Puebloan (or Anasazi) peoples.

Earth Tours (☎435-691-1241; www.earth-tours.com; trips per person from $150; ☺Mar-Oct; 🐾) offers fun and informative half- and full-day area hikes, plus 4WD trips into the backcountry.

✕ 🛏 p285

The Drive » Though Boulder is only 32 miles (50 minutes) south of Torrey, you have to cross over 11,317ft-high Boulder Mountain to get there. Tight switchbacks climb quickly up into the pine-forested treeline. The road is maintained, but do note that you can expect snow at these elevations from November through May.

--- --- --- --- --- --- ---

⑥ Torrey

Old pioneer homestead buildings line the main street of this quiet town as, in the distance,

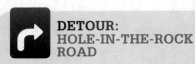

DETOUR: HOLE-IN-THE-ROCK ROAD

Start: ❷ Escalante

Almost as soon as the saints arrived in Salt Lake Valley, the second Mormon church president Brigham Young encouraged pioneers to settle every inch of the Utah Territory. Looking for a shortcut to more hospitable lands, in 1879 more than 200 pioneering Mormons followed this southeasterly route. When the precipitous walls of Glen Canyon on the Colorado River blocked their path, they blasted and hammered through the cliff, creating a hole wide enough to lower their 80 wagons through by rope – a feat that is honored by the road's name. An open-air memorial just west of Escalante town tells the story in greater detail. Today the 57-mile (one-way) road is still dusty and desolate.The last 7 miles require 4WD, and even then it can take almost as long to traverse those as the first 50. The road stops short of the actual lowering site. Hikers can trek out and scramble down past the 'hole' to Lake Powell in less than an hour. Sorry, no elevators to bring you back up.

red-rock cliffs catch the sunset light beautifully. The primary industry here long ago shifted from logging and ranching to outdoor tourism. Most visitors to Capital Reef National Park (11 miles away) sleep and eat here – you should do the same.

Hondoo Rivers & Trails (☎800-332-2696, 435-425-3519; www.hondoo.com; 90 E Main St), one of southern Utah's longest-operating backcountry guides, offers half-, full- and multi-day hiking, 4WD, rafting, horseback riding or combo trips.

✗ ⊨ p285

The Drive » Torrey sits 1300ft above Capitol Reef, and is usually about 10°F (6°C) cooler. The 11-mile cruise through canyonlands to the valley park is all down hill from there.

- - - - - - - - - - - -

TRIP HIGHLIGHT

❼ Capitol Reef National Park

Sixty-five million years ago when the earth's surface buckled and fell, the 100-mile Waterpocket Fold was created. Today **Capitol Reef National Park** (☎435-425-3791, ext 4111; www.nps.gov/care; cnr Hwy 24 & Scenic Dr; admission free, 7-day scenic drive per vehicle $5; ⊙24hr, visitor center & scenic drive 8am-6pm Apr-Oct, to 4:30pm Nov-Mar) protects a cross-section of geologic history that is downright painterly: chocolate-red cliffs, yellow sandstone arches, giant cream-colored domes and stark gray monoliths.

Make sure to take the 8.2-mile, one-way **Scenic Drive** along the fold. You first pass through Mormon pioneer fruit and nut orchards, which you can freely pick from in season. The historic **Gifford Farmhouse** is a small homestead museum, where if you're lucky you can buy orchard-fruit-filled minipies. At the end of the road, **Capitol Gorge Trail** (2.5 miles round-trip) leads past ancient petroglyphs. Follow the spur trail to the **Pioneer Register**, where names carved in the rock date back to 1871.

Eating & Sleeping

Bryce Canyon City ❶

✖ Bryce Canyon
Pines Restaurant   American $$

(☎435-834-5441; www.brycecanyonmotel.
com/bryce-restaurant.html; Hwy 12; breakfast
& lunch $5-12, dinner mains $10-19; ⊙6:30am-
9:30pm Apr-Nov) A classic, rural Utah, meat-
and-potatoes place. Homemade pies and soups
here are so good.

▄ Bryce Canyon Resort   Motel $$

(☎435-834-5351, 800-834-0043; www.
brycecanyonresort.com; cnr Hwys 12 & 63;
r $99-189, cabins $159-210; ❋ 🕾 ⊠ 🐾) Choose
between deluxe rooms, with newer furnishings
and extra amenities, and cabins at this roadside
motel complex. ATV outfitter and restaurant
on-site.

Escalante ❷

✖ Cowboy Blues   American $$

(530 W Main St; sandwiches & mains $9-20;
⊙11am-10pm) Family-friendly meals here
include BBQ ribs, steaks and daily specials like
burritos or meatloaf. The only place in town with
a full bar.

▄ Canyons Bed & Breakfast   B&B $$

(☎866-526-9667, 435-826-4747; www.
canyonsbnb.com; 120 E Main St; r incl breakfast
$135-165; ❋🕾) Upscale cabin-rooms with
porches surround a shaded terrace and gardens
where you can enjoy your breakfast each
morning.

▄ Circle D Motel   Motel $

(☎435-826-4297; www.escalantecircledmotel.
com; 475 W Main St; r $65-75; ❋🕾🐾) It's just
a nicely updated, older motel, but the friendly
proprietor goes out of his way to accommodate
guests.

Boulder ❺

✖ Burr Trail Grill
& Outpost   Modern Southwestern $$

(http://burrtrailgrill.com; cnr Hwy 12 & Burr
Trail Rd; dishes $8-18; ⊙grill 11am-2:30pm &
5-9:30pm, outpost 7:30am-8pm Mar-Oct; 🕾) We
like the eclectic dishes and homey vibe at the
Grill, where locals come to chat and chew. Next
door, the Outpost is a local art gallery as much
as it is a gift shop and cafe.

▄ Boulder Mountain Lodge   Lodge $$

(☎435-335-7460; www.boulder-utah.com; 20 N
Hwy 12; r $110-175; ❋ @ 🕾) An ideal place for
day-hikers who want to return to high-thread-
count sheets, plush terry robes and an outdoor
hot tub. Hell's Backbone Grill (p282), on site, is a
southern Utah must-eat.

Torrey ❻

✖ Capitol Reef Cafe   American $$

(☎435-425-3271; www.capitolreefinn.com;
360 W Main St; breakfast & lunch $6-12, dinner
mains $16-22; ⊙7am-9pm Apr-Oct) Whenever
possible, this cozy cafe uses local and organic
ingredients in its vegetable-heavy dishes. Area
trout and locally made pies are a hit.

▄ Austin's Chuckwagon Motel   Motel $

(☎435-425-3335; www.austinschuckwagon-
motel.com; 12 W Main St; r $75-85, cabins $135;
⊙Mar-Oct; ❋🕾⊠🐾) Rustic outside, motel
rooms inside have same-as-everywhere style
but are well-maintained. Having an on-site
general store, deli and laundromat is nice.

▄ Torrey Schoolhouse B&B   B&B $$

(☎435-633-4643; www.torreyschoolhouse.
com; 150 N Center St; r incl breakfast $118-148;
⊙Apr-Oct; ❋🕾) Dressed-down in country
elegance, each light, airy room in this huge
former schoolhouse has high ceilings and well-
chosen antiques.

Mesa Arch *Suspended over a spectacular view*

Moab & Southeastern National Parks

27

Hiking, biking, rafting, riding (four-wheelers or horses): Moab and the surrounding parks and extensive public lands are activity central. Adrenaline, anyone?

TRIP HIGHLIGHTS

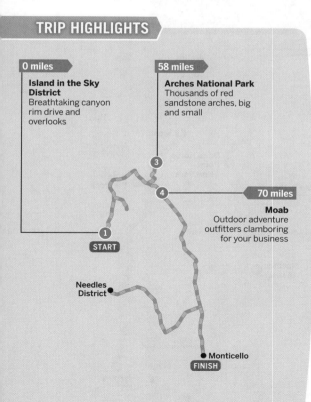

0 miles

Island in the Sky District
Breathtaking canyon rim drive and overlooks

58 miles

Arches National Park
Thousands of red sandstone arches, big and small

70 miles

Moab
Outdoor adventure outfitters clambering for your business

START

Needles District

Monticello
FINISH

4 DAYS
114 MILES / 183KM

GREAT FOR...

BEST TIME TO GO

April and October have the most temperate weather, and there are many events going on.

 ESSENTIAL PHOTO

The quintessential Utah picture: Delicate Arch in Arches National Park.

 BEST FOR FAMILIES

Both Arches and Canyonlands National Parks have short trails and junior ranger packs.

Moab & Southeastern National Parks

Stare at the swirling pattern long enough and you'll swear you can see the red rock move. Hiking through Utah's southeastern parks, you get to test your limits and bear witness to the earth's power at its most elemental. Here the story of wind and water is written in stone.

TRIP HIGHLIGHT

① Island in the Sky District

Roads and rivers make inroads into the 527-sq-mile desert of **Canyonlands National Park** (www.nps.gov/cany; 7-day per vehicle $10, tent & RV sites without hookups $10-15; ⏱24hr), but much of it is still untamed wilderness. Vast canyons divide the park into disparate sections. Think of **Island in the Sky** (☏435-259-4712; Hwy 313, Canyonlands National Park; ⏱visitor center

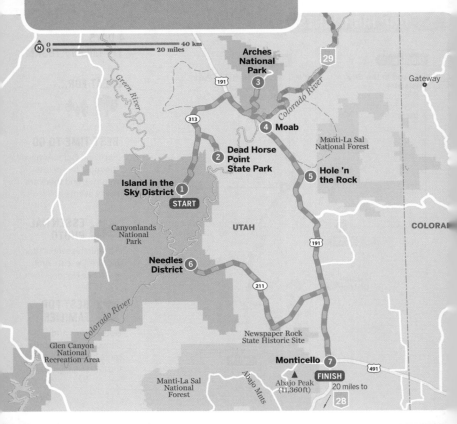

8am-6pm Mar-Oct, 9am-4pm Nov-Feb) as the overview: an RVer's special, with paved drives and easy-access lookouts. Here narrow, serpentine valleys tipped with white cliffs loom high over the Colorado and Green Rivers.

A good short hike here is the half-mile loop to oft-photographed **Mesa Arch**, a slender, cliff-hugging span framing a picturesque view of **Washer Woman Arch** and **Buck Canyon**. Grand View Overlook trail (2 miles round-trip) follows the canyon's edge and ends at a praise-your-maker precipice atop the mesa.

The Drive » Dead Horse Point State Park is a short detour off slow and scenic Hwy 313, 11 miles northeast of Island in

LINK YOUR TRIP

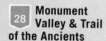

28 Monument Valley & Trail of the Ancients

From Monticello, drive 20 miles south to Blanding to start a trip around the ancient-site-filled, far southeastern Utah.

29 Dinosaur Diamond Prehistoric Byway

Start a tour of Jurassic-era formations and fossils in Moab.

the Sky. Note that though your trip begins at Islands, you'll be spending all the nights of this trip 42 miles away in Moab.

② Dead Horse Point State Park

The views pack a wallop at **Dead Horse Point State Park** (www.stateparks.utah.gov; Hwy 313; park day-use per vehicle $10, tent & RV sites $20; ☺ park 6am-10pm, visitor center 8am-6pm Mar-Oct, 9am-4pm Nov-Feb). At the end of a four-mile drive you can peer down 2000ft to the Colorado River and 100 miles across a mesmerizing stepped red-rock landscape. (You might remember this epic vista from the final scene in *Thelma & Louise*.) Legend has it that cowboys blockaded the narrow entrance to the mesa to corral wild horses, and that they forgot to release them upon leaving. The stranded equines died within view of the unreachable Colorado River below, hence the park name. Ranger-led geology talks are presented daily March through October at the point. To escape the small (but sometimes chatty) crowds, take a walk around the mesa rim.

The Drive » Retrace your tracks back along Hwy 313 and then follow Hwy 191 south to Arches; it's 26 miles total.

TRIP HIGHLIGHT

③ Arches National Park

More than 2000 red sandstone arches – ranging from 3ft to 300ft wide – cover the relatively compact **Arches National Park** (☎435-719-2299; www.nps.gov/arch; Hwy 191; 7-day per vehicle $10; ☺24hr, visitor center 7:30am-6:30pm Mar-Oct, 9am-4pm Nov-Feb). Add to that mazelike fins and rock-topped spires and you have one wondrous park.

There is one main road (19 miles one-way) with scenic stops, and two short spurs. In the **Windows section** several arches can be seen from the pavement. Quick walks lead to other named formations, such as **Sand Dune Arch** (0.4-mile round-trip). To get to the park's most famous feature, **Delicate Arch** itself, take the three-mile round-trip trail near Wolfe Ranch or you can overlook it from the viewing area. At the end of the main road **Devils Garden** marks the beginning of a two- to 7.7-mile round-trip hike that passes at least eight arches.

Advance reservations (at least a day or two) are necessary for the free, twice-daily ranger-led hikes into the maze of rock that is the **Fiery Furnace**. Be prepared for fun scrambling up and over boulders, chimneying down between rocks and navigating narrow ledges.

The Drive ≫ Red-rock cliffs surround you on all sides as you drive the five miles into the town of Moab.

- - - - - - - - - - - -

TRIP HIGHLIGHT

④ Moab

Southeastern Utah's largest community (population 5093) bills itself as the state's recreation capital – and man, does it deliver. The numerous outfitters here can help you find just about any type of outdoors adventure imaginable. Try **Sheri Griffith Expeditions** (📞800-332-2439; www.griffithexp.com; 2231 S Hwy 191) for river rafting – family floats to class IV Cataract Canyon rapids. **Poison Spider Bicycles** (📞800-635-1792, 435-259-7882; www.poisonspiderbicycles.com; 497 N Main St) will outfit you for mountain biking on the area's Slickrock Trail. **Farabee's Jeep Rental & Outlaw Tours** (📞877-970-5337; www.farabeesjeeprentals.com; 1125 S Highway 191) specializes in 4WD rentals and trips. **Moab Desert Adventures** (📞877-765-6622, 435-260-2404; www.moabdesertadventures.com; 415 N Main St) offers climbing, canyoneering and multisport packages.

Canyonlands Field Institute (📞800-860-5262, 435-259-7750; http://canyonlandsfieldinst.org; 1320 S Hwy 191) leads all-ages interpretive hikes and canoe tours. And **Red Cliffs Lodge** (📞866-812-2002, 435-259-2002; www.redcliffslodge.com; Mile 14, Hwy 128) has daily horseback trail rides.

The town itself is a pleasant place chock full of restaurants and motels. Look for Southwestern souvenirs around the intersection of Main and Center Sts. On a rainy day, you might peek into the **Museum of Moab** (www.moabmuseum.org; 118 E Center St; adult/child $5/free; ⊙noon-5pm) to learn more about pioneer and Native American history.

🍴 🛏 p293

The Drive ≫ Businesses get fewer and farther between until Moab ends abruptly in desert nothingness at its southern extent. Hole 'n the Rock is only 12 miles along.

- - - - - - - - - - - -

⑤ Hole 'n the Rock

What didn't Albert and Gladys Christensen do? He was a barber, a painter, an amateur engineer and a taxidermist; she was a cook (their house once contained a restaurant) and lapidary jeweler. But what's really amazing is that they did all this while making their home in a 5000-sq-ft cave. An

CALLAHAN GALLERIES/GETTY IMAGES ©

Dead Horse Point State Park

NEWSPAPER ROCK STATE HISTORIC SITE

This tiny, free recreation area showcases a large sandstone rock panel packed with more than 300 petroglyphs attributed to Ute and Ancestral Puebloan groups during a 2000-year period. The many humanoid and animal figures are etched out of the black, mineralized surface called desert varnish, making for great photos – late afternoon light is best. Follow the raised boardwalk along the cliffside to see them all. The site lies 12 miles west of Hwy 191 en route to Canyonlands – Needles District.

unabashed tourist trap, **Hole 'n the Rock** (www. moab-utah.com/holeintherock; 11037 S Hwy 191; tours adult/ child $6/3.50; ⏰9am-5pm; ♿) is decorated in knockout 1950s kitsch. The couple lived in the blasted-out home until 1974. Today in addition to the cave, there's a yard full of small wooden buildings with shops, a hodgepodge of metal art and a small exotic animal zoo.

The Drive » Following Hwy 191 south 30 miles the views are in the distance and the road moves fast. The next 42 miles on Hwy 211 cross rugged park land. Scan the sheer cliffs on the right side as you go along; they're a favorite with rock climbers.

- - - - - - - - - - - - - - - -

❻ Needles District

The district is named for the thin sandstone chimneys jutting skyward in the desert. Here on the canyon floor, the jagged terrain is so different from Island in the Sky, it's hard to believe they're both part of Canyonlands National Park (p288). Keep your receipt, because entry to one is good for the other.

Needles District (☎435-259-4711; Hwy 211; ⏰8am-6pm Mar-Oct, 9am-4:30pm Nov-Feb) receives half as many visitors as other area parks, so it's a great place to get away from it all – especially if you have 4WD or a mountain bike. Fifty miles of off-road trails (permit required) crisscross the vast landscape.

Cave Spring Trail (0.6-mile loop, easy to moderate) is especially popular with kids. The path leads up ladders and over slick rock to an abandoned cowboy camp. The handprint pictographs on the last cave's walls are haunting. To get among the namesake needle formations **Chesler Park – Joint Trail** is an 11-mile loop hike through desert grasslands, past towering red-and-white-striped pinnacles and between deep, narrow slot canyons.

The Drive » Backtracking along cliffside Hwy 211 to Hwy 191, turn south. The valley opens up then narrows as you gain elevation getting closer to the mountains outside Monticello, 27 miles further along.

- - - - - - - - - - - - - - - -

❼ Monticello

In the foothills of the Abajo (Blue) Mountains, Monticello sits at 7022ft, a good 3000ft higher (and 10°F cooler) than Moab. If you're hungry after hiking in the Needles, your closest eating options are here. The town is pretty little; the **San Juan Visitor Center** (☎435-587-3235, 800-574-4386; www. southeastutah.com; 117 S Main St; ⏰10am-4pm Mon-Fri Nov–mid-Mar, 8am-5pm daily mid-Mar–Oct) has a similarly diminutive museum of local pioneer history.

Spring wildflowers and fall tree foliage are a novelty among the arid canyonlands of this region. But there they are just west of the town boundaries in the 1.4-million-acre **Manti–La Sal National Forest** (www.fs.fed.us/r4/mantilasal; off N Creek Rd; admission free; ⏰24hr), which rises to 11,360ft at Abajo Peak. **Abajo-Harts Draw**, off N Creek Rd, is the closest recreation area with trails and campgrounds.

🍴 🛏 p293

Eating & Sleeping

Moab ④

✖ Desert Bistro   Southwestern $$$

(📞435-259-0756; http://desertbistro.com; 36 S 100 West; mains $20-50; ⏰5:30-10pm Mar-Nov) Stylized preparations of game and seafood are the specialty at this welcoming, white-tablecloth restaurant inside an old house. Everything is made on site, from freshly baked bread to delicious pastries. Great wine list, too

✖ Love Muffin   Cafe $

(www.lovemuffincafe.com; 139 N Main St; dishes $6-8; ⏰7am-2pm; 📶) Early-rising locals buy up many of the daily muffins – such as the 'breakfast' with bacon and blueberries. Not to worry, the largely organic menu at this vibrant cafe also includes creative breakfast burritos and sandwiches.

✖ Moab Brewery   American $$

(www.themoabbrewery.com; 686 S Main St; mains $10-22; ⏰11:30am-10pm Mon-Thu, 11:30am-11pm Fri & Sat) Choosing from the list of microbrews made in the vats just behind the bar area may be easier than deciding what to eat off the vast and varied casual American menu.

🛏 Aarchway Inn   Motel $$

(📞800-341-9359, 435-259-2599; www.aarchwayinn.com; 1151 N Hwy 191; r incl breakfast $129-169; ❋📶🏊) Space sets this sprawling motel apart: humongous standard rooms, family suites and the largest heated swimming pool in town. The playground, basketball court and nature trails are great for kids.

🛏 Adventure Inn   Motel $

(📞866-662-2466, 435-259-6122; www.adventureinnmoab.com; 512 N Main St; r incl breakfast $80-105; ⏰Mar-Oct; ❋📶) A great little indie motel, the Adventure Inn has spotless rooms (some with refrigerators) and decent linens, as well as laundry facilities. There's a picnic area on site; no hot tub.

🛏 Sunflower Hill   Inn $$

(📞800-662-2786, 435-259-2974; www.sunflowerhill.com; 185 N 300 East; r incl breakfast $165-225; ❋📶🏊) Kick back in an Adirondack chair amid the manicured gardens of the rambling 100-year-old farmhouse and an early 20th-century home that make up this inn. All 12 guest quarters have a sophisticated country sensibility.

Monticello ⑦

✖ MD Ranch Cookhouse   American $$

(📞435-587-3299; 380 S Main St; mains $10-25; ⏰11am-9pm Mar-Oct) Service can be a bit slow, but the homestyle ribs, sandwiches and steaks are pretty darn good for a rural town in the middle of the desert.

✖ Peace Tree Juice Cafe   Cafe $$

(516 N Main St; mains $8-20; ⏰7:30am-4pm daily, plus 5-9pm May-Sep) A colorful cafe in a former home, Peace Tree serves more than the requisite breakfasts and juice drinks. In season, dinners might include 'Nona's' lasagna and portobello mushroom burgers.

🛏 Abajo Haven Guest Ranch   Lodge $

(📞435-979-3126; www.abajohaven.com; 5440 N Cedar Edge Ln; cabins $79) Outdoor adventure in the Abajo Mountains. Stay in nicely rustic cabin (king and two single beds each), then have an old fashioned cook-out and go on a guided hike to ancient sites just an hour and a half from your cabin.

Moki Dugway *Hairpin turns and hair-raising heights*

Monument Valley & Trail of the Ancients

28

Extreme desert isolation has preserved rocky natural wonders and numerous Ancestral Puebloan sites in far southeastern Utah and into Arizona.

TRIP HIGHLIGHTS

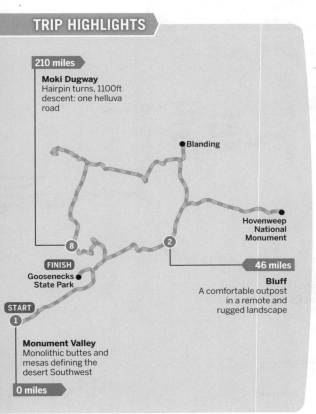

210 miles

Moki Dugway
Hairpin turns, 1100ft descent: one helluva road

● Blanding

● **Hovenweep National Monument**

46 miles

Bluff
A comfortable outpost in a remote and rugged landscape

FINISH
Goosenecks State Park ●

8

2

START
1

Monument Valley
Monolithic buttes and mesas defining the desert Southwest

0 miles

5 DAYS
262 MILES / 422KM

GREAT FOR...

BEST TIME TO GO
October through April to avoid searing heat.

 ESSENTIAL PHOTO

Monument Valley's monolithic buttes at sunrise or sunset.

 BEST FOR ANCIENT SITES

Hire a guide in either Bluff or Monument Valley to get you off the beaten track and see rock art and ruins.

295

Monument Valley & Trail of the Ancients

Capturing the sheer scale of Monument Valley in a photo poses a big challenge. The best perspective shots have clouds or the moon in the background or something such as cactus or juniper trees in the foreground. To make the many shades of deepest red stand out, avoid the harsh noon sun and either use a polarizing filter or adjust your white balance accordingly.

❶ Monument Valley

Don't worry if you feel like you've seen this place before. Monument Valley's monolithic chocolate-red buttes and colossal, colorful mesas have starred in countless films, TV shows and commercials. The most famous formations are visible from the 17-mile, rough-dirt **scenic drive** looping through **Monument Valley Navajo Tribal Park** (☎435-727-5874; www.navajonationparks.

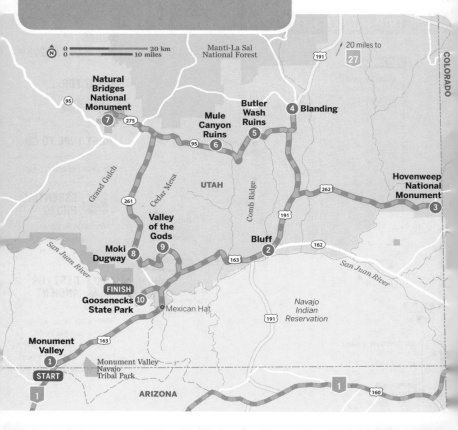

org/htm/monumentvalley.htm; adult/child $5/free; ⏲ drive 6am-8:30pm May-Sep, 8am-4:30pm Oct-Apr; visitor center 6am-8pm May-Sep, 8am-5pm Oct-Apr), **down a four-mile spur road south of Goulding's Lodge** (📞435-727-3231; www.gouldings. com; Hwy 163; r $180), **which has a small museum and offers tours. The park and scenery straddle the Utah–Arizona line.**

The only way to get into the backcountry to see rock art, natural arches and coves is by taking a Navajo-led tour by foot, horseback or vehicle. Easy-going guides have booths in the parking lot at the visitor center. Tours are peppered with details about Dine culture, life

LINK YOUR TRIP

1 Four Corners Cruise

In Monument Valley pick up this trip to continue exploring the geological wonders and Native American ancestry of the region.

27 Moab & Southeastern National Parks

One hundred miles north of Bluff, Moab is your base for outdoor activity near Arches and Canyonlands National Parks.

on the reservation and movie trivia.

✗ 🛏 p301

The Drive » The monument's mesas diminish in your rearview mirror as you head north, crossing the San Juan River and continuing along its valley the 45 total miles to Bluff, Utah.

- - - - - - - - - - - - - - - -

TRIP HIGHLIGHT

② Bluff

Tiny tot Bluff (population 258) isn't much, but a few good motels and a handful of restaurants – surrounded by stunning red rock – make it a cool base for exploring. We've set up the trip for two nights in Monument Valley, two here in Bluff and one in Mexican Hat or back in the Valley. But distances are short enough that you could spend every night in Bluff and take daily forays.

Descendants of the town's pioneers re-created a log cabin settlement called **Bluff Fort** (www.hirf.org/bluff. asp; 5 E Hwy 191; admission free; ⏲ 9am-6pm Mon-Sat). Three miles west of town on public lands, the accessible **Sand Island petroglyphs** (www.blm.gov; Sand Island Rd, off Hwy 163; admission free; ⏲ 24hr) were created between 800 and 2500 years ago.

A few outfitters in town lead backcountry excursions that access rock art and ruins. **Far Out Expeditions** (📞435-672-2294; www.

faroutexpeditions.com; half-day from $125) offers single and multiday hikes. **Wild Rivers Expeditions** (📞800-422-7654; www. riversandruins.com; 101 Main St; day trip adult/child $175/133), a history- and geology-minded outfit, rafts along the San Juan. And **Buckhorn Llama** (📞435-672-2466; www. llamapack.com; per day $400) leads five- and six-day, llama-supported treks.

✗ 🛏 p301

The Drive » The best route to Hovenweep is the paved Hwy 262 (past Hatch Trading Post, turn off on to Hwy 191 and follow the signs). From Bluff to the main entrance is a slow, 42-mile drive total (1¼ hours).

- - - - - - - - - - - - - - - -

③ Hovenweep National Monument

Meaning 'deserted valley' in the Ute language, the archeological sites of **Hovenweep National Monument** (📞ext 10 970-562-4282; www.nps.gov/hove; Hwy 262; park 7-day per vehicle $6, tent & RV sites $10; ⏲ park dusk-dawn, visitor center 8am-6pm Jun-Sep, 9am-5pm Oct-May) exist in splendid isolation. Most of the eight towers and unit houses you'll see in the **Square Towers Group**, accessed near the visitor center, were built from 1230 to 1275 AD. Imagine stacking each clay-formed block to create such tall structures on tiny ledges. You could easily spend a half day or more hiking around the gorge's ruins. Other sites, which lie across the border in Colorado, require long hikes.

The Drive » Bluff is the only base in the area, so you'll have to drive both to Hovenweep and back in one day. Moving on to Blanding, 28 miles north of Bluff, Hwy 191 is a rural road unimpeded by too many twists or turns.

------

④ Blanding

A special museum elevates small, agriculturally oriented Blanding a little above its totally drab name. The **Edge of the Cedars State Park Museum** (www.stateparks.utah.gov; 660 W 400 N; adult/child $5/3; ⊘9am-5pm Mon-Sat) is where you can learn more about the area's ancients, with its trove of archeological treasures that have been gathered from across southeastern Utah. Outside, climb down the rickety ladder into a dark, earthy-smelling ceremonial kiva (an Ancestral Puebloan ceremonial structure) c AD 1100. Can you feel a power to the place? (Just ignore the encroaching subdivision noise.) **Blue Mountain Artisans** (www.facebook.com/pages/Blue-Mountain-Artisans; 215 E Center St; ⊘11am-6pm Wed-Sat) sells professional photographs of area archeological and geological sites, plus local jewelry.

GIORGIO FOCHESATO/GETTY IMAGES ©

✕ p301

The Drive » Heading west on Hwy 95, the scenery gets up close and personal. Butler Wash is only 14 miles along on free public lands; look for the signs.

------

⑤ Butler Wash Ruins

No need of hike days into the backcountry here: it's only a half-mile tramp to views of the freely accessible **Butler Wash Ruins**, a 20-room cliff dwelling on public lands. Scramble over the slickrock boulders (follow the cairns) to see the sacred kivas, habitation and storage rooms associated with the Ancestral Puebloan (or Anasazi) Kayenta group of northern Arizona c 1300 AD.

Monument Valley

The Drive » Continue west on Hwy 95, after the road veers north, look for a sign announcing more ruins – about 25 miles along.

6 Mule Canyon Ruins

Though not particularly well preserved or evocative, the base of the tower, kiva and 12-room **Mule Canyon Ruins** sit almost roadside. Pottery found here links the population (c 1000 to 1150 AD) to the Mesa Verde group in southern Colorado.

The Drive » Continue along through the cliffs and canyons of Hwy 95 until you branch off on to the even smaller Hwy 275. The monument is 26 miles west of Mule Canyon.

7 Natural Bridges National Monument

The views at **Natural Bridges** (www.nps.gov/nabr; Hwy 275; park 7-day per vehicle $6, tent & RV sites $10; ⏰24hr, visitor center 8am-6pm May-Sep, 9am-5pm Oct-Apr) are of a white sandstone canyon (it's not red!). All three impressive and easily

TAKE ONLY PICTURES

Sadly enough, many invaluable archeological sites in the area have been vandalized by thieves. Even casual visitors do irreparable damage by climbing on old dwelling walls or picking up 'just one' little pot shard. The old maxim 'take only pictures' bears repeating. Do not touch, move or remove any artifacts; it's against the law. The best way to explore ancient backcountry sites is with a well-informed, responsible guide.

accessible bridges are visible from a nine-mile winding **Scenic Drive** loop with overlooks. The oldest is also the closest: take a half-mile hike to the beautifully delicate **Owachomo Bridge**, spanning 180ft at only 9ft thick. Note that trails to Kachina and Siapu bridges are not long, but they require navigating super-steep sections or ladders. Near the end of the drive, don't skip the 0.3-mile trail to the **Horsecollar Ruin** cliff dwelling overlook.

The Drive >> Ochre-yellow to reddish-orange sandstone canyons surround you as you wend your way south on Rte 261. To your right is **Cedar Mesa-Grand Gulch primitive area**, a seriously challenging wilderness environment. To drive the 36 miles to Moki Dugway will take at least an hour.

TRIP HIGHLIGHT
8 Moki Dugway

Along a roughly paved, hairpin-turn–filled section of road, **Moki Dugway** descends 1100ft in just three miles. Miners 'dug out' the extreme switchbacks in the 1950s to transport uranium ore. Note that the road is far from wide by today's standards, but there are places to pull out. You can't always see what's around the next bend, but you can see down the sheer dropoffs. Those afraid of heights (or in trailers over 24ft long), steer clear.

The Drive >> At the bottom of the dugway, prepare yourself for another wild ride. The turn off for Valley of the Gods is less than five miles ahead on your left.

9 Valley of the Gods

Think of the gravel road through the freely accessible **Valley of the Gods** as a do-it-yourself roller coaster, with sharp, steep hills and quick turns around some amazing scenery. Locals call it 'mini-Monument Valley'. Download the public lands office pamphlet from www.blm.gov to identify the strangely shaped sandstone monoliths and pinnacles (Seven Sailors, Lady on a Tub, Rooster Butte...). Allow an hour-plus for the 17 miles between highways 261 and 163. Do not attempt it without 4WD if it's rained recently.

The Drive >> Once you emerge from the valley, follow Hwy 163 back west and take the little jog up Hwy 261 to the Goosenecks State Park spur, a total of 8 miles away.

10 Goosenecks State Park Overlook

Following the 4-mile spur to **Goosenecks State Park** (http://stateparks.utah.gov; Rte 261; admission free; ☉24hr) brings you to a mesmerizing view. From 1000ft above you can see how the San Juan River's path carved tight turns through sediment, leaving gooseneck-shaped spits of land untouched. The dusty park itself doesn't have much to speak of besides pit toilets and picnic tables.

Eating & Sleeping

Monument Valley ❶

✕ Stagecoach Dining Room $$

(mains $8-27; ⏰6:30am–9:30pm Central Time, shorter hours in winter) Goulding's restaurant is a replica of a film set built for John Ford's 1949 western *She Wore a Yellow Ribbon*. Tuck into the steaks or Navajo tacos piled high with chile and cheese.

🛏 Goulding's Lodge   Motel $$

(📞435-727-3231; www.gouldings.com; r $205-242, cabins $92, tent sites $26, RV sites $5; ❄🛜🏊🐕) This historical hotel a few miles west of Monument Valley has modern rooms, most with some view of the megaliths in the distance. Each has a DVD player so you can rent one of the many movies shot here.

🛏 View Hotel   Hotel $$$

(📞435-727-5555; www.monumentvalleyview.com; Hwy 163; r $209-265, ste $299-329; ❄@🛜) Probably the most aptly named hotel in Arizona. Rooms that end in numbers higher than 15 (for example 216) have unobstructed panoramas of Monument Valley below. Wi-fi available in the lobby only; restaurant on site.

Bluff ❷

✕ San Juan River Kitchen   New Mexican $$

(www.sanjuanriverkitchen.com; 75 E Main St; mains $14-20; ⏰5:30-10pm Tue-Sat) The inventive, regionally-sourced Mexican-American dishes here use organic ingredients whenever possible. Don't skip the homemade chipotle chocolate ice cream.

✕ Twin Rocks Cafe & Trading Post   Native American $$

(913 E Navajo Twins Dr; mains $6-18; ⏰7am-9pm) A full diner-style menu is available, but we recommend trying fry bread (deep-fried dough) as part of a breakfast sandwich or wrapped up as a Navajo taco.

🛏 Desert Rose Inn   Motel $$

(📞888-475-7673, 435-672-2303; www.desertroseinn.com; Hwy 191; r $105-119, cabins $139-179; ❄@🛜) Wood porches wrap completely around a dramatic, two-story log building at the edge of town. Quilts on pine beds add to the comfort of extra large rooms and cabins.

🛏 Recapture Lodge   Motel $

(📞435-672-2281; www.recapturelodge.com; Hwy 191; r incl breakfast $70-90; ❄@🛜🐕) A locally owned, rustic motel with super-knowledgeable staff who can help out with trek planning. There's plenty of shade around the small pool and on the property's 3½ miles of walking trails.

Blanding ❹

✕ Fattboyz Grillin   American $$

(www.facebook.com/pages/Fattboyz-Grillin; 164 N Hwy 191; mains $7-18; ⏰noon-9pm Mon-Sat) Good barbecued ribs, sandwiches and burgers. A Brian Kirby burger has it all: beef patty, barbecued pork, cheese *and* chile.

Mexican Hat

✕ Old River Grille   Diner $

(http://sanjuaninn.net; Hwy 163; mains $7-15; ⏰7am-9pm) Southwestern home cooking here includes some Navajo Nation dishes.

🛏 San Juan Inn   Motel $

(📞800-447-2022, 435-683-2220; www.sanjuaninn.net; Hwy 163; r $85-100; ❄) The cliffside motel perches high above the San Juan River. Rooms are pretty basic, but are the nicest in town. Trading post on site.

Dinosaur National Monument
Amazing fossil finds

Dinosaur Diamond Prehistoric Byway

29

Take a trip back in time to when Allosaurus walked the earth. Cruise through this incredibly fossil-rich landscape, then dig into the many museums and quarries to learn more.

TRIP HIGHLIGHTS

220 miles

Vernal
Another excellent dino museum; great overview film

200 miles

Dinosaur National Monument
More than 1600 pieces stick out of a wall of bones

5 4

● Rangely

● Price
FINISH

2

Moab ●
START

Fruita
Hands-on dinosaur museum fun and interpretive hikes

90 miles

SIX DAYS
351 MILES / 565KM

GREAT FOR...

BEST TIME TO GO
May and September have temperate weather, but activities for kiddos happen June to August.

ESSENTIAL PHOTO
A lower leg bone big as your body at Dinosaur National Monument.

BEST FOR FAMILIES
Digging to find 'dinosaur bones' at the Dinosaur Journey museum.

303

Dinosaur Diamond Prehistoric Byway

Imagine the most remote and rugged place you've seen. Driving the diamond you'll conquer high plateaus, traverse scenic canyons and cross tall mountains. Though arid now, in the late Jurassic period (154 to 147 million years ago) this mostly Morrison Formation terrain was a lush, subtropical forest. Eighty different vertebrates have been found within this one region. Utah and Colorado combined represent the most complete fossil record in the US.

❶ Moab

Situated between two national parks and surrounded by even more public land, Moab makes a good base for outdoor adventure. If you want to track area dinosaurs, pick up the topical pamphlets from the **Moab Information Center** (www. discovermoab.com; cnr Main & Center Sts; ⏱8am-7pm Mon-Sat, 9am-6pm Sun). The half-mile **Mill Canyon Dinosaur Trail**, 15 miles north of town, follows a Jurassic-era stream bed where fossils and petrified

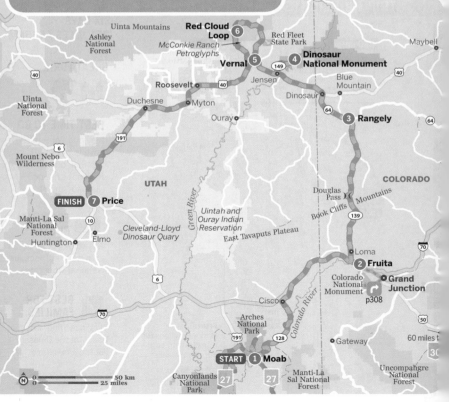

wood are to be seen. Plus there's a detour to a track site. **Comb Ridge Sauropod Trackway**, 23 miles north, contains four different sets of fossilized footprints.

Numerous outdoor operators lead excursions into the region. **Adrift Adventures** (800-874-4483, 435-259-8594; www.adrift.net; 378 N Main St; tours per person from $65) offers 4WD trips that focus on prehistoric sites – both dinosaur bones and ancient rock art. With **Canyonlands by Night and Day** (800-394-9978, 435-259-2628; www.canyonlandsbynight.com; 1861 N Hwy 191; sound & light show adult/child $69/59), an evening dinner cruise

LINK YOUR TRIP

27 Moab & Southeastern National Parks

Before your dinosaur odyssey, spend a few activity-filled days exploring the national parks around Moab.

30 San Juan Skyway & Million Dollar Highway

For incredible vistas and old mining towns, detour 105 miles southwest on Hwy 50 to start this trip in Ouray, Colorado.

down the Colorado comes complete with a sound and light show.

The Drive » Two miles north of Moab, follow the long and windy River Rd (Hwy 128) through the Colorado River gorge for 44 miles (1¼ hours) before exiting at Cisco, which is a further 42 speedy, interstate miles from Fruita.

- - - - - - - - - - - - -

TRIP HIGHLIGHT

❷ Fruita

Two miles inside the Colorado state line, stop at the **Trail Through Time** (www.blm.gov; 1-70, exit 2, McInnis Canyons National Conservation Area; ☉dawn-dusk), the best of four interpretive dinosaur trails around town. On the 1.5 mile loop you can learn loads about the prehistoric landscape from interpretive panels, touch in-situ bones and, in summer, check out the active **Mygatt-Moore Quarry**.

Maybe it's the desolation of the dry, rumbling country; maybe it's the lack of anything man-made in your view. Whatever the reason, it seems entirely possible to imagine dinosaurs roaming **Fruita Paleontological Area** (www.blm.gov; Horsetheif Rd, off Kings View Rd; admission free; ☉dawn-dusk). A half-mile loop trail leads past helpful signs illustrating the environment and the six dinosaurs found here during 100 years of off-and-on excavation.

Dinosaur Journey (970-858-7282; www.museumofwesternco.com; 550 Jurassic Ct; adult/child $8.50/6.50; ☉9am-5pm May-Sep, 10am-4pm Mon-Sat, from noon Sun Oct-Apr; ♿) is a fantastic little family-friendly museum where kiddos can make their own dinosaur tracks, dig for bones and be surprised by a spitting and spurting, animatronic dilophosauruses. Unlike many big-city museums, the fossils here are actually from the region.

✕ 🛏 p309

The Drive » Backtracking 4 miles west on I-70, take exit 15 north to CO 139. You start out in Loma, but soon enough the grey cliffs emerge and the road rises to wind it's way up and over Douglas Pass (8268ft). Driving the 71 miles to Rangely will take an hour and a half.

- - - - - - - - - - - - -

❸ Rangely

South of Rangely, **Canyon Pintado National Historic District** (www.blm.gov; CO 139; admission free; ☉24hr) protects the ancient archeology of the area's Freemont and Ute cultures. Seven rock-art sites are easily accessible off CO 139. Stop at the South Orientation Center sign (mile 52.8) for information or pick up a interpretive brochure at the **Rangely Chamber of Commerce** (970-675-5290; www.rangely.com; 209 E Main St; ☉1-5pm Mon-Fri). The latter also has a list of other rock-art sites scattered along area backroads.

An oil-service town, Rangely itself isn't much to look at, but its handful of motels and restaurants make it a good stop en route to Dinosaur National Monument.

✖ 🛏 p309

The Drive » Follow CO 64 out of Rangely, through a stark landscape; after 18 miles be sure to turn east (right) on Hwy 40 to get to the Colorado section of the monument.

TRIP HIGHLIGHT

④ Dinosaur National Monument

Straddling the Utah–Colorado state line, **Dinosaur National Monument** (www.nps.gov/dino; off Hwy 40; 7-day per vehicle $10; ⏰24hr, Quarry Visitor Center 8am-6pm mid-May–late Sep, 9am-5pm late Sep–mid-May, Canyon Area Visitor Center 9am-5pm June–early Sep, 10am-4pm Sat & Sun mid-Apr–May) protects one of North America's largest dinosaur fossil beds, discovered here in 1909. Though each state's section is beautiful, Utah has the bones.

Start at the **Canyon Area Visitor Center** in Colorado where you can pick up an interpretive brochure for the **Harpers Corner Scenic Drive** (31 miles one way), which cruises from 5921ft to 7625ft with several overlooks along the way.

Thirty miles west in Utah, absolutely do not miss the **Quarry Exhibit** (Dinosaur National Monument; ⏰9am-4pm), which is an enclosed, partially-excavated rock wall with more than 1600 actual bones sticking out – an amazing, almost unbelievable sight to see. (The area was once a stream bed where remains collected.) Follow the **Fossil Discovery Trail** (2.2 miles round-trip) to touch a few more rock-bound giant femurs and such.

The Drive » From the Utah side of the national monument, Vernal is 15 miles away via UT 149 and Hwy 40.

TRIP HIGHLIGHT

⑤ Vernal

The only town of any size around, Vernal, UT, serves as the gateway for the national monument. Not that you'd notice with a giant pink sauropod statue welcoming you or anything.

The informative film at the **Utah Field House of Natural History State Park Museum** (http://stateparks.utah.gov; 496 E Main St; ⏰9am-5pm Mon-Sat; ♿) provides a great all-round overview of the region's paleontological history. Interactive exhibits, expert interview videos, and, of course, giant mounted fossils, further tell the story.

✖ 🛏 p309

JOHN & LISA MERRILL/GETTY IMAGES ©

Kayaking at the Dinosaur National Monument

DETOUR: COLORADO NATIONAL MONUMENT

Start: ❷ Fruita

The **Colorado National Monument** (☎970-858-3617, ext 360; www.nps.gov/colm; Hwy 340; 7-day per vehicle $10; ⏲24hr, visitor center 9am-6pm) is the crown jewel of the Western Slope, a place where the setting sun seems to set fire to otherworldly red-rock formations and hikers test themselves against a starkly beautiful environment. Rising 2000ft above the river valley, these colorful canyons expose the geologic history of the area. Learn more about the different sedimentary layers at the visitor center, then step out to overlook the stratification in real life.

The monument contains a variety of hiking trails starting on the 23-mile **Rim Rock Drive**, most of them relatively short, such as the half-mile hike starting from the **Coke Ovens Trailhead** or a quarter-mile stroll starting at the **Devils Kitchen Trailhead**. The park's highest, **Black Ridge Trail** (5.5 miles one way) traipses up and down through the Morrison Formation of Jurassic dinosaur fame. The west entrance to this 32-sq-mile scenic wonder is 2 miles south of Fruita, off I-70.

The Drive ≫ Travel 10 miles north of Vernal on Hwy 191 to Red Fleet State Park. A further 12 miles north, turn west on Red Cloud Loop and follow signs up and around and down through forests where you may see deer and elk. You'll reach McConkie ranch at Dry Fork after 40 miles.

❻ Red Cloud Loop

Take a slowly scenic, 74-mile drive on the Red Cloud Loop backway to explore the ancient environs. Check out hundreds of fossilized dinosaur tracks at **Red Fleet State Park** (☎435-789-4432; http://stateparks.utah.gov; admission $7; ⏲6am-10pm Apr-Oct, 8am-5pm Nov & Dec). The 200ft of **McConkie Ranch Petroglyphs** (Dry Fork Canyon Rd; by donation; ⏲dawn-dusk) are also fascinating. Generous ranch owners built a little self-serve info shack with posted messages and a map, but be advised that the 800-year-old Fremont Indian art here requires some rock-scrambling to see. Being on private land has really helped; these alien-looking anthropomorphs are in much better shape than the many that have been desecrated by vandals on public lands. Before you go, stop at the **Dinosaurland Tourist Board** (☎800-477-5558; www.dinoland.com; 134 W Main; ⏲9am-5pm Mon-Fri) for pamphlets on this and other regional driving tours.

The Drive ≫ Red Cloud Loop ends where you started, in Vernal. From there follow Hwy 40 west through several small towns before you turn south at Hwy 191. The next 50 miles (one hour) snake through canyons and over ridges to reach Price. For Cleveland-Lloyd quarry, take CO 10 south to the Elmo-Cleveland turnoff and follow signs 15 miles east on dirt roads.

❼ Price

Though limited in scope, the **College of Eastern Utah Prehistoric Museum** (www.museum.ceu.edu; adult/child $5/2; ⏲9am-5pm Mon-Sat) has worked to make their fossil displays a bit more dynamic. Get directions there for the remote **Cleveland-Lloyd Dinosaur Quarry** (☎435-636-3600; www.blm.gov; off Hwy 10; adult/child $5/2; ⏲10am-5pm Thu-Sat late Mar-Oct), 32 miles south of Price. More than 12,000 bones have been taken from the ground there; the largest concentration of which belonged to meat-eating allosaurs. Excellent exhibits examine why so many of one species was found in one place. Salt Lake City is 110 miles northeast.

Eating & Sleeping

Fruita ②

✗ Aspen Street Coffee   Cafe $

(📞970-858-8888; 136 E Aspen Ave; dishes $2-8; ⏰6:30am-5pm Mon-Sat, 7am-1pm Sun; 📶) Simple wraps, strong coffee and homemade baked goods make this a great spot to fuel up before a hike or a drive.

✗ Hot Tomato Cafe   Pizza $$

(📞970-858-1117; www.hottomatocafe.com; 124 N Mulberry St; small pizzas $12-16; ⏰11am-9pm Tue-Sat) The liveliest place in town, Hot Tomato attracts a fun mix of outdoorsy mountain-biker types, vacationing families and local diners. The excellent thin-crust pizza here is made with organic flour and fresh toppings.

🛏 Balanced Rock Motel   Motel $

(📞970-858-7333, ext 4; http://balancedrock-motel.com; 126 S Coulson St; r $50-80; ❄️📶) Tidy and well-maintained, Balanced Rock proves an excellent value. The two-story, exterior-access indie motel is popular with area mountain bikers.

Rangely ③

✗ Mexican House   Mexican $$

(624 Market St; dishes $10-18; ⏰11am-9pm) Piping hot chips and tasty cabbage *pico de gallo* salsa start off every meal at this decent little Mexican joint. Try modern favorites like shrimp tacos as well as more traditional enchiladas.

🛏 Blue Mountain Inn & Suites   Hotel $$

(📞970-675-8888; www.bluemountaininn-rangely.com; 37 Park St; d $140; 🅿️🍽️📶♿) A timber-framed entrance and indoor pool with stone fireplace help make this the best low-rise hotel anywhere near the Colorado side

of Dinosaur National Monument. The French chef at the cafe outdoes himself, with desserts especially.

Vernal ⑤

✗ Backdoor Grille   Cafe $

(87 W Main St; mains $5-8; ⏰11am-6pm Mon-Sat) For homemade soup, a crusty panini and a good read, stop into Backdoor Grille, at the rear of Bitter Creek Books.

✗ The Porch   Southern $$

(www.facebook.com/theporchvernal; 251 E Main St; lunches $8-12, dinner mains $14-22; ⏰11am-2pm & 5-9pm Mon-Fri, 5-9pm Sat) Southern US favorites done right. The chicken fried steak and blackened shrimp taste just like a Louisiana grandmother would make.

🛏 Econo Lodge   Motel $

(📞435-789-2000; www.econolodge.com; 311 E Main St; r $69-99) Reasonable motel rooms can be hard to find in this town; these will do.

🛏 Holiday Inn Express & Suites   Hotel $$

(📞435-789-4654; www.vernalhotel.com; 1515 W Hwy 40; r incl breakfast $100-170, ste $130-200; ❄️📶♿) One of the town's newer chain hotels, the HI Express has loads of amenities (fitness center, business center, laundry). Kids laughter usually fills the indoor pool.

🛏 Landmark Inn & Suites   Motel $

(📞888-738-1800, 435-781-1800; www.landmark-inn.com; 301 E 100 S; motel r incl breakfast $129-169, B&B $80-100; 📶) Contemporary comforts like plush mattresses and flat-screen TVs come standard in the upscale motel rooms, and there's an unattended B&B in a big house across the street.

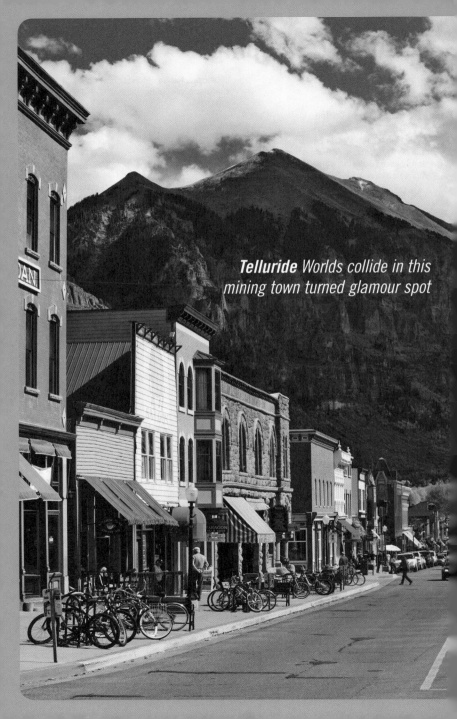

Telluride *Worlds collide in this mining town turned glamour spot*

San Juan Skyway & Million Dollar Highway

30

Encompassing the vertiginous Million Dollar Highway, the San Juan Skyway loops southern Colorado, traveling magnificent passes to alluring Old West towns.

TRIP HIGHLIGHTS

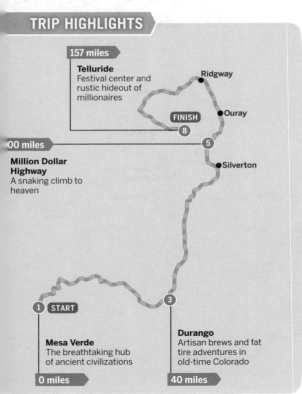

157 miles

Telluride
Festival center and rustic hideout of millionaires

Ridgway

 FINISH

Ouray

00 miles

Million Dollar Highway
A snaking climb to heaven

Silverton

1 START

Mesa Verde
The breathtaking hub of ancient civilizations

0 miles

3

Durango
Artisan brews and fat tire adventures in old-time Colorado

40 miles

6–8 DAYS
157 MILES / 253KM

GREAT FOR...

BEST TIME TO GO
Visit from June to October for clear roads and summer fun.

ESSENTIAL PHOTO
Snap Mesa Verde's dramatic cliff dwellings.

BEST FOR FOODIES
The farm-to-table options in Mancos and Durango.

311

Classic Trip

San Juan Skyway & Million Dollar Highway

30

This is the west at its most rugged; of a landscape of twisting mountain passes and ancient ruins, with burly peaks and gusty high desert plateaus, a land of unbroken spirit. Beyond the thrills of outdoor adventure and the rough charm of old plank saloons, there remains the lingering mystery of the region's earliest inhabitants whose awe-inspiring cliff dwellings make up Mesa Verde National Park.

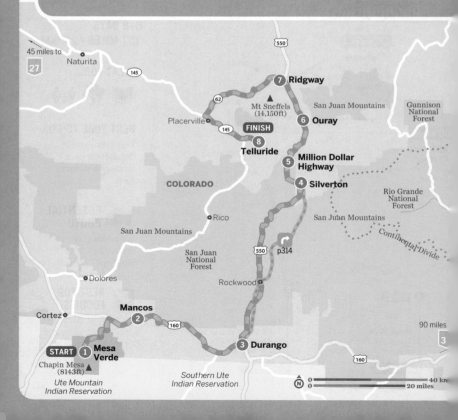

TRIP HIGHLIGHT

① Mesa Verde

More than 700 years after Ancestral Puebloans left, the mystery behind their last known home remains. Amateur anthropologists love it; the incredible cultural heritage makes it unique among American national parks. Ancestral Puebloan sites are scattered throughout the canyons and mesas, perched on a high plateau south of Mancos, though many remain off-limits to visitors.

If you only have a few hours, stop at **Mesa Verde Visitor &**

LINK YOUR TRIP

27 Moab & Southeastern National Parks

It's a three-hour drive from Telluride. Take CO-145 north to CO-90 west, which becomes UT-26 west. It ends at UT-141, head north.

31 Colorado's High Country Byways

From Durango it's a four-hour drive on the CO-160 to Alamosa; from here take the CO-285 north to Great Sand Dunes National Park.

Research Center (☎800-305-6053, 970-529-5034; www.nps.gov/meve; North Rim Rd; ⊙8am-7pm daily Jun–early Sep, 8am-5pm early Sep–mid-Oct, closed mid-Oct–May; ﹝ﺡ﹞) and drive around **Chapin Mesa** where you can take the short walk to the easily accessible Spruce Tree House, the park's best-preserved cliff dwelling.

If you have a day or more, buy tickets in advance for popular ranger-led tours of Cliff Palace and Balcony House. These active visits involve climbing rung ladders and scooting through ancient passages. The heat in summer is brutal – go early if you want to hike or cool off at the informative **Chapin Mesa Museum** (☎970-529-4475; www.nps.gov/meve; Chapin Mesa Rd; admission included with park entry; ⊙8am-6:30pm Apr–mid-Oct, 8am-5pm mid-Oct–Apr; ﹝P﹞﹝ﺡ﹞) near Spruce Tree House.

The Drive » Entering Mesa Verde, go immediately left for the visitor center. Return to the main access road. It takes 45 minutes to reach the main attractions on Wetherill Mesa and the road is steep and narrow in places. Leaving the park, head east on US-160 for Mancos, exit right for Main St and follow to the intersection with Grand Ave.

② Mancos

Blink and you'll miss this hamlet embracing the offbeat, earthy and slightly strange (witness the puppets dangling through the roof of the local coffee shop). With a vibrant arts community and love for locavore food, Mancos is the perfect rest stop. You will find most points of interest in a three-block radius. These include a distillery, custom hat shop, galleries and good cooking. During the last Friday of each month, the Arts Walk fires up what locals deem 'downtown.'

The area's oddest accommodations is **Jersey Jim Lookout Tower** (☎970-533-7060; r $40; ⊙mid-May–mid-Oct), a watch tower standing 55ft high with panoramic views. This sought-after lodging is 14 miles north of Mancos at 9800ft. It comes with an Osborne Fire Finder and topographic map.

The Drive » Drive east on US-160. Reaching Durango turn left onto Camino del Rio and right onto W 11th St in 0.5 miles. Main Ave is your second right.

TRIP HIGHLIGHT

③ Durango

A regional darling, Durango's style straddles its ragtime past and a cool, cutting edge future where townie bikes, caffeine and farmers markets rule. Outdoor enthusiasts get ready to be smitten. The **Animas River** floats right through

Classic Trip

town; float it or fly-fish it, while hundreds of mountain bike rides range from scenic dirt roads to steep single track. When you've gotten your kicks, you can join the summer crowds strolling **Main Avenue**, stopping at book shops, boutiques and breweries.

Leave town heading north on the **San Juan Skyway** (US 550), which passes farms and stables as it starts the scenic climb toward Silverton. Bring your hunger to the family-run **James Ranch** (Animas River Valley; mains $6-13; ⏰11am-7pm Mon-Sat) just 10 miles out of Durango. The

outstanding farmstand grill features the farm's own organic grass-fed beef, cheese and fresh produce market. Steak sandwiches and focaccia cheese melts with caramelized onions simply rock. Kids dig the goats. Thursday features Burgers & Bands from July to October (adult/child $20/10). A two-hour farm tour ($18) is held on Mondays and Fridays at 9:30am and Tuesdays at 4pm.

✕ 🛏 p319

The Drive ≫ Take Main Ave heading north. Leaving Durango it becomes US 550, also part of the San Juan Skyway. James Ranch is 10 miles in on the right side. A band of 14,000-ft peaks become visible to the right and frequent pullouts offer scenic views. Before Silverton the road climbs both Coal Banks Pass (10,640ft) and Molas Pass (10,910).

DETOUR:
NARROW GAUGE RAILROAD

Start: ❸ Durango

Climb aboard the steam driven **Durango & Silverton Narrow Gauge Railroad** (☎970-247-2733, toll-free 877-872-4607; www.durangotrain.com; 479 Main Ave; adult/child return from $85/51; ⏰departure at 8am, 8:45am & 9:30am; ♿) for the train ride of the summer. The train, running between Durango and Silverton, has been in continuous operation for 123 years, and the scenic 45-mile journey north to Silverton, a National Historic Landmark, takes 3½ hours one-way. Most locals recommend taking it one way and returning from Silverton via bus, it's faster. It's most glorious in late September and early October when the Aspens go golden.

---

❹ **Silverton**

Ringed by snowy peaks and proudly steeped in tawdry mining town lore, Silverton would seem more at home in Alaska than the lower 48. At 9318ft the air is thin, but that discourages no-one from hitting the bar stool.

Explore it all and don't shy away from the mere 500 locals – they're happy to see a fresh face. It's a two-street town, but only respectable **Greene Street**, now home to restaurants and trinket shops, is paved. One block over, notorious **Blair Street** was a silver rush hub of brothels and boozing establishments, banished to the back street where real ladies didn't stroll.

Stop at the **Silverton Museum** (☎970-387-5838; www.silvertonhistoricsociety.org; 1557 Greene St; adult/child $5/free; ⏰10am-4pm Jun-Oct; 🅿 ♿), housed in the old San Juan County Jail, to see the original cells. It tells the Silverton story from terrible mining accidents to 'saloons, alcohol, prostitution, gambling, robbery...there were many opportunities to die violently.'

Most visitors use Silverton as a hub for jeep tours – sketchy mining roads climbing in all directions offer unreal views. In winter,

Silverton Mountain

(☏970-387-5706; www.
silvertonmountain.com;
State Hwy 110; daily lift ticket
$49, all-day guide & lift ticket
$99) offers experts some
serious powder skiing on
ungroomed terrain.

🍴 p319

The Drive » Leaving Silverton
head north on US 550, the
Million Dollar Highway. It
starts with a gentle climb but
becomes steeper. Hairpin turns
slow traffic at Molas Pass to
25mph. The most hair-raising
sections follow, with 15mph
speed limits in places. The road
lacks guardrails and drops are
huge, so stay attentive. Pullouts
provide relief between mile
markers 91 and 93.

TRIP HIGHLIGHT

⑤ Million Dollar Highway

The origin of the name
of this 24-mile stretch
between Silverton and
Ouray is disputed – some
say it took a million
dollars a mile to build
it in the 1920s; others
purport the roadbed
contains valuable ore.

Among America's most
memorable drives, this
breathtaking stretch
passes old mine head
frames and larger-
than-life alpine scenery.
Though paved, its blind
corners, tunnels and
narrow turns would
put the Roadrunner on
edge. It's often closed in
winter, when it's said to
have more avalanches
than the entire state

LOCAL KNOWLEDGE: COLORADO'S HAUTE ROUTE

An exceptional way to enjoy hundreds of miles of
single track in summer or virgin powder slopes in
winter, **San Juan Hut System** (☏970-626-3033;
www.sanjuanhuts.com; per person $30) continues the
European tradition of hut-to-hut adventures with
five backcountry mountain huts. Bring just your
food, flashlight and sleeping bag – amenities include
padded bunks, propane stoves, wood stoves for
heating and firewood.

Mountain-biking routes go from Durango or
Telluride to Moab, winding through high alpine
and desert regions. Or pick one hut as your base.
There's terrain for all levels, though skiers should
have knowledge of snow and avalanche conditions
or go with a guide. The website has helpful tips and
information on rental skis, bikes and (optional)
guides based in Ridgway or Ouray.

of Colorado. Snowfall
usually starts in October.

Leaving Silverton, the
road ascends Mineral
Creek Valley, passing the
Longfellow mine ruins
one mile before **Red
Mountain Pass** (11,018ft),
with sheer drops and
hairpin turns slowing
traffic to 25mph.

Descending towards
Ouray, visit **Bear Creek
Falls**, a large turnout
with a daring viewing
platform over the
crashing several hundred
foot falls. A difficult
eight-mile trail here
switchbacks to even
greater views – not for
vertigo sufferers.

Stop at the **lookout**
over Ouray at mile
marker 92. Turn right for
the lovely **Amphitheater
Campground** (☏877-444-

6777; http://www.recreation.
gov; US Hwy 550; tent sites $16;
🕑Jun-Aug).

The Drive » The Million
Dollar Highway makes a
steep descent into Ouray and
becomes Main St.

⑥ Ouray

A well-preserved mining
village snug beneath
imposing peaks, Ouray
breeds enchantment.
It's named after the
legendary Ute chief
who kept the peace
between the white
settlers and the crush
of miners invading the
San Juan Mountains
in the early 1870s, by
relinquishing the Ute
tribal lands. The area
is rife with hot springs.
One cool cave spring,
now located underneath

Classic Trip

WHY THIS IS A CLASSIC TRIP
CAROLYN MCCARTHY, AUTHOR

This trip is Colorado at its most breathtaking, with winding country roads and spunky mining towns backed by the chiseled San Juan mountains. Want to feel the Wild West? Try making small talk with the barkeeps and hotel hosts in Ouray, Silverton and Telluride. In these parts, every 19th century saloon or historic hotel has a ghost story to share. Check out the bullet holes in Telluride's New Sheridan bar.

Above: Durango & Silverton Narrow Gauge Railroad
Left: Spruce Tree House, Mesa Verde
Right: Hiking near Telluride

FRANZ-MARC FREI/CORBIS ©

RUSS BISHOP/GETTY IMAGES ©

WHIT RICHARDSON/GETTY IMAGES ©

the **Wiesbaden** (📞970-325-4347; www. wiesbadenhotsprings.com; 625 5th St; r $132-347; 🐕🛜🏊) hotel, was favored by Chief Ouray. Now you can soak there by the hour.

The annual Ouray Ice Festival draws elite climbers for a four-day competition. But the town also lends thrills to hikers and 4WD fans. If you're skittish about driving yourself, **San Juan Scenic Jeep Tours** (📞970-325-0089; http:// sanjuanjeeptours.com; 206 7th Ave; adult/child half-day $59/30; 👶) takes open-air Jeeps into the high country, offering special wildflower or ghost town trips. It's worth hiking up to **Box Canyon Falls** (off Box Canyon Rd; adult/ child $4/2; ⏰8am-8pm Jun-Aug; 🅿👶) from the west end of 3rd Avenue. A suspension bridge leads you into the belly of this 285ft waterfall. The surrounding area is rich in bird life – look for the protected black swift which nests in the rock-face.

🛏 p319

The Drive » Leave Ouray heading north via Main St, which becomes US 550 N. It's a flat 10-mile drive to Ridgway's only traffic light. Turn left onto Sherman St. The center of town is spread over the next half-mile.

TELLURIDE FESTIVALS

For information see www.visittelluride.com/festivals-events.

Mountainfilm (late May) A four-day screening of high-caliber outdoor adventure and environmental films.

Telluride Bluegrass Festival (late Jun) Thousands enjoy a weekend of top-notch rollicking alfresco bluegrass going well into the night.

Telluride Film Festival (early Sep) National and international films are premiered throughout town, and the event attracts big-name stars.

---

⑦ Ridgway

Wide open meadows backed by snowcovered San Juans and the stellar Mt Sneffels, Ridgway is an inviting blip of a burg. The backdrop of John Wayne's 1969 cowboy classic *True Grit*, today it sports a sort of neo-Western charm.

Sunny rock pools at **Orvis Hot Springs** (☎970-626-5324; www.orvishotsprings.com; 1585 County Rd 3; per hour/day $10/14) make this clothing-optional hot spring hard to resist. Though it gets its fair share of exhibitionists, a variety of soaking areas (100 to 114 degrees F) mean you can probably scout out the perfect quiet spot. Less appealing are the private indoor pools lacking fresh air. It's nine miles north of Ouray, outside Ridgway.

The Drive » Leaving town heading west, Sherman St becomes CO 62. Take this easy drive 23 miles. At the crossroads go left onto CO 145 S for Telluride. Approaching town there's a traffic circle, take the second exit onto W Colorado Ave. The center of Telluride is in 0.5 miles.

TRIP HIGHLIGHT

⑧ Telluride

Surrounded on three sides by mastodon peaks, exclusive Telluride was once a rough mining town. Today it's dirtbag-meets-diva – where glitterati mix with ski bums and renowned music and film festivals create a frolicking summer atmosphere.

The very renovated center still has palpable oldtime charm. Stop into the plush **New Sheridan Bar** (☎970-728-3911; www.newsheridan.com; 231 W Colorado Ave; ⊙5pm-2am) to find out the story of those old bullet holes in the wall and the plucky survival of the bar itself, even as the adjoining hotel sold off chandeliers to pay the heating bills during waning mining fortunes.

Touring downtown, check out the **free box** where you can swap unwanted items, the tradition is a point of civic pride. Then take a free 15-minute **gondola** (⊙7am-12am; 🚻) ride up to the Telluride Mountain Village, where you can rent a mountain bike, dine or just bask in the panoramas.

If you are planning on attending a festival, book your tickets and lodging months in advance.

✕ 🛏 p319

Eating & Sleeping

Durango ❸

✖ East by Southwest   Fusion, Sushi $$$

(📞970-247-5533; http://eastbysouthwest.com; 160 E College Dr; sushi $4-13, mains $12-24; ⏰11:30am-3pm & 5-10pm Mon-Sat, 5-10pm Sun; 📶 🚼) Locals rave about this hip enclave serving pan-Asian and creative sushi in a congenial low-key setting. The food rocks, but don't skip the sake cocktails.

✖ Ska Brewing Company   Brewpub $$

(📞970-247-5792; www.skabrewing.com; 225 Girard St; mains $7-13; ⏰11am-3am Mon-Wed, 11am-3pm & 5-8pm Thu, 11am-8pm Fri) Ska ranks among Colorado's finest brews. This tasting-room bar was once just a production facility, today it gets packed with locals after work. Its onsite restaurant, the Container, serves delicious brick oven pizzas, heaping sandwiches with local beef and cheese, and fresh salads.

🛏 Rochester House   Hotel $$

(📞970-385-1920, toll-free 800-664-1920; www. rochesterhotel.com; 721 E 2nd Ave; d $169-229; 😊❄🛜) Influenced by old Westerns, with movie posters and marquee lights, this adorable hotel splices the new West with old Hollywood. Rooms are spacious and breakfast is served in an old train car. There's a free summer concert series in the courtyard, Wednesdays at 4:30pm.

Silverton ❹

✖ Montanya Distillers   Pub $$

(www.montanyadistillers.com; 1309 Greene St; mains $6-13; ⏰12pm-10pm) Dangerous bartenders at this mod bar on Greene St can talk you into anything while crafting exotic cocktails with homemade syrups, berries and its very own award-winning rum. With a fun atmosphere, especially the rooftop deck in summer. Order a fruit and cheese plates or the famous house spinach and artichoke dip.

Ouray ❻

🛏 Box Canyon Lodge & Hot Springs   Lodge $$

(📞970-325-4981, 800-327-5080; www. boxcanyonouray.com; 45 3rd Ave; r $110-165, apt $278-319; 🛜) Not every hotel offers geothermal heated rooms, and these are spacious and accommodating. The real treat here is four wooden spring-fed hot tubs, perfect for a romantic stargazing soak. Book well ahead.

Telluride ❽

✖ La Cocina de Luz   Mexican, Organic $$

(www.lacocinatelluride.com; 123 E Colorado Ave; mains $9-19; ⏰9am-9pm; 📶) Lovingly serving organic and Mexican, it's no wonder that the lunch line runs deep at this healthy *taquería*. Perks are a salsa and chip bar, handmade tortillas and margaritas with organic lime and agave nectar. With vegan, gluten-free options too.

✖ New Sheridan Chop House   Modern American $$$

(📞970-728-4531; www.newsheridan.com; 231 W Colorado Ave; mains from $19; ⏰5pm-2am) For an intimate dinner on embroidered velvet benches. Start with a cheese plate, from there the menu gets Western, for example pasta with wild mushroom and sage. Carnivores should try the elk shortloin in a hard cider reduction. For a treat, end with a flourless dark chocolate cake in fresh caramel sauce. Service is superb.

🛏 Telluride Town Park Campground   Campground $

(📞970-728-2173; 500 E Colorado Ave; campsite vehicle/walk-in $23/15; ⏰mid-May–mid-Oct; 🛜) Right in the center of town, this lovely spot has 20 sites with great views, some river beaches and bathhouse access. It fills up quickly in the high season.

Aspen World-class skiing and
mountain adventures

Colorado's High Country Byways

31

This breathtaking trip takes you from Colorado's front range to the high-country byways that connect Rocky Mountain National Park with the continental divide and scudding mountains of the south.

TRIP HIGHLIGHTS

333 miles

Aspen
Old money, glitz, glam, and Colorado's most dramatic peak

29 miles

Boulder
The People's Republic walks to a beat all its own

START
● Denver

80 miles

Rocky Mountain National Park
Up in the skyway, heaven's splendor is everywhere

9 **FINISH**

Great Sand Dunes National Park
Colorado's wind-whipped desolation angel

540 miles

5–7 DAYS
540 MILES / 869KM

GREAT FOR...

BEST TIME TO GO

June to September for clear roads, wildflowers, aspens and great views.

 ESSENTIAL PHOTO

Maroon Bells.

 BEST FOR WILDLIFE

Capture Colorado's signature peak in all its alpenglow glory.

31 Colorado's High Country Byways

This high-country Rocky Mountain thriller brings wild-world explorers across the continental divide through hair-pin turns, lost alpine lakes, exhilarating landscapes, broken-down mining towns and some of the state's most tanned and toned resorts and cities. You'll climb to 12,096 feet, dusty-bottom your way past towering snowcapped peaks, finally ending in a vast sand-dune wonderworld of arching skies, howling winds and surreal landscapes.

1 Denver

Spirited and urbane, Denver is the West's cosmopolitan capital, and well worth a day of exploration (see p338). This city is blessed with great museums, tons of sunshine and spectacular parks and bike trails.

✗ ⨼ p327

The Drive ⟫ Take I-70 N on this 45-minute drive, veering west onto US 36 W, which will take you past the worthwhile **Butterfly Pavilion** (www. butterflies.org; 6252 West 104th Ave; adult/senior/child

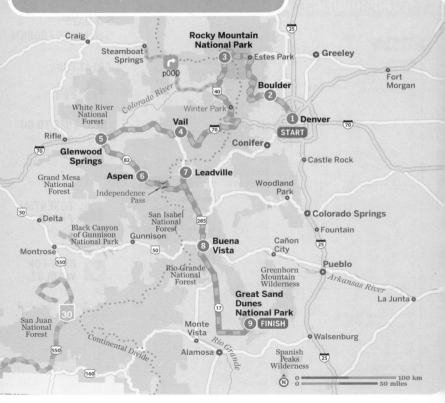

$9.50/7.50/6.50; ⏱9am-5pm; P) , on your way to crunched-out Boulder.

- - - - - - - - - - - - - - - - -

TRIP HIGHLIGHT

② Boulder

Tucked up against its soaring signature Flatirons, this idyllic college town has a sweet location and a palpable eco-sophistication.

If you only have a couple of hours, head straight to **Chautauqua Park** (www.chautauqua.com; 900 Baseline Rd; admission free; ⏹HOP 2) for some of the best hikes and views on the Front Range. Then it's down past the stroll-worthy **University of Colorado at Boulder** (CU; ☎303-492-6301; www.colorado.edu; Euclid Autopark;

LINK YOUR TRIP

15 **Enchanted Circle & Eastern Sangres**

Head directly south on bumpy backroads to Toas, joining the New Mexico crimson-hued Enchanted Circle.

30 **San Juan Skyway & Million Dollar Hwy**

From the Great Sand Dunes National Park, head up to Hwy 50 and past the mysterious Black Canyon of the Gunnison to Ouray.

parking per hour $1.50-3; ⏱tours 9:30am & 1:30pm Mon-Fri, 10:30am Sat; P) ; ▯203, 204, 209, 225, AB, B, DASH, DD, DM, GS, J, SKIP, STAMPEDE) campus to the **Boulder Creek Bike Path** (admission free; ⏱24 hr;) and its riverfront parks. The pedestrian-only **Pearl Street Mall** (www.boulderdowntown.com; Pearl St, btwn 11th St and 14th St; P) ; ▯203, 204, 205, 206, 208, 225, AB, B, BOLT, DASH, DD, DM, GS, JUMP, N, Y) is lively and perfect for strolling.

✗ p327

The Drive » From downtown head west on Canyon Blvd (Colorado 119) winding your way up Boulder Canyon, past towering rock formations and the Barker Reservoir to the hippie mountain enclave of Nederland. From there, it's north on the stunning Peak-to-Peak Hwy 72, past Long's Peak to Estes Park, the eastern entrance to Rocky Mountain National Park. It'll take two to four hours.

- - - - - - - - - - - - - - - - -

TRIP HIGHLIGHT

③ Rocky Mountain National Park

With one foot on either side of the continental divide and behemoths of granite in every direction, **Rocky Mountain National Park** (☎970 586 1242; www.nps.gov/romo) takes you to the wild-tufted top of the United States.

Estes Park (☎800-443-7837, 970-577-9900; www.visitestespark.com; 500 Big Thompson Ave; ⏱9am-8pm daily Jun-Aug, 8am-5pm

Mon-Fri, 9am-5pm Sat, 10am-4pm Sun Sep-May;), with its fun main drag and plethora of kitsch shopping, is a necessary stop into the park. From there, head into the park to the **Moraine Park Museum** (☎970-586-1206; Bear Lake Rd; ⏱9am-4:30pm Jun-Oct), before deciding on your route through the park and a day hike.

⌷ p327

The Drive » On this day-long drive from downtown Estes, head into the park on US 34 (generally open late May to October, depending on snow). From there, it's down past the fun resort town of **Grand Lake** (☎800-531-1019, 970-627-3402; www.grandlakechamber.com; cnr West Portal Rd & Hwy 34; ⏱9am-5pm Mon-Sat, 10am-4pm Sun Jun-Aug) and the Winter Park Ski area, over **Berthoud Pass** (www.berthoudpass.com; Hwy 40), up I-70, over the heart-trembling **Vail Pass** (day/season pass $6/50), and down into Vail.

- - - - - - - - - - - - - - - - -

④ Vail

If you have a day, hop on the **Vail to Breckenridge Bike Path** (www.fs.usda.gov) and ride it for as far as your lungs will take you. You can also grab the **Eagle Bahn Gondola** (☎970-476-9090; www.vail.com; Lionshead Plaza; per person $25; ⏱8am-5pm winter, 9am-6pm summer;) to a cool mountain top summit, try a round at the **Vail Golf Club** (☎888-709-3939; www.vailrec.com; 1778 Vail Valley Dr; 9-/18-holes $55/90

May-Oct), a ride at the **Stables** ([☎]970-476-6941; www.vailstables.com; Spraddle Creek Rd; rides 1/2/3/hr $65/90/160; [☺]May-Sep; [👤]), or a soar with **Vail Valley Paragliding** ([☎]970-845-7321; www.vailvalleyparagliding. com; per person $185-250) or **Zip Adventures** ([☎]970-926-9470; www.zipadventures. com; 4098 Hwy 131, Wolcott; per person $150; [☺]mid-Apr–Nov; [👤]).

[🛏] p327

The Drive ❯❯ From Vail, it's a straight hour-long shot west along I-70 to Glenwood Springs. Along the way, you pass through the amazing Glenwood Canyon, as you marvel at the hanging bridge construction and fractured canyon walls.

BRENT WINEBRENNER/GETTY IMAGES ©

❺ Glenwood Springs

Perched at the confluence of the Colorado and Roaring Fork Rivers at the end of Glenwood Canyon, **Glenwood Hot Springs** ([☎]970-947-2955; www.hotspringspool.com; 401 N River St; admission adult/child $19.25/11.75, lower rates off peak; [☺]7:30am-10pm late Jun-Aug, from 9am Sep-May; [👤]) have been a travel destination for centuries. The Ute Indians meditated in steamy **thermal caves** ([☎]970-945-0667; www.yampahspa. com; 709 E 6th St; admission incl towel rental $12; [☺]9am-9pm) here, then called Yampah (Great Medicine). Before or after your hot springs or thermal caves treatment, you can rent a

bike with **Canyon Bikes** ([☎]800-439-3043; www. canyonbikes.com; 319 6th St; half-day rental per adult/child $19/15; [☺]8am-8pm Jun-Aug; [👤]) or charge Class III and IV rapids with **Colorado Whitewater Rafting** ([☎]800-993-7238; www.coloradowhitewaterrafting. com; 2000 Devereux Rd; half-day adult/child $52/42; [☺]May-Aug; [👤]) through Glenwood Canyon.

[🛏] p327

The Drive ❯❯ From Glenwood cruise south through the Roaring Fork Valley on CO-82 for about 40 miles to Aspen. The further up the valley you go, the bigger the homes. Stop in old mining towns such as

Carbondale and Basalt, to ground yourself before hitting glitzed-out Aspen.

TRIP HIGHLIGHT

❻ Aspen

Aspen is a singular town unique to the world. An intoxicating cocktail of cowboy grit, Euro panache, Hollywood glam, Ivy League brains, fresh powder, live music and lots of money.

In summer, winter, spring or fall, the ski resorts of **Aspen Mountain** ([☎]800-525-6200; www.aspensnowmass. com; lift ticket adult/child $117/82; [☺]9am-4pm

Rocky Mountain National Park

Dec–mid-Apr; 🚶), **Aspen Highlands** (📞970-925-1220; www.aspensnowmas.com; Prospector Rd; Aspen Mountain day pass summer $28, 1-day winter lift ticket adult/child $114/79; ⊘9am-3.30pm; 🚶), **Snowmass** (📞866-352-1763; www.aspensnowmass.com; Aspen Mountain day pass summer $28, 1-day winter lift ticket adult/child $114/79; ⊘lift 8am-3:30pm; 🚶) and **Buttermilk** (📞800-525-6200, 970-925-1220; www.aspensnowmass.com; Buttermilk Rd & Hwy 82; Aspen Mountain day pass summer $28, 1-day winter lift ticket adult/child $114/79; ⊘8am-3:30pm; 🚶), offer world-class skiing and

mountain adventures. Hikers won't want to miss a day-trip to the **Maroon Bells** (📞970-925-3445; www.fs.usda.gov; Maroon Creek Rd; ⊘9am-5pm Memorial Day-Oct; 🚶) – quite simply one of the most beautiful mountains in the world. Downtown Aspen has some of the West's best restaurants, as well as plenty of galleries and the noteworthy and eyebrow-raising **Aspen Center for Environmental Studies** (ACES; 📞970-925-5756; www.aspennature.org; Hallam Lake, 100 Puppy Smith St; ⊘9am-5pm Mon-Fri; P 🚶).

🍴 🛏 p327

The Drive » During the summer, it'll only take a few hours to go over Independence Pass (CO-82) to Leadville. Wintertime, you'll need to backtrack clear to Vail to get here on the slow road. No matter which route you take, this is spectacular country.

- - - - - - - - - -

7 Leadville

Leadville was once the second biggest city in Colorado. But unlike other historic towns with mining roots, Leadville never made the switch to resort status.

Dive into town history at the **Healy**

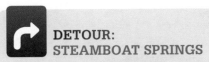

DETOUR: STEAMBOAT SPRINGS

Start ❸ Rocky Mountain National Park

You can easily extend your trip by heading west from Grandby on US 40, to the ski resort and peaced-out mountain village of Steamboat Springs. When you're in town, don't miss hikes and bikes in the nearby wilderness, followed by a soak in **Strawberry Park Hot Springs** (📞970-870-1517; www.strawberryhotsprings.com; 44200 County Rd; per day adult/child $10/5, camping sites $55, cabins $65; ⏰10am-10:30pm Sun-Thu, to midnight Fri & Sat; 👪), Colorado's best.

House Museum and Dexter Cabin (www.historycolorado.org; 912 Harrison Ave; adult/child 6-12yr $6/4.50; ⏰10am-4:30pm mid-May–Sep), before a wilderness outing to the nearby **Mt Massive Wilderness Area**, **Twin Lakes** (📞719-486-9345; www.twinlakescolorado.com; 6411 Hwy 82; r $95-125; ⏰May-Oct 1; 🅿😊❄📶), **Ski Cooper** (📞800-707-6114; www.skicooper.com; Hwy 24; lift ticket adult/child $47/27; ⏰9am-4pm Dec–mid-Apr; 👪) or the **Matchless Mine** (E th Rd; adult/child 6-12yr $7/3, combo ticket with Mining Hall of Fame $10/5; ⏰9am-5pm, Jun-Sep).

The Drive » It's only a couple hours' drive straight south from Leadville to Buena Vista, you could spend a few days exploring here. First, you pass the headwaters of the Arkansas, as you descend into the Arkansas River Valley. The Collegiate Peaks tower to your right, while Buffalo Peaks Wilderness is well worth a stop on your left.

❽ Buena Vista

With 14,197ft **Mt Princeton** (📞719 539 3591; www.summitpost.org; Mt Princeton Rd; ⏰best Jun-Sep; 👪) and the rest of the **Collegiate Peaks** providing a dramatic backdrop to the west, and the icy Arkansas River with its Class II and IV rapids best explored with **Buffalo Joe's Whitewater Rafting** (📞866-283-3563; www.buffalojoe.com; 113 N Railroad St; half-/full day adult $64/98, child $54/78; ⏰May-Sep; 👪) rushing by the boulder-filled hills east of town, Buena Vista certainly lives up to its name. Whether you're after hiking, biking, paddling, achy-bones-soaking at **Mt Princeton Hot Springs Resort** (📞888-395-7799; www.mtprinceton.com; 15870 Co Rd 162; day pass adult/child from $18/12, rooms/cabins from $124/164; ⏰8am-10pm; 👪🐾) or simply

stupendous landscapes, this is a town that has adventure playground written all over it.

🛏 p327

The Drive » It gets pretty flat for a while, but don't worry, as you head down more than 100 miles south to the Great Sand Dunes, things start to get more interesting at every mile marker. Salida is a fun hometown worth a stop along the way.

`TRIP HIGHLIGHT`

❾ Great Sand Dunes National Park

For all of Colorado's striking natural sights, this sea of sand is a place where nature's magic is on full display.

At the center of the **park** (📞719-378-6399; www.nps.gov/grsa; 11999 Hwy 150; ⏰8:30am-6:30pm summer, shorter hours rest of year; 👪) is a 55-sq-mile dune of sand surrounded by rigid mountain peaks on one side and glassy wetlands on the other. After long drives on the straight highways of high plains or twisting byways through the Rocky Mountains, it's a bit unnerving to find yourself so suddenly standing amid the landscape of the Sahara. While you're here, take a while to head out for a hike or mountain bike, or continue north to the spectacular **Crestone Needle** (📞866-351-2282; www.crestonevisit.com; 116 S Alder St; ⏰hours vary).

Eating & Sleeping

Denver ❶

🍴 Root Down   Modern American $$$
(📞303-993-4200; www.rootdowndenver.
com; 1600 W 33rd Ave; small plates $7-17, mains
$18-28; ⏰5-10pm Sun-Thu, 5-11pm Fri & Sat,
10am-2:30pm Sat & Sun; 🚗) In a converted gas
station, chef Justin Cucci has undertaken one
of the city's most ambitious culinary concepts,
marrying sustainable 'field-to-fork' practices,
high-concept culinary fusions and a low-impact,
energy efficient ethos.

🛏 Curtis   Boutique Hotel $$
(📞303-571-0300; www.thecurtis.com; 1405
Curtis St; d $159-239; 🐕❄@📶; 🖥15 RTD)
Pop culture is worshiped at this boutique joint
that also sells happy relaxation. There are 13
themed floors and each is devoted to a different
genre of American pop culture.

Boulder ❷

🍴 The Sink   Pub $
(www.thesink.com; 1165 13th St; mains $5-12;
⏰11am-2am, kitchen to 10pm; 👶; 🖥203, 204,
225, DASH, SKIP) Waiters bob and weave under
the low-slung, graffiti-scrawled ceiling of the
Sink, a Hill classic that's been around since
1923. Robert Redford even worked here!

Rocky Mountain National Park ❸

🛏 Stanley Hotel   Hotel $$$
(📞970-577-4000; www.stanleyhotel.com;
333 Wonderview Ave; r from $199; P📶❄) A
favorite local retreat, this best-in-class hotel
served as the inspiration for Stephen King's
famous cult novel *The Shining*.

Vail ❹

🛏 The Sebastian   Hotel $$$
(📞800-354-6908; www.thesebastianvail.com;
16 Vail Rd; r summer/winter from $230/500;

P❄📶❄❄) Deluxe and modern, this
upscale lodging is the latest addition to the Vail
scene and its list of amenities is impressive,
including a mountainside ski valet, goddess spa
and adventure concierge.

Glenwood Springs ❺

🛏 Sunlight Mountain Inn   Lodge $$
(📞970-945-5225; www.sunlightinn.com; 10252
County Rd 117; d $90-149; ❄) A stone's throw
from Sunlight Mountain Resort's ski area, this
adorable mountain lodge has 20 Western-style
rooms with fireplaces and quilted bedspreads.

Aspen ❻

🍴 Pine Creek Cookhouse   American $$$
(📞970-925-1044; www.pinecreekcookhouse.
com; 12700 Castle Creek Rd; year-round lunch
and summer dinner mains $13-41, dinner prix-fixe
with ski tour/sleigh $90/110; ⏰11:30am-
2:30pm daily, 2:30-8pm Wed-Sun; 🚗👶)
Think gorgeous log-cabin restaurant serving
outstanding, fresh fusion fare, set 11 miles up
Castle Creek Canyon past the old mining town
of Ashcroft.

🛏 Viceroy   Hotel $$$
(📞970-923-8000; www.viceroysnowmass.
com; 130 Wood Rd; studios summer/winter
from $175/625; P❄📶❄❄) By far the best
choice in Snowmass...and with incredible $95
summer rates, it's the best deal in all of Aspen
(it's the local rate, but just tell them you're a
local – staff want you to have it).

Buena Vista ❽

🛏 Liars' Lodge B&B   B&B $$
(📞719-395-3444; www.liarslodge.com; 30000
Co Rd 371; r $138-168, cabin $265; 📶) This
airy, spectacularly set log cabin is perched on
a finger of the Arkansas River, so close that the
river will sing you to sleep.

Highway 50 Easy to see why it's 'the loneliest road in America'

Highway 50: The Loneliest Road

32

Wanted: Intrepid travelers not afraid of empty spaces. Must be history lovers willing to embrace the weird. Adventurers preferred.

TRIP HIGHLIGHTS

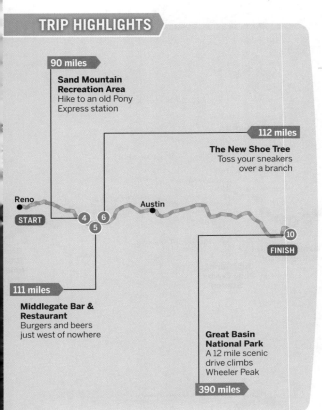

90 miles

Sand Mountain Recreation Area
Hike to an old Pony Express station

112 miles

The New Shoe Tree
Toss your sneakers over a branch

Reno
START
④ ⑥
⑤

Austin

⑩
FINISH

111 miles

Middlegate Bar & Restaurant
Burgers and beers just west of nowhere

Great Basin National Park
A 12 mile scenic drive climbs Wheeler Peak

390 miles

3 DAYS
390 MILES / 628KM

GREAT FOR...

BEST TIME TO GO

Spring for snowcapped mountains, fall for colorful leaves.

ESSENTIAL PHOTO

Take a shot of Hwy 50 rolling toward the South Snake Range.

BEST FOR HISTORY

Old Pony Express stations link visitors to the past.

Highway 50: The Loneliest Road

Ah, central Nevada. Miles and miles of high-desert scrub where the view is always the same. Or is it? Look closely and you'll see subtle reminders of earlier wayfarers. Prehistoric tribes left rock carvings. The Pony Express abandoned its stone stations. Chunks of the Lincoln Hwy, established in 1913 as the nation's first transcontinental road, bake in the sun. And what do modern travelers abandon? Check out the New Shoe Tree.

❶ Reno

Nicknamed 'The Biggest Little City in The World,' Reno is the best place to rest up, load up and blow some cash before entering the sandy wilds of the Great Basin, a series of bowl-shaped depressions between the Sierra Nevada Mountains and the Rockies. Downtown, try your luck at the mining-themed **Silver Legacy** (www.silverlegacyreno.com; 407 N Virginia St), one of several casinos on Virginia St, then walk south to the

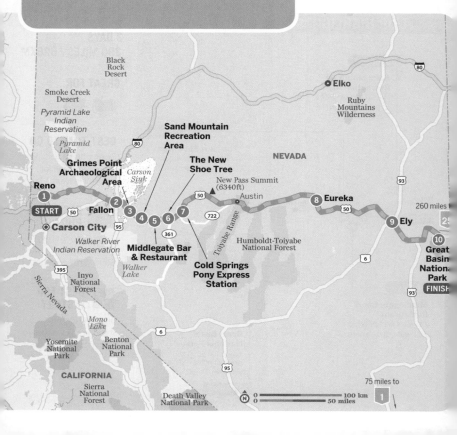

Riverwalk District (www.renoriver.org) to watch kayakers run Class II and III rapids at the 1.5-mile **Truckee River Whitewater Park** (www.reno.gov). Enjoy the river view while you can; rivers don't flow to the sea in the Great Basin. They meander into lakes, marshes and squishy sinks.

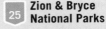 p335

The Drive ≫ Hop on I-80 east. In Sparks, just east of Reno, fuel up on gas and Elvis kitsch at **Sierra Sid's Casino** (200 N McCarran Blvd, off I-80), which exhibits guns and jewelry owned by Elvis. From I-80, pick up Hwy 50A east in Fernley.

- - - - - - - - - - - - - - - -

❷ Fallon

Look up and you might spot an F-16 flying over Fallon, home of the US Navy's Topgun fighter pilot school. On the ground, dragsters

LINK YOUR TRIP

❶ Four Corners Cruise

To loop through the Four Corners region, drop south on Hwy 93 to Las Vegas.

㉕ Zion & Bryce National Parks

Trade mountain peaks for fiery spires by driving I-50 east to I-15 south in Utah.

compete at the **Top Gun Raceway** (☎775-423-0223; www.topgunraceway.com; adlut/child $10/5) between March and September. The **Churchill County Museum** (☎775-423-3677; www.ccmuseum.org; 1050 S Maine St; admission free; ☺10am-5pm Mon-Sat, closes 1hr earlier Dec-Feb) is a bit like Fallon's attic. Here you can see a Paiute hut and a Model T Ford, learn about the hardships of pioneers and flip through an impressive collection of historic photographs. You can also reserve tickets for tours of **Hidden Cave** here.

The Drive ≫ Head east on Hwy 50 for 7 miles You'll pass cattle, barbed wire fences and a methamphetamine warning sign or two.

- - - - - - - - - - - - - - - -

❸ Grimes Point Archaeological Area

A 0.75-mile interpretative trail at this **archeological site** (☎775-885-6000;

www.blm.gov/nv; admission free; ☺24hr) loops past 200 or so petrolgyphs, or rock carvings, some of them dating back 9000 years. For another archeologically significant site, follow the entrance road back to **Hidden Cave**, a possible cache site in prehistoric times. A short but steep interpretive trail leads to the cave (closed without a guide), or you can join a free, docent-guided cave tour on the 2nd and 4th Saturdays of the month. They begin at 9:30am at the Churchill County Museum (p331).

The Drive ≫ Continue east about 16 miles. In the spring, the pavement ahead might shimmer in the heat while snowy mountains beckon in the distance.

- - - - - - - - - - - - - - - -

 TRIP HIGHLIGHT

❹ Sand Mountain Recreation Area

That 600ft-high yellow monolith? That's **Sand**

I SURVIVED HWY 50 CERTIFICATE

For travelers who like a challenge, the Nevada Tourism Commission has issued a *Hwy 50 Survival Guide* (www.travelnevada.com/travel-guides). The guide includes a basic map, details about Hwy 50 towns and a postcard. Your goal? To get the postcard stamped in five communities along the route. Return the completed card, and you'll receive a personalized 'I Survived Hwy 50' certificate along with a pin. Pre-order a survival guide at www.ponyexpressnevada.com or pick one up at chambers of commerce, hotels, motels and gas stations along the route.

Mountain ([phone]775-885-6000; www.blm.gov/nv; admission free for brief, non-motorized use; ⊙24hr), a 1.5-mile by 2-mile sand dune. And if you think it might be a peaceful place to ponder nature, roll down your window. Yep, that's the sound of swarming ATVers revving their dune buggies. They're a mesmerizing sight as they zip up and down the dune.

The ruins of the **Sand Springs Pony Express Station** (admission free) are also here. British explorer Sir Richard Burton stopped at the station in 1860. He described it as '...roofless and chairless, filthy and squalid, with a smoky fire in one corner and a table in the centre of an impure floor, the walls open to every wind and the interior full of dust.' Nice!

Covered by sand for a century, the station was rediscovered by archeologists in 1976.

The Drive » Continue 21 miles east. The Pony Express Re-Ride recreates the full run every June (www.xphomestation.com).

TRIP HIGHLIGHT

❺ Middlegate Bar & Restaurant

What's the marquee menu item at this wood-plank watering hole (p335)? The Middlegate Monster, a 1⅓ lb burger that's hard to finish unless you're one of the Navy Seals passing through or dropping in – sometimes they arrive by helicopter. A former stage stop, and later a Pony Express station, Middlegate is a fine place to loiter. Add your dollar bill to the collection on the ceiling.

✕ p335

The Drive » Continue on Hwy 50 and drive east. About a mile ahead on the left is a cottonwood tree and a dirt pull-off. If you get to Hwy 722, you've gone too far.

TRIP HIGHLIGHT

❻ The New Shoe Tree

The branches of this towering cottonwood, known as the **New Shoe Tree**, are draped with knotted pairs of sneakers. The old shoe tree, which was larger, was cut down a few years ago. This one? It's kind of ugly, it's kind of weird, and it's kind of our favorite sight on the drive.

The Drive » Because Nevada was so desolate, Pony Express riders traveling through the state changed horses only three times and covered a distance of about 90 miles. Continue east.

❼ Cold Springs Pony Express Station

A two-mile trail leads to the stone ruins of another Pony Express station, **Cold Springs**. A Hispanic rider, Jose Zowgaltz was mortally wounded in an Indian ambush just north of here, but he did make it into the station. In a separate incident, Indian warriors killed the station master.

The rock foundations of the second Cold Springs Station are across Hwy 50, just south. It doubled as a stage coach stop and later a telegraph station.

The Drive » Hwy 50 twists up to the 6348ft New Pass Summit

THE PONY EXPRESS

Wanted: Young, skinny, wiry fellows not over 18. Must be expert riders willing to risk death daily. Orphans preferred.

The Pony Express (1860–61) was the FedEx of its day, using a fleet of young riders and swift horses to carry mail between Missouri and California in an astounding 10 days. Each horseman rode full-bore for almost six hours – changing horses every 10 miles – before passing the mail to the next rider. The Pony Express lasted only 18 months, made obsolete by the telegraph.

SABRINA DALBESIO/GETTY IMAGES ©

The New Shoe Tree One of the Southwest's many roadside oddities

LOCAL KNOWLEDGE: COLD SPRINGS PONY EXPRESS STATION

The Bureau of Land Management calls the vault toilet at the Cold Springs Pony Express Station 'The Loneliest Rest Stop on the Loneliest Road.' But we hear it gets a lot of use.

then drops into another basin. Another climb leads into the Toiyabe Mountains. Austin, once a mid-19th-century boomtown, is now home to a few frontier churches and old buildings.

8 Eureka

In the late 19th century, $40 million worth of silver was extracted from the hills around Eureka. Pride of place goes to the **county courthouse** (☎775-237-5540; 10 S Main St; admission free; ⏱8am-5pm Mon-Fri, closed 12-1pm), with its handsome pressed-tin ceilings and walk-in vaults, and the beautifully restored **opera house** (☎775-237-6006; 31 S Main St; ⏱8am-5pm Mon-Fri, closed 12-1pm), also dating from 1880, which hosts an art gallery and concerts. The **Eureka Sentinel Museum** (☎775-237-5010; 10 N Monroe St; admission free; ⏱10am-6pm Tue-Sat Nov-Apr, 10am-6pm daily May-Oct) displays yesteryear newspaper technology and colorful examples of period reportage.

The Drive » Continue east over rolling scrubby hills and watch for deer. It's 77 miles to Ely.

9 Ely

The biggest town for miles around, Ely was established as a mining town in the 1860s. Its old downtown has beautiful regional history murals and awesome vintage neon signs.

Downtown, kitsch lovers will dig the Hotel Nevada (p335); its funky casino and eclectically Western lobby are worth a look even if you don't spend the night. The bar defines the term 'local color.' You can also buy 'I Survived the Loneliest Road' t-shirts here.

The **Ely Renaissance Village** (www.elyrenaissance.com; 150 Sixth St; ⏱10am-4pm Sat Jul-Sep) is a collection of 1908 period homes built by settlers from France, Slovakia, China, Italy and Greece.

✕ 🛏 p335

The Drive » Continue east on Hwy 50.

TRIP HIGHLIGHT

10 Great Basin National Park

Near the Nevada–Utah border, this uncrowded national park (☎775-234-7331; www.nps.gov/grba; admission free; ⏱24hr) encompasses 13,063ft Wheeler Peak, rising abruptly from the desert and creating an awesome but compact range of life zones and landscapes. A seasonal 12-mile scenic drive twists up to the summit.

Hiking trails near the summit take in superb country made up of glacial lakes, groves of ancient bristlecone pines (some more than 5000 years old) and even a permanent ice field. June through August, stick around for the **Dark Rangers** astronomy programs (Tuesday, Thursday and Saturday nights). The guided **full-moon hikes** are also popular.

The main **visitor center** (☎775-234-7331; ⏱8am-4:30pm) sells tickets for guided tours (adult $8 to $10, child $4 to $5) of Lehman Caves, which are brimming with limestone formations. Reservations are recommended. Next to the visitor center, a simple cafe stays open from May through October.

The Great Basin Visitor Center, near the village of Baker, is open mid-April though October.

🛏 p335

Sleeping & Eating

Reno ❶

✕ Great Basin Brewing Co
Brewery $$

(www.greatbasinbrewingco.com; 5525 S Virginia St; mains $8-19; ⏰11am-midnight Sun-Thu, 11am-1:30am Fri & Sat) This busy place serves five flagship beers with 13 seasonal brews and has a nice selection of Belgian ales. Pub grub includes burgers, sausage sandwiches, pizza and fish tacos. It's three miles south of downtown on Virginia St.

✕ Old Granite Street Eatery
American $$

(📞775-622-3222; www.oldgranitestreeteatery.com; 243 S Sierra St; lunch $9-14, dinner $11-26; ⏰11am-11pm Mon-Thu, 11am-midnight Fri, 10am-midnight Sat, 10am-4pm Sun) A lovely place for organic and local comfort food, old-school artisanal cocktails and seasonal craft beers. The community table is fashioned from a barn door.

🛏 Peppermill
Casino Hotel $$

(📞866-821-9996, 775-826-2121; www.peppermillreno.com; 2707 S Virginia St; r/ste Sun-Thu from $70/130, Fri & Sat from $170/200; 🅿❄@🛜❄) The popular Peppermill boasts Tuscan-themed rooms in its newest 600-room tower, and has almost completed a plush remodel of its older rooms.

🛏 Sands Regency
Casino Hotel $ $

(📞775-348-2200; www.sandsregency.com; 345 N Arlington Ave; r Sun-Thu/Fri & Sat from $29/69; 🅿❄🛜❄🏊) The exterior is a little tired, but the rooms are fine, decked out in a cheerful tropical palette. Empress Tower rooms are best.

🛏 Wildflower Village
Motel; B&B $

(📞775-747-8848; www.wildflowervillage.com; 4395 W 4th St; hostel $30, motel $55, B&B $125; 🅿❄@🛜) This artists' colony on the western edge of town has a tumbledown yet creative vibe. Individual murals decorate the facade of each room, and you can hear the freight trains rumble on by.

Middlegate Bar & Restaurant ❺

✕ Middlegate Bar & Restaurant
Restaurant $$

(www.middlegatestation.net; 42500 Austin Hwy, cnr Hwys 50 & 361; mains $6-17) Play a little pool, chat with the fry cook, enjoy a juicy burger and see who strolls through the door.

Ely ❾

✕ La Fiesta
Mexican $$

(700 Ave H; lunch special under $8, mains $9.25-26; ⏰11am-9pm; 🅿) It's a little dark and ho-hum, but the enchiladas are deliciously cheesy, it serves beer and you'll get a solid meal.

🛏 Hotel Nevada
Hotel $

(📞888-406-3055, 775-289-6665; www.hotelnevada.com; 501 Aultman St; r $50-125; ❄@🛜) From the lobby over-stuffed with animal mounts and Old West memorabilia to the celebrity-named rooms, the Hotel Nevada is fun. In the rooms, decor is more simple than chic, but the staff seems on the ball. The bad? The smoky casino and quirky showers. If the online reservation system says full, still call; it may have rooms.

Great Basin National Park ❿

🛏 Campgrounds
Campground $

(📞775-234-7331; www.nps.gove/grba; primitive camping free, tent & RV sites $12) Five developed campgrounds are available on a first-come, first- served basis. Lower Lehman Creek and Strawberry Creek are open year-round; the others are open in warmer months, typically April/May through October.

STRETCH YOUR LEGS
LAS VEGAS

Start/Finish: Bellagio

Distance: 1.8 miles/2.9km

Duration: Four hours

This loop takes in the most dazzling sites on the Strip: the canals of Venice, the graceful Eiffel Tower, the world's tallest Ferris Wheel and a three-story chandelier. And remember, objects on the Strip are further away than they appear.

Take this walk on Trips

Bellagio

For floral inspiration, pause in the lobby at the ever-stylish **Bellagio** (www.bellagio.com; 3600 Las Vegas Blvd S) to admire the room's showpiece: a Dale Chihuly sculpture composed of 2000 hand-blown glass flowers in vibrant colors. Just beyond the lobby, the **Bellagio Conservatory & Botanical Gardens** (admission free; ⏰24hr) dazzles passers-by with gorgeously ostentatious floral designs that change seasonally. If you're hankering for fine art, see what's on display at the **Bellagio Gallery of Fine Art** (adult/student/child $16/11/free; ⏰10am-8pm), which hosts blockbuster traveling exhibits.

The Walk ≫ Walk north on S Las Vegas Blvd and cross E Flamingo Rd. Caesar's Palace will be just ahead on your left.

Caesar's Palace

It's easy to get lost inside this labyrinth-like Greco-Roman **fantasyland** (www.caesarspalace.com; 3570 Las Vegas Blvd S) where maps are few (and not oriented to the outside). The interior is captivating, however, with marble reproductions of classical statuary, including a 4-ton Brahma shrine near the front entrance. Towering fountains, goddess-costumed cocktail waitresses and the swanky haute-couture of the Forum Shops ante up the glitz. For lunch, consider the fantastic **Bacchanal Buffet** (www.caesarspalace.com; 3570 Las Vegas Blvd S), a gastronomic celebration of global proportions.

The Walk ≫ Continue north on Las Vegas Blvd S, passing the Mirage. At night, its faux-Polynesian volcano erupts. Just north, take the walkway over Las Vegas Blvd S.

Venetian

The spectacular **Venetian** (www.venetian.com; 3355 Las Vegas Blvd S; gondola ride adult/private $19/76) is a facsimile of a doge's palace, inspired by the splendor of Italy's most romantic city. It features roaming mimes and minstrels in period costume, hand-painted ceiling frescoes and full-scale reproductions of the Italian port's famous landmarks. Flowing canals, vibrant piazzas and stone walkways attempt to capture the spirit of La Serenissima Repubblica, reputedly the home of the world's first casino. Take a **gondola ride** or stroll through the atmospheric **Grand Canal Shoppes**.

The Walk » It's a 0.7-mile trek to Paris, but sights along the way should keep it interesting, particularly the $55 million LINQ shopping and entertainment district set to open in December 2013. It will be home to the 550ft-tall High Roller, billed as the world's tallest Ferris wheel.

Paris-Las Vegas

Evoking the gaiety of the City of Light, **Paris-Las Vegas** (www.parislv.com; 3655 Las Vegas Blvd S) strives to capture the essence of the grand dame by re-creating her landmarks. Fine likenesses of the Opera, the Arc de Triomphe, the Champs-Élysées, the soaring Eiffel Tower and even the Seine frame the property. The signature attraction is the **Eiffel Tower Experience** (702-946-7000; adult/child from $11.50/7.50; 9:30am-12:30am Mon-Fri, to 1am Sat & Sun, weather permitting). Ascend in a glass elevator to the observation deck for panoramic views of the Strip, notably the Bellagio's dancing fountains.

The Walk » Walk a short distance south on Las Vegas Blvd S. Cross Las Vegas Blvd S on Paris Dr.

Cosmopolitan

The twinkling three-story chandelier inside this sleek addition to the Strip isn't purely decorative. Nope, it's a step-inside, sip a swanky cocktail and survey your domain kind of place, worthy of your wildest fairy tale. A bit much? Not really. Like the rest of Vegas, the **Cosmopolitan** (www.cosmopolitanlasvegas.com; 3708 Las Vegas Blvd S; 24hr) is just having fun.

The Walk » From here, walk north on Las Vegas Blvd S to catch the dazzling choreographed dancing fountain show at Bellagio's.

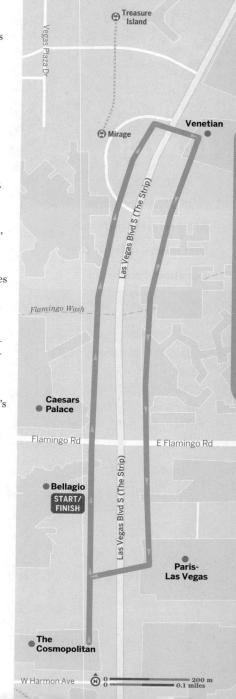

STRETCH YOUR LEGS
DENVER

Start/Finish: Highlands

Distance: 4 miles/6.4km

Duration: Four hours

The Mile High City has some of the best walking paths in the nation, world-class art museums, brewpubs aplenty, urban white-water parks, Rocky Mountain–chic boutiques and eateries, and a new urban scene that is transforming this classic Western city.

Take this walk on Trips

Highlands

One of Denver's top up-and-coming neighborhoods, Highlands sits conveniently next to I-70, offering a birds-eye vantage of the city, B-Share bicycles (if you prefer to bike this route), and free two-hour parking. In the hipper-than-thou Lower Highlands neighborhood check out some cool boutiques, raucous brewpubs and great lunchtime restaurants, like **Linger** (☎303-993-3120; www.lingerdenver.com; 2030 W 30th Ave; mains $8-14; ☺11:30am-2:30pm, 4pm-2am Tue-Sat, 10am-2:30pm Sun), before heading into the city.

The Walk >> Trundle over to the 16th St pedestrian bridge that will take you over I-70, past John McEnroe's pile of public art known as National Velvet, and across another pedestrian bridge to Commons Park.

Commons Park

Affording views of the city and a bit of fresh air, spacious and hilly Commons Park has bike paths, benches, river access, and plenty of people-watching. A lyrical curving stairway to nowhere known as Common Ground by artist Barbara Grygutis is an undeniable centerpiece. The stairway is just east of the pedestrian bridge over the Platte River.

The Walk >> Cruise straight through the park to the massive and hard-to-miss Millennium Bridge.

Millennium Bridge

A defining piece of city infrastructure, the Millennium Bridge is the world's first cable-stayed bridge using a post-tensioned structural construction (yowsa!). If the technical jargon goes over your head, you'll be impressed enough by just looking up – the sweeping forms of the cables and white mast are a dramatic sight against Denver's consistently blue sky.

The Walk >> Stop on the bridge to take in the views of Coors Field and Union Station, before plunging down into the chaos of Lower Downtown (LoDo).

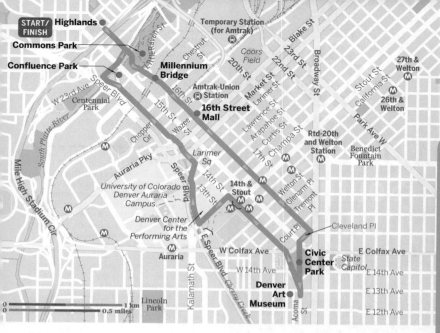

16th Street Mall

The 16th Street Pedestrian Mall is an unavoidable tourist trap, with plenty of T-Shirt shops, plus a few good restaurants and bars and some decent public art on display. The funkier LoDo, around Larimer Sq, is the best place to have a drink or browse the boutiques.

The Walk » Cruise south on 16th St to the end of the pedestrian mall. From there, it's a quick scurry across Colfax Ave to Civic Center Park. To save time, hop on the free bus that runs the entirety of the mall.

Civic Center Park

In the shadow of the State Capitol's golden dome, Civic Center Park hosts lounging drifters, politicos yammering into Bluetooth headsets and some of the most iconic public sculptures in the city, including the 1920 Bronco Buster, whose model was arrested for murder before the statue was finished. If you have time, head over to the State Capitol for a free tour, plus a photo opp on the 13th step that sits exactly a mile above sea level.

The Walk » Continue south past the whimsical Yearling statue (how did that horse get onto that chair?), more public art and the post-modern Denver Library, before you hit the iconic Denver Art Museum.

Denver Art Museum

If you are only going to visit one museum in Denver, this is it. The DAM puts on special avant-garde multimedia exhibits. The Western American Art section of the permanent collection is justifiably famous. The landmark $110-million Frederic C Hamilton wing, designed by Daniel Libeskind, is simply awesome. If you run out of time, grab a B-Cycle here to pedal back to Highlands along the Cherry Creek Bike Path.

The Walk » Go past the Convention Center's Big Blue Bear, continuing west down Champa St to past the Denver Performing Arts Complex and its signature Dancers statue. From there, take the Cherry Creek Bike Path all the way to Confluence Park and Highlands.

Driving in Southwest USA

The interstate system is thriving in the Southwest, but a well-maintained network of state roads and scenic byways offers unparalleled opportunities for exploration.

Driving Fast Facts

➡ **Right or Left?** Drive on the right.

➡ **Legal Driving Age** 16 (New Mexico: 15½)

➡ **Top Speed Limit** 85 mph (Hwy 130 between Austin and San Antonio, TX)

➡ **Best Bumper Sticker** We're all here because we're not all there (Jerome, AZ)

DRIVER'S LICENSE & DOCUMENTS

All drivers must carry a driver's license, the car registration and proof of insurance. If your license is not in English, an official translation or an international driving permit (IDP) is highly recommended. You will also need a credit card to rent a car.

INSURANCE

Liability insurance covers people and property that you might harm in an accident. For damage to your own rental vehicle, a collision damage waiver (CDW) is available for about $22 to $27 per day. If you have liability and collision coverage on your vehicle at home, it might cover damages to rental cars; inquire before departing. Additionally, some credit cards offer reimbursement coverage for collision damages when you use the card to rent a car; again, ask before departing. There may be exceptions for rentals of more than 15 days or for exotic models, jeeps, vans and 4WD vehicles.

Note that many rental agencies stipulate that damage a car suffers while being driven on unpaved roads is not covered by the insurance it offers. Check with the agent when you make your reservation.

RENTING A CAR

Rental cars are readily available at airports and many downtown city locations. Rates usually include unlimited mileage, but 'unlimited' can actually be capped. Dropping off the car at a different location is usually more expensive than returning it to the place of rental. Larger companies don't require a credit card deposit, which means you can cancel without a penalty if you find a better rate. Since deals abound and the business is competitive, it pays to shop around.

Most companies require that you have a major credit card, are at least 25 years old and have a valid driver's license. Some national agencies may rent to drivers between the ages of 21 and 25 but may charge a daily fee.

The following companies operate in the Southwest:

Alamo (www.alamo.com)
Avis (www.avis.com)

Budget (www.budget.com)
Dollar (www.dollar.com)
Hertz (www.hertz.com)
National (www.national.com)
Thrifty (www.thrifty.com)

BORDER CROSSING

Cities and towns in Arizona where you can cross the Mexican–US border include San Luis (south of Yuma), Lukeville (Hwy 85), Nogales and Douglas. From New Mexico, travel south to El Paso, TX, to reach Ciudad Juarez. US Customs and Border Protection tracks current wait times (see http://apps.cbp.gov/bwt) at every border crossing.

Bring your passport if you are crossing the border. Foreign visitors should review US entry requirements at the State Department (www.travel.state.gov) and the US Customs and Border Protection (www.cbp.gov) websites.

MAPS

Detailed state highway maps are distributed free by state governments. Call or send an email to state tourism offices (typically through their websites) to request maps or pick them up at highway tourism information offices when you enter a state on a major highway. For exploring Native American reservations in the Four Corners region, buy the popular AAA Indian Country map. It's for sale at **Books 'n' More** (⊙8am-8pm Jun-Aug, vary rest of the year), which is across the plaza from Grand

Road Trip Websites

American Automobile Association (AAA; ☑800-222-4357; www.aaa.com) Provides maps and other information, as well as travel discounts and 24-hour emergency assistance for members.

America's Byways (www.byways.org) Descriptions and maps for designated national scenic byways.

Gas Buddy (www.gasbuddy.com) Find the cheapest gas in town.

Southwest USA Playlist

Border Town Chris Whitley

Rocky Mountain High John Denver

Take it Easy The Eagles

Texas, Texas Red Meat

Viva Las Vegas Elvis Presley

Canyon Visitor Center on the South Rim, and from various outlets online.

ROADS & CONDITIONS

Be extra defensive while driving in the Southwest. Everything from dust storms to snow to roaming livestock can make conditions dangerous. Near Flagstaff, watch for elk at sunset on I-17 – they like to soak up warmth from the blacktop (or so we heard). Elk can weigh between 500lb and 900lb.

Distances are great in the Southwest and there are long stretches of road without gas stations. Running out of gas on a hot and desolate stretch of highway is no fun, so pay attention to signs that caution 'Next Gas 98 Miles.'

Road conditions for interstates and rural highways are typically very good. Unpaved roads to ghost towns, petroglyph sites, and remote trailheads are generally well-graded but can be challenging after storms or if they lead to very remote sites. Unpaved roads across Indian reservations are of varying quality. Consider using four-wheel drive vehicles for extended trips on dirt roads and ask locally about conditions.

For updates on road conditions, call ☑511 (excluding Texas) while traveling within the state, or call one of the following:
Arizona (☑in-state 511, 888-411-7623; www.az511.com)
Nevada (☑in-state 511, 877-687-6237; www.nvroads.com)
New Mexico (☑in-state 511, 800-432-4269; http://nmroads.com)
Southern Colorado (☑in-state 511, 303-639-1111; www.cotrip.org)
Texas (☑800-452-9292)
Utah (☑in-state 511, 866-511-8824; www.commuterlink.utah.gov)

ROAD RULES

Driving laws are slightly different in each state, but all require the use of safety belts. In every state, children under five years of age must ride in a child safety seat secured by proper restraints.

The maximum speed limit on all rural interstates is 75mph, with Texas and Utah allowing higher speeds on a handful of specified sections of road. The speed limit drops to 65mph in urban areas in Arizona, Colorado, Nevada and Utah. New Mexico and Texas allow urban interstate drivers to barrel through at 75mph. But no matter your location, watch for speed limit signs requiring a lower speed than the maximums listed here.

Texting while driving is banned for all drivers in Colorado, Nevada and Utah. Hand-held cell phone use is banned in Nevada.

PARKING

Public parking is readily available in most Southwest destinations, whether on the street or in parking lots. In rural areas and small towns it is often free of charge. Many towns have metered parking, which will limit the amount of time you can leave your car.

Parking can be a challenge in urban areas. Street parking is limited so you will probably have to pay to leave your car in private lots. See the City Guides, p26, for more information about parking in Las Vegas, Phoenix, Santa Fe and Austin.

FUEL

Gas stations are common in urban areas and along interstates. Many are open 24 hours a day. Small-town stations may be open only from 7am to 8pm or 9pm.

Road Distances (miles)

	Amarillo, TX	Austin, TX	Bryce Canyon NP, UT	Carlsbad, NM	Cortez (Mesa Verde NP), CO	Denver, CO	Grand Canyon (North Rim), AZ	Grand Canyon (South Rim), AZ	Las Vegas, NV	Phoenix, AZ	Reno, NV	Salt Lake City, UT	Santa Fe, NM
Austin, TX	495												
Bryce Canyon NP, UT	835	1250											
Carlsbad, NM	285	480	820										
Cortez (Mesa Verde NP), CO	540	960	390	530									
Denver, CO	435	930	565	580	380								
Grand Canyon (North Rim), AZ	750	1175	130	740	340	690							
Grand Canyon (South Rim), AZ	695	1110	290	685	370	675	210						
Las Vegas, NV	855	1300	250	850	570	755	270	280					
Phoenix, AZ	705	1005	430	590	400	790	340	220	290				
Reno, NV	1305	1740	565	1295	840	990	680	725	450	735			
Salt Lake City, UT	880	1300	260	870	350	520	390	520	420	710	520		
Santa Fe, NM	280	700	660	270	280	390	530	470	640	520	1080	630	
Tucson, AZ	735	890	540	480	470	890	470	350	410	120	855	820	560

Driving Problem-Buster

What should I do if my car breaks down? Call the service number provided by the rental-car company, and it will make arrangements with a local garage. If you're driving your own car, its advisable to join AAA (p341), which provides emergency assistance.

What if I have an accident? If serious damage occurs, you'll have to call the local police (☎911) to come to the scene of the accident and file an accident report, for insurance purposes.

What should I do if I get stopped by the police? Always pull over to the right at the first available opportunity. Stay in your car and roll down the window. Show the officer your driver's license and automobile registration. For any violations, you cannot pay the officer for the ticket; payment must be made by mail or internet.

What happens at a border patrol checkpoint? The 'stop side' of the checkpoint is the route going from the south (Mexico) to the north (USA). You may be waved through; otherwise, slow down, stop and answer a few questions (regarding your citizenship and the nature of your visit) and possibly pop your trunk and roll down your window so that the officers can see into your car.

What if I can't find anywhere to stay? In summer it's advisable to make reservations in advance. Most towns have tourist information centers or chambers of commerce that will help travelers find accommodation in a pinch. Public lands managed by the Bureau of Land Management and the forest service often allow dispersed camping, which means you can camp where you want on undeveloped land as long as you stay 900ft from a developed water source and follow other guidelines (www.blm.gov).

At most stations, you must pay before you pump. The more modern pumps have credit/debit card terminals built into them, so you can pay right at the pump. At more expensive, 'full service' stations, an attendant will pump your gas for you; no tip is expected.

SAFETY

When leaving the car, travelers are advised to remove valuables and lock all car doors, especially in urban areas and at isolated trailheads. Be extra careful driving on rural roads at night, which may not be well-lit and may be populated by deer, elk, livestock and other creatures that can often total your car if you hit them.

RADIO

Arizona On the Hopi reservation KUYI (88.1FM) plays reggae, honky tonk, Cajun and Native American music, with Hopi news.

New Mexico KTAO (101.9FM) in Taos is a solar-powered station airing Native American music, astrology reports, local news, outlaw country and world music.

Texas In Lubbock, KDAV (1590AM), where Buddy Holly once worked, plays nothing but classic rockabilly.

BEHIND THE SCENES

SEND US YOUR FEEDBACK

We love to hear from travelers – your comments help make our books better. We read every word, and we guarantee that your feedback goes straight to the authors. Visit **lonelyplanet. com/contact** to submit your updates and suggestions.

Note: We may edit, reproduce and incorporate your comments in Lonely Planet products such as guidebooks, websites and digital products, so let us know if you don't want your comments reproduced or your name acknowledged. For a copy of our privacy policy visit lonelyplanet.com/privacy.

AUTHOR THANKS

AMY C BALFOUR

Many thanks to BLM maestro Chris Rose for his Nevada insights and Elvis knowledge, Robin Tellis at the Grand Canyon, Sara Benson, Dan Westermeyer, Justin Shephard, Tracer Finn, Jim Christian, Catrien van Assendelft, Alex Amato, Mike Roe, Lewis Pipkin and fellow adventurers Sandee McGlaun, Lisa McGlaun, Paul Hanstedt and Grand Canyon power-walker Karen Schneider.

MICHAEL BENANAV

I'd mostly like to thank Kelly and Luke, who always let me go, and always let me come back.

GREG BENCHWICK

Special thanks to my friend and commissioning editor Suki, my coordinating author and the rest of the Lonely Planet team. And, of course, to my supercalifragilisticexpialidocious research partner, a little Miss Violeta Ezcurra Benchwick.

LISA DUNFORD

I appreciate all the kindred spirits I've met on the Utah road over the years. Thanks especially to Trista Kelin Rayner and Lyman Hafen.

MARIELLA KRAUSE

Thanks to Gene Brenek for taking that epic road trip through West Texas with me. And thanks to Lonely Planet editor Suki Gear for sending me to West Texas in the first place. I knew I'd either love it or hate it, and it turns out I love it.

CAROLYN MCCARTHY

I'm indebted to the good people of the Rocky Mountains. Special thanks to Lance and his Ouray friends for the bed and BBQ. Many thanks go out to the talented Rachel Dowd and virtual beers go out to all my colleagues for being the best to work with.

RYAN VER BERKMOES

Thanks to Lonely Planet's Suki Gear in Oakland for giving me the chance to continue living a Texas adventure that started in 1997. Huge thanks go to my dear friend Justin Marler and Laura. And just like the multi-purpose onion ring, I love all things Golden.

THIS BOOK

This 2nd edition of Lonely Planet's Southwest USA's Best Trips guidebook was commissioned in Lonely Planet's Oakland office, and researched and written by Amy C Balfour, Michael Benanav, Greg Benchwick, Lisa Dunford, Mariella Krause, Carolyn McCarthy and Ryan Ver Berkmoes. The last edition (*Arizona, New Mexico & the Grand Canyon Trips*) was written by

Becca Blond, Aaron Anderson, Sara Benson, Jennifer Denniston, Lisa Dunford, Josh Krist and Wendy Yanagihara.
Commissioning Editor Suki Gear
Coordinating Editor Kate Whitfield
Senior Cartographer Alison Lyall
Coordinating Layout Designer Lauren Egan
Managing Editors Bruce Evans, Brigitte Ellemor
Managing Layout Designer Chris Girdler

Assisting Editors Carly Hall, Monique Perrin, Amanda Williamson
Assisting Cartographers Jeff Cameron, Mick Garrett
Assisting Layout Designer Carol Jackson
Cover Research Naomi Parker
Internal Image Research Kylie McLaughlin
Thanks to Anita Banh, Ryan Evans, Larissa Frost, Corey Hutchison, Genesys India, Jouve India, Trent Paton, Kerrianne Southway, Gerard Walker

PUBLISHER THANKS

Climate map data adapted from Peel MC, Finlayson BL & McMahon TA (2007) 'Updated World Map of the Köppen-Geiger Climate Classification', Hydrology and Earth System Sciences, 11, 1633¬44.

Cover photographs: Front (clockwise from top): Arches National Park, Utah, Alan Copson / AWL; Chile pepper ristra, New Mexico, Sabrina Dalbesio; Wigwam Motel, Holbrook, Arizona, Danita Delimont / Alamy.
Back: Colorado River and Grand Canyon, Arizona, Momatiuk - Eastcott / Corbis

INDEX

Ryan Ver Berkmoes Ryan grew up in Santa Cruz, California, the sort of goofball beachtown place that made him immediately love Port Aransas. An inveterate wanderer, he was most at home on the hundreds of miles of Texas backroads he traversed for this book. Whether it was discovering a forgotten town on Texas Hwy 70 or driving to the literal end of the road to (happily!) check out still another empty Gulf Coast beach, he relished every click on the odometer.

My Favorite Trip 24 **Heart of Texas** for the wide open spaces that are iconic of the American Southwest. Tumbleweeds, unbroken horizons and ribbons of lonely asphalt.

Read more about Ryan at:
www.lonelyplanet.com/members/ryanvb

Greg Benchwick A Colorado native, Greg's been all over the Centennial State. Greg taught skiing in Vail, walked through fire-pits in campsites across the state and attended journalism school in Boulder. He calls Denver's Highlands home.

My Favorite Trip 31 **Colorado's High Country Byways** takes me over Independence Pass from Aspen to Leadville, past towering alpenglow peaks and quaking trees and shimmering lakes.

Lisa Dunford Moving every two years put Lisa on the road at a young age – and she's been traveling ever since. From the first time she saw the incredible red rocks of Utah nearly 10 years ago, she's been returning over and over again.

My Favorite Trip 25 **Zion & Bryce National Parks** for amazing Zion hiking and the perfect park town of Springdale.

Read more about Greg at:
www.lonelyplanet.com/members/gbenchwick

Read more about Lisa at:
www.lonelyplanet.com/members/lisa_dunford

Mariella Krause Mariella first fell in love with Austin when she checked out the UT campus during her junior year of high school. After college, she intended to live 'everywhere,' but felt so at home in Austin that she accidentally stayed for 15 years. Mariella will always consider Texas home, and she still sprinkles her language with Texanisms whenever possible, much to the amusement of those who don't consider 'y'all' a legitimate pronoun.

My Favorite Trip 22 **Big Bend Area Scenic Loop** because there's so much to see, including far-away constellations, funky art installations, mysterious ghost lights, and even bears.

Carolyn McCarthy Carolyn fell for the Rockies as an undergraduate at Colorado College, where she spent her first break camping in a blizzard in the Sangre de Cristo Range. For this title she sampled the craft beers of four states, tracked wolves and heard even more Old West ghost stories. Carolyn has contributed to over 20 Lonely Planet titles, specializing in the American West and Latin America, and has written for *National Geographic, Outside, Lonely Planet Magazine* and other publications.

My Favorite Trip 30 **San Juan Skyway & Million Dollar Highway** – nothing beats southern Colorado in summer!

Read more about Carolyn at:
www.lonelyplanet.com/members/carolynmcc

OUR WRITERS

OUR STORY

A beat-up old car, a few dollars in the pocket and a sense of adventure. In 1972 that's all Tony and Maureen Wheeler needed for the trip of a lifetime – across Europe and Asia overland to Australia. It took several months, and at the end – broke but inspired – they sat at their kitchen table writing and stapling together their first travel guide, *Across Asia on the Cheap*. Within a week they'd sold 1500 copies. Lonely Planet was born.

Today, Lonely Planet has offices in Melbourne, London and Oakland, with more than 600 staff and writers. We share Tony's belief that 'a great guidebook should do three things: inform, educate and amuse'.

Amy C Balfour, Co-ordinating Author Amy has hiked, biked, skied and gambled her way across the Southwest. In Nevada, her favorite meal was a burger at Middlegate Station on the Loneliest Road. At Grand Canyon National Park she enjoyed a return trip to Phantom Ranch, hiking down the South Kaibab Trail from the South Rim and up the Bright Angel. Amy has authored or co-authored more than 15 books for Lonely Planet and has written for *Backpacker*, *Every Day with Rachael Ray*, *Redbook*, *Southern Living* and *Women's Health*.

My Favorite Trip 32 **Hwy 50: The Loneliest Road** for Pony Express history, offbeat attractions and the Middlegate burger.

Read more about Amy at:
www.lonelyplanet.com/members/amycbalfour

Michael Benanav Michael came to New Mexico in 1992, fell under its spell, and ended up moving to a village in the Sangre de Cristo foothills where he still lives. He's spent years exploring the mountains, deserts and rivers here as a wilderness instructor – and has driven all over state, on all kinds of roads, to reach them. Aside from his work for Lonely Planet, he's authored two non-fiction books and writes and photographs for magazines and newspapers.

My Favorite Trip 13 **Georgia O'Keeffe Country** for the colors, and the joy of the drive itself.

Read more about Michael at:
www.lonelyplanet.com/members/mbenanav

 ## MORE WRITERS

Published by Lonely Planet Publications Pty Ltd
ABN 36 005 607 983
2nd edition – Feb 2014
ISBN 978 1 74179 8128
© Lonely Planet 2014 Photographs © as indicated 2014
10 9 8 7 6 5 4 3 2 1
Printed in China

MIX
Paper from responsible sources
FSC™ C021741

Paper in this book is certified against the Forest Stewardship Council™ standards. FSC™ promotes environmentally responsible, socially beneficial and economically viable management of the world's forests.